Inventing Secondary Education

Inventing

Secondary

Education

The Rise of the High School in Nineteenth-Century Ontario

R.D. GIDNEY

W.P.J. MILLAR

McGill-Queen's University Press
Montreal & Kingston • London • Buffalo

© McGill-Queen's University Press 1990
ISBN 0-7735-0746-9 (cloth)
ISBN 0-7735-0787-6 (paper)

Legal deposit second quarter 1990
Bibliothèque nationale du Québec

Printed in Canada on acid-free paper

This book has been published with the help of a grant from
the Social Science Federation of Canada, using funds provided by the Social Sciences and Humanities Research
Council of Canada.

Canadian Cataloguing in Publication Data

Gidney, R.D. (Robert Douglas), 1940–
    Inventing secondary education
    Includes bibliographical references.
    ISBN 0-7735-0746-9 (bound) –
    ISBN 0-7735-0787-6 (pbk.)
    1. Education, Secondary – Ontario – History –
    19th century.   I. Millar, W.P.J. (Winnifred Pheobe
    Joyce), 1942–   .   II. Title.

LA418.06G43 1990   373.713   C89-090455-3

Composed by Typo Litho composition
Linotron Times Roman, 10/12.

To our parents,
Mildred and Graham Millar,
Harry Gidney,
and
In Memoriam
Mary Catherine Gidney

Contents

Tables

Acknowledgments

The origins of this book go back at least a decade and during that time we have inevitably incurred many intellectual debts to friends and colleagues in Canada and abroad. Our first foray into the world of the nineteenth-century high school was made in partnership with the late Douglas A. Lawr and the notes he collected in the middle 1970s have contributed substantially to the research base for the last few chapters of this book. A decade after his death our own work continues to be informed by the quality of his scholarship and his insights into the role of the high school in small communities in both nineteenth- and twentieth-century Ontario.

In the summer of 1986 we accepted an invitation to give a series of lectures at Monash University, in Australia, and used that occasion to formulate many of the ideas presented here. Without the criticisms, conversations, and comparisons raised by our Monash colleagues, and above all by Dick Selleck and Marjorie Theobald, this would have been a much inferior work and might not have been completed at all. At the Faculty of Education, The University of Western Ontario, R.J. Clark, G.R. Lambert, and J.D. Purdy have provided unfailing companionship and at an early stage helped us collect some of the data that appears in chapter 6. Gordon Darroch, of York University, kindly allowed us to use the Darroch/Ornstein occupational classification code and also provided thoughtful and thorough criticism of our quantitative work, as did Fred Ellett and Chad Gaffield. Our friends Don Gutteridge and Patrick Harrigan waded through the entire manuscript and their comments and criticism were an invaluable help. Conversations with Richard Aldrich, Bruce Curtis, and Alison Prentice have been invariably stimulating and productive. Chris Clark, John Graham, Kate Gutteridge, Donna Hollands-Hurst, Pam Hurley, and Shirley Lassaline have all, at one time or another, given us much-needed research assistance. And Kathy Taylor's help with the data analysis was indispensable. To all these people, our thanks; to the reader, a reminder that our errors are ours alone.

This book would not have been possible without the unflagging moral and financial support of Paul Park, erstwhile Dean of the Faculty of Education, The University of Western Ontario, and his faith in us was much appreciated. Some of the early research for the project was also funded by the Social Sciences and Humanities Research Council of Canada. Nor could the book have been written without the kindness, courtesy, and competent assistance of many archivists, especially those at the Archives of Ontario, the United Church Archives, Queen's University Archives, the University of Western Ontario Regional Collection, and the National Archives of Canada. An earlier version of chapter 4 was published in 1985 in the *Canadian Historical Review* and is reproduced here with permission of the University of Toronto Press.

Our daughter, Catherine Anne, has not only worked for us as a research assistant but has also put up with interminable discussions and occasionally outright disagreements about issues rooted in a distant past that she was, at that time at least, only dimly aware of. Throughout it all she exercised patience, tolerance, and good humour. Moreover, as a high school student during the years this book was being written, she served as a constant reminder of the way in which the past informs the present. To her, our special thanks.

The first London grammar school. Built around 1840 at the Forks of the Thames, it was used for decades and repeatedly condemned in the 1860s by the grammar school inspectors. From the early 1850s on, it was hopelessly outclassed by the tax-supported central school, which also offered the elements of an English and classical education. (Courtesy UWORC)

London's new collegiate institute, built in the 1870s when the high schools and collegiate institutes were becoming a distinct, identifiable, and sometimes impressive part of the urban landscape. (J.G. Hodgins, *Schools and Colleges of Ontario*, Toronto 1910, vol. 1)

The new high school in the village of Welland; according to a proud contemporary account, "the structure, which stands in the midst of spacious grounds, is of red brick trimmed with white ... two stories in height, with a basement used as the caretaker's residence ... well furnished, and ... heated throughout by hot air from a huge furnace in the basement." (Quoted in Suzanne Tanguay, *The History and Development of Welland High and Vocational School*, Welland 1975. Picture courtesy Welland Public Library)

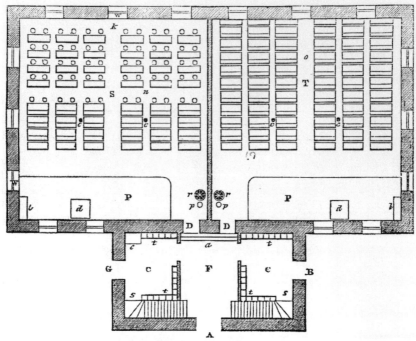

The first floor of a model grammar or union school as envisaged by the Education Office in the 1860s. The school would have accommodated two hundred pupils in three separate classrooms. The plan included a hot-air furnace, fourteen feet of blackboard space in each room, cupboards (b), and a raised platform and desk for the teachers (P and d). (Courtesy AO, J.G. Hodgins, *The School House*, 1857)

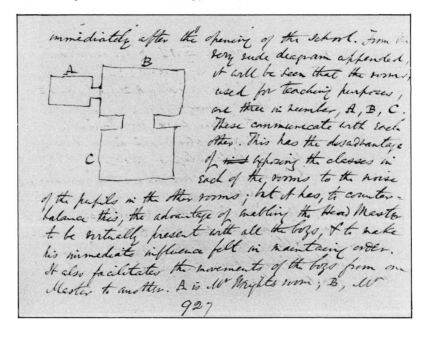

[On the roll 29th May, 55 (32 boys, 23 girls).
[On the roll 29th Oct., 55 (34 boys, 21 girls).

In May, only four of the girls in the school were taking Latin; and, in October, only seven. Mr Checkley appears honestly to leave the girls to their free choice in this matter. The girls are all grown up to an age at which it is suitable for them to be in an advanced school. In consequence of his having obtained the co-operation of his brother, Mr Checkley no longer needs the assistance of the female teacher, who was at first engaged to take a superintendence of the girls. In the school arrangements, the boys and girls are to some extent separated, as the accompanying Diagram shows: the waved line being a partition; the girls occupying the position A; and the boys, the position B; while Mr Checkley's throne, or post of observation, is at C. Mr Francis Checkley has a separate room, which has been comfortably fitted up. Mr F. Checkley has the principal direction of the Mathematical department, over which his attainments and past experience qualify him especially to preside — the Rev. Mr Checkley having himself no great taste for Mathematics. (1 ... in Homer (formerly; not reading Greek at present)

Segregating the sexes: the arrangement at the Barrie grammar school, 1867. Barrie had two teachers and two rooms. One, as G.P. Young describes and sketches it here, was divided by a partition in order to separate "to some extent" the boys from the girls. The teacher's "throne or post of observation" is at C. (Courtesy AO, GIA, vol. 4)

Left: Galt grammar school in 1868, described and sketched by G.P. Young in one of his manuscript reports. Even Tassie's large, well-known school hardly approached the Education Department's ideal. (Courtesy AO, GIA, vol. 4)

A crude "organizational chart" of the school system in Port Hope, 1868, by G.P. Young. The two ward schools (M and N) offered the first reader only; the children then attended the central school, a union grammar and common school. Note the segregation of the sexes, and the separation of the grammar and common school classes. (Courtesy AO, GIA, vol. 4)

BURLINGTON LADIES' ACADEMY.

Report of Miss _ _ _ _ _ _ Scholarship and Deportment, at the Burlington Ladies' Academy, during the Term ending _ _ _ _ _ _ 184 .

STUDIES.	MERIT.	DEMERIT.
Deportment,	6	11.
Spelling,	7	
Reading,	7	
Writing,		
English Grammar,	6½	
English Composition,		
Modern Geography,		
Arithmetic,		
Ancient Geography,		
Sacred History,		
General History,		
Watts on the Mind,		
Natural Philosophy,		
Chemistry,		
Physiology,	6½	
Astronomy,		
Mental Philosophy,		
Moral Do.,		
Rhetoric,		
Botany,		
Philosophy of Natural History,		
Geology,		
Kame's Elements of Criticism,		
Paley's Evidences,		
French,	6½	
German,		
Latin,		
Drawing,	6½	
Painting, (water colors,)		
Oil Painting,		
Embroidery,		
Piano Forte,		
Vocal Music,	5	
Guitar,		
Calisthenics,		

From the merit column on this page, the Parents may form a correct idea of Miss Medora Bull's proficiency in her several Studies during the past Session. Her Standing is highly creditable to her, and she will doubtless make an excellent Scholar.

Her demerit is all for minor delinquencies, with the exception of which her deportment has been amiable and praiseworthy.

D. C. VanVliet
Principal

EXPLANATION.—No. 8 denotes perfect ; 7, excellent ; 6, very good ; 5, good ; 4, medium ; 3, poor ; 2, bad ; 1, very bad ; 0, entirely neglected. These numbers indicate the pupil's proficiency in her several studies, only so far as they have been pursued by her. Each lesson is accurately marked, varying form 1 to 8, according to the manner in which it is recited. At the close of the Term, these numbers are added, and their sum divided by the number of lessons recited : the quotient gives the average number for each lesson, as shown in the Merit column.

A report card from a girls' private school, 1847. Note the long list of accomplishments available at the school as well as the range of academic subjects. (Courtesy AO, MU19)

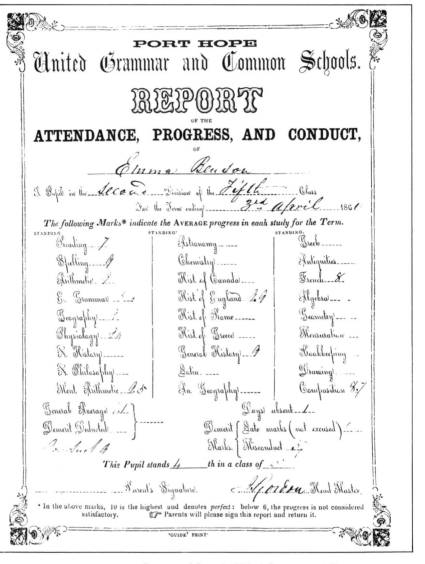

Report card from the United Grammar and Common Schools, Port Hope, 1860. A lawyer's daughter, Emma Benson was sent to the union school, which offered a solid academic education but few of the accomplishments available at the Burlington school. (Courtesy AO, MU119)

Intermediate, or Class II Non-Professional, Examination.

This Document gives the holder NO AUTHORITY TO TEACH in a Public or High School.

N° 3743

It is hereby Certified that *James A. Dickinson* having passed the Intermediate Examination held at *Richmond Hill* on the *5th 9th July* is entitled to the standing of a pupil in the Upper School.

Frank N. Tudell
Deputy Minister of Education.
pro Secretary

Dated at the Education Department,

Toronto, *11 Aug* 18*80*

NOTE.—If the holder of this is a candidate for a Public School Teacher's Certificate, he may (on satisfactory proof of age and character) be admitted by the Inspector to a County Model School to be trained for a 3rd Class Professional Certificate; but if he has already taught with success for one year in a High or Public School, he is eligible for admission to a Normal School to be trained for a 2nd Class Professional Certificate, on application to the Deputy Minister.

	SUBJECTS OF EXAMINATION.	Marks. Possible	Marks Awarded.
Group I.	Arithmetic.	100	42
	Algebra	100	43
	Euclid.	100	62
Group II.	English Grammar,	180	74
	Composition,	75	30
	Dictation.	45	39
Group III.	History.	100	63
	Geography.	100	64
	English Literature.	100	45
Group IV.	Natural Philosophy.	110	56
	Chemistry.	110	41
	Book-keeping.	80	54
	Latin.	200	
	French.	200	
	German.	200	
	Grade awarded		B

Almost unknown in the schools before the 1860s, paper credentials and student records came of age in the last third of the nineteenth century. The Intermediate Certificate, awarded for success at the Intermediate examination, allowed students to proceed to Upper School or to teacher training. For a few years it was also the basis for awarding provincial grants by payment by results. Note the low pass marks; it took a few decades to establish 50 per cent as the conventional norm for a pass. (Courtesy G.M. Dickinson)

Owen Sound Collegiate Entrance Examination

Maud Graham

The following is the number of marks obtained by you in each subject at the recent Examination for admission to the Collegiate Institute, Owen Sound. Dec. 1897

	Maximum marks	Marks obtained
READING	50	48
DRAWING BOOKS	25	22
EXAM. PAPER (*Drawing*)	25	21
WRITING	20	15
ORTHOGRAPHY & ORTHOEPY	55	22
LITERATURE	105	75
ARITHMETIC	105	63
GRAMMAR	105	77
GEOGRAPHY	80	52
COMPOSITION	105	84
HISTORY	80	2?
TOTAL	755	58?
MINIMUM FOR PASS	377	
FAILED		
PASSED		✓
RECOMMENDED		

Please show this card to parents and teachers.

Entitled to 3 years Scholarship. F. W. MERCHANT, Principal.

The high school entrance examination was the litmus test for both successful pupils and teachers in the public schools, and the symbolic terminal point of the public school program. This is one side of a postcard mailed to candidates by the principal of the Owen Sound collegiate institute, informing them of their results. (Maud Graham scrapbook, in possession of authors)

The Owen Sound Collegiate Institute.

RECORD FOR 1892.

For six years in succession the Owen Sound Collegiate has passed more candidates at the University and Departmental Examinations for Teachers' Certificates than any other school in the Province. The following is the record of the number of pupils passed at the examinations of 1892:

University Matriculation 10

(Seven candidates obtaining an aggregate of 23 honors, 12 First Class and 11 Second Class. One candidate winning a general proficiency scholarship.)

First year University Examination.. 3

Matriculation in Medicine 3

Senior Leaving Examination 13

Junior Leaving Examination.................. 38

Primary Examination 42

Art School Examinations, about 200

The following are the names of the successful candidates at the Matriculation, Leaving and Primary Examinations:

UNIVERSITY MATRICULATION.

ALEX. M. DEWAR—First Class Honors in Mathematics, French, German: Second Class in English. Winner of Fifth General Proficiency Scholarship.

R. W. ALLIN—First Class Honors in Mathematics, French and German.

MISS MAUD GRAHAM—Second Class Honors in English, French, German.

ARTHUR R. HAMILTON—Second Class Honors in Mathematics, English, History and Geography.

RICHARD HOWEY—First Class Honors in Chemistry, Zoology, History and Geography; Second Class Honors in English, French, German.

FRANK HUTCHISON—First Class Honors in Chemistry.

JOHN W. LITTLE—First Class Honors in English, History and Geography; Second Class Honors in Classics.

Examination results, Owen Sound collegiate institute, 1892. By the end of the 1880s, examination results, more than anything else, measured the reputation of a school. This first page of a printed leaflet announces the achievement of successful students, but first it trumpets the record of excellence established by the principal and teachers of the school. After her success in the entrance exam five years earlier, Maud Graham achieved the distinction of being the only girl in her class to pass university matriculation. She continued her studies at the University of Toronto. (Maud Graham scrapbook, in possession of authors)

Owen Sound collegiate institute science laboratory, 1888. Owen Sound was one of a handful of outstanding collegiates in the 1880s and early 1890s. Among the reasons for its success was civic pride and public investment in such modern and still uncommon facilities as this science laboratory. (Courtesy AO, *AR*, 1888)

Inventing Secondary Education

CHAPTER ONE

Introduction

Like many other modern institutions, the Ontario secondary school is an invention of the second half of the nineteenth century. As its very name implies, it is one part of a more extended system of education organized into three successive stages, with the secondary and post-secondary sectors built atop the elementary or primary school. Each sector is responsible for particular age groups and particular levels of learning. The secondary school deals with teenagers already educated well beyond the rudiments of literacy. Its curriculum is tightly linked to, and is mainly a more advanced or specialized version of, the curriculum taught in the elementary school. Similarly, the upper boundary of the secondary school is clearly defined by, and articulated with, the point at which the third stage of the system begins.

The modern Ontario secondary school is also a public school. Though there is a small private sector, which includes a handful of prestigious boarding schools, the vast majority of secondary schools are day schools, financed and controlled by local and provincial educational authorities. Except for the Roman Catholic schools, the public secondary sector is secular or, at least, non-denominational. As well, the schools are comprehensive in scope: they educate both boys and girls, and offer a variety of different programs of study within a single building.

Before the 1850s, however, secondary education, in the sense we have just described, did not exist. Boys and girls were educated in sexually segregated institutions. Schools were founded, financed, and controlled mainly by churches, voluntary groups, and private individuals, not by local or provincial governments. Different sorts of schools were established to offer distinct types of curricula. And however diverse they might be in other respects, most schools offered what would now be identified as both elementary and secondary education to children whose ages might range anywhere from five or six to their late teens.

In their attempt to render the past intelligible to modern readers, historians have tended to minimize these differences by assimilating the past to the present. The common school is treated as an early form of primary school. The grammar school is said to be akin to a secondary school. Despite the presence of large numbers of non-matriculants, the colonial university is treated like a modern undergraduate college. The problem with this approach is that it masks the important shifts in the organization of education that took place in the middle decades of the nineteenth century, and obscures the emergence of what were essentially new, or at least profoundly different, institutions. Nowhere is this more true than in the case of secondary education. The Upper Canadian grammar school, for example, was not, in the modern sense, a secondary school, nor was it conceived as a second stage in a general system of education. Rather it was, by intent at least, a special-purpose classical school that took boys immediately after they had learned the rudiments and gave them both an "elementary" and "secondary" education. The common school was not simply an elementary school but one that was expected to teach both the three Rs and more advanced subjects alike.

Before the 1860s, moreover, all of the terminology we use to describe the organization of education was in flux and lacked the fixed meanings we take for granted today. The word "elementary" was in common use throughout the first half of the nineteenth century. It did not, however, refer to a particular sort of school but to the subordinate or rudimentary parts of any form of education. The common schools taught elementary and other subjects. The grammar schools provided an elementary classical and English education. Both sorts of schools might be described as offering elementary education in contradistinction to the superior education furnished by a university or collegiate school. For example, a correspondent to the *Globe* in 1856 divided the educational system into two parts, higher and elementary, and then wrote of "our system of Elementary – Grammar and Common School – education."[1]

Two other now familiar words, "primary" and "secondary," had been borrowed from European school systems during the nineteenth century. By the 1850s "primary" had come into common, though not precise, use as a synonym for elementary education generally or for the early stages of an elementary education. Even then it was not so well established that it had eliminated other contenders – for example, as late as 1859 one board of school trustees used the word "initiatory" as well as "primary" to identify the early stages of learning in its schools.[2] Nevertheless, in the two decades before Confederation "primary" was already well on the way to becoming a standard part of the lexicon. But "secondary" was not. Despite the millions of words spilled on education in the mid-nineteenth century, we have located no more than a handful of instances where the term was used by Upper

Canadians. And even in those few cases, "secondary" carries a meaning quite different from its twentieth-century definition. In his report on elementary education in 1846, for example, Egerton Ryerson, Upper Canada's chief superintendent of education, used the word "secondary" to identify a stage in the organization of Prussian and French education.[3] However, he apparently considered it a foreign word or a word meant to describe a foreign institution, and did not employ it when articulating his own vision of the organization of Upper Canadian education, reverting to more familiar or specific terms such as "grammar school." In 1847 he used the word in a fashion which at first sight appears modern but which in context carries another meaning altogether.[4] The word also appears in a long quotation from the president of Harvard College reprinted in the *Journal of Education for Upper Canada* in 1853, but here secondary education is assimilated to "higher education" and is to be provided in colleges.[5] A few years earlier, on the other hand, Ryerson had written of the need to classify pupils better by organizing "the primary, secondary and senior departments of the common school."[6]

"High school" was yet another term coming into common use at mid-century. Sometimes it was used synonymously with "grammar school" as, for example, when Ryerson wrote that the grammar school ought to be the "high school of the city – the intermediate school between the common schools and the university."[7] Sometimes it was identified as distinct from the grammar school but above the elementary schools.[8] Sometimes it was used as a cover term for all departments and subject levels beyond the teaching of the three Rs.[9] Some people used it to identify a level of teaching for which other people used the terms "union" or "central" school.[10] And where a precise meaning is given it can hardly be equated with "secondary" education. In Paris, according to its local superintendent, "a High, or Union school will be established ... to contain all the pupils *in* and beyond the Third [Reading] Book"; in Hamilton in 1861 pupils entered the "High School" when they had progressed "as far as the second division" of the prescribed common school program.[11] Neither the second division nor third book can easily be categorized as "secondary," and this usage reminds us of the derivation of the term: "high school" comes from "higher school" or "high English school," an institution that offered something beyond the rudiments but that was indefinite as to precisely what. Speaking in the legislature in opposition to the abolition of the professional faculties at the University of Toronto in 1853, George Brown remarked that nothing could "be more desirable than to secure for our country the benefit of a high school of surgery and medicine"; similarly, in condemning the ambitions of "petty" institutions like Victoria College, he called for the establishment of "a high school in Toronto," by which he meant a proper university, "free from sectarianism, where high education should be taught."[12] At or before Confederation, in other words, the term "high school" was a residual term referring to an institution that might teach a varying list of subjects at varying levels of difficulty to a wide age range.

Much the same might be said of the term "academy." One finds it used to identify a school *building* in which a common school, grammar school, or both, might be taught.[13] One finds it juxtaposed against the classical grammar school as a school that offered a modern curriculum.[14] Sometimes it was used as a synonym for a grammar school, and sometimes as the name of an institution that taught everything from the three Rs through an undergraduate curriculum.[15] Another common mid-nineteenth-century phrase was "intermediate school," but there is contradictory usage here as well. While it was normally used to identify grammar schools, or any school between the common school and the university, we find the local superintendent writing of Hamilton in 1861 that "the present organization of the City schools embraces a grammar school, a central or high school, three intermediate and six primary schools."[16] Similarly in 1864 Ryerson remarked to a correspondent that "every principal city and Town in the neighboring States has its High School, as well as its Primary and Intermediate Schools."[17]

Upper Canadians, it must be emphasized, were not alone in lacking a fixed meaning for secondary education. Before the 1860s the word "secondary" was rarely used anywhere in the English-speaking world.[18] And even when the term was used, it did not refer to a school designed for a particular age or curricular level.[19] Following European usage, it referred to a school that catered to a particular social class, and usually, but not always, one that prepared boys for the universities and professions.[20] Almost without exception such schools took boys at quite young ages and taught them what we would now consider to be both secondary and elementary education, including in some cases the elements of literacy. A different meaning was attached to "secondary" in some parts of the United States. In 1840 for example, Philadelphia opened a number of "secondary" schools where pupils were sent from the "primary school" at about age eight; if pupils completed the course at the secondary school they might then go on to the "Central High School."[21] And in passing, Pavla Miller provides a wonderful definition from the state of South Australia: "According to the Inspector General's rough rule of thumb, all schools charging a weekly fee should be considered as primary schools, and those that charge a quarterly fee of more than say 13 shillings ... should be considered secondary schools for the purposes of the [1875 Education] Act."[22] Finally, in a recent study of English middle-class schools, John Roach remarks that "the major problem, from the point of view of the late twentieth century, in discussing both the grammar and private schools of ... [the nineteenth century] is that no clear dividing line existed between elementary and secondary education ...

Almost every combination of ages and levels of study can be found with the result that the term 'secondary education' as we use it today is an anachronism."[23]

In Upper Canada, as elsewhere, in sum, the "term secondary education" was rarely used until the last third of the century and, if used at all, might refer to a type of school very different from our understanding of the term. Education simply was not organized as a tripartite set of vertically integrated stages. "Secondary education" was indeed being invented during the last half of the nineteenth century, and some of its roots lie in the middle decades of the century. But to use the term "secondary education" to describe, in any precise way, any of the schools of mid-nineteenth-century Upper Canada is not only anachronistic, but a misleading anachronism at that.

By the 1880s, nonetheless, education in Ontario had been largely reconstructed, and virtually all of the characteristic features of the modern secondary school had been put in place. Our aim in this book is to chart the transition from traditional to modern institutions that occurred between the 1840s and the 1880s. As our title indicates, our central concern lies with the development of the modern secondary school. But more broadly, we hope to account for some at least of the origins of the tripartite organization so characteristic of modern education systems. In the chapters that follow we will focus on four sets of questions. First, there is the problem of explaining the organization of education in early Upper Canada. If the conventional elementary-secondary dichotomy does not help to explain it, how then are we to make sense of it? Second, given that there was in fact a pre-existing set of institutions organized in one particular way, why did Upper Canadians change it? Why, in other words, did they invent secondary education, in the sense of a linked, sequential, second stage of a tripartite system? Third, given the fact that middle-class education in much of the English-speaking world was provided in non-government schools, why did Upper Canadians place their secondary schools in the *public* sector? Why did they behave more like the Americans or Scots in this respect than like the English or Australians? And finally, why did secondary education become coeducational and comprehensive? Once again, there were models elsewhere that pointed in very different directions – to separate schools for boys and girls, and, as well, to separate schools for the different programs of study. Why in Ontario did the sexes come to be educated together? And why were programs of study that led to different vocational outcomes lodged under the same roof?

Before we begin our argument, some preliminary comments are in order. During the nineteenth century, in Ontario as well as in other parts of the English-speaking world, secondary or superior education was conventionally associated with the education of the upper and middle classes. Thus this book is primarily concerned with the schools that educated these classes and not with the growth of the education system generally. While we will have a good deal to say about the common schools, our focus falls almost exclusively on the senior classes and not on the lower grades where the great masses of children were to be found, or on the development of common school policy as such. Equally we have largely ignored Upper Canada College and the small number of late-nineteenth-century girls' and boys' boarding schools. In several cases such schools have their own historians, and to deal with them adequately would have made this book much longer than it is. But beyond that, we have chosen to focus primarily on the Upper Canadian grammar schools not only because these institutions eventually became the public secondary schools of the late nineteenth century, but also because, of all our educational institutions, they are perhaps the least well known. Historians have copiously documented the growth of the common schools and universities throughout the period but have largely ignored, and misunderstood, the development of the grammar schools. Even then we have not attempted to provide a full narrative account of the history of the grammar schools. Much has been omitted before 1840 and after 1880. Rather we are primarily concerned here to offer an explanation of the decline of traditional institutions and habits of thought, and the emergence of modern institutional forms.

Throughout the book we will often use the phrase "the middle class" and a preliminary comment is in order here as well. In this study the middle class includes merchants and other proprietors, professionals, public officials, and clerks, along with substantial farmers and those artisans and craftsmen who had won some degree of prosperity from their work. To put it another way, it includes the people who could afford the opportunity costs and other expenses of keeping their children in school for a few years longer than the majority of Upper Canadians, and whose children formed the clientele of the senior classes in the common schools, the grammar schools, and the colony's various private and collegiate schools. We recognize that this is a loose definition, and one, perhaps, that is theoretically unsatisfying. Anything more fine-grained, however, simply cannot be fruitfully applied to our analysis of superior education in Upper Canada. Just as there are no clear borderlines to the middle class itself, so there are none when it comes to schooling. As we will see in chapter 6, some of the wealthiest individuals in the community sent their children to the public grammar schools and some did not. And similarly there were always grammar school students whose parents were poor, though undoubtedly they would have been defined as the respectable poor. The majority of our school users fell somewhere in between.

While we are not, then, committed advocates of the two-class model of social stratification, we do not have the sources from the middle decades of the nineteenth century to discriminate between the school-related behaviour of the Upper Canadian elite and the more general run of well-off and modestly prosperous members of society. For example, very few private school registers from the period have survived and thus we cannot analyse the effect of fine distinctions of occupation and wealth on attendance patterns at different private schools or between the private and the public sector.[24] Thus our middle class is really not "middle" at all, but synonymous with such contemporary usages as the "respectable classes" or the "middle classes."[25] It includes in other words *all* of the better-off portions of Upper Canadian society. This, of course, is essentially identical with Michael Katz's "business class" and we prefer to use the phrase "middle class" mainly on the grounds that it is more familiar, and perhaps a little more socially inclusive.[26] In a majority of cases, moreover, we are dealing with schools in relatively small communities, where social distance was less pronounced; if we were dealing with Toronto alone or even the handful of other cities, it might be more important or more useful to distinguish between upper- and middle-class behaviour. In order to avoid, in any case, as many stylistic infelicities as possible, and to reduce the number of qualifiers to the minimum, we will observe the following rule throughout the book: references to schools, to public opinion generally, and to people's beliefs, habits, and assumptions are to be read as references to middle-class schools, opinion, or beliefs unless we note otherwise.

In the early chapters of this book the reader will come across references to an intensive study of five southwestern Ontario grammar schools. All of the details about this part of our work and our findings about the schools, and the communities where they were located, are described in chapter 6. The phrase "the abc's" was more commonly used by contemporaries than "the three Rs" but because of its familiarity we have chosen to use the latter term to refer to the rudiments of literacy and numeracy. Since the terms common school and grammar school were generic terms we have also borrowed the English phrase "grant-aided" to identify those common and grammar schools that received local tax support and/or legislative grants. This also helps us to avoid, as much as possible, using "private" versus "public," which was not a common juxtaposition in the period before 1860.

And finally, two brief notes for readers who are not familiar with Ontario history in the nineteenth century. The territory that is now Ontario has had three names in law: Upper Canada from 1791 to 1840, Canada West from 1841 to 1867, and Ontario from 1867 on. Conventional usage however tends to use only two – Upper Canada to 1867 and Ontario after that – and we will do likewise. Secondly, a brief word of introduction to Egerton Ryerson. An influential Methodist minister, newspaper editor, at different times political reformer and conservative, pioneer public servant, prolific author, controversialist, and moralist, Ryerson was also chief superintendent of education in Upper Canada from 1846 to 1876, the three formative decades in the history of the Ontario school system.[27] Though Ryerson was responsible in a general way to the cabinet of the provincial parliament, there was no minister of education and thus he had great discretionary powers and wide administrative latitude. He did not always get what he wanted, nevertheless, and the development of the secondary school is a case in point. Despite his unceasing efforts for more than twenty years, Ryerson was unable to impose the "one best system" of superior education on the province. In the end, the politics of education would give most of the victories to his opponents. But even if the schools never became exactly what he wanted them to be, his beliefs and activities cast a long shadow across this narrative, as indeed they do over Ontario education itself.

CHAPTER TWO

Patterns of Educational Provision in Upper Canada

Upper Canadian education was organized around a set of interlocking educational and social assumptions – assumptions about the best pedagogical practices, the uses of schooling, and the nature of social relations. None of them was invented in the colony itself. They had been imported as part of the immigrants' cultural baggage from Britain and America, and transplanted to the new environment. But regardless of their particular origins, they were of critical importance in structuring the pattern of educational provision in Upper Canada. The colony's educational institutions were constructed in conformity with these assumptions, which governed the relationships between different sorts of schools, and determined the ways in which Upper Canadian families used their schools.

Throughout the colony's history, Upper Canadians made a distinction between the rudiments of literacy taught to beginners, on the one hand, and the rest of the curriculum, taught to all other pupils, on the other. Indeed if there was such a thing as a two-stage notion in Upper Canadian education, it was captured in this dichotomy. Upper Canadians inherited the idea that very young children learning the elements of reading and writing constituted a distinct subgroup of the pupil population. That is, they shared the view, long held elsewhere, that beginners, who could not yet learn from books and who had not yet mastered the disciplines of classroom life, merited special classes and teaching techniques. [1]

When for example in 1840 King's College Council drafted a model set of regulations for the district grammar schools, it assumed that boys would attend these schools from the outset of their education. But beginners were to be assigned to a "preparatory form," which was to precede the "first form." [2] Thus while the grammar schools were expected to provide the first elements of reading and writing, there was, nonetheless, an implicit assumption that a grammar school education proper did not include the rudiments. Precisely the same distinction was made at Upper Canada College in 1836: a "Preparatory School" intended for "the preparation of those pupils who are not qualified to join the lowest College Form" taught pupils the elements of Latin, and English reading, spelling, and writing.[3] Similarly, in a letter written in 1845 to the editor of the *Patriot*, a correspondent voiced his complaints about the general state of the grammar schools, including the fact that "children were often sent to them unable to read or write." Among the reforms he suggested was "the exclusion ... of those children who should be attending common schools or Preparatory schools, under the management of females who are often better qualified than men to be instructors of boys under seven or eight years of age."[4] One finds much the same distinctions being made in the private-venture and proprietary schools for both boys and girls. Though the smaller schools especially rarely excluded beginners, the advertisements and circulars tell of lower fees and separate departments for younger children.[5]

In early Upper Canada the distinction between beginners and the rest was rarely crystallized into separate institutions for each. Schools were generally too small or too poor to provide separate teachers for beginners, let alone separate buildings. Yet there was a clear tendency in that direction. Separate departments and "preparatory classes" are one indication. Another was the exclusion of younger children where the size and success of a school warranted it. When it opened its doors in 1836, Upper Canada Academy took all comers, beginners and more advanced pupils alike; but as numbers grew during the 1840s, its successor, Victoria College, limited its preparatory classes to those who had already acquired the three Rs.[6] The same is true of other institutions. Typically, the Toronto Academy, founded by the Free Church in 1846, began by including the three Rs but by 1852 had eliminated the rudiments, announcing that no pupil was to be admitted "till he can read and write English fluently."[7]

The distinction between beginners and the rest has always lent some apparent plausibility to the view that the elementary-secondary dichotomy is an appropriate categorization for Upper Canadian schools. But it is at best, we suggest, crude and misleading. Where ages are given, the dividing line is highly variable – sometimes at seven or eight, sometimes at ten, occasionally at twelve – and the curricular basis is generally the rudiments of literacy. Nor was the division institutionalized in separate schools. The grammar school taught the three Rs as did the common school, and both taught more besides. So indeed did most other schools – academies, colleges, and private-venture schools alike. If the elementary-secondary dichotomy existed at all, it was embryonic and overlaid by other kinds of assumptions which played a more important part in structuring Upper Canadian education.

But if the terms elementary and secondary are unhelpful, it does not follow that the division between beginners and the rest is of marginal interest. In fact it helps focus our attention on one of the fundamental fault-lines in nineteenth-century education. On the one side there were the elements of literacy and numeracy, skills acquired almost universally in Upper Canada regardless of social class, sex, religion, or ethnicity. On the other side lies what we might term "the discretionary sector" of education – the sector constituted by those schools, or parts of schools, which offered a curriculum more advanced than literacy, and attended by that minority of pupils who remained in school longer than the norm.[8] It is out of the discretionary sector that modern secondary education would begin to emerge in the middle decades of the nineteenth century.

Among the fundamental assumptions which informed the discretionary sector was the notion that the curriculum could be subdivided into two broad categories. There were the studies that constituted "superior education" on the one hand, and the studies of a "common" or "ordinary" education on the other. Once again, however, it must be emphasized that this distinction cannot be reduced to the elementary-secondary dichotomy, nor is it even a prototype. "What is meant by a common school education?" one newspaper editor asked rhetorically in 1834.

This question has never been answered. Some think it enough that their children learn to read; others will insist on writing; many will be content with reading, writing and arithmetic. Others will add to this list, grammar, geography, history – perhaps, practical mathematics, physics, astronomy, mechanics, rural economy – with several other branches ... In short, where shall the limit be fixed? Who shall prescribe the boundaries beyond which the common school education shall never extend? It is evident upon reflection, that the phrase common school education is a very indefinite one.[9]

Writing in 1847, Egerton Ryerson cast his curricular net even more widely: a "plain English education" of the kind given in "every good common school" should include

reading and the principles of the English language; arithmetic; elementary geometry or Knowledge of Forms, geography and the elements of history; natural history and agricultural chemistry; writing, drawing and vocal music; bookkeeping, especially in reference to Farmers' accounts; religion and morals.[10]

For girls, an ordinary education would include most of these subjects and, almost invariably, plain needlework as well.[11]

Both an ordinary and a superior education included the three Rs, and both included a variety of higher studies – those subjects begun after children had mastered the rudiments and which composed the curriculum of the discretionary sector. A "superior education," then, was not simply a second or more advanced stage of education. Though it usually lasted longer than an ordinary education, that was not integral to its meaning either. Rather it was a different *kind* of education: its curriculum included a number of special subjects which clearly distinguished it from a common or ordinary English education.

For boys, a superior education consisted of those studies constituting a liberal education. And the mark of a liberal education was, above all, a knowledge of the language and literature of Greece and Rome. These were not the only valued subjects in such an education. Mathematics was usually considered essential as well. Natural philosophy, history, geography, and English grammar and composition were routinely included, and in many schools so indeed were such practical subjects as bookkeeping, geometrical drawing, and commercial arithmetic.[12] Nevertheless, since at least the Renaissance, the study of the classics was virtually coterminous with the acquisition of a liberal education. In Europe and in Britain the classics were seen as the best subjects for training the mind to think clearly and logically. They were also the subjects that gave access to the great corpus of philosophical, political, scientific, and aesthetic literature which constituted the foundations of Western thought. As a distinguished historian of the classical inheritance has put it, for the educated classes of Europe and Britain the language and literature of Greece and Rome remained "as points of cultural and intellectual self-reference throughout the nineteenth century."[13]

In Upper Canada, as in Britain, the classics were not seen simply as two subjects amongst a number of other equally valued subjects. Rather they were treasured as the pre-eminent means of training the mind and furnishing it with worthwhile knowledge. Reviewing two new Latin texts – and that in itself is a gauge of the distance between his world and ours – George Brown, the editor of the *Globe*, wrote in 1850 that "it is now generally acknowledged that the study of the ancient classics of Greece and Rome is essential to the full development of the mind – to the formation of correct taste, and to the attainment of right views of the connexion that exists between language and thought."[14] Almost without exception the classics were required subjects for entry to the colonial universities as indeed they were in Britain. They were the crucial prerequisites that distinguished a learned profession from an ordinary occupation. A liberal education was the mark of a gentleman and gave its possessor, in his own eyes at least, a special claim to political and social leadership. As Egerton Ryerson described the distinction in 1842, "an English education" was "requisite to the ordinary duties of life"; "a classical and scientific education" was "requisite to professional pursuits; and I may add, necessary to extensive and permanent success in any of the higher employments to which one may be called by the authorities or voice of his country. The latter includes the former; and the union of both is essential to individual and national greatness."[15]

At least among the Upper Canadian "clerisy" – the respectable clergy of the Anglican and Presbyterian churches, the members of other learned professions, college and grammar school teachers, educational policymakers, and others of like mind – classical learning was not seen as narrowly bookish or merely ornamental. Indeed, as the preceding passage by Ryerson indicates, classical studies were pre-eminently useful. A Queen's College professor put it this way in 1848: the study of Latin and Greek was "a great engine of mental culture" which gave students "an advantage in the prosecution of more practical studies which those only can understand who have profited by it."[16] Classical studies were, according to a trite but illuminating student oration at Victoria College in 1838, "peculiarly adapted to the development of the intellectual faculties" because they enlarged the conceptions of mind, improved the memory, rendered more acute the discriminatory powers, improved a student's eloquence, and had a number of practical applications for doctors, lawyers, and the clergy besides.[17] The mental culture and discipline derived from studying the classics were routinely considered to best "qualify young persons to discharge the duties of the magistry and other public situations ... and to furnish a sufficient supply of intelligent and well-informed persons to meet the future exigencies of the state."[18] While the dominant place of classics in the curriculum was beginning to come under attack at mid-century, and the volume of criticism would mount each decade thereafter, Upper Canadian educators still overwhelmingly endorsed the notion that classics was the supreme expression of the best in educational practice and, for boys at least, the *sine qua non* of a liberal education.

A SUPERIOR EDUCATION for girls differed from that of boys in some fundamental ways. Girls too would learn the three Rs and the more advanced parts of an English education, studying many of the same subjects as boys. But along with the "solid" or academic subjects, they would also take a variety of "ornamental" studies that might include fancy needlework, drawing and painting, instrumental music, dancing, French, and other modern languages. The extent to which any of the solid or ornamental subjects would be pursued depended on parental wealth and preferences, but whether a girl's education was limited to a small private day school that offered only a limited range of subjects, or she was sent to one of the larger boarding schools and kept there for a prolonged period, the solid and ornamental subjects went hand in hand. If she enrolled in the senior form of a sophisticated and serious institution like the Burlington Ladies' Academy in 1845, she might study Paley, the English classics, Latin, and moral philosophy. But she would also learn "wax fruit and flowers," embroidery, instrumental and vocal music, and Female Manners.[19]

This "accomplishments curriculum," as it has come to be known, was to be the subject of much criticism in the later nineteenth century, and historians have denigrated it as well, dismissing it as trivial and frivolous.

In recent years, however, such judgments have been challenged and the quality as well as the constraints of the accomplishments curriculum have been reassessed.[20] The case for a distinct curriculum for girls arose out of the notion of the separate spheres appropriate to men and women. A woman's proper sphere, as we know from a decade or more of historical research, was primarily in the home as wife, mother, and homemaker, though it also extended beyond the domestic circle to the church and the voluntary association, for she was seen not only as prime mover in the domestic sphere but also as the moral lever of society generally.[21] The accomplishments curriculum, both solid and ornamental, was designed to prepare girls for the roles they would play in later life. It was not intended to lead on to paid work, since middle-class women (and indeed most married women) did not engage in paid work in the nineteenth century. Thus criticism that it debarred women from credentials that led to middle-class occupations, while quite correct, is essentially misconceived. Its whole point and purpose lay elsewhere.

Thoughtful exegesis on the nature of women's education is not common in Upper Canada but there is a fine statement of the ideal written in 1865 by a Mrs Holiwell, who ran a ladies' school in Toronto. For Mrs Holiwell, the aim of education was to produce a woman who was useful, moral, cultivated, and polished. By useful, she referred to the skills of managing a household, and she believed that kind of training was almost entirely the responsibility of the home, not the school. Morality too was best left to the home, with the church and school playing subsidiary roles. Similarly with polish, which could only really be acquired by mixing in good society. Knowledge and accomplishments, however, were the special domain of the school, and she outlined her curriculum in the following way. A girl should acquire

so much familiarity with History and Geography, Ancient and Modern, that she will readily understand most historical allusions, and the connexion of the present age in its politics and philosophy with the past, and I would have her acquire such a method of studying these subjects as would make it easy at any time to take up a particular history of a particular period or country, and master it with the least waste of time. Also such a knowledge of her own language that her correspondence may be correct and elegant; her diary, memorandum book, and album mirrors that reveal an educated mind. I would have her Arithmetic comprehensive, that in business transactions she could control results, and not feel herself at the mercy of the shopkeeper and the workman, as is often the case. I would add to these attainments, an acquaintance with the Sciences and Literature, that she may not look with an ignorant eye on the wonders of that world of which she forms a part, and when thrown among the learned and scientific she may follow the conversation with pleasure, even when forbidden to assist.

... [The accomplishments include] a good knowledge of the Theory and Practice of Music, and such cultivation of the voice as the individual talent will permit. My own taste would lead me to desire no other accomplishment, if the musical talent were really superior, and very highly cultivated; should it, however, be only moderate, it would be as well to add Drawing or Painting, or both; and if musical taste were altogether wanting, I would prefer that a pupil devote herself altogether to Drawing, as the time spent over the Piano will be only wasted. The Modern Languages should never be neglected in a thorough course of education. French has a particular claim on us as Canadians, with half of our fellow-subjects speaking that tongue, and Italian and German might be added advantageously, especially if the young pupil showed no preference for art.

Dancing, and various kinds of Needle Work, are easily attainable by all, and should rather be looked upon as amusements, than matters requiring serious application. [22]

It is not difficult, it must be said, to find school prospectuses which list a greater range of subjects than does Mrs Holiwell, or which appear to conform more closely to modern notions of what a good curriculum should include. But what is of special value in her statement is not simply the list of subjects but her description of their purposes. On the one hand the curriculum she proposes is neither trivial nor frivolous. What the Australian historian Marjorie Theobald says of the accomplishments curriculum generally is true of Mrs Holiwell's: "Its roots in the humanistic philosophy of the ancient liberal arts tradition are apparent"; it was, in effect, "a gender variant of a liberal education." [23] Yet on the other hand, this is not a curriculum which can easily be assimilated to modern standards. Science is for intelligent conversation and appreciation of the world around her. Music is for display and entertainment. English is for elegance. Arithmetic is for dealing with tradesmen. Her curriculum, it might be said, lacks the essential elements of academic rigour; put another way, it is not narrowly bookish, scholastic, or credentials-driven. Its purpose was not qualifications for work but to cultivate such qualities as usefulness, good taste, civility, sociability. [24] Knowledge was important in achieving those ends but "subjects" did not constitute ends in themselves, and education counted for something else than a paper chase.

We are not arguing, we want to insist, that this curriculum was politically or vocationally liberating; clearly, it was not. It was, indeed, one of the social forms which maintained inequalities of gender in the first three-quarters of the nineteenth century. The accomplishments curriculum, however, deserves to be assessed on its own terms and not judged according to the canons of late nineteenth-century (male) academics, schoolmen, and other people who thought memorizing Latin verbs and physics more worthwhile and more educative than studying the piano, drawing, or fancy needlework. To dismiss this curriculum as "mere accomplishments" is not only to give vocationalism an unwarranted legitimacy as the central focus in the construction of the curriculum but it is also to devalue the study of art and music in particular – two constitutive elements of human experience. Indeed, it remains an unanswered question in curriculum history as to just how these two traditional liberal arts were reduced, for both men and women, to options and frills in modern education.

Mrs Holiwell's essay on an appropriate curriculum for girls was, of course, a statement of an ideal, and we have no clear idea about how many schools pursued such a program. There were undoubtedly schools which offered little more than the three Rs and one or two of the accomplishments, superficially taught. On the other hand, there were also schools throughout the century which offered girls a rich menu of intellectual fare. Equally, families might differ in the extent to which they valued an extended education for their daughters; generations, indeed, might differ in the same way. An exchange of letters between W.W. Baldwin and his son Robert concerning the education of Robert's teenage daughter Maria illustrates this latter point nicely. In the spring of 1843 Robert had decided to send her to the Quebec Seminary and proposed a formidable list of the subjects he expected her to study there. Maria, already a diligent student of German, French, and a variety of other subjects, quailed at the list and turned to her grandfather for advice. W.W. intervened with some trepidation but suggested to Robert that his demands might be excessive, and the focus of her studies misdirected.

in general my opinion as to female education of the present day as far as I can see (my view being extremely narrow) – I think the most important of all objects (that of preparing young ladies to make good wives) is too much neglected – nature has designed the woman for this special duty – embellishments and accomplishments properly bestowed and acquired simply give grace to those duties in the hands of a well educated girl.

In his reply Robert assured his father that he had no intention of trying

to make her a professor of any Science whatever ... You know perfectly well what all the *ologies* mean when in a programme of a Ladies School – and the extent to which they profess to teach them which I take to be merely such a knowledge of each as will prevent their falling into absurd blunders in casual reference to them. To this extent I should be sorry to have either of my daughters any more than my sons ignorant of any one of the branches of knowledge the list of which seems to have alarmed you – Beyond this I am not desirous of going, though if the natural taste of the individual led to a further pursuit of any of them I certainly would rather encourage than repress it without allowing its hard name to frighten me.

When W.W. returned to the subject, Robert's response was more acerbic. He objected to the implication that he was "inclined to pitch the standard too high and to forget the sphere of social life in which Providence has destined women to move." Neither was the case, he insisted, and "if I have erred in the power and have overrated the mental capabilities of the sex I can only attribute it to having received my early impressions of its powers from what I felt to belong to my dear Mother." Maria also had traits, Robert continued, which reminded him of his deceased wife, "who if she had not a mind of fully the same force and power as my dear Mother, was far from being deficient in certain of those qualities, and had assuredly all others which make a husband happy."[25]

Father and son, then, could disagree on the breadth and depth of the education that Maria should receive, and they may also have held different views on the relative "force and power" of the female mind. But both agreed on one fundamental issue – the purpose of female education was to prepare for woman's distinctive social role. On that point, moreover, they were entirely in accord with virtually all contemporary opinion. And it was that conviction which, above all, underpinned the near-universal assumption in Upper Canada that the content of a superior education for girls would be different from that appropriate for boys.

A THIRD FUNDAMENTAL ASSUMPTION, which follows from the last, was that schools should be segregated by sex. Though economics and settlement patterns often ensured that good intentions would come to nought, the preference for sexual segregation appears to have been well-nigh universal, amongst the middle classes at least.[26] It may not have been considered essential in the case of small children, for even in some of the better ladies' schools there were junior classes enrolling boys as well as girls.[27] But for older boys and girls, public opinion seems to have overwhelmingly favoured separation, and for two distinct reasons.

First, as we have just seen, there were profound differences in the kind of curriculum suited to the two sexes. While both boys and girls might need to study the core subjects of an English education, girls did not need classics, or mathematics, or commercial subjects – subjects that prepared for occupations, careers, and the public arena. And even the same subjects might be given different biases when taught to boys and girls. Because there was no common curriculum, then, the sexes could not be educated together, except perhaps for the rudiments. But coeducation posed moral dangers as well. The "practice of assembling children of both sexes promiscuously in the same apartment" was repeatedly condemned by contemporaries, and such fears reinforced the imperatives of curricular differentiation.[28] Parents who could afford to exercise choice generally voted with their fees to maintain their daughters in separate establishments. Within the limits of the pressures to keep taxes low, public authorities attempted to maintain separate classes or schools for boys and girls. The vast majority of private schools were single-sex, and where such teachers operated coeducational establishments they often went out of their way to emphasize the segregation of the sexes: the advertisement for the Rev. McMullen's Ladies' and Gentlemen's Academy at Picton, for example, assured parents that "the schools are kept distinct in separate buildings, the pupils never meeting except at meal times."[29]

THE ASSUMPTION that schools should be socially segregated seems to have been no less pervasive. As in other early nineteenth-century societies, most Upper Canadians – or at least most of those who mattered – took it for granted that social classes or ranks were both necessary and inevitable. Not only was a hierarchical structure sanctified by the political theory of the day, but the embryonic science of economics was proving beyond reasonable doubt that the majority of men would inevitably remain poor and that to tamper with the social system was therefore a fraud and a delusion.[30] "The present age," John Strachan remarked,

has demonstrated that no great and decided amelioration of the lower classes of society can be reasonably expected; much improved they certainly may be, but that foolish perfectability with which they have been deluded can never be realized ... In times of tranquillity the people may be better instructed, the laws may be made more equal and just, and many new avenues of enjoyment may be opened; but labour is the lot of man, and no system of policy can render it unnecessary, or relieve the greater portion of mankind from suffering many privations.[31]

The sense of class consciousness in Upper Canada was substantially sharpened by those other victims of social change in nineteenth-century Britain, the middle-class emigrants forced to flee to the colonies. Though they are sometimes described as "gentry," this is almost always a misnomer. Generally they were people on the fringe of middle- or upper-middle-class life who for various reasons had suffered a decline in their fortunes. There were those who left because of business failure.[32] There were others who could no longer support a family at home.[33] There were half-pay officers unable to maintain respectability or educate their children.[34] There were clergymen "destitute of interest or patronage," governesses, schoolteachers, and clerks who could not afford to marry on their salaries, and a remarkable number of surgeons and other medical men belonging to the lower rungs of the profession.[35] If there were a handful who went to the bush for adventure, they were far outnumbered by those who were failures at home, and had no place to turn except, in Eric Hobsbawm's words, "to that dustbin of the unwanted and unsuccessful, the colonies."[36] They came to Upper Canada in substantial numbers and profoundly influenced the tone and style of Upper Canadian life far into the nineteenth century.[37] They brought needed skills, and cultural capital that ranged from substantial libraries to pianos. They also brought with them a sense of class-consciousness sharpened by their own bitter experiences at home. To quote out of context an apt phrase of George Orwell's, though they owned no land, "they felt they were landowners in the sight of God."[38] They had been forced to leave Britain because, as Susanna Moodie put it, they "could not labour in a menial capacity in that country where they were born and educated to command."[39] Many of these middle-class immigrants were not wealthy and would never become so, though they would usually secure for themselves reasonably comfortable professional, business, or administrative occupations. But their particular backgrounds and social assumptions reinforced more conventional impulses towards a ranked, hierarchical society in Upper Canada.

Their attitudes towards schooling reflected the same biases. Consider, for example, the case of Mrs Read of March Township in the Ottawa valley. In 1827, Hamnett Pinhey, a leading light in the area, received the following cryptic note from Mrs Read, informing him

that when she opened a study [school] for the benefit of her own children and those of her immediate neighbours (her equals) she did not open a charity school, for certainly if she gave her time to her poor neighbours it would be gratis. Her imperative duties leave her no time for such charitable purposes but Mr P having much more leisure she thinks it would be certainly better spent than in insulting a Lady.

Mystified by this, Pinhey passed the note on to her husband, which elicited a second letter detailing her grievance. Pinhey had advised the housekeeper of a friend to send her son to Mrs Read's little school on the grounds that "one hour spent under Mrs Read's tuition would be better for her son than six days spent at a School on the other side of the river and that it was a pity her son should get the *Yankee Whine*. A smile passed over my countenance at the joke," Mrs Read concluded,

but a pang went to my heart that *you* should for a moment encourage the presumption of the woman to think that her son is a fit school companion for my Daughters. It brought to mind the Fable of the "Boys and the Frogs" – "It may be play to you but death to us" for at this moment from our unfortunate situation the lower class are sufficiently inclined to an equality – you have now lent them your authority to lower us.[40]

Similarly, the dangers of mixed schools were noted by Judge Powell's wife in 1817. She was, she told a friend, worried about sending her granddaughter to a particular teacher in York who

from what I have heard does not possess that extreme vigilance respecting the conduct of her Pupils out of the School Room, which I think full as necessary as attention to them when they are in it; - another thing is objectionable to me; there can in this place be no distinction of classes; - this objection does not arise from Aristocratic pride but from the conviction that the vulgar habits of home, are more likely to become contagious, than to receive correction by example.[41]

Given such attitudes, it is not surprising to find attempts being made in some Upper Canadian communities to establish select schools under the Common School Act of 1816.[42] We know, as well, that in a few villages there were separate common schools for the children of half-pay officers and those of other townsfolk.[43] We have cases of parents withdrawing their children from grammar schools because the school contained "scholars of a very low class ... feeling indignant that their children should attend the same school."[44] And we have complaints like this one from some school reformers in the Eastern District: "the gentry of the country consider it a disgrace to themselves, and a degradation of their children that they should be taught in the common schools; that they are consequently at great expense keeping teachers in their own families or sending their children to boarding schools."[45]

The ability to translate a preference for social segregation into reality was always compromised in Upper Canada. No matter how sharp the sense of class distinction might be, it was of little import if parents lacked the resources to purchase segregated education and had no choice but to send their children to a mixed-class school. Moreover the social thought of the period was not one-dimensional. England prided itself on having an open society compared to continental countries. Scotland took particular pride in the "lad o' parts" who climbed out of the lower orders with the aid of the parish schoolmaster, went on to the university, and distinguished himself in Scottish letters or science. Similar themes abound in early American history: it is what Jefferson referred to when he wrote of creating a school system that would rake the genius from the rubbish. The conviction that in the good society aristocracies of both birth and talent must exist led John Strachan, in his early educational plans for Upper Canada, to include provisions "to open the way to the poorer inhabitants to a liberal Education for their promising children."[46] And many others would share Strachan's belief that ladders of educational opportunity must be built to complement the existing ladders of patronage, charity, and the economic opportunity of an expanding commercial society. Strachan himself was living proof that men could rise from stonemason's cabin to prince of the Church. There were other examples too: one thinks of Sandfield Macdonald, the son of a small farmer, educated first in the local common school and then by Hugh Urquhart at the Cornwall grammar school until he was ready to be apprenticed at law.[47] But, as Asa Briggs reminds us, "the rungs of the ladder did not move; it was individuals who were expected to do so."[48] If some men climbed the ladder in Upper Canada, the fact still remains that the colony was a stratified society, that stratification was sanctioned by both prevailing political and economic theory, and that schooling was expected to reflect and to help preserve it.[49]

YET ANOTHER FUNDAMENTAL ASSUMPTION in shaping the structure of Upper Canadian education was that schools were extensions of, and subordinate to, families. Parents were instrumental in creating or sustaining most schools, the curriculum and patterns of attendance were subordinated to families' social and economic strategies, and the idea of the good school was modelled closely on that of the ideal Christian family.

First, much of the schooling available in Upper Canada was the immediate creation of parents who banded together to found and maintain schools through co-operative effort or who ensured the survival of private-venture teachers through their tuition fees. The village academies – Grantham or Bath for example – were initially financed on joint-stock principles and organized by leading local families. Fathers, moreover, commonly served as trustees of the schools their children attended, hiring the teacher and supervising the progress of the pupils.[50] Indeed the expansion of the so-called state schools was often due more to parental initiatives than to government. The conversion, in the 1840s, of Grantham Academy into the publicly funded St Catharines grammar school was largely the product of the same men who had founded and directed the academy's fortunes throughout the 1830s, and who had educated their own children there.[51]

Moreover, to an extent almost inconceivable today, parents determined what was to be taught to their children and how long they would attend. There were, as we have already suggested, cultural traditions about what must be learned in school and about the hierarchy of esteem among subjects: literacy and numeracy were universally taken for granted as essential skills, while the classics were treated with a good deal of deference. But within these broad limits, and in the absence of any authority which could impose prescribed curricula, parental wishes and plans for their children dominated the curriculum.

For boys, the subjects they studied tended to be vocationally oriented. If for example a boy was to enter law or medicine he had to be able to pass the Latin examination prescribed by the Law Society or the Medical Board.

For the Anglican or Presbyterian ministry he might also need a little Greek. Hence boys destined for these occupations usually began to study the classics at a relatively early age, often at the same time as they learned the English rudiments, and the classics occupied a considerable portion of their time. In other occupations, however, classics were unnecessary. An apprenticeship to a surveyor or a civil engineer might require advanced mathematics but no classics. A man intent on training his son for business might want neither classics nor higher mathematics but simply a sound English and commercial education. Thus it was largely a boy's occupational destination that determined which subjects he took and how long he stayed in school. William Hamilton Merritt was a man who could well afford an extensive education for all his boys; but what they studied in fact hinged on their future occupations. Commenting on the progress of his sons in a letter to his father-in-law, he remarked that he was "thinking of giving the eldest a classical education and bringing up William and Thomas to business, with an English education only. William is willing to commence Latin if I please, but ... much time is lost in learning the languages unless a profession is in view."[52]

The strength of parental influence in curricular choices can be measured in a clash over the matter at Upper Canada College. The college authorities had constructed a prescribed program of studies which took the student concurrently through a series of English subjects, classics, arithmetic, and mathematics. It was the kind of program which was dear to the hearts of the nineteenth-century clerisy and which educational conservatives of any generation might describe as well-rounded; yet it also included vocationally oriented subjects like commercial arithmetic and bookkeeping. But in 1831 a group of Toronto citizens, including several successful businessmen, petitioned the lieutenant-governor, demanding changes to suit those parents "who do not desire to have them [their sons] instructed in the Classics." What they wanted instead was "to have their sons Educated in the College in such branches of an English education as will qualify them for discharging with efficiency and respectability, the scientific, and other business of Tradesmen and Mechanics."[53] The college authorities bowed to public pressure despite misgivings and created the "partial course" – the name itself indicates what the schoolmen thought of it – which allowed students to study "English composition, History, Geography, Writing, Arithmetic, Mathematics, French, Geometrical drawing and Bookkeeping" without tackling Latin or Greek. It proved a popular innovation. In the middle and late 1830s the partial course attracted anywhere from a quarter to a half of the senior students in the school.[54] The course remained a prescribed program; parents could not pick and choose individual subjects as they could at most other schools in the colony. But not even Upper Canada College, with its institutional independence assured by its endowments, could entirely resist parental pressures to shape the curriculum to their own purposes.

There were undoubtedly parents, as there have always been, to whom learning was its own reward and who introduced their sons, and occasionally even their daughters, to the classics not just for vocational purposes but because they wanted their children to inherit the full panoply of the Western intellectual tradition. It was perhaps this impulse that animated Alexander Macdonell when in 1828 he told his son to work hard, for a good education not only "opens the doors to the learned professions [and] to the formation of the mind [but] qualifies the Gentleman to be an ornament to society."[55] Nor was William Hamilton Merritt's assessment of the value of classical learning narrowly utilitarian. Writing to his wife in 1835 he described his ambitions for one of his sons: "I want him to turn his attention wholly to the Law – acquire a classical education until 16 and by the time he is 21 years of age or before, he will be qualified to practise. My motive is not to make him a lawyer merely to gain a livelihood, or make money. I shall endeavour to instil nobler sentiments in his mind."[56]

Nonetheless, in the relatively few cases where surviving family papers contain information on parental motives for sending boys to school, the concern about providing a boy with a secure occupational future seems paramount and appears to have been the main determinant of the kind of education he might receive. If one of Merritt's boys was to be provided with a lengthy classical education, another, less given to learning, was not kept in school but was rather to be sent for a year "either to Lower Canada or New York then placed 1 year in a store in Montreal where he may with diligence be competent to enter a store here [in York] and in one or 2 years after commence for himself."[57] Donald MacLeod, a half-pay officer who emigrated to Upper Canada in 1845 and bought a prosperous farm in Vaughan Township, has left a rich record of his struggles to provide a future for all four of his boys. He prepared his eldest son to inherit the family farm. This was his patrimony and his schooling had been limited to a simple English education. His second son was kept at Upper Canada College long enough to obtain a good English education along with mathematics and then apprenticed to a civil engineer. The two younger boys attended a variety of private masters and Upper Canada College and were then sent to university, one to prepare for an apprenticeship in law and the other for the ministry. The education of his three younger boys cost MacLeod dearly, but to bestow "great and respectable professions" on them was one of his greatest satisfactions in life.[58]

Within the same family, then, different children might be sent to different schools, for different lengths of time, to study radically different subjects. But there were also differences amongst families, arising from differing occupational, cultural, or social characteristics. Schooling, like money, land, or interest, was one element of what E.P. Thompson has called "the grid of inheritance" – one form of patrimony a father might bestow on a son or daughter to preserve or advance a family's security, status, or continuity. "We have," writes Thompson, "the particular inheritance practices of families, and the grid of law, custom, expectation, upon which these practices operate. And these grids differ greatly between social groups."[59] Land was the focus of one such grid. The family business was another. In his study of the social origins of the late nineteenth-century business elite, T.W. Acheson suggests another – the Scottish artisan's habit of investing in an apprenticeship rather than prolonged schooling for his sons.[60] Schooling was yet another form of patrimony. Anglican and Presbyterian clergymen in Upper Canada, for example, were not by any means wealthy but they provided many of their sons with a classical education which opened the doors to the professions. Indeed, professional occupations generally were massively overrepresented in the grammar schools and colleges of Upper Canada, as they were elsewhere in the same period.[61] As farmers looked to land, and merchants to the family business, to secure the fortunes of the next generation, so other social groups looked to schooling to preserve or enhance a family's position into the next generation.

Schools were not only created by families and subordinated to their economic and social strategies, they actually mimicked the character of the family itself. Grant-aided or private, Upper Canadian schools tended to have no more than one or two teachers and a student body no larger than a modern class. Even as late as the mid-forties, the grammar schools commonly had fewer than thirty pupils,[62] the private schools made a virtue of advertising the limited numbers of pupils they took, and if we can judge by the advertisements, a substantial number of children were educated at home or in the homes of clergymen and others who took in a few boarders to educate with their own children. Thus, barring a handful of exceptions such as Upper Canada College, the schools tended to be small and intimate, more the size of families than of modern schools, an arrangement where "parental" or constant supervision could be exercised. Where possible it was select in its choice of pupils so as to exclude unwelcome influences. The teacher was often a relative, friend, or friend of friends; and lacking these kinds of personal credentials, teachers routinely depended on clergymen and other respectable people to make their names known and to establish their reputability.[63]

"The metaphor of the family," in Alison Prentice's felicitous phrase, was no accidental feature of Upper Canadian schooling.[64] After a century of habituation it is difficult to recapture an historical moment when schooling, divorced from its ties to family values and characteristics, was viewed with suspicion. Yet as late as the mid-1860s, one prominent Toronto teacher could write that "many persons, who estimate education highly, entertain a deep-rooted distrust, if not aversion to schools."[65] Judging by the comparative number of small private schools for girls and for boys – far more for the former than the latter – this aversion may, by mid-century at least, have been more potent when it came to girls' education, where a familial educational environment was more congruent with the values, skills, and accomplishments that girls were expected to acquire for the future. But before mid-century there is evidence to suggest that, at least for some Upper Canadians, the aversion to schools held for both boys and girls. Describing Edward Blake's early education, his mother wrote that "his dear Father disliking schools, Edward received a desultory sort of education for some years – in the morning while dressing gave him his Latin lesson himself, which consisted of some lines of Virgil to be read off fluently in English and written out neatly by the evening. For the grammar we had a Tutor, and the English branches devolved on me."[66] In a letter to Egerton Ryerson written in 1843, R.B. Sullivan described the education of his son as follows.

You do him injustice in supposing that he has been *at school*. A private tutor attended at my house who knew and taught nothing but Latin and by my own desire he attended to nothing else – consequently Willy cannot write or read writing, and is perfectly ignorant of many things which every younger boy knows but he has made no small progress during his hour a day in the Latin, and as to loose reading of every book that came in his way, I never met a child who has seized with such avidity all kinds of books.[67]

And Donald MacLeod, the Vaughan Township farmer and half-pay officer whom we have already met struggling to educate three of his boys, commented to a friend that, having tried both, education in domestic settings – at home or in clergymen's families – was generally to be preferred to large schools: "The greatest number of Publick Schools resemble the Tropics. We hear of a few that, in the former, get case-hardened to meet and overcome the buffets of this mental toil ... ; those that sink under the ordeal ... are never favourably heard of."[68]

At this distance, and given the paucity of sources, it is not easy to reconstruct the reasons for this antipathy to schools. In the case of boarding away from home, parents seem to have been uneasy about breaking the natural ties of affection within the family, about the health of their offspring placed amongst large numbers of other children, and above all about the loss of influence over their moral and religious training.[69] As for day schools, where some of these considerations did not apply with such force, parents were still concerned about the quality of instruction in large classes and the bad examples which might be set by other children.[70] Whatever the mix of reasons, the metaphor of the family was intended to mitigate the dangers schools could pose.

It is important, however, not to push the metaphor too far. From the beginning it was recognized that sending children into a public arena for their education – that is, to a "public" school – had advantages that a home or "private" education could not provide. First, there was the fact that schools were specialist institutions. Parents had a variety of pressing duties to perform and these made it difficult to allocate adequate time to the instruction of their children. In a letter home to Scotland, the Presbyterian clergyman Mark Stark wrote that "this busy summer has sadly interfered with my attention to the children's lessons. Agatha [his wife] does what she can but she cannot do all and they are much behind what they ought to be."[71] There was also the matter of acquiring special skills. Unlike William Hume Blake or Mark Stark, few parents could teach a boy Latin. And presumably other parents had neither the time nor the knowledge to teach their children such arcane subjects as commercial arithmetic, bookkeeping, French, or piano.

Sent to the right school, moreover, a child could make valuable social contacts not possible within the domestic circle or in the local village academy. The Orangeville merchant William Roe could have obtained a less expensive but still select education for his girls either in Toronto or nearer home. Yet he spent nearly £100 a year during the early 1840s to send them to Mrs Cockburn's, one of a trinity of Toronto schools – the others were Mrs Goodman's and Miss Purcell's – that were to Upper Canadian girls what Upper Canada College was to boys. Our knowledge of these three schools is limited, but the occasional glimpse is revealing. We have a list of boarders (there were also day pupils) at Mrs Cockburn's in 1839 and, though most of the girls cannot be identified with any precision, they included the Misses Chisholm, Ridout, Powell, and Woodruff, along with the two Roe girls and two daughters of David Thorburn.[72] We have, too, the reminiscences of Mrs Elizabeth Grover, who attended Miss Purcell's school in the early 1830s.[73] Miss Purcell at that point took no day pupils; the school consisted solely of twelve boarders. Among them, Mrs Grover claimed, were "young ladies of Canada's first families." John Strachan's daughter was an ex-pupil and the daughters of Philip VanKoughnet and Bishop Mountain were Mrs Grover's contemporaries. The school was "Church of England and the Catechism and Collects were to be learned and the Bishop [sic] [Archdeacon Strachan] taught us on Sunday afternoon." Like the Anglican boys at Upper Canada College, Miss Purcell's girls attended St James' Cathedral for Sunday services and one of the highlights of Mrs Grover's school life was the day the girls were invited to Lady Colborne's bazaar at Government House, where the halls were lined with soldiers and filled with Toronto's best, young and old. Schools like Upper Canada College and Miss Purcell's provided an environment where the right young men could not only meet each other but meet the right young ladies as well and thus lend a hand in consolidating the network of local elites that ruled the colony.

Finally, there were the pedagogical and disciplinary advantages schools were reputed to have over home education. In the late 1820s, for example, John Strachan pointed out that young boys learned more easily and quickly when they attended school with older ones and saw them learning the same lessons beforehand. "It is in this," he concluded, "that the advantage of a public over a private education is most easily and strikingly illustrated."[74] Despite his father's antipathies, Edward Blake was finally sent to school because, wrote his mother, he "never liked regular studies and after a time" his tutor "informed us he thought Edward required the stimulus of a public school."[75] Similarly R.B. Sullivan finally turned to Ryerson and Victoria College because what he thought his son now needed was "kind discipline and regular habits of thought and study."[76] In a letter of 1840 to her son John about the education of his daughter, Ann Macaulay wrote that she was

glad you begin to think it necessary to send Annie to school, I have been grieved to see her kept so long from it, the system of home teaching does not do where the mother has not time or ill-health prevents from constant attention especially where there is but one child to attend to, she is now near 6 years old and cannot read yet, she is a compleatly spoilt child and all I have heard speak think so too, it is full time to commence a strict course and subdue her wilfulness or you will have a hard trial by and by.[77]

Summarizing his own views of the relative pedagogical advantages of public and private instruction, Mark Stark wrote that

many of the advantages or disadvantages of public and private education depend upon the character of the child – as well as the mode of treatment but I think that generally speaking more instruction *may* be communicated in a limited time by private tuition than can possibly be done in a public school even with the best system but that the great advantage of the latter consists in the regular habits of attention and steady application together with a greater drawing forth of character by intercourse and competition with others of various character and talents.[78]

Given the tension that existed between the aversion to formal schooling and the recognition of its instrumental and disciplinary value, it is not surprising that teachers often promised to provide a setting where "the advantages of a Public School will be combined with a Private Education."[79] And as Alison Prentice has explained, the metaphor of the family was invoked with special intensity where boarding was concerned. "The government of the school is parental," the prospectus for the Burlington Ladies' Academy proclaimed in 1845.[80] "Our discipline," John Strachan proclaimed of Trinity College, "is of the mildest form, consistent with those limitations which are absolutely necessary to the companionship and intimate association of so many young and ardent spirits, living in the same family ... For such reasons, our discipline partakes much of domestic control."[81] In 1846 the teacher of a Toronto girls' school announced that she would take twelve young ladies into her family, "the object being to unite the benefits of School Discipline and elegant deportment, with the advantages of Home Education."[82]

The familial model meant, above all, the model of the *Christian* family. In discussion about education and in the advertisements for schools, the importance of religious teaching and a religious atmosphere was a pervasive refrain. "Arrangements for boarders," one private-venture teacher announced, "will approach nearly to those of a well-regulated family, in which religious exercises will be prominent."[83] Another promised to give "utmost attention to the religious and literary interests of their pupils."[84] An Anglican clergyman offered to take "four young gentlemen as pupils who should be treated in every respect as members of his own family" and give them a classical and English education: "the strictest attention would be paid to morals and manners, and it would be the endeavour of the advertiser to instil into the minds of his pupils the sound religious principles, which form the only safeguard in the path of life."[85]

Schools, in sum, were assumed to be closely in tune with the interests and concerns of families. Almost without exception, schooling in Upper Canada had to be purchased directly by parents – through subscriptions or tuition fees, or both. Thus the school was expected to be responsive not simply to some abstract social entity but directly to those who purchased its services. The curriculum had to be sensitive to parental plans for their children. Schools were expected to be organized according to the preference for sexual and social segregation. And schools were expected to reflect and reinforce the patterns of authority, standards of care, and values that characterized the ideal Christian home.

Upper Canadians also assumed that the responsibility for founding and sustaining schools would be borne by a variety of social institutions, not just by the state. This does not mean, however, that they were opposed in principle to state intervention. There were always some advocates of the view that any education beyond that for the poorest classes should be left entirely to the free market.[86] Unlike England, however, where such opinions were potent – in part precisely because so much upper- and middle-class education was already provided for by endowed institutions – few Upper Canadians took a firmly ideological stance on the matter. Their attitude was, rather, government financing if necessary, but not necessarily government financing. Thus the debates in the legislature and the press tended to focus on whether or not government funding of a particular sector was needed, and if so from what source of funds.[87]

Before mid-century, however, it did not follow that financial aid should be given *exclusively* to institutions run by government. Nor was it assumed that government was necessarily the proper agency to formulate educational policy or administer the schools. Indeed the word "public" had not yet become synonymous with government or the state. Though schools akin to our notion of state schools had existed from 1807 and 1816 when the first grammar and common school legislation was passed, government aid was also extended to denominationally controlled academies and colleges as well. In the mid-1840s, the Wesleyan Methodists, Egerton Ryerson included, could see nothing inconsistent in urging that denominational colleges and their preparatory schools should form an integral and grant-aided part of a national system of education.[88] And even schools that received no grant were considered by some to be "public" rather than "private" institutions. When George Brown described the Free Church's Toronto Academy as "a merely private institution and therefore not entitled to public funds," a correspondent replied that this was "a perverted use of the terms *private* and *public*. The seminary, as all must see, is virtually, if not formally, a public one, conducted on thoroughly Catholic principles, extensively approved by the community and conferring substantial benefits on a very considerable body of the youth of Canada, of all leading denominations."[89]

The preceding paragraph also reminds us that throughout the first half of the nineteenth century, the churches remained major participants in the educational enterprise. The shortage of clergymen and the mix of denominations in most communities limited the extent to which the clergy were directly involved in the common schools. The influence of the churches in middle-class education, however, was pervasive. Clergymen were the masters in many of Upper Canada's grammar schools.[90] They opened large numbers of private-venture schools throughout the first half of the century.[91] Denominations funded and sustained most of the colony's colleges and boarding schools. Eminent clergymen made government policy for education: Upper Canada's "ministers of education" from 1815 to 1876 were all clergymen – John Strachan, Robert Murray, and Egerton Ryerson.[92] Lesser lights served as school visitors and trustees of private and grant-aided schools alike.[93] By the early 1830s it was already clear that no one denomination would shape Upper Canadian education to its own ends. The colony was too pluralistic for that. But growing denominational rivalries and the historic prerogatives of the churches over superior education especially led all the major denominations to engage in college and school founding in the middle decades of the nineteenth century. Indeed it is well to remember that in the provision of collegiate and preparatory education, the state was the interloper on ground historically occupied by the churches, and it was the credibility and competence of the state that had yet to be established. Why should a high school be under denominational rather than non-denominational control? an editorial in the Episcopal Methodist newspaper asked rhetorically in 1855. "We reply, the public generally has more confidence in an institution under the control of a religious body, who may be responsible for its moral character, and who will interest themselves in its efficacy than in one under the management of a municipal corporation, or the government itself."[94]

The absence of any *a priori* assumptions about the primacy of government in founding schools or directing educational policy, and the amorphous meaning of "public" institutions, left room for initiatives from many directions – from private philanthropy, cooperative voluntary effort by local groups of parents and other interested parties, joint-stock ventures, denominational fund-raising, and business ventures by private individuals, as well as school founding, and funding, by government itself. Or, put another way, the market, the state, the churches, and families themselves were all engaged in the provision of Upper Canadian education.

With so many agencies involved, the free play of people's preferences and customs with respect to size, religion, sexual or social segregation, future occupations, and the like produced a system characterized by a high degree of institutional variety along with great diversity in the experience of education itself. Though by our standards all schools were small, the numbers of pupils ranged from the handful of boarders in home schools or in the elite girls' boardings schools, through the grammar schools with their twenty or thirty pupils, to large schools like Victoria College or Upper Canada College, which by the mid-1840s had a hundred, and nearly two hundred, pupils respectively.[95] The preference for sexual segregation produced different schools for boys and girls, each of which offered substantially different programs of study. There were, as well, schools that offered an exclusively classical regimen, and those that offered no classics at all; schools with a formal prescribed program of studies, and those where parents were free to select, and pay for, each subject studied by their children. There were schools where non-denominational religious teaching was the norm but also schools tinctured with particular brands of Christianity. And, as we have just suggested, the schools varied by type of foundation. There were those like the grammar schools or Upper Canada College which were primarily maintained by government funds, village academies run on joint-stock principles, denominational colleges funded by the donations of the faithful, and schools sustained by the private enterprise of teachers.[96]

Though we know too little about it, what evidence survives points to a no less striking range of educational experience among middle-class children. The program of studies at Upper Canada College in the mid-1830s was consonant with our own understanding of school organization – a set of forms or grades with a group of subjects all students took, and two "streams," the classical or preparatory, and the "partial" or commercial.[97] By way of contrast there was the Eastern District grammar school at Cornwall, taught by the Rev. Hugh Urquhart, who in 1839 had thirty-one

scholars studying everything from Greek and Latin down to the three Rs –
a state of affairs typical of the district grammar schools in the 1830s.[98] And
that again needs to be set against the experience of the young Edward Blake,
taught by his father and mother.[99] There was the female department of
Upper Canada Academy, which not only taught the accomplishments but
also offered an extensive academic program to a large number of girls –
forty-eight in 1841 – who boarded in the same building and even took some
classes with an even larger number of boys, though strictly forbidden from
"conversing, corresponding, or in any way associating together, save in the
case of Brothers and sisters, and that by a written permission of the Principal."[100] There were the girls who, because there was no other choice,
attended one of the village grammar schools with their brothers and studied,
perforce, whatever the teacher offered. There were Miss Purcell's twelve
boarders, and young Annie Macaulay, whose father paid £20 a year

in connection with Mrs Creighton to a young woman who teaches her and Miss
Creighton from 12 to 2 every day. They meet at present at Mrs Creighton's. Annie
also has commenced dancing. Mr Yeo attends a private class twice a week at Mrs
Draper's where a few little ones assemble. I should expect her also in the course of
the winter to get lessons in music – she begins to have a very good notion of
spelling.[101]

The variegated pattern of Upper Canadian schooling – the sheer diversity
of institutions and experiences – comprised a fundamental characteristic of
colonial education. It was not mere chaos, however. The structure conformed
to the various assumptions we have been discussing thus far: the preference
for sexual segregation, for example, or the family-like setting of most
schools. The structure of Upper Canadian education was also shaped by the
interplay of these assumptions. The hierarchy of prestige amongst institutions, for example, was produced by the way in which notions about curriculum and class overlapped each other. And the system of "tracking" or
"streaming" was based on a mix of beliefs about sexual segregation, "the
grid of inheritance," and the nature of the curriculum.

However diverse the schools might be in some respects, they were generally sorted into two categories: common and superior. This distinction
was derived in part from the kind of curriculum each type of school offered.
But no less important, it was rooted in the notion that there should be different
forms of education for the different social classes.   The common schools
provided boys and girls with an "ordinary" or "plain" or "common" English
education. They might or might not be grant-aided, for prior to mid-century
the phrase "common school" was not yet synonymous with a grant-aided
school and was applied to private schools as well.[102] They might or might
not be sexually segregated. They might offer no more than the rudiments,

or in the urban areas offer a higher English and commercial education as well. What distinguished the common school from other schools was what it did not do: the common school did not teach the classics or the accomplishments. These latter subjects were the preserves of the superior schools – the grammar schools, ladies' schools, seminaries, private academies, and so forth.

Consider the relationship between the grammar schools and the common schools. The grammar schools often began, like the common schools, with the rudiments of English literacy, taught the ordinary branches of an English education, and often advanced a pupil's knowledge of English or arithmetic or history no further than, or not even as far as, the common school.[103] Yet along with the college, the grammar school was repeatedly identified by contemporaries as part of the system of *superior* education. The reason is simple. The grammar school offered not just a common or English, but a classical education. It was, as Ryerson described it in 1849, the first stage in a system of liberal studies.[104] Thus the grammar school – even the most lowly country school with perhaps only a few pupils learning the rudiments of Latin while all the rest studied nothing but English and commercial subjects – had an ambience and bestowed a status that no common school could aspire to. The grammar school, by virtue of its identification with classical teaching, shared in an educational enterprise that conferred a liberal education and gave access not simply to "jobs" or ordinary occupations but to "professions," the only proper occupations of liberally educated men.[105]

To reiterate, the hierarchy of educational institutions was not founded on bundles of discrete subjects, some of which were more difficult than others or which could only be mastered by older students. Rather the superior place of the grammar school arose from the value contemporaries placed on the educative function of classical studies and the fact that classics alone gave access to the universities and professions. The grammar schools ranked higher than common schools in the educational hierarchy because of a complex of social and educational values which distinguished between a liberal and an ordinary education, and liberal and ordinary subjects. The grammar school offered the former; the common school, the latter.

But the principle of hierarchy, we have said, turned on a dual axis – not just on curriculum but on social class as well. The grammar school not only taught classics, it educated the respectable classes. Many of its pupils, nonetheless, never actually studied the classics – never, indeed, progressed much beyond the level of a good common school education. But they received that education in the grammar school, deriving added status from being educated in a school associated with liberal learning and, in turn, lending prestige and authority to the superior claims of the school. The common school, on the other hand, was, as one contemporary put it, a place "where the children of common people are admitted at a common rate of

fees for common branches of Education." [106] Class and curriculum combined
to define the common school as an inferior institution in the hierarchy of
esteem. Or another example: in a letter of 1839 to a Presbyterian journal,
a correspondent wrote of the educational needs of Upper Canada this way:

we want Colleges for the learned professions, Grammar schools for the middle classes
and common schools ... for the great body of the people. In all civilized countries
there have been, and no doubt always will be, three classes, or ranks in society –
all attempts at the levelling principle to the contrary notwithstanding; and if so, there
ought to be three classes of schools to correspond. [107]

At mid-century, then, the hierarchy of educational institutions was shaped
by overlapping assumptions about class and curriculum. These were not
entirely consistent with each other, since, in the "right" school, a commercial
or even a plain English education might be graced with the title "liberal"
or "superior." But before mid-century, this inconsistency caused contemporaries no concern. A superior education was thought at one and the same
time to be an induction into a particular curriculum, and that education
appropriate to a particular class. If we are to use the phrase at all, it is only
in this sense that the contemporary European usage of "secondary" should
be applied to Upper Canada's superior schools. They were not second stage,
but secondary because of what and whom they taught.

The combined effects of class and curriculum, then, created a fundamental
fault-line in Upper Canadian education. A minority of children received a
more extended and a different kind of education from that of the vast majority
of their contemporaries. But superior education was itself internally differentiated as well. One important basis for differentiation, as we have already
seen, was sex. Segregation by sex does not definitionally track children
towards different futures, since a society may well have sexually segregated
schools in which a common curriculum is taught. But obviously, this was
not the case in Upper Canada. Though boys and girls might share the three
Rs and some other parts of an ordinary English education, this common
core was succeeded by different programs of study. Boys pursued the classics
or commercial subjects; girls learned the accomplishments. Two sorts of
educational programs ran parallel to each other, upwards from the rudiments
and towards different vocations.

A second sharp distinction existed between classical and non-classical
studies. It was part of the conventional wisdom at the time that the study
of Latin and Greek, if it was to have any value at all, had to commence
early and be pursued intensively. [108] Ideally, classics were begun concurrently with the English rudiments and continued to occupy a substantial
proportion of time throughout the rest of a boy's education. That is to say,
one did not complete an English or elementary education and then move on

to such subjects as classics; rather a pupil began both a classical and an English education at the same time. The classical school or department was thus a specialized track or stream which ran upwards from the rudiments and culminated in matriculation into a college or a professional society. Inevitably, however, the pedagogical demands of learning Latin and Greek rendered the classical program inaccessible to all but those who began classics at an early age. Transfer from the upper reaches of a common school or from any other school which only taught English or commercial subjects was in principle impossible. Thus the two basic programs of study – classical or preparatory on the one hand and "modern," English, or commercial on the other – tended to be tightly insulated from each other. A pupil began one or the other at an early age, and each led on to different destinations in life.

Accessibility to either stream was obviously limited by wealth and social class: most pupils did not move beyond the rudiments. But for those who did continue in school, the sharp separation between programs operated to differentiate the kind of education received by individual members of the same family and by different social groups. A classical education might be given by a father to the sons who would not inherit the family business or farm. Professionals or others without real property might give all of their boys a full classical education in lieu of any other form of patrimony. Tracking was not, in other words, driven simply by wealth and class. Consider again the petition in 1831 by the group of Toronto parents, including several notable businessmen, for changes in the curriculum at Upper Canada College.[109] These were people who could afford the costs of an expensive education, who could well have given their sons a classical education, but who demanded the creation of a non-classical stream because their sons were intended for business, not the professions. Upper Canada Academy (the predecessor to Victoria College) had a similar division between the Classical Program and the "Commercial Department" which excluded classics and prepared for "the business of life, either as Merchants, Engineers, or Mechanics."[110] The point here is that if we are to understand the organization and functions of superior education we need to look beyond the horizontal divide between the social classes to the vertical fractures that channelled middle-class children towards their various occupational and social destinations.[111]

While different tracks can be identified, however, no general rule dictated whether or not a particular track was to be housed exclusively in a separate institution. A few of the early grammar schools required all students to take classics, and John Strachan's primer on the proper organization of the district grammar schools recommended that classics be taught to all, though all pupils would take English and commercial subjects as well.[112] More generally, however, the schools were multi-purpose. Upper Canada College, as we have seen, had dual tracks imposed upon it. Upper Canada Academy not only had classical and commercial departments but offered the accomplishments to girls as well.

Like so many generalizations in this chapter, moreover, our discussion of tracking ends with some essential qualifications. The rigidities of the program differentiation were real enough but there were also a number of ways around them. The plethora of evening and other single-subject private-venture schools provided alternative ways of acquiring knowledge. If a boy did not learn his Latin in a grammar school, he might learn it from a private master, and a young man might be able to hurry the process along with the aid of a hired "crammer." Or a school might teach only commercial subjects, or only the mathematical skills necessary for surveying, architecture, or engineering.

Moreover, sharp distinctions between English and liberal programs of study and even between girls' curricula and boys' tended to be most successfully maintained in the larger towns, and in schools supported either by high fees or large subsidies. In smaller communities especially, sexual segregation, distinct tracks, and required programs of study were often diluted by the pressing necessity to take any pupil who could pay the fees and to teach any combination of subjects that parents were prepared to pay for.

At mid-century, then, Upper Canada's education system was characterized by institutional variety, by institutional hierarchies based on both curriculum and class, and, where possible, by curriculum-related streaming designed to provide specialized forms of education. These structural characteristics entailed substantial curricular overlap as grammar schools, girls' schools, and common schools alike all taught the three Rs and the other elements of a plain English education. The overlap was even more extensive between the grammar and common schools, since often enough the only curricular difference between them was the addition of classics in the former. The structure also entailed competition between different types of institutions for students and their fees. It meant as well the coexistence of single-track and multi-purpose institutions, sometimes in the same locality. To modern eyes, it appears to be hardly a "system" at all. It was, nonetheless, largely consonant with the assumptions about education held by contemporaries. If it appears somewhat disorderly to us, that is precisely because we wear the blinkers of a very different set of assumptions inherited from the revolutionary changes in educational thought and practice that took place in the second half of the nineteenth century.

CHAPTER THREE

The Provision of School Places: The Roles of Demand and Supply

If the structure of the discretionary sector was moulded by the educational assumptions of Upper Canadians about how schooling was to be organized, its growth was determined by the interaction of the demand for education and the supply of school places. For a variety of reasons, an increasing number of individuals and families sought opportunities to obtain more advanced levels of education. At the same time, churches, private individuals, and government were all active in promoting the establishment of schools, thus making the discretionary sector more accessible to more people. Cumulatively, these activities led to a massive increase in both school places and enrolments during the first three-quarters of the nineteenth century.

There is now a substantial theoretical literature devoted to explaining changes in school enrolments, much of it focused on growth since World War II, and most of it the product of economists and sociologists rather than historians. Their models and methods cannot always be fruitfully applied to the nineteenth century, in large part because the sources are either lost or do not provide sufficient grist for sophisticated quantitative analysis. And this is especially true for the discretionary sector before the 1880s, when a significant proportion of schools and enrolments lay outside the public sector and for which no certain statistics exist. Nonetheless it is still worth considering the relevance of these insights in the light of the evidence that does survive.

There are, for example, a number of helpful hypotheses that attempt to explain why there is growing demand for greater amounts of education by individuals and families. Perhaps the most familiar of these is the human capital thesis – the notion that individuals invest in schooling in order to acquire knowledge and skills that can be converted into good jobs and income. As the economy becomes more complex, so the argument goes, and as jobs require more skills, families or individuals will invest in more schooling in order to acquire the necessary skills, and indeed will be forced to do so if they are to keep pace with others in a changing economy. Thus as industrialization proceeded in the nineteenth century, and as technology grew, so more and more families sent their children to school and kept them in school longer. This hypothesis has now been largely rejected as a general explanation for the expansion of enrolments, particularly because so many jobs in the new economy required less knowledge or skill than before, not more.[1] Nonetheless it remains useful if it is applied to some occupational sectors only, and is broadened to include not just skills but educational credentials as well.[2]

During the middle decades of the nineteenth century, there were an increasing number of jobs available in what we would now describe as white collar and professional occupations (see general table 1). The number of doctors, for example, more than doubled between 1851 and 1861, and doubled again in the next decade. The number of lawyers increased by nearly as much. The ranks of clergymen increased more slowly, but steadily nonetheless. The number of bookkeepers and clerks climbed rapidly as the size and scope of business and industry advanced. The supply of druggists and schoolteachers multiplied as well. The absolute numbers employed in such occupations were not large, but the rate of increase each decade was generally higher than that of the workforce as a whole, and between 1851 and 1871 it tended to be much higher.

The steady growth of such occupations, which were tied to the discretionary sector in education, provided an economic base for the expansion of higher studies in the common and grammar schools. The Medical Board, the Law Society, the Anglican and Presbyterian churches all required candidates to learn a modicum of Latin, Greek, or both before they began their professional studies.[3] Classics, mathematics, and French were part of the matriculation standards at all of the Upper Canadian colleges.[4] To begin an apprenticeship with a provincial land surveyor, a boy was required, by law, to appear before a board of examiners and demonstrate his knowledge of "vulgar and decimal fractions, the extraction of Square and Cube root, of Geometry, plane Trigonometry, Mensuration of Superficies, and the use of Logarithms."[5] Clerks needed more than the rudiments of literacy and numeracy: the "help wanted" columns of the time often specified "a good common school education," while bookkeepers might need more specific skills.[6] The growth of private-venture evening schools specializing in vocational skills in the two decades around mid-century, along with the large commercial colleges in the 1860s, also testifies to the demand that existed for marketable business and commercial skills.[7] Thus there is good reason to think that the search for marketable skills and credentials played a part in driving discretionary-sector enrolments upwards in the middle decades of the nineteenth century.

A related explanation for rising demand is the consumption hypothesis, which treats schooling as a normal good and predicts that as income rises, people will purchase increasing amounts of it. In the extant American literature, as Grubb and Lazerson remark, this is a central explanation for expansion at the turn of the century, and it is probably relevant for Upper Canada as well.[8] The number of prosperous Upper Canadians was growing in the decades around mid-century and there is no shortage of evidence that prolonged schooling for both girls and boys was closely related to a family's prosperity.[9] Schooling was not just about getting good jobs; it was also a sign of respectability and prosperity maintained or achieved. Acquiring the right kind of education, moreover, was something to be pursued for its own sake and for the prestige it conferred independent of its economic value. A liberal education was not simply a prerequisite for entry to a profession or some other occupation; it was also an education that made Gentlemen, just as the accomplishments made Ladies.[10]

There is yet another factor that needs to be considered as well. Michael Katz and Ian Davey write that "the economic benefits of school attendance accrue from the differential advantage it bestows. That is, two levels of educational attainment always coexist: that reached by most people and that by a fortunate minority. It is the distance between the two rather than their intrinsic qualities which counts."[11] By mid-century, literacy was almost universal and, over the next two decades, the common schools became tuition-free. As the number of children in the early grades rose, as access to the higher grades became easier, and as the grammar schools multiplied, the spiral of educational qualifications probably had the same effect as it does today. If in 1822 a printer sought an apprentice who only needed to know how to "read and write and cast accounts," later advertisers sought a good common, or even a liberal, education.[12] And by the 1860s the cry of professions overcrowded had already become a familiar refrain as, indeed, had the solution. Law, which in the 1860s already had the highest entry standards of any profession in Upper Canada, was experiencing "a disastrous increase in lawyers and students." What then should be done? "Let the benchers, instead of making only 2 books of Horace and 3 of Geometry the test of admission into the Society, compel all candidates to undergo a severe written examination ... in English, Ancient and Modern History, Classics and Mathematics."[13] Not to be outdone, the Medical Board introduced a matriculation requirement in Greek in 1866.[14] While we cannot even be certain that there is in fact a causal connection, it is at least reasonable to think that the attraction of the professions explains some of the enrolment increases in Latin and Greek that took place in the 1850s and 1860s, and the rising ratio of senior students to beginners in these subjects. To maintain a superior economic or social advantage, individuals and families had to invest greater amounts of time and money than they had before. But this, in turn, provoked a further rise in demand. As Fred Hirsch argues, each time some individuals in the crowd gain a better view by standing on tiptoe, "others are forced to follow if they are to keep their position."[15]

If the human capital thesis is the optimistic version of the relationship between schools and jobs, the decline of alternatives to schooling is its pessimistic face. In the former, children are *pulled* into schools by the promise of obtaining marketable knowledge and skills. In the latter, children are *pushed* into schools by the disappearance of apprenticeships in skilled trades, by the growth of "dead-end" and therefore unattractive unskilled occupations, or by the decline of easy-entry unskilled jobs open to young people.[16] In Upper Canada's industrializing towns the "decline" thesis is of limited relevance, since the pattern is rather the reverse – with the growth of industrial employment in the 1860s, the teenage sons of skilled artisans and labourers actually left school for work in greater numbers than they had the decade before.[17] Jobs pulled them *out of* school. But the thesis does have relevance in other cases. In our five southwestern Ontario towns, there is some evidence to suggest that artisans and small businessmen may have been using the grammar schools to move their boys out of these occupations and into those which would come to constitute the new middle class – a shift which Mary Ryan has documented for upper New York state but which still needs more careful consideration than we are able to give it in this book.[18]

The thesis is also pertinent for rural Upper Canada. By the late 1850s, not only was the province running out of new farmland but changes in crops, production methods, and foreign competition encouraged a long-term trend towards larger farms worked by fewer hands. As Joy Parr has put it, these combined changes "dashed the hopes of many rural sons and daughters who had aspired to independent proprietorship."[19] It was not so much that jobs disappeared in the countryside – indeed there was a growing demand for wage labour – but that many young people were not prepared to become agricultural labourers with no hope of ever owning a farm. With the help of their families, they moved instead to the North American West or emigrated to the industrializing cities and towns. Many entered factory work, which was almost always better paid than wage labour in the countryside. Many others, we suggest, used the increasing availability of the common and grammar schools to acquire the skills they needed to become clerks, teachers or professionals, or to enter other white collar occupations. Though the Tipperary Irish migrants to Upper Canada preferred to buy their boys a farm, Bruce Elliott writes, it was also a common heirship strategy to provide younger sons with the financial support necessary for a prolonged education and professional training.[20] Complaining bitterly about the local school trustees' decision to substitute a cheap but inferior teacher for a better one, Judith Shore explained to Ryerson that she was "a widow, a resident freeholder in S.S. No. 6, I have five sons to provide for, and as I feel unable to provide a farm for each, I have been trying to educate one of them for business, he was getting along very well at school, and had commenced studying bookkeeping, but our trustees put away the teacher."[21]

In the two decades after 1850, over a quarter of grammar school students came from outside the town where the grammar school was located, sons and daughters of farmers living in the nearby townships.[22] Such students were commonly reported to be more serious than town children and more likely to enrol in the more advanced classes: "pupils from the country," said one grammar school master, "are generally *select*, the *elite* of the youth; they have generally some profession in view and prosecute their studies with an ardour mostly unknown to the youth of the Town."[23] It was not just the scions of respectable and successful farmers who tried to use schools to make the transition to city life. In 1856 the editor of the *Leader* condemned what he saw as the growing aversion of too many rural youth to life in the country:

This aversion is most clearly seen in the number of applications for clerkships in the different railway companies, and in all the Departments of the Government. We took the trouble on a recent occasion to inquire into the number of unaccommodated applications in one of the Railway offices. And, strange as it may seem, we found the number to be upwards of four hundred and fifty for clerkships alone. A closer examination showed that the great majority of the applicants were lads from the rural districts – who having acquired in the Common Schools the rudiments of arithmetic and English Grammar and having acquired at the same time a disgust for agricultural labour, had come to the cities with gentlemanly aspirations and views.[24]

ALTOGETHER, THEN, there are a variety of hypotheses that are useful in explaining the growing demand for education, and thus rising enrolments, in the discretionary sector. All of them, however, imply that new school places were created in response to a pre-existing demand for superior education. But, says Sheldon Rothblatt, "there is a tendency in the history of education generally to assume demand when the supply side may be the crucial variable."[25] Though he was writing about the expansion of higher education in nineteenth-century England, Rothblatt's remark is pertinent for Upper Canadian schooling as well. The supply of schooling was not, in any straightforward sense, a simple market response to the demand for skills or qualifications. Rather, schools were established for a wide variety of reasons that were unrelated, or only loosely related, to the actual level of demand for school places. And the existence of new school places generated its own demand by making schools more economically and geographically accessible. At the very least, in other words, supply must be considered as a variable potentially independent of the level of demand.

Upper Canada's churches were one important source of supply. All of the churches needed to provide a steady stream of clergymen for the colony's growing population. The Anglican and Presbyterian churches required their clergymen to have both classical and formal theological education, and thus colleges that made provision for arts and theological training were essential to them. Other denominations might have much lower minimum educational qualifications for their clergy, but they were increasingly aware that their ministers had to keep pace with the rising educational levels of their own laity, and also be prepared to meet the challenges of nineteenth-century scepticism. Why did the Baptists need a Theological Institution? asked one leading advocate in 1853.

The extraordinary activity of the press, which is so marked a peculiarity of this age, presents a twofold claim upon the ministry ... *Formerly*, the progress of error was slow, and it was exposed, or its force was spent, before it reached the masses. *Formerly*, the assaults of infidelity on the truth could only affect a limited circle; and it was enough, if there were a few accomplished defenders of the faith, in high places and in seats of learning. But *now*, a humble preacher of the gospel can scarcely find a remote hamlet, in which the oppositions of science, falsely so called, the quibbles of a deistical literature, and the pretensions of a visionary philosophy have not preceded him![26]

A second reason for denominational school-founding was the education of the laity. A growing number of prosperous farmers, merchants, and professional men were seeking day and boarding schools for their sons and daughters. It was important not only that such schools be academically sound but that "an evangelical influence shall preside both in the school and in the boarding establishment."[27] No less important, however, was the fear that if children were sent to schools of a rival denomination, they would be forever lost to the faith of their fathers. "It has become a question with many of us," the editor of the *Advocate* wrote in 1846, "whether the Methodist Episcopal Church in Canada shall have an Academy, or Institution of learning where our sons and daughters can receive a proper literary education without too great a sacrifice or alienation of feeling." To attend the schools founded by others, even the Wesleyans' Victoria College, was a risk: "It is better ... that our young men should go to the States ... than to attend Victoria College; for at the institutions in the states they will at least be treated with respect, while the reverse will be the case at Cobourg, unless they can be persuaded to leave the M.E. Church."[28]

The imperatives of professional training and lay education often blended nicely. Candidates for the ministry needed not only theological instruction but a solid preliminary classical and English education. A day or boarding school would at one and the same time secure these ends, offer an education in a suitable environment to the laity, and perhaps subsidize the costs of theology courses as well. The interrelationships between these three motives were spelled out in 1846 by the college committee of the newly established Free Church, which was then engaged in founding Knox College and the Toronto Academy.

In the report of last year, it was stated that Mr Esson, out of his own zeal in the cause of education, had, with the assistance of some of the students, opened a school for boys, in which the elements of classics and other branches were taught, combined with a scriptural training. This school Mr Esson abandoned, because he could not conduct it and do anything like justice to the department of his Professorship. But he conducted it long enough to prove that such an institution may be most fitly combined with the College, and most profitably worked in harmony with it ... The committee believe that many parents throughout the country, as well as in Toronto, would rejoice to send their children to such an institution. We contemplate that it should stand prominently forward as a religious school, in the best sense of the phrase, and we do not doubt that, both directly and indirectly, it would confer important advantages on the church. Though in no sense formally designed to be a nursery to the Divinity Hall, it is not too much to expect, that, through the Divine blessing, some of its pupils might have their hearts touched with Divine grace, and so be led to consecrate themselves to the work of the ministry.

But, important as are these considerations, there are others which go more directly to recommend the connection of such a school with our College. These are – *first*, the assistance which it would give to our College in educating in the elements of classical learning those who, admissible to the College in so far as character and views to the ministry go, are yet, from the want of early training, unfit at first to enter into its classes; and, *secondly*, the assistance which such a school would receive from the College. It is evident, that, with one Head Master, who might himself have a seat in the College, the school might require, for a time at least, no other assistants than some two or three of the most advanced students. [29]

During the middle decades of the century, such motives led all of the large denominations to found schools, colleges, or both. By the early 1840s, for example, the Church of Scotland had established both Queen's College and Queen's College School in Kingston. [30] The Wesleyan Methodists had opened Upper Canada Academy in Cobourg in the mid-1830s and transformed it into Victoria College early in the 1840s. Even after it received its charter as a university, however, it continued to have a preparatory department far larger than the undergraduate department itself. [31] The Anglicans created Trinity College and Trinity College School; the Episcopal Methodists, Belleville Seminary; the Baptists, the Canadian Literary Institute at Woodstock; and the Free Church, not only Knox College with both a theological and preliminary course, but between 1846 and 1852, the Toronto Academy. There are other examples besides. It must be emphasized, moreover, that these schools did not constitute a minor or peripheral part of the total provision for superior education in Upper Canada. With an enrolment of 82 in 1852, Queen's College School was far larger than most of the grant-aided grammar schools. In 1851 the Toronto Academy had 170 pupils and throughout the early 1850s Victoria had 150 preparatory students. In other words, these three schools alone had enrolments in the early 1850s equal to something more than 10 per cent of the total enrolment in the grant-aided grammar schools.[32]

The churches were also important in another way. Committed to the principle that a good preliminary education was valuable for future ministers, church leaders were articulate advocates of the expansion of superior education throughout the province. However useful a denominational academy or college might be in completing the education of ministerial candidates, it was no substitute for good local schools accessible to the general run of young men who heard the call. "Among the circumstances that here probably tended to limit our supply of students," the editor of the *Canadian United Presbyterian Magazine* wrote in 1854,

we may mention next, the deficiency of means, in many parts of the province, for attaining the necessary preparatory education. It is true there has been for a long time, in Toronto, a classical academy, of a very high order [Upper Canada College]. But in the first place, numbers are not in circumstances to come to the city and maintain themselves here, and pay, moreover, the ample fees demanded; and secondly, and chiefly, the kind of education there given is not precisely that most suitable for the generality of our students. Far be it from us to speak slightingly of the advantages of a thorough classical education; but ... nothing can be more preposterous than the idea of a youth, turned probably 20, and with no other language than his mother tongue, commencing his studies, and devoting, we suppose, 7 years to the minutiae of Latin and Greek prosody, and the details of heathen mythology, ancient geography and half-fabulous history. It is a much more brief, compendious, and withal more useful, preparatory course to which, generally speaking, our students must betake themselves. Now we know that numbers have really found it difficult, situated as they have been, to get such preparatory training as they required. It is satisfactory to be able to say that this *desideratum* is in the way of being rapidly supplied. Grammar schools are being planted generally in the country; and if they fulfil the expectations entertained of them, they will leave little to be complained of on this score.[33]

The churches, in other words, not only founded schools themselves, but church leaders contributed editorials, addresses, and arguments that helped make public opinion, and with it, politicians, sympathetic to the expansion of local facilities for superior education.

Yet another fruitful source of supply was civic boosterism. The civic leaders and editors of villages and towns across the province vied with each other not only for industries and railroads but for schools and colleges as well. The leading inhabitants of Streetsville agreed in 1839 to create a joint-stock company that would raise a building and hire teachers for a combined common, grammar, and ladies' school. They explained that they had several reasons for doing so, among which was to contribute to the growth of the village. "We may not be able to bring a Court-house or Gaol to our Village … but we may, through the blessing of God … open in it such a fountain of useful learning as might induce children, and even families, to flock to it."[34] Three decades later the editor of the *Brantford Expositor* rang the same changes. London was trying to obtain one of the new Normal Schools about to be established, but

the Forest City has really no claims on Government favor. Besides it is not central enough. Already there are more public institutions there, educational and others, than are required. London has been pampered so much that she has waxed arrogant and selfish. Two colleges and a huge asylum for the insane are not, it seems, enough for her. We do not think, however, that the proposed Normal School will be located there. Any one can see, in a moment, by glancing at the map, that, except Stratford, Brantford is the most central spot in the peninsula, and the most accessible. But no one, who has ever visited Stratford, will say that it is a fit locality for a Normal School, while our town is especially adapted for such a purpose. The situation of Brantford on the fruitful and picturesque banks of the Grand River is unrivalled; the climate is admirable and healthy; there is ready access by rail in all directions. But with all these advantages, our claims will not be recognized unless we take the trouble to make them known at head-quarters.[35]

For their part, schools and colleges were quick to take advantage of their eager civic suitors. When, during the 1850s, the leaders of Victoria College were considering a new site for the college, they showed all of the exploitive instincts attributed to late nineteenth-century manufacturers in extracting concessions from municipal councils. The college should of course be located in the best place for the whole Conference, said the editor of the *Christian Guardian*; "at the same time, however, … other things being equal, liberal offers of pecuniary means will be allowed to exercise a proper influence on the choice of location."[36] However cynical, this was a realistic assessment of the situation. The editor of the local newspaper urged his fellow citizens to offer "every encouragement" to Victoria to stay in Cobourg, while individuals from other towns offered sites and money as an incentive to Victoria to leave Cobourg.[37]

If town leaders were unable to attract a denominational boarding school or a grant-aided grammar school, they could do what the citizens of Streetsville had done – start a school on their own. The academy begun at Bath in 1811, taught by Barnabus Bidwell, for example, originated from the determination of leading local residents to have something more than the three Rs available for their children. A subscription was taken up, a building obtained, and the school opened with an ambitious curriculum consisting of the three Rs, "speaking, grammar and composition, the learned languages, penmanship, geography and other branches of a Liberal Education." Though the academy languished during and after the War of 1812, it was revived by subscribers in the 1820s and by the mid-thirties had a substantial two-storey building and was offering a common, commercial, and classical education to local children.[38] The Grantham Academy in St Catharines, the Ancaster Literary Institution, and the Newburgh Academy were founded the same way. Acting on the joint-stock principle, the subscribers bought shares that entitled them to vote for the trustees who would run the institution. The shares produced – or were supposed to produce – enough money to acquire adequate buildings, hire teachers, and provide a broader curriculum than was possible in the rural schools.[39]

In the decades before mid-century, however, by far the most common source of education in urban areas was the school begun by one or two individuals as a straightforward business venture.[40] Until the late 1820s such schools had rarely been found outside of York or Kingston but in the thirties and forties the growing population of other urban communities attracted a steady flow of people prepared to risk opening private-venture schools in the hope that they could make a living solely from the tuition fees their pupils paid them. Many of these schools were simply common schools, charging the same fees as the grant-aided common schools and teaching little more than the three Rs. But others taught a much wider range of subjects and charged fees similar to those of the grammar schools and academies. In the late twenties and early thirties, for example, Kingston had two important grammar schools. One was the government-aided Midland district school; the other the Kingston grammar school, begun by a Presbyterian minister and supported mainly by Presbyterians who viewed the former institution as an Anglican preserve. The Kingston grammar school taught the usual course of English and classical subjects and among its students counted John A. Macdonald, Oliver Mowat, J.H. Cameron, and a future principal of Upper Canada College.[41] In Toronto in the mid-thirties, Thomas Caldicott, assisted by two younger teachers, ran a school that sometimes had as many as eighty students. Its curriculum included the three Rs, bookkeeping, drawing, geography, trigonometry, navigation, algebra, history, Latin, Greek, French, natural philosophy, and the mechanical arts. For the three Rs, Caldicott charged fifteen shillings a quarter; for more advanced subjects, thirty shillings or two pounds.[42]

The superior private-venture schools outside the major urban centres had much the same characteristics. A small number appear to have been primarily residential and charged fees for tuition and boarding similar to the fees at Upper Canada College or Upper Canada Academy – the Newmarket,

Caradoc, and Barrie academies are examples.[43] Most, however, were primarily day schools for local children. At Amherstburg in the late twenties, for example, the Rev. Alexander Gale, a Presbyterian minister, ran a school for more than thirty boys and girls, over half of whom were studying Latin, with six or seven engaged in Greek and advanced Latin.[44] At Maitland, a teacher offered the three Rs for fifteen shillings a quarter, and the commercial and classical subjects for the usual two pounds.[45]

The private-venture schools were especially important in providing for the education of middle-class girls. Reluctant to send their girls to the common schools, or even to the grammar schools in the relative handful of places where they had been established, parents throughout the province turned to the only local alternative and patronized the little "Ladies' Schools" that multiplied everywhere after the 1820s. Toronto always seemed to have a dozen or more. In the thirties and early forties, villages like Ancaster, Bath, Belleville, Perth, Newmarket, and London all had ladies' schools; Niagara had three; Cobourg five.[46]

Once again, some of these schools were simply single-sex common schools, offering only the three Rs and plain needlework. But others had a far more extensive curriculum – academic subjects that included history, geography, mathematics, and French, along with the "female arts" of plain and fancy needlework, screen painting, embroidering in silk, music, dancing, and singing. The fees were generally similar to those of the grammar schools, with music and French replacing Latin and mathematics as the most expensive subjects. Some schools had limited boarding facilities, usually costing twenty-five or thirty pounds a year.

Our knowledge of these schools is almost entirely limited to the barebones advertisements published in the local newspapers, and we are no better off with respect to the private-venture teachers themselves. We can assume that the minority of schools that persisted over many years were profitable but we cannot even guess at how good a living they provided. We know little about the teachers or why they taught. The Misses Brown, who began a long-lived school in Toronto in 1844, were presumably contributing, like their brother George, to the survival of a family still weighed down by the debts of business failure in Scotland.[47] Featherstone Osler's wife and others like her probably taught to supplement a clergyman's inadequate salary.[48] Mrs Goodman was a career teacher with twenty years' experience in England and Quebec City before she opened her Toronto school.[49]

We have been able to locate only a few cases where it is possible to go beyond this sort of inference. The Skirving family emigrated from Scotland in 1833 and settled on a farm near York. Within six months the father died, leaving a wife and six girls to fend for themselves. They were fortunate in having good connections in Toronto to help them through the crisis and two sons arrived from Scotland to assist them as well. In 1834 one of the girls became a governess and Mrs Skirving opened a school in York Mills. The clientele, however, was not numerous enough to support a large family, and, after two more unsuccessful attempts in Aurora and Weston, she finally moved to Toronto in 1840. Here she ran a school with the assistance of her older daughters until she died in 1846.[50] Other women opened private schools for much the same reason. Some were more successful than Mrs Skirving; some were not. Needing to support herself after the death of her doctor-husband in 1822, Mrs Cockburn moved from Quebec City to York and opened a ladies' school. She brought with her letters of reference and introduction from Bishop Mountain which won her the active support of Lady Maitland, the wife of the lieutenant-governor. That, in turn, helped attract a well-heeled clientele and the school became one of the most prestigious and expensive in the colony, as well as one of the most enduring of the private-venture schools, lasting until at least the mid-1840s.[51] Marianne Fuller, along with her two daughters, on the other hand, tried opening a ladies' school in Simcoe in the late 1850s after the death of her husband, but "got very little encouragement," she told Ryerson in a letter appealing for aid. "We kept on until last Spring, then my daughter who taught French went out as a governess, my other daughter continues to teach at home having two younger sisters to educate."[52] The Rev. Mark Stark's future wife underwent a remarkably similar experience. Her father, forced by a business failure to emigrate, died shortly after settling in Upper Canada, leaving a wife and family unprovided for. One of the girls became a governess in Lower Canada, an older boy took a job in a store, while mother and another daughter opened a school in Dundas.[53] If these few examples are any indication, women opened private-venture schools to supplement family funds, to work at the only career respectable women could attempt, or to support a family in widowhood. It is a tragedy that we know so little about these numerous schools and the determined and sometimes highly successful women who ran them.

Two other forms of private-venture teaching are worth noting. First, there was the work of the educated clergy of the Anglican and Presbyterian churches. By the thirties it was common for the village and country clergy or their wives to take a few students into their homes to teach them English and classical subjects, or for the girls, the appropriate graces. By the mid-forties, it appears from the advertisements in *The Church* that most of the Anglican clergy in fixed parishes were taking a few students. No doubt it was done primarily to supplement their incomes; but at the same time it helped spread the availability of superior education into country areas where private-venture schools were uneconomic.[54] Secondly, there were the evening or part-time schools primarily devoted to technical training of one kind or another. In Kingston in 1835 one could attend an evening school to study architectural drawing and land surveying. One of the teachers at the Home

district school offered a few special classes in 1836 "in the various departments of Mechanical and Ornamental drawing." At Cobourg in 1844 "a
Gentleman, lately from England, by profession a civil engineer, would be
happy to give instruction ... in Mathematics, Arithmetic, Surveying and
Engineering Drawing." And there was a steady stream of advertisements
for short courses in such subjects as shorthand, bookkeeping, and penmanship.[55]

Until the 1840s the private-venture school had been the dominant form
of schooling available in urban Upper Canada, providing an ordinary common school education for "the humbler classes" as well as select and superior
education for those above them. With the expansion of the grant-aided
common schools after 1841, however, the number of private-venture common schools declined rapidly. By mid-century the voluntary sector consisted
largely of select and superior schools, some of which offered only the
rudiments of an English education to boys or girls while others taught a
wide range of accomplishments to girls, or classical and mercantile subjects
to boys. Catering to the respectable classes of the towns and cities, nonetheless, and attracting as well those parents from the countryside who could
afford not only tuition fees but the costs of boarding, the private-venture
schools remained an important part of the pattern of educational provision
in mid-century Upper Canada.

THE SUPPLY OF SCHOOLING in the discretionary sector also expanded as a
result of government policy. As early as the 1790s the colonial authorities
had tried to make provision for grammar schools and a university, while
the grant-aided common schools, established in 1816, had never been restricted to teaching the rudiments alone. Virtually from the beginning of
settlement, then, government played an important role in fostering schools
that offered the higher branches of an ordinary and a liberal education.

The early intervention of government in Upper Canadian education arose
from two political imperatives. First there was what might be described as
the supply side of the human capital thesis. Just as the churches had to
invest in education if they were to ensure a continuing flow of trained
clergymen, so government invested in schools and colleges to ensure a supply
of skills necessary to maintain itself and, more broadly, the institutions of
civil society. The colony needed lawyers, judges and JPs, land surveyors,
doctors, civil servants, and a variety of other occupations that involved the
acquisition of skills traditionally transmitted through schooling. Thus from
first settlement onwards, the colonial leaders took it for granted that schools
and colleges must be encouraged by legislation and subsidy.

It was not just skills that were wanted, however, but appropriate values
and beliefs. That is to say, colonial leaders were not simply concerned with

manpower training but with the creation of moral and political consensus. In 1792 Simcoe wanted schools established in Upper Canada because the only alternative was the republican schools to the south. In a famous passage on the need for a university, John Strachan argued that since Upper Canada had no landed aristocracy, the law would become "the most powerful profession" in the colony. It was, therefore, "of the utmost importance" that law students

should be collected together at the University, become acquainted with each other ... and acquire similar views and modes of thinking, and be taught by precept and example to love and venerate our parent state. It is surely of great consequence that a class of intelligent men belonging to a profession which offers the highest inducements of reputation, wealth, influence, authority and power, should be actuated by sentiments and feelings of attachment to the British Empire.[56]

Such sentiments, moreover, were not the preserve of a few Compact Tories but rather the conventional view of most of those who spoke for church or state. In 1848, the second principal of Victoria College, Alexander MacNab, described the character of the education imparted there as

truly *British*. As we have long been fully committed, in our own mind, to the sentiment that youth should be educated for their *country*, as well as for themselves, every effort is made to make those under our care acquainted with the nature of the institutions, social and civil, which distinguish our glorious Empire.

While mere *party politics* are never mentioned within these walls, sentiments of true patriotism and sound loyalty are constantly inculcated.

Although it would be beneath the dignity of a public institution of this kind to meddle, to the slightest degree, with the local party questions of the day, yet, in our judgment, it is a duty we owe to our God and our country, especially in these times of commotion and change, to use every means in our power to give to the youth committed to our care a proper bias in relation to those institutions which, for ages, have been the glory of the land.[57]

The long history of the attempt to establish a university in Upper Canada reflects the conviction that it was part of the duty of government to ensure the production of a future generation of young people who were equipped with the skills and the values to provide wise leadership for the colony. There were, as well, government-funded grammar schools in all the district towns to introduce boys to the elements of a classical education and to prepare them for the university. The grant-aided common schools were, of course, not intended to produce leaders, but they were nonetheless expected to promote loyalty and to teach not just the rudiments but more advanced

English subjects as well, to that minority at least who stayed in school a little longer than the rest.

The cumulative effects of the growing demand for advanced studies and the school-founding activities of government, churches, and private individuals can be read in the record of expanding enrolments and schools. Before the 1840s the surviving evidence is too scanty to allow us to measure growth in any but the crudest way. From that decade onwards, however, statistics collected by the Education Office, along with a variety of other sources, give us an increasingly full picture of the number of pupils and schools involved in the discretionary sector of Upper Canadian education.

Because they were outside the emerging state system, we know least about enrolments in the private-venture and proprietary schools. Moreover there is no way of determining precisely how many of their students were studying elementary or advanced subjects. Our attempt to calculate the size of the private sector is described in appendix A. At mid-century, we have argued, it was primarily urban, it enrolled about 16 per cent of all urban pupils, and in the larger towns and cities this figure rose as high as 30 per cent or more. Enrolments in private schools increased over the next two decades but at a far slower rate than either the grant-aided schools or the age group five to fifteen. If the school advertisements are any guide, most of the schools taught older pupils, studying the higher subjects and the accomplishments, but they also taught beginners. There is no way of determining the proportion of each. Indeed, often the best we can do with the private schools is to retreat to words like "many" and "some." They cannot be neglected because of that, however. The non-aided schools constituted a substantial part of middle-class education at mid-century, and deserve attention especially because of the role they played in the superior education of middle-class girls.

We are on somewhat better ground when we turn to the grammar schools. We know the exact number of schools from the beginning because the disbursement of the grant for each school was recorded annually in the Blue Books. But enrolment figures are suspect, or at least incomplete, until mid-century, since many schools never bothered to file the required reports. Immediately after the grammar school act of 1807, four schools were founded, and by 1838 there were thirteen of them with at least 300 pupils and probably more.[58] By 1845, there were twenty-five schools with a total enrolment of something less than a thousand.[59] By 1850, fifty-seven schools enrolled 2000 pupils. A decade later, there were eighty-eight schools with 4500 pupils, and on the eve of the School Act of 1871, just over a hundred schools with 7300 pupils. Put another way, grammar school enrolments doubled during the 1850s, and increased by nearly 200 per cent between 1851 and 1871. As general table 3 demonstrates, this growth rate was substantially higher than that of either the total population aged five to fifteen or of the ten to fifteen age group alone. Reliable figures on enrolment by subject do not begin until 1855, but over the succeeding decade, the number of grammar school pupils enrolled in Latin and Greek rose substantially.[60] No less important, however, enrolment in modern or practical subjects increased steadily: English studies were almost universally pursued in the grammar schools, practical or commercial arithmetic became as common as Latin, and significant numbers of students took science and bookkeeping as well (see general table 4).

While most historians recognize the importance of the private and grammar schools for the provision of higher studies in Upper Canada, there is still a tendency to assume that the common schools did little more than teach the three Rs. Thus the range of the common school curriculum deserves some special notice here. Until the late 1840s most common schools, and especially those in rural Upper Canada, probably did not offer more than the three Rs, but there were always some teachers willing and able to teach a few pupils the elements of mathematics, English composition, bookkeeping, and very occasionally the classical languages as well. Throughout the 1830s the common school reports submitted to the legislature routinely record a few schools each year which offered the higher branches of mathematics, Latin, French, and even Greek as well as the more usual English subjects.[61] In 1843, the common school commissioners in Ancaster township reported that in general the schools taught only English reading, grammar, writing, arithmetic, history, geography, etc. At the school in the village of Ancaster, however, "besides the above branches shall be taught Mathematics and Bookkeeping, the Latin, Greek, and French languages – Pupils from any part of the township will be received at this school for these higher branches without any extra charge if within the age."[62] Similarly, the local superintendent for Toronto reported that "in several of the [common] schools, Bookkeeping, Geography, Grammar and History form part of the daily studies – while in one or two Latin and Elementary Mathematics engage the attention of a few of the Senior pupils."[63]

There was, as we have already tried to suggest, nothing wayward about such developments. The content of a common or ordinary English education was always ill defined and could be expanded or contracted to suit the views of the speaker. Generally it did not include the classics but even here no sharp distinctions can be drawn, since by ancient tradition the Scottish parochial schools had included classics in their curriculum, a tradition that was carried to Upper Canada by clergymen and other Scottish emigrants.[64] By the 1840s, many cities and towns in the northeastern United States had already established high schools that extended a common school education far beyond the rudiments. And it was uncommon in Upper Canada to find spokesmen for the view, so widely held in England, that grant-aided elementary schools should offer little more than the three Rs.

Egerton Ryerson had always had a particularly expansive view of the role of the common school, and, once in command of the common school system, he introduced a series of measures that made it easier for local boards to provide for the upward extension of their schools.[65] The landmark school legislation of 1846 had continued the practice of dividing the cities and towns into a number of school sections, each with its own trustees – a situation which, however suited to the countryside, was neither necessary nor efficient in urban areas. The next year, then, new legislation created a single board of common school trustees for each incorporated city, town, and village. The act also gave the trustees broad powers to determine the kind of schools that were established, and Ryerson urged them to use this clause to create a gradation of schools – primary, intermediate, and high – to provide for the wants of all children in the town.[66]

Secondly, Ryerson established a set of standards and compulsory examinations that differentiated amongst teaching certificates, identifying those teachers who were capable of teaching the higher subjects and those who were not.[67] While small or poor rural school sections might choose to hire a cheap and minimally qualified teacher holding only a third-class certificate, any school section could select one with the academic skills to teach more advanced subjects. Again, advanced instruction was paid for by the combined sum of the government grant and local taxes, just as the rudiments were. What this meant was that school boards could not, and did not have to, charge special tuition fees for the higher subjects. After 1850, moreover, in either town or country, trustees did not have to consult ratepayers or anyone else if they wished to hire a first-class teacher or build a central school offering an advanced English education.

Finally, as a legally defined common school program of studies began to emerge, its bounds were kept coincident with expansive notions about the content of a common school education. Initially there was no specified program of studies, but simply indicative programs garnered from the standards set for teachers' examinations, lists of authorized texts, and the studies taught at the Model School.[68] In 1858, however, the Council of Public Instruction recommended a program of studies for the common schools consisting of three divisions. The third or highest division incorporated the fourth and fifth National Readers, geometry and algebra, natural philosophy, mensuration, trigonometry, and a variety of other studies we would now define as secondary-level work.[69] Though not a compulsory program, it was nonetheless a potent symbol, indicating the broad range and high level of attainment the common schools, at their best, were intended to provide. Indeed it substantially overlapped the grammar school program and even overlapped parts of the first year at University College.[70] Together with the other three measures it indicated that policymakers intended the common school to be far more than a primary school.

But what about Latin and Greek, which were the hallmarks of a liberal education? Could classics be taught in a common school? On this point, policy was somewhat more uncertain. There is good evidence to suggest that Ryerson did not intend to allow the urban common schools to teach Latin and Greek. In 1847 his commentary on the right of urban boards to create any "description" of schools refers to different schools for the sexes or denominations, and to different levels of schooling, but to the higher English or mercantile subjects only.[71] And in 1854 J.G. Hodgins, Ryerson's right-hand man, told a correspondent that "the Common School Act does not contemplate the establishment of a classical department in connexion with the common schools in Cities and Towns." Moreover, Hodgins continued, the government grant and the matching local school taxes which made up the Common School Fund could only be spent to pay common school, not classical, teachers.[72] From 1850 onwards, nonetheless, the trustees' right to establish any "description" of school was interpreted in such a way as to allow urban boards to organize a classical school or department.[73] To pay for it they simply raised the required amount, from local sources, over and above the costs of running the common school proper. This applied only to incorporated urban areas, however. Though Latin was occasionally taught in a few rural schools before mid-century, it was rarely taught after that, and official policy discouraged it.[74] The motive seems to have been entirely related to the character of the rural school itself – usually a single-room, single-teacher institution catering to all ages and already offering an extensive English education. As Ryerson explained in 1855,

it requires all the time and attention of a teacher to conduct an English elementary school properly and efficiently; and he ought not to divert a considerable portion of his time in teaching two or three pupils Latin and Greek to the disadvantage of the great body of the pupils and their parents. If certain parents wish to have their children taught Latin and Greek, and do not wish to send them to one of the schools established for that purpose, and if the teacher of a common school is competent to teach Latin and Greek, then such parents can employ him to teach their children out of school hours and pay him for doing so.[75]

About the only limit that Ryerson set for the common schools, then, was that country common schools could not teach classics or French. Beyond that, official policy gave the common schools a broad curricular mandate.

In both town and country, boards of trustees were quick to exploit the opportunities this mandate provided. With the publication of detailed statistical returns from 1852 onwards, it becomes possible to trace in systematic fashion the growth of higher studies in the common schools. The pertinent tables report enrolments by classes that correspond to the various Irish National Readers. These, in turn, can be linked to one of the three divisions of the program of studies, which also listed the other subjects children were expected to study. The third or highest division covered the fourth and fifth readers, and thus, while the choice is somewhat arbitrary, the numbers in these two readers are tolerable indicators of enrolments in the senior branches of a common school education. As general table 5 indicates, in the two decades after 1850, fourth- and fifth-class enrolments increased by over 150 per cent for the province as a whole, and by over 300 per cent in the urban areas. Indeed, if one considers only the fifth or highest class, the increase in enrolments was still something more than 200 per cent.

No school, it must be emphasized, was required to offer the subjects of the third division or to have any but a teacher holding a third-class certificate – a minimal qualification that would not have enabled a teacher to cope with much more than the rudiments.[76] And yet throughout rural Upper Canada there was a rapid growth in the number of highly qualified teachers. In 1852, when the relevant statistics first became available, only 11 per cent of rural teachers held first-class certificates. By 1861, however, the figure was 29 per cent and by 1869, 45 per cent.[77] Even in the countryside, in other words, large numbers of teachers were qualified to teach higher arithmetic, elementary mathematics such as algebra and mensuration, and the other subjects listed in the third division of the prescribed common school program.

We suspect, though we have no means of verifying it, that large numbers of these first-class teachers were employed in villages and hamlets too small to be incorporated, and therefore to be recorded separately from the surrounding rural areas, but large enough to generate a demand for schooling above the rudiments and also to provide a tax base generous enough to pay the salary of a good teacher. We are not, in other words, arguing that the bulk of rural children had access to the most highly qualified teachers. The figures are impressive nonetheless. By 1861 nearly 40 per cent of all rural pupils were enrolled in the two highest readers, and in the fifth book alone, 20 per cent were enrolled (general table 6). The number of pupils in such subjects as algebra or bookkeeping was much smaller, probably because most county teachers did not have time to attend to such subjects and also cope with the vast mass of other children only learning their letters or reading in the first three books. Thus some of the more specialized subjects of the common school curriculum were difficult to obtain in the rural school, and if pupils were to continue their studies they had to go to the larger common schools of the villages or towns, to the nearest grammar school, to a denominational academy, or indeed, to a local "crammer" – a clergyman or other educated person who might drill the student in enough classics or mathematics to prepare for the professional or college matriculation examinations.[78] Despite these limitations, however, it is clearly misleading to conceive of schooling in rural Upper Canada as a featureless plain marked by no form of education superior to the three Rs.

What was true of the countryside was even more true of urban Upper Canada. By 1861, 65 per cent of teachers in incorporated villages, 74 per cent of those in towns, and 83 per cent of those in Upper Canada's five cities held first-class certificates – all figures that would rise over the course of the next decade. About 31 per cent of all urban students were enrolled in the two highest readers, though the percentage was somewhat less in the cities alone (general table 6). Enrolments in the fifth reader stood at 14 per cent for all urban areas. The fact that these figures are lower than those for the counties should not be misread, however. In rural Upper Canada little else was available; in all of the larger urban areas there were other kinds of schools to draw senior pupils away from the higher grades of the common school. If, for example, one combines the 1861 enrolment figures for both common and grammar schools, senior enrolments were much higher – upwards of 45 per cent of total enrolments in Upper Canada's incorporated villages, and 39 per cent in the towns.

There was another important difference as well: despite lower percentages in the fourth and fifth readers, urban common schools always had higher enrolments than did rural schools in the more specialized subjects such as algebra, mensuration, and bookkeeping. This was a consequence of the greater specialization of teachers that accompanied the spread of graded common schools during the 1850s. The search for efficient ways to organize the hordes of youngsters entering the schools, in the urban areas especially, had led to the practice of dividing large groups of children into smaller units based on age, attainments, or some combination of both, and assigning each group to one teacher.[79] Each group could then be passed along from one teacher to the next in some systematic way and according to some common criteria. Since teachers themselves were increasingly finely graded according to their own levels of learning, and matched to the accomplishment of pupils, it was but a short step to crown the common school with a teacher holding a first-class certificate, and have her, or (more usually) him, take responsibility for all of the more advanced subjects. In this fashion, age level and curriculum level increasingly intertwined.

Grading was institutionalized in one of two ways – by the creation of a large central school that brought all the higher classes of a town together in a single building, or by the construction of several multi-classroom ward schools. The central schools were particular favourites of Ryerson's and have received much attention from historians, but whatever their other merits, they did not necessarily result in higher enrolments in advanced subjects than were to be found in the ward schools of other communities. In 1861, for example, the ward schools in Kingston and Toronto were as successful as London's central school in keeping pupils enrolled in third division subjects.

In the early 1850s a handful of urban boards took advantage of the clause that allowed them to offer classics in the common schools. Hamilton, London, and Brantford are the best-known examples, though there are others besides.[80] Hiring a classical master crowned the work of the common school and made it a truly comprehensive institution, providing the full range of education from the three Rs to preparation for university matriculation. These were new kinds of schools, in other words, combining the subjects of both an ordinary and liberal education, and extending their curriculum from the rudiments to advanced English, commercial, and classical studies.

Had these schools been widely emulated, the development of the modern high school in Ontario would have had a very different history, resembling more closely, for example, the predominant American pattern, where the high school department grew upwards from the lower rungs of the common school, and where both kinds of school were under the control of the same board. It would, moreover, have pitted the grammar and common schools in direct competition against each other. Such competition did indeed occasionally happen, but in the main, the course of events flowed in a different direction. Even the Hamilton, London, and Brantford central schools abandoned their classical departments, and left Latin and Greek to be taught in the local grammar schools. In the end, indeed, all of the higher work of the common schools would be abandoned as the common and grammar schools came to be organized in a sequential rather than a parallel fashion. But what is important here is the fact that during the 1850s and 1860s at least, the common schools played an important role in the provision of advanced instruction throughout Upper Canada.

The discretionary sector, in sum, grew steadily throughout the middle decades of the nineteenth century. The number of schools that offered not only the rudiments but more advanced work multiplied, and enrolments in the higher subjects grew at rates rarely matched until the explosive growth of secondary and higher education in the 1960s. Enrolments in classical studies climbed steadily; so, presumably, did enrolments in the accomplishments taught in the private schools, though that is more difficult to verify. But there was also a significant expansion in "moderns" – in English and commercial subjects, practical arithmetic and applied mathematics, science, and modern languages. In this, Ontario was no different from other parts of the world, for the rise of modern studies was an international phenomenon. It can be found in the emerging high schools of the United States, in the growth of the higher grade schools in England, in imperial Germany, colonial Queensland, or South Australia.[81] Indeed, it was during the last half of the nineteenth century that non-classical studies came of age and laid claim to a central place in the school curriculum, a matter that will preoccupy us in other parts of this book.

CUMULATIVELY, WE HAVE SAID, both demand and supply account for the massive expansion of the discretionary sector in the first three-quarters of the nineteenth century. What remains unclear is the relative importance of each. Presumably both demand and supply are important variables in understanding the multiplication of enrolments and schools. There have to be schools *and* pupils to attend them. Either factor can act as a constraint on growth. Nonetheless, if there was rising demand for advanced education in nineteenth-century Upper Canada which drove enrolments up, it occurred in an environment where school places were plentiful, and in an atmosphere conducive to making schools ever more widely accessible. Our own sense of things is that throughout the middle decades of the nineteenth century, the supply of school places actually ran well ahead of the level of demand.[82] And that, in turn, was to play an important part in reshaping the structure of the discretionary sector by weakening the viability of the private-venture and proprietary schools, thus loosening the grip of voluntarism on middle-class education, and by encouraging the grant-aided grammar schools to accommodate broader purposes and a new clientele.

CHAPTER FOUR

The Failure of Voluntarism and the Transition to Public Education

The expansion of the discretionary sector in the middle decades of the nineteenth century was accompanied by a fundamental change in the *source* for the supply of school places. In early Upper Canada the provision of superior education was mainly the work of individuals, churches, and voluntary associations. Until the 1840s at least, government played a very limited role, and non-aided superior schools were far more numerous than those that received government grants. During the two decades around mid-century, however, the initiative began to shift to the state. Increasingly after 1850 it would be government rather than other agencies that would supply the vast bulk of school places. And this transition from voluntarism to the state would be of fundamental importance in shaping the future structure of superior education in Ontario.

Though few Upper Canadians were resolutely opposed to government intervention as a matter of principle, they generally assumed that most middle-class education should be, and would be, maintained by voluntary means. In part this preference arose from the sheer familiarity of voluntarism to Upper Canadians and immigrants alike: throughout most of the English-speaking world, private-venture and proprietary schools, whatever their precise labels, were the common resort of those who could afford educational choice or prolonged schooling. Voluntarism reflected and reinforced widely held values as well. The small private-venture schools, as we have already suggested, mimicked the character of the family itself in its intimate size, its "parental" supervision, its selective nature, and its ability to accommodate denominational religious instruction. Dependent on fees for their very survival, moreover, the voluntary schools tended to be directly responsive to parents' curricular preferences. Beyond that, the denominational and private-venture schools provided separate facilities for educating boys and girls, and could, far more easily than grant-aided schools, preserve the social segregation that many parents preferred.

The mid-century voluntary school was also sustained by the broader social values attached to the notion of respectability. For some people it was the business of parents to look after their children, in education as in other things; to pay for a child's schooling was a moral duty and a material proof of independence.[1] For English immigrants especially, grant-aided common schools carried the taint of the charity school, a fit place only for those who could not look after themselves.[2] In the words of one mid-century school-man, "respectable people – those who could afford to send elsewhere – hesitated to expose their children to the pernicious influences" of the common schools.[3] Because they charged higher fees, the grant-aided grammar schools tended to be more select in their clientele; still, as public institutions they were formally open to all and consequently at least some parents refused to use them, opting for local private grammar schools instead.[4]

In the years immediately around mid-century, in sum, traditional means of school provision survived despite the steady expansion of state-aided schools. Voluntarism continued to supply a substantial proportion of the school places in the towns and cities. Aside from the grant-aided grammar schools, it provided most of the schooling considered appropriate for middle-class children. And its appeal lay not only in customary ways of doing things but in the familial and broader social values it helped sustain.

IT PROVED, NONETHELESS, remarkably difficult to maintain a broadly based voluntary sector in mid-nineteenth-century Upper Canada. This was due to a variety of internal weaknesses that plagued both private-venture and pro-prietorial schools. But above all it was due to the failure of the voluntary sector to obtain sources of financial support to supplement income from fees and thereby ensure that the schools were accessible, stable, and educationally efficient.

Until at least mid-century, a middle-class education was an expensive investment. To provide a child with an elementary education in a select school, to ensure that a daughter acquired the academic and ornamental accomplishments requisite to her station, to school a boy in the classics or give him an advanced English and commercial education, demanded a con-siderable outlay of cash in a country that was cash poor, and the costs increased proportionally if two or more children were involved. Those fortunate enough to live in one of the larger urban areas might have a variety of day schools to choose from, including a grant-aided grammar school and several select schools; still, they could expect fees for "a good English education" to range from ten or fifteen shillings to £2 or £3 a quarter – this at a time when the maximum fee in a grant-aided common school was three shillings ninepence for the same period of about three months; and indeed when many common schools were abolishing fees altogether. In smaller communities, the choice was far more limited. In the 1840s grammar schools had only just begun to expand beyond the district (or county) towns. While select schools were widely established, they might not be adequate to complete a child's education, especially in the case of boys. Thus the availability of a suitable education often depended on a parent's ability to pay boarding as well as tuition fees in another town. Boarding was especially costly. Only a few fee bills and school accounts survive in the family papers, but what remains is illuminating. In the mid-1830s Hamnett Pinhey, an Ottawa Valley businessman, paid £55 to send his son to Upper Canada College for three terms.[5] Between 1839 and 1844 William Roe, a Newmarket lumber merchant, paid over £110 a year to have his two daughters educated at Mrs Cockburn's school in Toronto.[6] In 1847 it cost Mark Stark £35 to send his boy to the Toronto Academy, and in 1850 A.N. Buell paid £30 per annum to Miss Woodhouse for the board and tuition of his daughter.[7] As the school advertisements in the newspapers indicate, moreover, these charges were typical. While there was some variation in the range of tuition fees in those towns where several schools competed for clientele, the costs of boarding varied little across urban Upper Canada.

From the 1830s to the 1860s there was a long series of complaints registered in both the private papers and the newspapers about high fees and, above all, boarding costs. The reaction in London and Kingston to the creation of Upper Canada College offers an early and spectacular example. In 1831 both towns sent petitions to the legislature protesting the centralization in Toronto of facilities for advanced education. The London petition wished the college every success, but pointed out nonetheless that

we cannot but feel that the great advantage which it offers can seldom be enjoyed by any of our children; useful, certainly it will be to the Home District and the Town of York, and perhaps to some youth brought up at other schools ... but very few parents are in circumstances in this part of the Province to benefit by the College and fewer appear inclined to send their children some hundreds of miles from home at so early an age as boys ought to enter a Classical school.

Our object therefore ... is to request that such an endowment may be granted to the school of the London District.[8]

The first eighteen signatures on this petition include eight JPS, two barristers, the treasurer of the district, a surveyor, an advocate, and the Clerk of the Peace. The Kingston protest was similar in content and social origin. These were clearly influential people in their communities and they were not poor. By the standards of most Upper Canadians, indeed, they were well off. But they had households to maintain, children to educate, and they did not feel themselves so rich as to be able to afford expensive boarding schools in distant towns. They needed good local schools to finish the education of their daughters and prepare their boys to enter a profession or some other respectable occupation. As George H. Markland, a leading and prosperous Kingstonian, remarked to John Macaulay in the late twenties, "you are quite right about the Schools, who are the people in the Province that can afford to send two or three boys first to a preparatory School and then to a University, both in the same place. The District Schools should have been made the preparatory Schools."9 Writing to a friend in Scotland in 1848, a prosperous farmer in Vaughan township explained that although his two younger sons had been attending Upper Canada College for several years, "my circumstances will not now allow me to continue ... Although I have got a good productive farm the expense of working it runs off with all its produce which barely pays the wages of servants."10 A few years earlier John Strachan had cautioned a potential emigrant against planning to start a ladies' school in Toronto: "there are so many schools here and comparatively so few people able to send their daughters from home."11 In a petition to the government pleading for a share in the grammar school fund, eighty-one householders in the village of Newboro explained that the nearest grammar school was thirty-five miles away and they "are unable to bear the expense of sending their children away to attend Schools of a higher order where a liberal education could be attained."12 Two decades earlier, in 1834, Mark Stark told his mother the same thing. He was unable to supplement a clergyman's income by keeping boarders because so few parents could afford such a luxury and it was, he added, a general problem: "A *very* nice English Family ... came to Ancaster to establish a school for young ladies but they are obliged to give it up for want of support. People here have not yet the money to pay for superior education."13 Our own analysis of the families who used the grammar schools in five southwestern Ontario towns in 1861 points to the same conclusion. Even amongst the wealthy, large families were more likely to use the grammar school for their children's education than small families. The latter could afford private tuition and most probably boarding expenses for their sons and daughters; the former, with more children to provide for, could not.14

Even when boarding fees were not a consideration, the costs of educating children could press against the limits of a father's income. Writing from Toronto to his mother in 1839, John Macaulay expressed his concern about the cost of sending his daughter to a local teacher:

Annie is not yet at school. Her mother went today to Mrs Blake's, in order to make all needful arrangements. The last thing she inquired was the terms – when lo! the lady teacher demanded how much do you think? *Only £20 a year!* This, of course, we could not dream of giving – I think it would have been almost sinful to accede to anything so very extravagant but in the meanwhile, I know not how Annie is to be taught.15

Regardless of whether he could afford it or not, however, Macaulay was forced to pay exactly that amount a year later in order to have Annie educated in the style expected for the daughter of a leading member of colonial society.[16] And one of the reasons that J.G. Hodgins was constantly in debt, and occasionally on the edge of banruptcy, in the 1850s and 1860s was the cost of sending his boys to Upper Canada College and then to university in Toronto.[17]

High costs, it must be emphasized, were not restricted to the voluntary sector; they were characteristic of all those schools that served the middle class – aided and non-aided schools alike. At mid-century, Upper Canada College with its massive government subsidy was no cheaper than a proprietary school like the Free Church's Toronto Academy, while the grant-aided grammar school in Toronto charged much the same fees as those private schools that catered to middle-class boys and girls. The same appears to have been true of other cities – Ottawa or London, for example – and of the smaller towns. It was, in other words, not just the voluntary sector that was expensive at mid-century, but middle-class education generally.

Whatever the burden high costs imposed on parents, however, the pertinent point is that high costs also undermined the voluntary sector itself. The private-venture schools were particularly vulnerable. Lacking any form of subsidy or external support, the success of a private-venture school depended entirely on a teacher's ability to balance expenses against fees. The teacher had to earn a living from the fees alone, and yet provide a classroom, heat, light, and other essential accoutrements, perhaps maintain space and provisions for boarders, and at the same time take only as many pupils as could be instructed effectively – a judgment that lay with the parents, not the teacher. The small number of pupils who could be managed by one teacher, or even a family of them, meant that fees were necessarily high. The combined effects of high fees and small numbers were outlined in 1839 by one Mrs Blackwood, an experienced teacher from England who had recently opened a school in Cornwall:

I have several young Ladies under my charge, belonging to the first families in the place; but although my terms are reasonable the income is not sufficient to enable me to meet the circumstances of many other highly respectable persons, whose means will not permit them giving to their children that education to which their standing in Society should entitle them – nor even, I may say, to give respectable support to myself.[18]

A decade later the editor of the *Christian Guardian* described the same problem:

It is well-known that where [schools] have been established by the enterprise of individuals, and depending solely for their support upon the tuition fees, that the fees have necessarily been so high as to exclude a large portion of the community for whose benefit they are designed ... and moreover, after struggling with difficulties for a time, have been compelled to relinquish their work, with perhaps the reward of a pecuniary loss. [19]

Thus the dilemma of the private-venture school: high fees excluded too many respectable people, while those who could afford the fees were too few to provide adequate remuneration for the teacher.

One consequence of this dilemma was that the private sector was extremely unstable. Using the newspapers and other sources for four Upper Canadian communities we have been able to track the longevity of some two hundred private-venture schools between 1830 and 1870. [20] Most of these schools were very short-lived, commonly closing down within one or two years of their establishment. Only a minority survived for five years or longer. And the smaller the community, the less the likelihood that they would survive for even five years.

The instability of the private sector was caused, in part at least, because supply outran effective demand. Schools, as we have already seen, were opened because respectable women were left without resources and they turned to the only acceptable avenue open to them. But even if they attracted a handful of students it might not be enough to sustain them and their children. We know in one or two cases that this is precisely what happened. [21] And though John Strachan was referring to governesses in the following piece of advice he gave to one woman, it might just as well have applied to those who tried to open a school: "So great has been the emigration of recent years amongst a portion of respectable families but decayed fortunes that the competition for every place that offers even a bare subsistence is most powerful." [22]

Instability did not arise from financial pressure alone: teachers died, married, or for a variety of reasons moved away or sought other employment. [23] Nonetheless, the delicate balance between costs and income meant that even successful schools were at constant risk. Bad times could lead to the temporary withdrawal of children from several families at once. Epidemics of sickness or changing educational fashions could decimate student ranks. So could the merest whisper of gossip, however malicious or ill founded. A hard-won profit margin could be wiped out by small enrolment fluctuations such as these and the teacher forced to close the school. [24]

As we ourselves noted some years ago, not all private-venture schools were ephemeral in nature. [25] Something like 30 per cent of our two hundred schools survived more than five years and some of these lasted ten or twenty years. Mrs Cockburn ran her school from 1822 until at least 1846. The school begun in 1844 by George Brown's two sisters lasted until at least 1860 and was kept up even after Isabella Brown married. [26] Mrs Crombie opened a ladies' school in Toronto in 1839 and continued to teach until

1855; the Misses McCord taught in Toronto for nearly thirty-five years. [27] Mrs T.C. Campbell taught from 1843 until at least 1862, first in Oshawa, then in Brockville, and finally in Toronto. [28] There are many other examples besides of schools being taught by both married and single women and providing them with what we must assume were secure incomes and careers. The fact of the matter is nonetheless that the majority of our two hundred schools survived for *less* than five years. And what may be of even more significance, the smaller the community, the less the likelihood that they would survive for even that long. In Upper Canada at least, the future shape of superior education was to be largely determined by the educational needs and political clout of people living in a large number of very small urban communities and it was in precisely those communities where voluntarism fared least well. [29]

Yet another problem for the private-venture schools was that limited resources left them open to charges of educational inefficiency. In the years around mid-century all middle-class education, government-supported and voluntary alike, might be expensive. But £50 invested in a boy sent to Upper Canada College bought boarding, tuition by a bevy of masters each responsible for and well qualified to teach their respective subjects, graded classes, academic options, and a variety of other services. The same amount invested in a daughter bought the two Misses McCartney – undoubtedly competent, certainly well recommended, but only two of them nonetheless to cover the whole of a girl's academic and ornamental education, and to provide, besides, supervision and parental care for the boarders. There were many private schools, the *Christian Guardian* remarked in 1863, but only two or three "which can afford to have a sufficient number of teachers to give an efficient education in all the useful and ornamental branches." [30]

In sum, the private-venture school was no cheaper than other kinds of schools and therefore no more accessible for respectable families of limited resources. For those who could manage the fees, it was markedly unstable. In the larger urban areas this might only mean that children would have to pass through the hands of a series of different teachers; in smaller communities the gap between the closure of one school and the opening of another might be months or years. And beyond that there were the charges of inefficiency. In mid-nineteenth-century Upper Canada, private entrepreneurship could not ensure that schools for middle-class children would be accessible, stable, or efficient.

The private-venture school, however, was not the only voluntarist option familiar to Upper Canadians. Another was the joint-stock or proprietorial school, run by trustees on behalf of a group of subscribers or a denomination and financed by the sale of shares or the solicitation of donations. The advantage this option offered lay in the creation of an endowment fund that could be used to circumvent the major defects of the private-venture school.

By subsidizing the total costs of a school, an endowment would not only guarantee a salary to the teacher but also make it possible to lower tuition fees and thus make the school both more stable and more accessible. It would also increase efficiency: the combination of increasing enrolments and an endowment would enable the trustees to hire more teachers and organize instruction more effectively. Or so at least the theory went, and indeed it worked well enough in other times and places.[31] Until at least the 1860s, however, it proved a frail reed in Upper Canada. The histories of most of the mid-nineteenth-century proprietary ventures can be pieced together and the recurring theme is initial enthusiasm measured in pledges and subscriptions, overcommitment on the part of founders or trustees, reluctance by the subscribers to pay up or renew their pledges, and a consequent flood of financial woes.

The problem did not lie in an inability to attract students. Most of the proprietary schools had large enrolments by the standards of the day.[32] Rather, it lay in the inability or unwillingness of large numbers of Upper Canadians to donate or subscribe the funds required. This was not a problem unique to the proprietary schools. The difficulties of financing Upper Canada's denominational colleges in this manner have been repeatedly documented by their historians, but at least the colleges were the urgent concern of influential and sometimes wealthy members of the various denominations. For the schools, it was a different matter. Community-based institutions like Grantham, Bath, and Ancaster academies, all founded in the 1830s, were in financial trouble from the day they opened their doors. Despite a larger potential base of support, the denominational schools suffered the same fate. The histories of the Wesleyans' Upper Canada Academy, the Baptists' Canadian Literary Institute, and the Episcopal Methodists' Belleville Seminary all tell of the crippling effects of commitments outrunning subscriptions and other forms of voluntary financial support.[33] The first Anglican attempt to found a female academy, in the early 1850s, failed because not enough subscribers could be found to buy the shares required even to open the institution.[34] And despite large enrolments and promising subscription lists, the Free Church's Toronto Academy, opening in 1846 at the beginning of a commercial depression, never recovered from its initial indebtedness. Clerical exhortations and desperate manoeuvres by the managers, which included compromising their voluntary principles by asking for government aid, failed to narrow the gap between income and expenses and the academy closed in 1854.[35]

Whether community or denominationally based, in sum, the problems of the proprietorial schools were the same. It proved very difficult, and in many cases impossible, to sustain them by voluntary means alone. Despite their best efforts, the trustees of Bath Academy warned in 1836, the survival of the school was at risk because they had "no other means than the uncertain aid of Voluntary Contributions, which from the want of capital in a new Country and various other causes cannot be relied on for that Steady and Effectual support so necessary to the usefulness of the Institution."[36] Two decades later, in an unusually perceptive summary of the problems of voluntarism, Philip Carman warned his Episcopal Methodist brethren against proceeding with any educational scheme financed by voluntary methods alone:

> For some years past I have had to do with a County Grammar School which school has been a kind of Seminary, there being a Male and Female department and Generally Two Teachers, the Principal say at a salary of £150 & the Preceptress from £50 to £75 per annum. The School has been well sustained, there being generally from 30 to 75 pupils, music, painting, drawing etc. being taught, the building rent-free and a Government grant of from £30 to £100 per annum, the last three or four years it has been £100 per annum. Notwithstanding all these advantages, with a popular Principal, the School is kept going with great difficulty and at times at a loss. Then again when we look at other similar institutions, how many have failed, and see the endowments they have and the difficulties they have, I cannot bring myself to believe that our Institution can possibly be kept going for any length of time without an endowment from some quarter even although it should be free from debt at the Commencement. But to begin with a heavy debt upon it at the rate of 8 or 10 percent interest with nothing but the cold charity of the Public to depend upon, I think would be presuming a little too much however. Looking at it in all its phases I must confess that with the knowledge I am in possession of respecting the liabilities and what can be made available to meet them it looks discouraging.[37]

But what was the alternative to reliance upon "the cold charity of the Public"? One obvious possibility was to turn to the state. As financial troubles accumulated, this was the response of many private-venture teachers and most proprietary school trustees. From the 1830s onwards, school founders petitioned the legislature, lobbied the politicians, and pleaded with government officials like Egerton Ryerson for grants to help maintain their schools.[38] A handful of schools, by virtue of their connection with chartered universities or powerful denominations, were successful in wringing grants from the state. In the main, however, and particularly after mid-century, government refused to provide the subsidies that might have enabled the voluntary sector to prosper.

The reasons for this are unclear because the question was never debated in either the legislature or the press. Certainly, it was not simply that the public authorities already supported one school system and did not want to support another. In the decade before mid-century, government support for superior or middle-class education was still haphazard at best. Grant-aided grammar schools for boys had only just begun to spread beyond a handful of district towns. Middle-class girls were utterly unprovided for. Most grant-aided common schools still taught only the rudiments and, in the urban areas, had not yet entirely supplanted the private-venture common schools. Policy too remained haphazard. On the one hand, the rights of proprietary schools to a share in public funds had been challenged in the legislature off and on since the early 1830s.[39] On the other hand, a number of private corporations had received grants and their claims had been justified on the grounds that they were "public" institutions, open to all and serving the public interest.[40] Ryerson himself vacillated about where responsibility for middle-class education lay, sometimes asserting that it fell to the state, and sometimes claiming that it should remain in the hands of families, churches, and private enterprise.[41] A central theme of his own rhetoric, moreover, was that voluntarism lay at the heart of the public system itself: government did not found schools for people; it aided, rather than supplanted, local initiative and voluntary effort.[42] Neither precedent nor principle, in other words, unequivocally militated against government grants to schools established and controlled by individuals, groups, or denominations, and maintained primarily by voluntary means.

From mid-century onwards, nonetheless, such grants were not forthcoming. The most likely explanation lies in the immediate exigencies of mid-nineteenth-century Upper Canadian politics. Two of the most divisive political issues of the period focused on grants in aid of education: the separate school and university questions. Both of these issues involved the legitimacy of state grants to denominational institutions, while the university question also raised another contentious issue – that of public grants to private charitable corporations. Grants given to the private and proprietary schools involved one or both of these questions depending on the character of the school, and the politicians were already all too familiar with the fierce passions raised by such issues. Thus, despite the fact that the cabinet undoubtedly had the power to extend individual grants to such institutions, neither tory nor reform administrators were prepared to do so. Though no reasons were ever recorded in its minutes or replies to the applicants, from the mid-forties onwards the executive council rejected a multitude of pleas for aid from private teachers as well as from institutions directly controlled by denominations, or even tinctured by denominational affiliation.[43] It was one thing to allow elected trustees to tax voters in order to provide advanced instruction, or to expand a grammar school system which had been established for decades and which, by mid-century, was administered by trustees who were broadly representative of the religious complexion of the community. It was another thing altogether to exacerbate existing political conflicts over the clergy reserves, the university, or the separate schools by opening new battlegrounds in order to save the voluntary schools. As Ryerson explained in 1853 to one private-venture teacher who applied for aid to save his school, "you must have observed that the policy of the Government (of both parties) during the last few years, has been not to make any new grant to any private or denominational School or Academy or College."[44]

The private-venture and proprietary schools, then, could look to neither the "cold charity of the public" nor the government for financial assistance. Constrained within the limits of their own resources, they were unable to hold the loyalties of those parents who could not afford the tuition or boarding fees the schools had to charge to remain solvent. Nor, to those who could afford the fees, could they offer stability, continuity, and educational efficiency. Faced with the inadequacies of familiar and traditional means of educational provision, Upper Canada's middle class adopted a simple but innovative solution: they put their children on the rates. That is, they created a new role for government, making it the direct instrument by which they could provide a suitable education for their boys and girls. Though the process was piecemeal, and extended throughout the middle decades of the nineteenth century, the main thrust of educational policy from 1841 to 1871 increasingly served the interests of middle-class families, and it was in their direction that the main current of public investment in education flowed.

This outcome should not surprise us. The politicians, government officials, school trustees, superintendents, and others who built and administered the school system were lawyers, doctors, clergymen, businessmen, civil servants, newspaper editors, and the like. They were also fathers. The failure of voluntarism was happening to them. Provincial politicians and local school trustees had a double stake: not only were they fathers themselves, but they were elected by constituencies made up, in large part at least, of fathers. The voters, for their part, were men who owned property or had income enough to entitle them to the franchise, and thus included those who complained about the high cost of boarding their boys in distant towns, and the "many respectable persons" who could not afford to pay Mrs Blackwood's fees for their daughters' education.

The extent to which parental and political interests could overlap is nicely illustrated in the case of W.H. Merritt and the Grantham Academy. Merritt had a personal stake in the academy: he had sent his sons to the school, contributed to its support, and served as one of its trustees. As well, friends and political supporters depended on it for the education of their children. During the 1830s Merritt had represented its interests in the assembly, and when it was near collapse repeatedly tried to obtain a grant for it. After a decade of experience with the vagaries of voluntarism, it is not surprising to find him in 1841 promoting the bill that made the grammar school fund available to towns other than the district capitals. Shortly thereafter it was Merritt who lobbied his friends in government to secure a grant for the academy, and as one of the trustees, negotiated the transfer of the building to a public board, thereby converting it into the St Catharines grammar school.[45]

The fit between parents, trustees, and policymakers was rarely as tight as this, but it was real enough. Grammar school parents themselves were, on the whole, a prosperous lot and included a cross-section of the kind of people who provided local leadership throughout the province.[46] Indeed, more than local leadership was involved: even in the handful of schools we have studied closely, two fathers of grammar school children in 1861 were MPS. As well, parents commonly served as school trustees. In Stratford in 1861 four out of five trustees had children in the school. In Strathroy it was three out of five and in Sarnia all of the trustees sent children to the grammar school. As a group, moreover, the trustees were influential people. During his first tour of the western half of the province in 1855, the grammar school inspector tallied the occupations of grammar school trustees and reported that out of a total of 186, 63 were clergymen, almost all either Anglican or Presbyterian; 40 were municipal officers or magistrates; 20 were doctors; and 6 were MPS.[47] All of these people, parents and trustees alike, were, of course, associated with established grammar schools, but we assume that they were also representative of those without adequate local educational facilities who would press so hard for the extension of grant-aided schools during the middle decades of the nineteenth century. In 1831, as we have already seen, the petitions from London and Kingston calling for more funding for local grammar schools and less for Upper Canada College were signed by leading members of these communities. Fifty years later, in 1879, an editor could comment in passing that those "who were supporters, and those interested in the success of the High Schools ... those who are doing so much for the moral, material and intellectual progress of the nation – represent the intelligence, the wealth, and to a great extent the *political power* of this country."[48] Whether they were seeking a grant to establish a new school, in other words, or additional grants or privileges to maintain it, the constituency of the grammar schools was a powerful political interest group that would influence the course of government educational policy from the 1840s onwards.

THEY MADE THEIR INFLUENCE FELT first in the multiplication of the number of grammar schools. Throughout the 1840s there was a frantic scramble to lay hands on a share of the grant given to grammar schools. Most of the historical record relating to this helter-skelter expansion survives, and the file constitutes a remarkable tale of political log-rolling in which civic boosters and combines of eager parents wrote their MPS, badgered the district councils, and petitioned the legislature for a portion of the grant. Local luminaries wrote their political friends in the executive council, and councillors themselves made sure that the importunities of important constituents were met. There was nothing subtle about the process. Newmarket wanted a grammar school, a friend of Robert Baldwin informed him in 1849. "The matter ... has been taken up ... by a large number of your best Friends and supporters" and a fine grammar school

will greatly redound to the credit of this portion of your Riding ... In employing your influence with the other portion of the Executive for the granting of a sum of money to assist in the building of a suitable edifice for the grammar school, I trust that you will bear in mind the fact that by granting a liberal sum, it will be the means of erecting a permanent monument, which will redound to your credit by a very large number of your political friends, as well as your enemies.[49]

The process of creating a new grammar school in the Wellington district in 1849 followed a similar course. Both Elora and Fergus had strong claims – large common schools in place, local financial support subscribed, and substantial petitions signed by residents of each town. The petition from Fergus warned that Elora was "on the edge of a wilderness," had a relatively new common school, and a teacher of doubtful quality; Fergus, on the other hand, had outstanding physical advantages, a fine common school, and a sound base of financial support. Elora, however, had one advantage that Fergus couldn't match: the support of A.J. Fergusson, a leading reform politician. In a private letter, Fergusson reminded Baldwin that Fergus was the residence of his political opponent in the last election. Fergusson also made the case for Elora to the cabinet and, no doubt, had a hand in a supportive letter from Malcolm Cameron as well. Elora got the school.[50]

These examples of school founding, it must be emphasized, were not atypical. In the years before 1853 the surviving record is full of similar examples, as rising towns and villages struggled to lay hands on the grammar school grant to ensure local provision for superior education, and to do it through a subsidy from government rather than by taxing themselves to pay for the higher branches of instruction to be taught in the local common school.[51] The end result was predictable: in only three decades, from thirteen to just over a hundred schools.

Outside of the district towns where the grant still amounted to £100, as it had since 1807, the size of the grammar school grant was relatively small and paid only a portion of a master's salary. But it was aggressively pursued nonetheless, for especially in very small communities it might make the crucial difference between the survival of a school and not having one at all. And local subscriptions might not be forthcoming without the assurance of the grant beforehand. "Lately I have been much occupied in procuring an endowment [grant] for a grammar school in this neighbourhood," the Rev. Featherstone Osler of Tecumseth township wrote his mother in 1851;

"having accomplished this, a suitable schoolhouse is to be erected by private subscription ... This will be a great matter for my troop of boys for I could not afford to send them all to ... boarding school and have not time to attend to their education at home."[52]

For men of moderate means like Osler, and especially those who lived in small communities, the importance of obtaining a share of the grant, it must be emphasized, was an urgent concern, for it was a crucial lever in providing boys with access to suitable professions and occupations. In his important work on the social characteristics of Upper Canada's first cohort of university students, David Keane points out that 69 per cent of all university entrants in the 1840s came from communities which had a grammar school or from a township in which such communities were located.[53] A handful of wealthy men might be able to bear the costs of private tutors or the expense of sending their boys to school in Toronto. Village clergymen, lawyers, doctors, retail merchants, and the like could afford no such luxuries. By 1859, a grammar school inspector noted, there were far too many grammar schools, and yet, he added, it was not difficult to understand why they had been established.

This undue increase in the number of schools has arisen mainly from the laudable desire of a few individuals in each town or village, to obtain if possible near their homes a classical training for their sons; hence the attempt not infrequently made to establish and open a school where a sufficient number of classical pupils cannot be obtained ... It should be observed, however, that while the establishment of new schools diminishes the income, and in some respects lowers the status and lessens the usefulness of the others, it has also the effect of disseminating more widely the privileges offered by such high schools and presents the opportunity of acquiring the rudiments of classical and mathematical knowledge, and thereby of attaining a university training to some, who would otherwise, from their circumstances, have been deprived of it.[54]

The grant brought not only greater accessibility but greater stability as well. Whatever their income from fees, grammar school masters were also guaranteed a salary from government funds. Fluctuations in enrolments did not close the school, and if the master died or moved elsewhere, the promise of the grant could be used to attract another. In the larger towns, moreover, fees and grants promised increasing efficiency. In the early 1850s the Toronto grammar school was no cheaper than the select day schools in the city. But it had two great advantages: it was a permanent institution, and it employed four full-time teachers as well as additional part-time instructors for French and bookkeeping.[55]

Voluntarism and state subsidies were not mutually exclusive in the mid-nineteenth century, and the expansion of grant-aided grammar schools did not mean the elimination of either voluntary effort or parental financial responsibility. Local people had to raise the money for a schoolhouse, tuition fees continued to be charged, and all additional operating costs except the teacher's share of the grant had to be paid for by voluntary contributions in one form or another. Indeed, until 1866 when local tax support became available, fees and subscriptions were as important to the survival of the school as government money. The crucial difference, particularly after the Grammar School Act of 1853, was that voluntary effort was now directed towards building schools which operated under the auspices of the state rather than to the preservation of an independent sector in Upper Canadian education.

It was not the expansion of the grammar schools alone, however, that served the interests of middle-class families. The expansion of the common school system catered to their interests as well. By 1850 legislation had already given urban boards the power to spend taxpayers' money on the creation of higher English schools, to charge the full costs of tuition in these schools to the ratepayers, and to unite common and grammar schools under a single board of trustees – a particular boon to smaller communities because it made it easier and cheaper for them to maintain facilities for advanced education. Local boards of trustees were quick to take advantage of these opportunities. To have a central school or a union school, paid for by government grants and local ratepayers, was a point of pride in the 1850s, and the movement spread rapidly through most of urban Upper Canada. In the common schools the curriculum was extended upwards, far beyond the requirements of basic literacy or numeracy. Better-qualified teachers were hired, despite the extra costs entailed, to teach more advanced subjects to older students. Boards attempted to recruit respectable girls by establishing separate female classes. Rules respecting cleanliness, appropriate dress, and the purchase of texts and supplies were introduced, keeping the riff-raff out and thus making the schools safer for the children of respectable families.[56]

As politicians and administrators shaped provincial law and local policy to fit the needs of their constituents, so middle-class parents exploited the new opportunities. Grammar school enrolments, as we have already seen, doubled in the 1850s and nearly doubled again in the next decade; and our own analysis of the social origins of the grammar school pupils during these two decades only confirms what contemporaries took for granted, that they were mostly children from the top half of the economic and social scales. It is no surprise to discover that middle-class children were being sent to school in increasing numbers in the mid-nineteenth century, or that they were being kept in school longer; this is already familiar from the work of historians in Canada and elsewhere.[57] Our point here is that this school-going population was being funnelled into grant-aided schools. Moreover, in the handful of cases where common school registers survive and have been analysed, the same phenomenon can be found. As Ian Davey and others have shown, the new central schools were particularly powerful magnets, increasingly drawing the middle classes into the public sector, and at the same time, undermining the viability of the voluntary schools. "The establishment of the new system of public schooling," Davey writes of the city of Hamilton, "had important ramifications for attendance patterns ... because it effectively destroyed most of the alternatives to public schooling in the city. Moreover it removed the stigma associated with attendance at the public schools."[58] The same phenomenon was noted by contemporaries as well. "For nearly twenty years," one private teacher explained to Ryerson in 1859, "I kept a most respectable private school in Kingston, which continued to flourish greatly, with scarcely any fluctuation till within the last three years. During that period the encouragement given to the public education system gradually injured my school until it no longer supported my family."[59]

We have no analysis for Toronto to match the work of Ian Davey on Hamilton. Nor do we have private school enrolment statistics for Toronto as we do for most other urban communities in the period.[60] But we do know that during the 1860s a vociferous debate was under way over the legitimacy of the respectable classes using the city's common schools, a debate which suggests in turn that slippage into the public system was occurring even though Toronto had no central school. The editorial and correspondence columns of the *Leader* in particular provided a forum for those who believed that the well off had no business feeding at the public trough. Prominent citizens, including members of the board of school trustees and city councillors, were accused of sending their children to the common schools; such people, said one irate correspondent, were "totally devoid of the moral honesty which would scorn to be dependent on the bounty of other agents."[61] The editor agreed. "In affording a free education ... to people able to help themselves, we are relieving them of parental responsibility ... entailed upon them by the Divine Being himself" and thus "contravening a settled law of nature" and "educating our people in immorality."[62] In response to such strictures, a "Parent and a Taxpayer" rang the changes that were taking place in attitudes and behaviour. Though well able to afford to pay for a private school, he wrote, not only did he prefer the common schools but it was his right to use them; and he considered it "insulting and impertinent" to be called morally dishonest when "my city taxes amount annually to a trifle less than forty dollars, a large proportion of which is for school purposes."[63]

Toronto may well have been a special case in respect to private school provisions as it was in so many other things.[64] The city's size, the concentration of wealth, the proportionately larger numbers of labourers and artisans, the sharper sense of class differences, and other factors besides may well have made private education more sought after and more economically viable. Yet even in Toronto, the impact of the shift into the public sector made itself felt. The declining numbers of students attending the Toronto Academy in the early 1850s was blamed, in part at least, on "the improvement of the City Schools, and from the greater facilities, perhaps, for acquiring a somewhat better education in the County [grammar] schools also. Some of the Directors are inclined to give up the Academy in consequence."[65] Nearly forty years later, in 1877, the same inexorable process was recorded by Augusta Miller: "a large free school," she informed a friend, "on the principle of the High School has opened near us on Berkeley Street called the Dufferin School. It has injured a good many little schools such as ours."[66]

Parents proved to be much more resistant, nonetheless, to sending their girls than their boys to the grant-aided schools. A grammar school was a traditional instrument for the education of boys, and even when it might not be the preferred solution, it was nonetheless a respectable place for a boy. To send a girl was a much more doubtful enterprise, since the grammar schools normally provided neither a suitable curriculum nor separate classes for girls. Thus those who could afford choices exercised them. Moreover, if the literary evidence is any guide, the aversion to the common schools seems to have been even stronger. As late as the mid-1860s it was still taken for granted by editors and correspondents to the newspapers that "our wealthy or well-to-do tradesmen, farmers, merchants and professional men, do not and will not, as a rule, send their daughters to the common schools."[67]

Yet the character of the voluntary schools continued to attract criticism as well. The private-venture sector remained unstable and hence unreliable. Attempts by successful schools to provide a more efficient education only resulted in higher fees.[68] For their boys, wealthy parents now had a variety of alternatives while those whose resources were limited could send them to the local grammar school or central school. But for girls, the choices were harder and the options more restricted. Amidst the general celebration of the progress of education so pervasive in the public rhetoric of the 1850s and 1860s, the lack of provision for middle-class girls stands out in the press and elsewhere as a recurrent source of bitter complaint.[69] As late as the mid-1860s, when the Anglican synod debated the question of founding its own girls' school, one of the strongest motives was that "the cost of education at private schools at present was too great for the generality of people in moderate circumstances."[70] The same point was made in a letter printed in the *Church Chronicle*: "What is to become of the daughters of those multitudes of good families, and especially us poor clergymen, whose annual income does not exceed $600 per annum. Must they lose their position or sink to a lower social level than they are naturally entitled to?"[71]

What was to become of them indeed? One option that parents increasingly exercised, though reluctantly, was to send their girls to the local grammar schools, a development we will return to in a later chapter. Another option had caused a good deal of consternation and public recrimination throughout the 1850s and 1860s. In the years around mid-century, convent schools had been founded in several Upper Canadian towns to provide an education for the daughters of respectable Roman Catholic families. Like most other voluntary schools, they were select, fee-charging, and single-sex institutions. But they were also subsidized by the church and by the religious orders themselves, and thus they could offer the advantages of subsidy – better facilities, lower fees, and a larger staff than a private-venture teacher could afford. They were not only much cheaper, as one of their proponents pointed out, but they were more efficient, for "the organization being larger is necessarily more perfect."[72] These advantages proved attractive to a number of Protestant as well as Roman Catholic families, or so at least it was claimed at the time. The outcry from Protestant zealots was predictable, and the "conversion" of one or two girls from prominent families gave an extra edge to the hysteria. We do not know the extent to which Protestant girls were actually sent to the nunneries, but in any case our interest in the phenomenon lies elsewhere. Like anti-popery in general, the nunnery panic had a tendency to concentrate the Upper Canadian mind wonderfully. The attraction of schools that were "hot-beds of Popery," designed to "ensnare the children of silly Protestants," gave increased urgency to the conviction that provision for female education was inadequate and that alternatives had to be created.[73]

During the 1860s some denominations like the Wesleyans and the Anglicans founded their own girls' boarding schools; others like the Baptists made a virtue of necessity and defended the principle of coeducation at their mixed boarding school.[74] But solutions like these were helpful only to those parents who either lived nearby or could afford to board their girls. As in the case of boys, accessibility for most people meant schools in the place where they lived. And for most people, that in turn meant the grant-aided schools, especially in those communities not large enough to sustain local private-venture schools.

Though more and more middle-class parents sent their children to grant-aided schools in the decades after 1850, this does not mean that the private sector disappeared. The preference for socially and sexually segregated schooling ran deep in the mid-nineteenth century, and if there were prosperous parents who made the adjustment to public education, there were always others who refused. In the five towns we have studied intensively, some 70 per cent of all parents with children between ages ten and twenty were British-born. These immigrant parents were, in the main, unfamiliar with grant-aided schools for the middle class, and if their numbers are representative for the rest of the province, it is perhaps not surprising to find that there were a significant number of children who continued to be sent away to boarding schools or who attended local private schools. Indeed the limited evidence available for the latter half of the nineteenth century suggests that in absolute terms both the number of private schools and enrolments actually increased. Though it may have become impossible in the smaller urban communities to sustain a private-venture school, such schools survived in the larger towns and cities, and at least a few prospered. From the late 1860s onwards, moreover, increasing wealth made it easier to initiate and sustain proprietorial ventures. Endowed with adequate funds, a new generation of denominational boarding schools established themselves as stable and efficient educational institutions serving those able to afford high day fees or the costs of boarding their sons and daughters away from home. [75]

If there was no absolute decline, however, it seems clear that there was a substantial relative decline. Our estimate for enrolments in the voluntary sector at mid-century was about one-third of all enrolments in the cities, and something less than that for all urban areas. By the 1870s, according to Department of Education statistics, this proportion had declined in the cities to something on the order of 10 per cent or less, and for all urban places to 5 per cent. Put another way, if the voluntary sector had continued to hold its mid-century share of the clientele, then it would have grown as fast as other comparable types of schools. In fact, the voluntary sector grew far more slowly than total common school enrolments, enrolments in the senior grades of the common schools, or grammar school enrolments (see appendix A, table A.3). The only sources for the period after the 1870s are the newspaper advertisements and the directories, which of course tell us nothing about enrolments. Where runs of either source stretch from mid-century to the 1890s, however, there are no significant increases in the number of schools. Despite the enormous increase in Toronto's population and wealth, for example, the 1896 city directory lists only a few more private schools than that for 1846. [76]

The transition from the private to the public sector was of crucial importance to the development of Ontario's educational system. Emerging state systems of education were common in the nineteenth century, but in the English-speaking world they were, often enough, limited to the elementary education of the lower classes. Had Upper Canada been wealthier, or its urban population less dispersed in small towns and villages, it might have paralleled developments in England or Australia where working-class education was provided by the state, and middle-class education by the churches and other forms of voluntarism. By the time enough wealth existed to sustain a viable system of middle-class voluntary schools in Upper Canada, however, the pattern was already fixed, and the new private boarding and day schools of the later nineteenth century became a conscious and expensive alternative to the state schools, used by only a minority of middle-class parents. Whatever the precise institutional forms that would evolve, it was increasingly clear from mid-century onwards that the clientele of the public system would include the middle class, and that the responsibility of the public schools would extend beyond the rudiments to the higher branches of instruction as well.

CHAPTER FIVE

The Development of the Grammar Schools, 1807–66

Until the 1840s, there were only a few grammar schools in Upper Canada, and compared to the voluntary sector, they played a modest role in providing superior education. In the two decades around mid-century, however, as people in small communities scrambled for a share of the government grant, the number of grammar schools multiplied relentlessly, rising from a handful in 1840 to nearly a hundred by the early 1860s. As their numbers grew, they increasingly became an indispensable part of the colony's system of education. But expansion took place without firm central direction, and thus the development of the grammar school was shaped by the needs of the parents who used them and by the dictates of local markets for education. The consequence of growth without regulation was of critical importance for the future. Customs and habits of thought took root amongst local school supporters which policymakers would later find impossible to dislodge, and these would influence the emerging structure of public education as much as any of the reform initiatives pursued by politicians or bureaucrats in the three decades after 1850.

THE HISTORY OF THE GRAMMAR SCHOOLS is as old as the colony itself. John Graves Simcoe, Upper Canada's first lieutenant-governor, believed that the creation of schools to educate the colony's elite was an essential prerequisite for its survival as a part of the British Empire. Without local schools, he warned, children would inevitably be sent to the United States, there to imbibe the destructive principles of republicanism and anti-British sentiments. During his short tenure in the colony, Simcoe had drafted a number of proposals for the establishment of grammar schools and a college in Upper Canada. But his entreaties for financial assistance received short shrift from the imperial government. To his superiors, such schemes were wildly overambitious in an infant colony. For the moment, he was told, Upper

Canadians would be best served by the establishment of schools at Quebec and Montreal, while the few Upper Canadians who needed a more advanced seminary could look to the rising college in Nova Scotia. Simcoe knew the neighbouring states were closer and cheaper even if those in Westminster did not. But in the midst of a European war, the authorities had no intention of providing financial help for Upper Canadian schools. Faced with this response, the most Simcoe ever accomplished was to authorize, without approval, a grant of £100 for the support of the Rev. John Stuart's grammar school in Kingston.[1]

If Britain would not finance Upper Canada's schools, were there resources within the colony? One alternative source of revenue, already being exploited in the United States, was land. In 1797, a joint address of the legislature requested the British government to appropriate a portion of the waste land of the Crown to the support of both a university and grammar schools. The imperial government agreed and requested the executive council to submit detailed plans for the proposal. These were completed and forwarded to Westminster in 1798.[2]

The council recommended that some five hundred thousand acres, or approximately ten townships, be set aside to support four grammar schools and a university. Two schools were to be founded immediately, at Kingston and Newark. The university and the other two schools would be established when demand required it. Each school was to have at least two masters, schoolrooms sufficient to accommodate a hundred boys, and living quarters for ten to twenty boarders. Salaries, buildings, and operating expenses were to be financed by sales and rents derived from the school lands. Half of the reserved lands were to be allocated to the future university, however.[3] The report made no reference to the governance of the schools but the colonial secretary instructed the lieutenant-governor to appoint six trustees besides himself, and to include among them the bishop of Quebec, the chief justice of Upper Canada, and the speaker of the assembly.[4]

It was a remarkable plan and if carried out would have resulted in the establishment of well-financed, educationally effective boarding schools rivalling the best in Britain and the United States. Unfortunately, nothing even remotely resembling those schools would exist until the founding of Upper Canada College in 1829. Though the five hundred thousand acres were indeed set aside at the beginning of the century, they turned out to be of no use in generating school revenues. "Since the reserves consisted," Lillian Gates remarks, "of completely undeveloped and unsurveyed townships, no rents could be obtained from them nor could they have been sold at a worthwhile price while the free grant system existed."[5] The very existence of the school reserves was gradually forgotten by all but a handful of government officials and it would be decades before they would begin to play an important role in the financing of Upper Canada's schools.

Since land could not be used to sustain institutions for superior education, government was left with only one alternative: appropriations from the revenues of the province. We know almost nothing about the political context of the attempts to secure and preserve that appropriation except what the barebones record of the legislative journals tells us. Opposition was strong enough to stop the passage of school bills in 1804 and 1805. Then, in 1807, the assembly reversed itself and passed the District Schools Act, which provided an annual appropriation of £100 for the salary of one grammar school teacher in each of the eight administrative districts in the colony.[6] The lieutenant-governor was to appoint trustees for each school. Subject to his approval, they hired and fired the teacher and drafted rules and regulations for the good government and maintenance of the school. In the following two years most of the new district schools went into operation. And as the number of districts multiplied in the following decades, so did the number of district grammar schools.

The government subsidy enabled a number of Upper Canadian towns to sustain a teacher capable of offering something more than the subjects of a common school education. That, one might argue, was no small achievement fifteen years after settlement. But compared to the plan of 1798 the act was a travesty. It multiplied schools far beyond immediate demand for superior instruction – setting a precedent, it must be remarked, that would characterize Ontario education throughout the nineteenth century. Politics had made that concession necessary, John Strachan would later say; the original promoters of the bill had proposed to establish only four schools, but the assembly insisted that what one district had all must have.[7] The act made no provision for raising or maintaining a building, and all operating expenses aside from the teacher's salary were left to the care of the local trustees, who themselves were utterly dependent on voluntary subscriptions and tuition fees to meet the needs of the school. Since no boarding facilities were provided, the advantages of the schools were largely limited to the communities in which they were located. For decades the district schools would remain hopelessly underfinanced, taught in dilapidated or unsuitable buildings, and inaccessible to most of the population. So flawed was the act that one can only assume its supporters believed it a temporary expedient until the school lands revenues became available. No one, presumably, imagined that it would stand almost without modification for fifty years.

The act, moreover, provoked sustained opposition from all except those who would immediately benefit by it.[8] There were professional men, merchants, and craftsmen struggling to support their own village schools while they watched neighbouring towns receive a substantial subsidy.[9] There were those throughout the rural areas who wanted help to support their common schools and felt that the grammar school act was no more than a subsidy cast in the lap of the rich, who needed and deserved it least.[10] The supporters of the act answered these criticisms as best they could. The small amount the legislature could afford, they argued, would hardly be of assistance to anyone if spread among the hundreds of common schools already established. The idea, moreover, that superior instruction could or should be brought to every man's door was preposterous: "with equal propriety might every man complain, who has not a church, a mill or a jail at his door."[11] Yet the defects of the act alienated even its erstwhile supporters, particularly in the new districts where, in the absence of classical pupils, the grammar schools were merely highly subsidized, highly priced common schools.[12]

Such diverse and widespread criticism very nearly brought the act down. In 1811 and 1812 bills actually passed through the assembly which would have abolished the district schools altogether had not the legislative council refused to assent to them.[13] But the price of preservation was the extension of subsidies to other schools. Several common school bills had already received substantial support in the legislature before the end of the War of 1812 and in 1816 the government would bow to pressure and appropriate the first annual grants in aid of common schools.

In part at least, the survival of the District Schools Act was due to the efforts of John Strachan, the Anglican clergyman and schoolmaster who was to influence all aspects of Upper Canadian educational policy. By 1820, Strachan had worked out a remarkably complete scheme of educational development for the colony. There was to be a university, the common schools were to be improved through a series of revisions to the act of 1816, scholarships would link the common and grammar schools to the university, and a General Board of Education was to be established to administer all of the colony's schools. In keeping with Strachan's establishmentarian views, however, the entire system was to be dominated by the Church of England, and Strachan himself was to be president of the General Board.[14]

For nearly two decades after 1815, Strachan would pursue this overall scheme with tenacious energy. The district schools, however, received very little attention from him. His only significant revision of the act of 1807 was the introduction of the scholarship system, linking the common and grammar schools, in the District Schools Amendment Act of 1819.[15] In itself this was a significant innovation, but it did nothing to improve the grammar schools *per se*. Given the continuing criticism of the grammar schools and his own reforming zeal, Strachan's laissez-faire attitude is somewhat surprising. Perhaps he feared that any major change would reawaken the abolitionism rampant before the war. Perhaps the district schools were simply his blind spot. He had, after all, conducted two schools under the act in a remarkably successful way and might not have recognized the defects that existed in the small country grammar schools. His assessment of them in 1815–19 was relatively optimistic; and not until 1828 when he actually visited many of them did he begin to express dismay at the buildings, the calibre of teaching, and the attainments of the pupils.[16] The only outcome of his visits, however, was a pamphlet on the proper organization and discipline of a grammar school that, however worthy, brought little in the way of immediate improvement.[17]

By 1828, in any case, Strachan was already under attack from the rising reform movement. The abolition of Anglican privilege in colonial education was a key aim of reformers, and as they won the ear of the colonial office, Strachan's policies were increasingly abandoned. His plans for a university were delayed indefinitely, and by 1833 the General Board was abolished. No substitute was put in its place, however. Though plans for the reform of education – the grammar schools included – were legion throughout the 1830s, the balance between executive and assembly, and between conservatives and reformers in the assembly, led to a stalemate not broken until after the rebellion of 1837.[18]

One thing was accomplished in the late twenties, however: the founding of Upper Canada College. Indeed, this was the immediate cause of the delay in opening the university. A new lieutenant-governor, Sir John Colborne, had recognized the political difficulties in proceeding with Strachan's plans, but there were also educational reasons for the delay. The district schools, he felt, were hopelessly inadequate as preparatory institutions. "It would be quite madness," he told the colonial secretary, "to proceed with the university when there is no tolerable seminary in the Province to prepare Boys for it."[19] In December 1828 – only a month after his arrival – Colborne told King's College Council that, as chancellor, he would not permit further moves to open the college until he had considered the alternatives more carefully.[20] Early in the new year he began to implement his own plans – the modification of the university charter and the establishment of a new, superior grammar school that would complete the work of the district schools and properly prepare students for the university.

Though he took the trouble to explain his intentions to both houses of the legislature and willingly complied with requests for information, the founding of what would become Upper Canada College was largely his own achievement. Anxious to see the school begin immediately, Colborne wrote home early in 1829, inviting the vice-chancellor of Oxford to select a principal and the senior staff.[21] He urged haste so that the college could commence early in 1830 and before the end of that year a highly qualified group of teachers had arrived in York, ready to begin their work. All were graduates, with high academic honours, of the English universities. They received handsome salaries and could take boarders besides. The college opened in temporary accommodations in January 1830. By that time a promising site had already been acquired and buildings were under construction that would house the college for the rest of the century.[22]

The immediate control of Upper Canada College was placed in the hands of the principal and staff, but general academic and moral supervision was exercised first by the General Board of Education and then, after 1833, by King's College Council.[23] The school was financed by two means. Its operating expenses were to be paid by an annual appropriation of £500 from the territorial revenues (in 1834 this was raised to £1000). Colborne also received permission to endow the school with some sixty-six thousand acres from the school reserves.[24] The administration of these lands was placed in the hands of King's College Council. Given the need for immediate funds to pay for buildings and other expenses, however, Colborne suggested that the college council make the requisite loans to the schools and in return receive patents to equivalent amounts of the land grant.[25] Thus began a pattern of indebtedness by Upper Canada College to the university that would plague the latter institution for decades. That, however, was for the future. By 1831, when the masters and boys occupied their new buildings on King Street in York, the school was already remarkably successful, drawing more than a hundred pupils from the best families in York and other parts of the province. With remarkable swiftness Colborne had met what he considered to be the colony's most urgent educational requirement – an efficient preparatory school staffed by men of the highest calibre, providing facilities for students from all parts of the province, relatively inexpensive because so heavily endowed, attracting the sons of the most respectable classes of society, and educating them in a distinctly Anglican and British environment.

Meanwhile the district schools continued, as they had during Strachan's ascendancy, to be virtually unadministered. Here, Colborne had nothing to offer by way of reform. The provincial authorities continued to pay out £100 annually to each district school – as the number of districts multiplied, the number of schools increased from eight in 1807 to thirteen in 1839 – but reports from the schools were submitted irregularly or in a few cases, not at all, so that information about their condition was hard to come by. By the late twenties, the government did not even have an up-to-date list of trustees, or any clear idea of how many pupils attended the schools. As for local administration, it was hardly better. Living in different parts of each district, the trustees rarely met, and thus annual examination or regular supervision of the teacher was often neglected. Death, disability, and removals from the district sometimes left the boards without a quorum for years at a time.[26] Thus from 1807 until 1838 the district schools were almost entirely left to the vagaries of local circumstance. In the larger towns they might well be good schools, offering the full range of a classical and English education, preparing boys for Upper Canada College or for the professions. Such schools could attract good teachers because the government salary and tuition fees together offered an income of £200 or more a year. Some masters supplemented that by boarding pupils in their own homes or by taking a few private students. By the thirties, most of the larger schools had acquired an assistant master, paid for out of fees, who taught a special subject or supervised the younger boys. In the smaller district capitals, the situation was very different. The teachers rarely had much income beyond the government salary, the pupils were fewer and most were enrolled in English subjects or the rudiments alone, and sometimes even girls were admitted in order to bring in enough revenues to sustain the school. The district schools became, in other words, whatever circumstances would permit and, within those limits, whatever the trustees who lived in the district town, the teacher, and the parents who used the school wanted them to become. [27]

In the wake of the rebellion, a conservative, loyalist legislature, in which council and assembly finally saw eye to eye, introduced changes to the act of 1807. New legislation, enacted in 1839, maintained the direct grant of £100 to the grammar school situated in each district town, but it also endowed the grammar schools with the school land reservation of 1798, which by this time was producing a small revenue. [28] The new funds were to be used for two purposes: to build proper schoolhouses, and to provide for the creation of new grammar schools in towns other than the district capital – the first time in Upper Canada's history that the expansion of these schools to more than one in each district was contemplated. New schools, however, were required to be located six miles beyond the district town and provide not less than sixty scholars. [29]

The act also created a centralized administrative framework for the schools. But power to make rules and regulations for the grammar schools was given not to an arm of government, but to King's College Council, still dominated by what other denominations at least saw as an Anglican oligarchy. The college council appointed a school committee which set about organizing the schools in a thorough way. In 1840, regulations were drawn up that set out the curriculum, the length of terms and vacations, the maximum fees, and some simple religious exercises. The curriculum was to be as far as practicable the same as that of Upper Canada College: a broad course that included English, French, history, and bookkeeping, as well as Latin, Greek, and mathematics. The council offered to help the schools find suitable head teachers; and it made a grant available to each school as a stipend for an assistant on condition that at least twenty pupils were learning Latin, that the regulations were observed, and that proper details of the assistant's qualifications were submitted. To enforce the regulations, the council proposed to appoint an inspector to visit the schools and examine the pupils. [30]

It was, on the face of it, a sensible piece of legislation that could not help but improve the schools. But it reverberated with the religious and political conflicts of the 1830s. A conservative legislature had put the schools under the thumb of John Strachan and the Anglican church through the medium of King's College. The Church of Scotland in particular was outraged and organized a series of petitions and protests to the legislature, while one of its most prominent laymen, William Morris, led the attack against the act in the new legislature created by the union of the Canadas.[31] Early in the session of 1841 a repeal bill passed both Houses easily. The whole apparatus of central control and supervision was removed, leaving policy and administration once again in the hands of the executive government but with no department assigned any particular responsibility for the grammar schools. Other provisions of the 1839 act were not repealed, however. The district schools were to continue to receive £100 each for the salary of the headmaster, as they had since 1807. As in 1839, the revenues of the school lands were to be devoted to the grammar schools, and spent to support assistant masters and to build proper schoolhouses in the district towns. If the executive council saw fit, however, grants could also be made to additional (or new) grammar schools in each district. But once again conditions applied: the six-mile rule remained, and the inhabitants had to provide a schoolhouse themselves along with fifty scholars before they were eligible for an additional grammar school grant.[32]

Between 1807 and 1839, then, grammar schools were "planted" by government in particular towns, and local people were left to make what use of them they could. In 1839, and again in 1841, legislation made expansion possible, and also shifted the initiative to the localities. A community could now raise a schoolhouse, guarantee a set number of scholars, and petition government for a share in the grammar school fund. It was this innovation that set off the expansionary fever of the 1840s and 1850s.

Some growth in numbers, it needs to be emphasized, would have been inevitable in any case. Neither the act of 1839 nor 1841 repealed the earlier legislation of 1807, and thus as the number of districts grew, and as counties were created after 1849, each new municipal capital was awarded its own grammar school. By 1853 there were twenty-six of these county or "senior" grammar schools as they came to be known.[33] Aside from this, however, the government was under no legal obligation to multiply the number of schools. It could have used the grammar school fund to improve existing schools – to build a schoolhouse and boarding facilities, purchase equipment and supplies, or pay the salaries of assistant masters. In other words the government might have chosen to create a relatively small number of well-endowed schools located in each county town, capable of providing an education similar to that of Upper Canada College – precisely the aim of the grammar school rules and regulations adopted in 1840 by King's College Council. In the early 1840s the Grammar School Fund was too small to achieve even that goal, but later in the decade, as the grammar school lands grew in value and were sold for a good price, the interest available from the capital multiplied rapidly. Between 1848 and 1849 alone it jumped 125 per cent, and by 1853 provided nearly £4000 annually to be spent on whatever goals the government wanted to pursue.[34]

As we have already seen, however, from early in the colony's history there was an ingrained preference for easy access, and for day schools, over more abstract notions of the high standards that might be achieved by a few well-endowed boarding schools. Leading schoolmen might have set their sights on English exemplars: protesting a threat to Upper Canada College's endowment in 1847, its principal and masters called upon government to nurture the college so that it might become "what will be more loudly called for than ever – the one great Public School of Canada."[35] But unless they lived in Toronto, local elites felt little enthusiasm for such centralizing policies, as the protests from London and Kingston against the initial establishment of Upper Canada College testified.[36] And those who lived outside the district or county towns felt much the same.[37] Thus the politicians and their constituents were in accord on the matter: access to superior education needed to be decentralized; local and cheap institutions were to be preferred to distant and expensive academies even if the latter could offer a better education. Given such preferences on the part of families who had children to educate, it is not surprising that politicians of all stripes catered to expansionary pressures. When it came to superior education, George Brown was no populist. He knew the value (and was the product) of good classical schools and he was a stout defender of a high-quality and centralized provincial university. But when he appealed to the electors of Kent and Lambton in 1851, it was the theme of geographical and social accessibility which rang through: "the Grammar Schools should be more numerous," his election platform read, "and the fees fixed at such a rate as to be within the reach of all classes."[38] Moreover it was not only provincial politicians who opted for expansion; the district and county councils, whose advice was routinely sought by the cabinet throughout the 1840s, almost always recommended the creation of additional grammar schools rather than investing the money in improving existing ones.[39]

It was within this context that the political log-rolling we examined in the previous chapter took place. The sheer increase in the number of schools, however, is only part of the story. The pressures of expansion were intense enough to whittle away even the few restrictions imposed by legislation. The act of 1839 had required sixty pupils and the related regulations twenty pupils in Latin. The act of 1841 required fifty pupils, with no classical stipulation. In 1846 the number was reduced to thirty. In 1851 it was lowered to twenty and the clause limiting the creation of grammar schools to areas six miles beyond the county town was repealed. The act of 1853 made no reference to minimum numbers at all.[40] What this meant was that increasingly through the 1840s and early 1850s even the smallest hamlets or unincorporated villages were eligible to receive the grant if only they could persuade the politicians to give it to them. And the politicians in turn found it difficult to resist, with the result, as one grammar school inspector would note in the 1860s, that in some small villages it was almost impossible to keep the school going because there was so little demand for superior education; indeed, he added, "I do not suppose that it was felt to be really needed at the time it was established. But a fear was entertained, that, if the school was not secured ... some rival village would rush in, and seize the prize."[41]

The politics of expansion also meant that there was no consistent relationship between the location of a school and urban growth. While almost all the cities and towns had grammar schools by 1861, only 50 per cent of the incorporated villages had one, while 29 per cent of the grammar schools were located outside incorporated urban communities – some in small but growing centres but others in already decaying hamlets. Scotland and Farmersville had made the most of their opportunities in the 1840s; Oshawa and Trenton had not. In 1861, the former still had grammar schools; the latter were without them.[42]

Unregulated growth threw up financial and administrative problems as well. Small schools in small communities meant a weak financial base. Too few pupils and the small amount they paid in fees, along with a grant divided too many ways, meant that village schools often could not afford adequate accommodation, supplies, or more than a single teacher to cope with all ages and everything from the three Rs to Caesar and Xenophon. The size of the grant, moreover, fluctuated from year to year because it was based on accumulated annual interest rather than a government appropriation. As a result, small schools that were barely viable one year were forced to close their doors when, in the next, their share of the grant decreased.[43] But big schools were hobbled as well. The pressure to subdivide the grant many times over meant that even large and successful schools had to look mainly to fees to survive. In 1849 the chairman of the York County Board of Trustees pleaded for a special grant of £200 for the district school in Toronto so that it could employ three masters instead of one and, at the same time, keep fees low "in order to render [it] more suitable than it is now to parties who desire for their children a superior commercial and classical education at a very moderate cost." The cabinet, however, replied that the act of 1841 stipulated that no more than £100 could be granted to any one grammar school.[44] Making the case to W.H. Merritt for a new act and larger grants, the headmaster of the St Catharines grammar school wrote that "the small amount of tuition fees together with the constantly decreasing Public Grant (owing to the erection of new schools as well as the division of the Counties) do not permit the employment of suitable assistance."[45]

The effectiveness of the administrative framework also deteriorated as the number of schools multiplied. Since 1807, the trustees had been appointed from all parts of the districts. Thus there were perennial difficulties in meeting on a regular basis to look after school business, and these difficulties only increased because the number of trustees multiplied along with the number of schools. By 1846, for example, the Johnston District had sixteen trustees and it proved nearly impossible for all of them to meet together at any time.[46] Moreover, as the number of schools multiplied trustees became confused about where their responsibilities lay: did they represent the interests of the school in their own locality or of all the schools in their district? The local records reveal increasing strain and competition amongst trustees over the allocation of money, the creation of new schools, and the disadvantageous position of the "junior" grammar schools, bereft of the £100 bounty inherited by the grammar schools in the district towns.[47]

The administrative system was no better at the centre, however. Throughout the 1840s, grammar school correspondence was handled by the Provincial Secretary's Office – a department of government that had wide responsibilities for official correspondence and secretarial work of all kinds, not just for the schools. Indeed it did no more for the grammar schools than pass on incoming correspondence to the executive council and relay its decisions.[48] There was, in other words, no one primarily responsible for either administration or policy matters except the cabinet itself, which was burdened by a multitude of other more weighty matters of state. Indeed the continuities with the period 1807–41 are marked: the grant was dispersed annually, but throughout the decade there were virtually no trustees' reports submitted on existing or new schools. By the late 1840s some order had been imposed: E.A. Meredith, the assistant provincial secretary, began to systematize the routine work of administering the grammar schools and was making regular recommendations to the executive council about what should be done in this or that case.[49] Nevertheless when Ryerson, who in 1853 was to assume responsibility for the grammar schools, applied to the cabinet for such basic and essential information as the amounts that were to be paid out to each school and the reports upon which payments were to be based, the provincial secretary replied, "I regret to say that the returns transmitted to the Government from the Boards of Grammar School Trustees throughout Upper Canada do not supply any statistical information respecting them of a satisfactory character."[50] Without adequate reports, let alone an inspectorate such as Ryerson had been fashioning for the common schools, the government never really knew what was going on in the localities, and thus could impose no accountability, financial or otherwise, upon them.

There was, however, one thing that did change in the 1840s: the grammar schools were gradually secularized, becoming steadily less embedded in the matrix of establishmentarianism that had characterized the schools before 1841. Technically, of course, no church had ever been legally established in Upper Canada. But the Church of England acted as though it was, the Church of Scotland claimed it was, and both churches were favoured to one extent or another by the colonial administration of the period. As was the case in England and Scotland, moreover, education in early Upper Canada was seen to be the responsibility of the church as much as, or more than, that of the state. The very notion of a liberal education included instruction in religious forms of knowledge. The churches assumed that part of their historic mission was to encourage the establishment of schools and colleges, and to supervise their work. Respectable clergymen were appointed as grammar school trustees and in most cases Anglicans and Presbyterians formed a majority of members on the grammar school boards. Most of the grammar school teachers before 1840 were clergymen, and John Strachan, at least, routinely used the grant as a way to supplement the salaries of his clergy by arranging to have local clergymen appointed grammar school masters as well.[51] And when government leaders needed advice on education, they turned to clergymen to give it – nearly half of those consulted by the education commission in 1839, for example, were ministers, while in the same year an admittedly tory legislature turned over the administration of the grammar schools to the Anglican-dominated King's College Council. As we suggested in an earlier chapter, in sum, the influence of the churches, in middle-class education especially, was pervasive.

Some of the key links between the churches and the grammar schools were broken as part of the more general reform of colonial administration that began in 1840. In particular, the practice of allowing working clergymen to serve as grammar school masters was ended between 1840 and 1842 on the grounds that it was impossible to do both jobs properly at the same time.[52] This step, in effect, severed the traditional tie between the congregation and its school that had so often characterized local relations between the church and education in Britain and in British North America.[53]

It was not primarily administrative reform, however, which led to the gradual decline of the churches' links to the grammar schools. Increasingly in the 1830s and 1840s, the religious pluralism of the colony made it politically impossible to maintain special privileges for one or two churches. The repeal of the Grammar School Act of 1839 had testified to that. It was not the forces of secularism that brought the act down but the angry petitions of influential Presbyterians and the attacks on it in the legislature by prominent laymen in the Church of Scotland.[54]

The dominant place of Anglican and Presbyterian clergymen amongst grammar school trustees, however, came to an end as a result of policies pursued by William Draper and Sir Charles Metcalfe, designed to broaden the base of support for moderate conservatism. Between 1843 and 1845, the ministry systematically remodelled the grammar school boards "with a view of placing them on a more enlarged footing, by the introduction of gentlemen of various religious persuasions."[55] Methodists, Congregationalists, and, where their numbers warranted it, Catholics were added to the boards throughout the province, and in order to make room for them, long-standing Anglican or Presbyterian members were dismissed.[56]

In the middle 1840s, it needs to be emphasized, this did not mean moving from clerical to lay boards. The majority of new appointments were clergymen, and clerical members continued to form majorities on all grammar school boards. It was, nonetheless, a delicate balancing act to get the mix of religious representation right, and as political affiliation and local patronage became more important in determining that mix, it became more difficult still. There is some evidence to suggest that under the reform party more laymen were being recommended than clergymen, and given the secularizing impulses of the Baldwin administration this is, perhaps, not surprising. When asked in 1848 to recommend new appointments for his eastern Ontario fiefdom, J.S. Macdonald argued that

the Rev. Mr Urquhart is the only clergyman named, and from the circumstances of his having acted in the capacity of chairman of the board for a number of years it is but right that he should be continued – Were I to name any other clerical gentleman I would be certain to give offense unless one from each of the numerous denominations in the District was included, and to have the Board composed of clergymen alone is a step which I am far from being disposed to recommend.[57]

In answer to a request from Robert Baldwin for nominations, James Hall supplied a list of four clergymen and eight laymen, though all were sorted by religion, ethnicity, and political affiliation, and a careful balance maintained.[58]

One suspects, in any case, that both conservative and reform administrations were anxious to be rid of the nuisance, and the political hazards, of trustee appointments, and both may have been sympathetic to lessening the degree of clerical influence of the boards. John A. Macdonald's abortive grammar school bill of 1847 included a clause for entirely secularized boards, of which the ministry would nominate only one member.[59] And both the grammar school bill of 1850 and the act of 1853 turned over the power of appointment to the new county councils.

Clerical influence did not, of course, disappear in 1850. Clergymen continued to be appointed in large numbers by the municipal councils, and the whole school system was, after all, run by a clergyman until 1876, advised by a Council of Public Instruction full of clergymen as well. Secularization in Upper Canada was a slow and in some cases at least an almost subterranean process. But it happened nonetheless. Working clergymen ceased to be teachers. Clerical trustees were in the majority as late as 1845; a decade later they represented only about 30 per cent of trustees.[60] And unlike the common school legislation from 1841 onwards, none of the grammar school acts ever made provision for grant-aided denominational schools.[61] Gradually, the grammar schools became, unequivocally, civil institutions. Along with the failure of the churches to sustain a network of denominational boarding or day schools, the secularization of the grammar school represented one more step in the larger story of the secularization of nineteenth-century society.

Whatever the progress of secularization, however, it did nothing to improve the general administration of the grammar schools. The schools varied in quality and in function. For one reason or another most of them were inadequately financed. Beyond that, administrative reform and financial accountability needed to be applied to the grammar schools as they were being applied to other departments of government during the 1840s. The politicians were not unaware of this. John A. Macdonald's grammar school bill of 1847 addressed all the educational, financial, and administrative issues but was withdrawn because its operation depended upon some of the provisions of his unsuccessful university bill of the same year.[62] Francis Hincks introduced another grammar school bill in 1850 which had been drafted by Egerton Ryerson at Hincks' request. It too offered solutions to most of the problems but was withdrawn in the face of opposition to increased taxation and to putting the grammar schools in Ryerson's hands.[63] In 1853, however, a new act passed without any apparent opposition, and it remained in place until additional legislation was passed in 1866.[64]

LIKE THE ABORTIVE BILL three years earlier, the act of 1853 was drafted by Ryerson and added another piece to the emerging educational system he had been fashioning since 1844. Paralleling the common school law, the Council of Public Instruction was given responsibility for making regulations for the grammar schools and Ryerson, as chief superintendent of education, became responsible for their administration. For the first time in their history the grammar schools became the responsibility of a particular department of government and a particular administrator. The £100 bounty was extended to all senior grammar schools, not just those established before the districts had been transformed into counties.[65] The Grammar School Fund, which continued to be based on the revenues of the school lands, was to be distributed to each county in proportion to its population. The county councils, instead of the Crown, were to appoint trustees for each grammar school. The grammar schools, by law, were required to offer a curriculum that included "all the higher branches of a practical English and Commercial Education," and also "in the Latin and Greek Languages so far as to prepare students for University College or any College affiliated to the University of Toronto, according to a programme of studies ... to be prescribed by the Council of Public Instruction."

All of these clauses had been carried over from the 1850 bill. But there were also three crucial omissions. A clause providing for an inspectorate was deleted, leaving Ryerson without field officers to supervise and enforce the will of the central authority. Far more important, however, the 1850 bill had made provision for compulsory local assessment by county councils, which would have rescued the grammar schools from their financial plight and put them on the same footing as the common schools. But just as in 1850, the taxation clauses were a major stumbling block, and thus they were omitted from the final version of the act.[66] Counties and cities were given permission to impose a rate for grammar school purposes but were under no obligation to do so. Local trustees, in other words, were left with no guaranteed sources of funds other than those they had had before – their share of the grant, and the tuition fees they could extract from parents who used the school. Finally, the 1850 bill made no provision for the further multiplication of schools; but in 1853, county councils were given authority to establish additional grammar schools subject only to modest limitations on the size of the available grant. And just to be sure there was no bureaucratic tampering with established schools, the act included a clause ensuring that all of them would continue to exist unless a change was approved by the local trustees. In sum, then, the act offered a partial solution to the administrative problems created by previous legislation, but promised no solution to the intertwined educational and financial problems that had plagued the grammar schools since 1807.

Traditionally in our historiography, the act of 1853 is treated as a symbolic turning point in the development of secondary education in Ontario, overshadowed only by the landmark act of 1871. We have reservations about both judgments, as will become apparent in the course of our argument. Certainly the act of 1853 laid the groundwork for a more effective administrative system and imposed some degree of accountability on the schools. But it also had some irretrievable flaws. Its financial clauses offered no substantial improvement over the acts of 1807 or 1841. More important, the act also lacked the regulatory teeth Ryerson needed to push the grammar schools in new directions. Indeed, it had to be reworked on both counts before he could carry through any major initiatives, and reworked it was in the act of 1865, legislation that has never received the recognition it deserves and that was at least as significant, and arguably more so, than the act of either 1853 or 1871.

Be that as it may, it is the lack of regulatory power that is pertinent here. Because the act of 1853 was so weak, it would take Ryerson not months but years to make any impact on the grammar schools. The new act came into force at the beginning of January 1854. Ryerson's first duties were to distribute the grant for that year and draft a set of rules and regulations for the schools. Accordingly, he wrote again to the provincial secretary, this time requesting the relevant statistical information for 1853, and adding that he had "as yet no information whatever to enable me to perform these new duties."[67] But as was the case a year earlier, the relevant information didn't exist. Moreover, the University of Toronto was in the midst of establishing new matriculation standards so that no rules governing the program of studies could be drafted. Thus the grant was apportioned as it had been previously, and the trustees were told to continue under the rules they themselves had already established until further notice. Ryerson did, however, distribute new and detailed forms for reports, which were to be submitted to him during 1855.[68] New regulations were then drafted and approved by the Council of Public Instruction in late 1854, approved by cabinet in February 1855, and circulated to trustees in March.[69] The regulations did not, however, take effect until fall term, 1855.[70] In a supplementary school act of that year, the legislature allocated a small amount to pay the salaries of two part-time inspectors, who were appointed in the summer and made their first provincial inspection in the late fall.[71]

None of the administrative mechanisms, then, even began to operate until the latter half of 1855. The first trustees' reports began to trickle in through the summer, the new regulations only came into force in the fall, and the first inspection was a whirlwind affair in which the inspectors had only an hour or two to devote to any one school, and did not visit others at all.[72] Thus it was only in late 1855 that enough information began to accumulate to allow Ryerson and his officials to assess the state of the grammar schools and the extent to which they conformed to the intention of the act and regulations.

The full force of the new broom in Toronto made itself felt slowly for other reasons as well. First, common school issues preoccupied the Education Office throughout these years – not only were the finishing touches being put on the policymaking and regulatory procedures for the common school system, but the separate school question was continually on the boil. Ryerson himself was out of the country from July 1855 to March 1856 and thus had little time to apply himself to the state of the grammar schools. The two inspectors were only part-time officials, and in the years after 1855 made only two-month forays into the countryside each year.[73] And finally we suggest that the focus of attention did not fall on the grammar schools in the middle and later fifties because everyone was awaiting new legislation to correct the flaws in the act of 1853. Ryerson and his officials had fully expected this to happen in 1855. Their proposal was to unite the grammar and common school boards in incorporated urban areas and thus give the grammar schools the same access to local taxation as the common schools. At the last moment, however, Macdonald withdrew the clause because of opposition from "a combination of parties in the House."[74] Though the evidence is sketchy, Ryerson apparently tried again in 1857, but once more the government drew back from any form of compulsory taxation to support the grammar schools.[75]

As the trustees' and inspectors' reports accumulated during the later fifties, Ryerson and his aides became increasingly dissatisfied with the state of the grammar schools, and determined to effect major reforms. This is a story we will return to. But our point in rehearsing the intricate details of grammar school administration in the middle fifties is to stress the limited and delayed effect of central initiatives in the years immediately following the act of 1853. Before the later 1850s the Education Office was only beginning to develop a "feel" for the diversity and complexity of the grammar schools, and no clear line of policy begins to emerge in the surviving records of the Education Office until at least the later 1850s.

The grammar schools, meanwhile, continued to multiply, from sixty-four in 1853 to eighty-six in 1861. Bereft of central direction, there was only the shelter of financial independence which could prevent enterprising trust- ees, teachers, or groups of parents from exploiting the grammar school grant as they saw fit, or shaping the schools to their own ends. As the number of schools increased, however, financial security proved illusory, with the consequence that the grammar schools became even more vulnerable to the pressures of local markets for education than they had been in the past. From 1853 the grammar schools had three potential sources for the revenue they needed: the grammar school grant, tuition fees, and municipal taxation *if* county and urban councils were willing to impose a grammar school rate. The combined amount that could be raised by the grant and tuition fees had already proved inadequate before 1853, and several things conspired to make the situation worse in the decade that followed. The policy pursued by the provincial cabinet during the 1840s of allowing schools to multiply without regard for the dwindling amount of the grant each school received was also pursued by nearly all the county councils, so that throughout the decade after 1853 new schools were continually laying claim to their share of a finite sum. Changes in local government boundaries added to the problem. When, for example, the Lincoln County trustees complained about a decline in their grant, Ryerson told them

I regret it as much as you can do ... But the diminution occurred from causes beyond my control ... The reduction was occasioned by the separation of the County of Welland from that of Lincoln. Before the separation, the apportionment was made to the United Counties as one, and as there was no grammar school in the County of Welland, the whole apportionment was distributed to the grammar schools in Lincoln; but on the separation ... I had to apportion to each county according to population, as required by law. Hence the reduction of the amount payable ... and I have no resources from which to add to it. [76]

Unlike the common school grant, moreover, the grammar school grant was not drawn from an annual appropriation by the legislature, but from the income of the grammar school land fund. But in 1857 the cabinet dipped into the fund to provide additional grants for municipal improvements, drawing off revenues desperately needed for the grammar schools. Ryerson protested vigorously but in vain: "the Grammar School Fund," he wrote,

is extremely poor – quite inadequate to the purposes for which it was intended; and to divest *one-fourth* of the proceeds of the sales of lands constituting that fund for public improvements is applying it to purposes wholly foreign to those for which these lands had been long since consecrated; and it is most injuriously keeping the fund down, while the number of grammar schools is yearly increasing, and the amount apportioned to each of them entirely too small.[77]

Tuition fees, moreover, could not easily be raised to compensate for a diminishing grant. Raising fees might very well drive pupils into the private sector, especially in the larger towns where such options still existed in the 1850s. But an even greater threat was the spread of tuition-free common schools. Good teachers, successful senior departments, and free tuition in an urban common school system could permanently cripple a grammar school or, indeed, devastate it. Just before the opening of the Hamilton Central School in 1853, for example, the local grammar school had 120 pupils; but "immediately after," the grammar school inspector reported, "it fell to 30. In October 1854 it had again increased to 50, when a classical master having been appointed in the Central School, the number was greatly reduced, and at last it was closed altogether."[78] The village of Brighton had both a grammar and a common school, a trustee explained to Ryerson in 1862; the former charged fees and the latter was free. "A new teacher has been appointed in the common school ... and he has introduced into the School, Algebra and other branches which I think ought to be taught only in grammar schools *in the same place*. If this be permitted the Grammar School will have to be closed as it is now barely self-supporting."[79]

Improvements in the state of the grammar schools, then, could not be expected from revenues raised by fees or the government grant. But could the grammar schools look to the county councils? In a handful of cases, the councils voted substantial annual grants to their grammar schools throughout the years between 1853 and 1866. York County Council is one example, Elgin and the united counties of Lanark and Renfrew are others.[80] Several more contributed one-time grants towards a building or to rescue a school on the verge of collapse. But most councils did nothing. Despite the fact that the grammar schools were legally *county* schools they were almost universally seen as urban institutions, and township councillors, or those from villages without grammar schools, were loath to raise funds for other people's schools. When, for example, trustees from Brampton appealed for aid to their township council, the response was that while Council is fully alive to the advantages likely to accrue from the estate of such an institution to persons living in the vicinity of it, and while they are willing to contribute personally towards that purpose, they cannot regard as just, the enforcement of a tax, in the benefits of which not more than one-tenth of such ratepayers will directly participate.[81]

Similarly in Brant, the county council "would not grant us one farthing for a schoolhouse," a trustee complained to Ryerson, "alleging that a grammar school would only benefit the town of Brantford, while the county would receive no benefit whatever from such an institution. It was with the greatest reluctance that the Council granted the small sum of £12 for paying the ordinary expenses of the Board of Trustees."[82]

Municipal councils in cities, towns, and villages also had the power to levy a rate for the grammar schools and this was much more common. While York County Council, for example, concentrated its funds on the smaller country schools in the county, the city of Toronto voted a substantial sum each year to aid the grammar school located there.[83] Some other communities, large and small, did the same. In many other cases, however, urban councils refused to support the schools on the grounds that they had no say in appointing the grammar school trustees, nor could they be guaranteed that their money would not be spent educating county children. A Hamilton trustee put the dilemma this way: "The county will not assist us with funds because we are within the city, the citizens having the principal benefit, and the city council will not assist because it is a county institution."[84]

The reluctance to provide tax support for the grammar schools, however, was more than a matter of squabbling over which jurisdiction was responsible. It was part of the larger question about the legitimacy of public funding for education which was being debated during the era. For the common schools, that debate focused on the question of abolishing tuition fees. As for the grammar schools, there was a long history of complaints about the injustice of taxing the whole population to pay for the education of those who could well afford to pay for it themselves. According to the editor of the *Perth Courier* in 1853, there was a good case for making the common schools free, since their aim was "to give good practical education to all," but no case for free grammar schools since "in a great many trades and occupations a classical education would be of no practical use" and thus it would be "manifestly unfair to tax the many for the benefit of the few."[85] A member of the Trenton Village Council put the point more pungently in 1866. "Three-fourths of the taxpayers," he told Ryerson,

are most willing to pay for common school education, but set their faces against paying for a Classical Education for any one. Those who wish to make *priests*, *doctors*, *lawyers*, or *Ministers*, are generally in independent circumstances, and in all justice and equity should pay for their Education, and not oppress the poor.[86]

In the years after the act of 1853, in sum, the grammar schools had to accommodate themselves to diminishing government grants, potent constraints on the amount they could raise by tuition fees, and in many cases, no assistance from counties or town councils. The impact of these financial pressures varied from place to place, creating dramatic differences amongst the grammar schools as their trustees and teachers cut their coats to fit their cloth.

THE DESTINY of a small number of schools was determined by exceptional circumstances both good and ill. The mere fact of being located too close to other grammar schools could place each of them in precarious circumstances, all vying for the same limited pool of pupils. In 1860, for example, the grammar school inspector offered this simple explanation for the inadequacies of two of the schools in Brant County: "Scotland is not more than five miles from Mount Pleasant and Mount Pleasant about the same distance from Brantford."[87] In 1855 Ancaster was found to be "in a very low state" for the same reason – it was "not more than 7 miles from Hamilton and within 4 miles from Dundas," both of which had good schools.[88] Other schools suffered from long-term competition with a well-established and reputable private school. The Kingston grammar school, for example, was constantly in trouble because it could not compete successfully with Queen's College school, and the same was true of Cobourg, competing against Victoria College's large preparatory school.[89] In yet other places, not enough classical pupils – even nominal pupils – could be found to meet the average attendance conditions of the grant. In the inspectors' view at least, such schools languished for years as mere infant or primary schools, often inferior to the local common schools; indeed, a few such schools, after struggling on for a year or two, simply closed down and never reopened.[90]

A few other schools became the captives of a particular faction. The London grammar school survived in what the inspectors thought was a state of intellectual torpor, controlled by a clique of Anglican trustees for the exclusive benefit of a few parents who refused to use the central school because it was "common" and tuition-free.[91] The Richmond grammar school, in the Ottawa Valley, was the elementary school of a community that for twenty years had refused – a singular exception – to comply with the common school acts or to tax itself for elementary schools.[92] As a result of a series of local (and strictly illegal) compromises, the Sandwich grammar school had, for decades, been the Protestant elementary school for the town, while the common school had served its Catholics, a fact uncovered only in the mid-fifties when the first central inspection was carried out.[93]

Exceptionally good or bad schoolteachers made an impact as well. An incompetent teacher could ruin a school that should otherwise have been successful; an outstanding one could rescue a school that might otherwise have been at risk. At Drummondville, a correspondent told Egerton Ryerson in 1861, a school "was commenced four years ago with 30 scholars and a fine prospect for more; but in consequence of the dissipated habits of its Head Master it completely broke down in a little more than a year."[94] On the other hand there is the case of Galt, where William Tassie reigned for decades, building a school that attracted pupils from all over the province and one that was often considered the finest grammar school in Upper Canada.[95] There were other similar, though less well known, cases. In the early 1860s, the Rev. F.W. Checkley turned a failing school in Barrie into a large boarding and day school with a staff of six teachers and an enviable record of preparing boys for professional and university matriculation examinations.[96] There was also the Cornwall school under the mastership of Rev. W.H. Davies, where forty-two of forty-seven boys were enrolled in Latin, ten of them at an advanced level, and sixteen were enrolled in Greek. "I may observe," wrote John Ambery after inspecting the school in 1860, "that in discipline and standard of studies the Cornwall Grammar School represents more than any other school in my section the idea of an English grammar school ... If the rest of the schools approached the same classical standard the University would soon be forced out of sheer shame to raise its present exceedingly depressing [matriculation] requirements."[97]

All of these schools, however, from Sandwich and Richmond to Galt and Cornwall, were exceptional and idiosyncratic cases. Of the hundred or so grammar schools established before 1870, only a few declined to mere primary schools or were closed down altogether. And only a few trustees and headmasters could maintain the kind of school Tassie created at Galt. Most schools fell somewhere in between. Lacking the critical mass of pupils to sustain a purely classical school, and without adequate subsidies to maintain their independence regardless of enrolments and tuition fees, the grammar schools had to appeal to the widest possible constituency, and cater to whatever local demand might exist.

"What is a grammar school?" J. Dunbar Moodie asked rhetorically in 1848. It was, he said, "a term ... not distinctly defined by law, but which is usually understood to signify a school in which the Classics are taught."[98] Increasingly in the decades around mid-century, however, this ceased to be a distinguishing characteristic of the Upper Canadian grammar school. During the 1840s particularly, the grant had often been given to schools which made no pretence of teaching classics. Both government and district councils had turned a blind eye to the ambitions of urban common school trustees who made a grab for the grammar school grant so that, without raising local taxes, they could subsidize the salary of a more qualified master who could teach the higher English subjects. There were a few outspoken critics of such practices. Moodie left us his definition of a grammar school in his report to the executive council on the claims of the village of Thurlow to a share in the grant. "It is evident," he concluded, that the object of the Act was to encourage a system of Education superior to that of the Common Schools, – but I am sorry to say, many individuals in the country seem to consider this aid as a boon granted to themselves, and they frequently apply the funds thus granted to paying the Teachers the common fees, and are thus enabled to get their children educated at a cheaper rate than at the *Common* Schools; while the instruction received by the children is in no respect superior.

In the particular case of the School in Thurlow, the Superintendent informs me, that the District Council considers it latterly only as a *Common* School, and therefore did not recommend that the allowance should be continued.

Moodie concluded by urging the cabinet to appoint someone to be responsible for the due application of funds granted under the act.[99] But before 1853 no action was taken to implement that recommendation. In the meantime, it was Thurlow that proved the exception rather than the rule: most of the investigations and complaints about the grant being given to mere common schools resulted in the grant being continued, not cut off. In the case of Demorestville, for example, everyone involved openly admitted that the school was a good village English school without any classical instruction and with a teacher unable to teach the classics, but neither the district council nor the cabinet recommended that the grant be cut.[100]

In other cases, and these appear to have been more common, village trustees sought the grant in order to subsidize the salary of a teacher qualified to offer both classical and English instruction.[101] By this means, common school trustees could provide instruction in the classics to the minority who wanted it without putting classics on the local rates; indeed, if the school was small enough they might obtain a teacher who could cope with classics, all of the rest of the pupils besides, and with the help of the grant actually reduce the cost to local taxpayers of his salary.

Thus it was that in the decade after 1855, when enrolment statistics first become available, Latin enrolments never rose much above an overall average of 50 per cent, and Greek stabilized at just under 15 per cent (see general table 4). The figures for Latin, indeed, may have been inflated, or at least rendered merely nominal, by the fact that in the late fifties and early sixties Ryerson was attempting to tie the grant to attendance in Latin, a formula that gave teachers and trustees a substantial incentive to maximize Latin enrolments. It was a frequent complaint of the inspectors that they did just that.[102] Whatever the exact figure in any case, large numbers of grammar school pupils never took Latin at all, using the school solely to study English and commercial subjects, a development some trustees and teachers actively encouraged. Many of these village schools may have served their communities well. But they were no longer grammar schools in the sense that Moodie meant. Unregulated expansion, and the financial problems it raised, helped blur traditional distinctions between an ordinary and a liberal education, and compromised the distinctive purpose of the grammar school.

The typical grammar school of the early 1860s was not a classical school but, as one contemporary put it, "a common school teaching classics."[103]

Some schools, moreover, continued throughout the period to take pupils only beginning to learn their three Rs. There were small communities where this was essential to the very survival of the school. "The grant is so small," a trustee of the Vienna grammar school wrote Ryerson, "and the fees which we can enforce so limited, that we find ourselves unable to engage the entire services of a master."[104] Thus he proposed to unite the grammar and common schools and employ a single teacher to do the work of both schools. In other cases, beginners were present because of the preference for social segregation. The master of the St Catharines grammar school explained that some of the younger pupils in his school

were the sons of the Trustees and others who would not send to our public or common schools. Hence if excluded from the grammar school they must resort to private schools, which would greatly injure our grammar school. In small towns and even in places of 6 or 7000 inhabitants like St Catharines the schools are dependent mostly on *fees from* students for support and will be doubtless until the School Act is so amended as to give the Trustees power to levy a tax equal to that possessed by the Trustees of common schools. To lessen the number of pupils then will be to cut short our revenue which at the most is not too great. If we receive *all* who apply we shall not probably have over 50, a number not too great for two teachers.[105]

THERE ARE HISTORIANS who argue that the origins of bureaucratic procedure in the Upper Canadian school system lay in an untoward, unwelcome, and unnecessary imposition by a few architects of educational change on a reluctant population, and that such procedures "would never have been sought or needed in the first place" had not the new common school legislation of the 1840s and 1850s "created a complex and frequently changing set of rules."[106] The history of the grammar schools during these two decades casts an ironic light on such assertions. The grammar school law hardly changed between 1807 and 1853, no complex set of rules was drafted to regulate a rapidly expanding system, and no central office existed until 1853 to mediate disputes or direct growth, and even then its effective powers were limited for some years to come. The results have already been described in various parts of the last two chapters. Directed by no other principles than log-rolling or patronage, expansion left some deserving communities without schools and gave them to others whether or not such schools were educationally or financially viable. The lack of central supervision allowed trustees to frustrate the intent of the legislature by using the Grammar School Fund to subsidize their common schools instead of raising the money from local ratepayers. Accountability in the expenditure of public money was entirely lacking. A few schools became the instruments of cliques. Others provided the means by which local elites preserved, at public expense, a socially segregated form of education. For a whole variety of reasons, trustees found themselves at war with one another, confused about their duties, and unable to carry out their legal obligations or even, in some cases, protect the educational interests of the communities they represented.

In such circumstances, trustees, teachers, and other local people sought advice, or the redress of their grievances, from anyone they thought could help. They might write the Provincial Secretary's Office, they might write Ryerson even though before 1853 he was powerless to intervene, or they might write an influential politician. Two examples from the Robert Baldwin papers illustrate the point nicely. A minority of the Talbot District grammar school trustees wrote Baldwin in 1848 to protest a resolution of the Board which "recommended the spoilation of the aid formerly given to the Grammar School at Port Dover; the trustees who live in Simcoe are being selfish and illiberal in wishing to deprive a rival small town of the means of keeping up its educational facilities." [107] In a second case, three new trustees from Whitby, members of the Board for the county of York, explained in panic that they had hired three teachers without being aware of a crucial clause in the act, assuming that other board members who "resided at Toronto ... knew the Law and were in possession of all necessary information on the subject." But they now found they could not legally expend public funds and were personally liable for the salaries of the teachers they had hired. [108]

The substantive issues raised in these two cases are not unusual in either the grammar or common school records of the period. Trustees frequently did not know the law, became involved in internecine disputes, or behaved in ways that prejudiced the interests of local minorities. In the case of the common schools, however, a bureau existed to inform, advise, arbitrate, order redress, and, when necessary, recommend adjustments to the law which would address recurring problems. In the case of the grammar schools, no such mechanisms existed. The legislation of 1807 had been designed to establish a single grammar school located in each district capital of Upper Canada. Each school was to be supervised by a small number of trustees and all schools were to receive exactly the same government grant of £100 – an adequate if not ample amount to support a qualified grammar school teacher. By mid-century, however, there had been a massive expansion in the number of schools. The number of trustees appointed to each district board had doubled or tripled, and though they not only lived in, but represented the interests of, different communities, they were collectively responsible for supervising the operation of two, three, or more schools. School finance was a quagmire. The annual grant was unpredictable and variable, it was inequitably distributed among schools, and in the vast majority of cases it amounted to far less than the sum needed to support a good teacher.

The problems these circumstances created were manifold, but in contrast to the common school system, nobody was responsible for sorting out difficulties, arbitrating conflicts, rendering advice, or ensuring that public policy was effectively and fairly executed. And thus when trustees or other people with a stake in the grammar schools needed help they could only fall back on measures of last resort. The Port Dover trustees pleaded with Baldwin to appoint additional trustees who would favour their interests over those of the town of Simcoe. The Whitby trustees begged Baldwin to pass "a special Bill through Parliament for the payment of the money if there is no other way of disposing of it. We cannot for one moment believe that the government will leave the trustees to pay the money out of their own pocket, which they must do, if not relieved by the Government or Parliament – We therefore do hope and trust you will do all in your power to relieve us from our present embarrassment."

The very extremity of such measures pointed to the need for mechanisms less heroic and uncertain than the arbitrary intervention of a leading politician or emergency legislation passed by the provincial parliament. Similarly, when the dispute over the grant to the Thurlow grammar school arose, local people had nowhere to go for arbitration except to the executive council itself, even though the dispute was hardly of such proportions as to warrant a place on its crowded agenda. Because no agency existed to collect the pertinent facts and make suitable recommendations, the cabinet, in turn, had no recourse but to appoint Dunbar Moodie, a local office-holder, to carry out a special investigation. If this had been an exceptional case such a measure might have been justified, but the dispute was one of a large number of recurring and routine grammar school problems which landed in the cabinet's lap. Not surprisingly, Moodie recommended that a permanent official be appointed to deal with such matters, and not surprisingly, cabinet eventually did just that.[109]

Certainly the origin of bureaucratic procedure was not the product of local demand alone; no one, indeed, has ever argued that it was;[110] it *also* arose from the more general political and administrative imperatives of an expanding Canadian state. But neither was a more effective legal and administrative system arbitrarily or unnecessarily imposed by the centre upon a hapless or unwilling populace. Rather it was pressed upon government in a multitude of letters and memorials sent to politicians and colonial officials by teachers, trustees, and other local people who sought a better framework within which to create and regulate the expanding system of local grammar schools.

To reiterate, then, if ever so-called democratic localism ran rampant, it was in the case of the mid-century grammar school. There was neither supervision nor any body of "complex and frequently changing set of rules" to implement policy, guide administration, adjudicate disputes, or ensure fair and equitable treatment of either individuals or communities. As the system expanded, new instruments were needed, and sought, by local people as well as by the central government to obtain those ends. As Michael Katz has noted recently, "Within a large organization, democratic procedures require bureaucratic forms."[111] While it is inappropriate to apply the word "democracy" to the mid-nineteenth century, his comment can be paraphrased to suit the circumstances: bureaucratic procedure was essential if public policy, including something even remotely approximating equity, was to be achieved under a system of representative and responsible government.

BE THAT AS IT MAY, there is no question that unregulated growth force-fed unplanned and unanticipated changes in the grammar schools. We have already noted just how far the mid-century grammar school had departed from the ideal type, defined by Dunbar Moodie as "a school in which the Classics are taught." In nearly all the schools it had become embedded habit to offer boys a wide variety of English or commercial subjects without requiring them to take classics as part of their studies, and in some cases, classics were not taught at all. But there was also a far more radical departure in the making. Increasingly girls were being routinely admitted as grammar school pupils, and this innovation, perhaps more than any other, marks a definitive break with the Georgian past.

It is not clear when girls began to attend the grammar schools. We know that some were sent to the district schools in the very early years of the century, but there is also scattered evidence to suggest that as the district capitals grew, and educational alternatives became available, most of the grammar schools tended to become exclusively male, the girls presumably being sent to private ladies' schools.[112] We suspect that the growth of female attendance occurred simultaneously with the expansion of the grammar schools into the smaller communities during the 1840s and early 1850s, but this is little more than guesswork since so few grammar school reports survive from that period. What we do know is that in 1855, when the first inspectors' reports and school registers were filed in the Education Office records, girls were already present in large numbers in the grammar schools. While there are no province-wide annual statistics available on the gender of grammar school pupils until the 1880s, we can use these two sources to indicate the growth of female enrolments and the proportion of pupils they represented.

In 1855 the inspectors reported that about half the schools in eastern Ontario, and a quarter of those in the western half of the province, had female students.[113] By 1866 the figure for the whole province was about 70 per cent, and by 1870, 90 per cent.[114] By the end of the sixties, in other words, the vast majority of Upper Canadian grammar schools were attended by girls as well as boys. There are no province-wide estimates before the mid-sixties of the proportion of pupils who were girls, but in the five south-western Ontario towns we have examined the girls made up 23 per cent of enrolments in 1855 and about 40 per cent in 1866. (For estimates of girls' enrolment statistics throughout the period, see general table 7.) The province-wide estimate for the latter year is about 37 per cent.[115] These overall figures, however, mask substantial variations. In 1866, some schools took no girls at all – Toronto, Kingston, and Galt, for example – while in others, girls represented 50 per cent or more of the student body. Of our five towns, Simcoe never had more than about 15 per cent girls. In Brantford and Stratford, on the other hand, they constituted about 30 per cent of enrolments between 1857 and 1866, and in Strathroy and Sarnia the figure was more like 50 per cent.

In the two decades after mid-century, then, not only did a growing number of grammar schools admit girls as students, but girls constituted a substantial proportion of enrolments. In the light of our repeated assertions that Upper Canadian parents and educators generally preferred schools that separated the sexes, the growth of coeducation calls for some explanation. Clearly, one cause lies in the economic constraints imposed by low population dens-ities. No one ever seriously suggested, for example, that the rural common schools could ever be anything but coeducational. And much the same was true of the villages and small towns: lacking the critical mass of people necessary to support private schools, and unwilling to tax themselves for the construction and maintenance of two entirely separate schools, one each for girls and boys, the education of the two sexes tended to be carried out in common. In the larger urban centres, trustees made valiant efforts to provide separate facilities for boys and girls, and many town and city boards did indeed do so, at least for the older students.[116] Yet overcrowding, the hard times of the early 1860s, and even the introduction of finer classification systems made it difficult to maintain the separation of the sexes.[117]

Whatever their preferences, moreover, many middle-class parents could ill afford the costs of sending their daughters to a private ladies' school. While they might resist sending them to a common school, the gap between wishes and horses made the local grammar school at least palatable, if less than ideal. Writing to a friend living in a country town who was concerned about the education of his four daughters, one Torontonian put it this way: "Grammar Schools are decidedly not the best institutions for girls; but situated as you are, they are the best you can get."[118] Settlement patterns and economic necessity, in other words, conspired to promote the spread of coeducation from early in the colony's history, and they remained pow-erful imperatives in the decades after mid-century.

This is not to suggest, however, that coeducation was accepted with equanimity. Many parents were not easily reconciled to mixed schools, did what they could to avoid them, and complained bitterly about the lack of alternatives. Repeated attempts were made to found denominational boarding and day schools for girls, and in the 1860s and early 1870s some of these were successful. Other voices were heard arguing for the allocation of public funds to subsidize the superior education of girls. "Why should one half of the population – the future companions and mothers – be utterly ignored?" the editor of the *Canadian Baptist* asked in 1860. "Why should *all* the public money given for higher education be expended exclusively on males?"[119] It was to become a common refrain over the next few years, and it was still being heard at the end of the decade. "Although we are all anxious that our boys should be properly educated," the editor of the *Leader* wrote in 1870,

Toronto possesses no schools within reach of the men of moderate means for the superior education of girls. Our admirable Common Schools offer ample facilities for elementary training, but beyond this no provision is made for females of the middle class. Without any desire to support half of what is said in support of "women's rights," we really fail to see why boys should be allowed to monopolize all the public provision made for higher education. Why should one man with a large family of boys have superior education provided for them, wholly or partially at the public expense, whilst another, whose children happen to be girls, must pay two or three hundred dollars a year each, for education frequently much inferior.[120]

There was no consensus about public funding, however. Throughout the 1850s and 1860s, opposition to any form of general taxation to pay for the superior education of those who were considered to be well off remained strong. Property taxes to support the grammar schools were adamantly opposed in the countryside particularly, as we shall see, and it is unlikely that rural voters would have taken any more kindly to proposals to fund equivalent schools for girls. Every common school board in the province, it is true, had the authority to establish separate schools for boys and girls and to tax property owners for their support. But even in large wealthy communities like Toronto, there was substantial resistance whenever proposals were made to create tax-supported higher schools primarily designed to cater to middle-class girls.[121] Given the divided state of public opinion, and the pressures on the provincial and municipal revenues in the late 1850s and 1860s, the legislature was unwilling to invest any more than it already did in middle-class education.

But there was, we suggest, another reason why the political will to fund separate girls' schools was lacking. While it may be true that most parents preferred sexual segregation in principle, it is also true that many of them were familiar with mixed schools and could accept them with some degree of equanimity. Mixed schools were not simply an esoteric colonial efflorescence. If they were unusual in England, they were common in Scotland.

The parish schools were mixed and so indeed were the burgh schools of most of the towns.[122] In the United States, coeducational academies and colleges were increasingly familiar institutions. From mid-century at least, a growing number of middle-class parents sent their girls to the central and grammar schools in Upper Canada – parents who were influential figures in their communities and in some cases members of parliament as well. This could not help but quell the fears others had about mixed schools and give coeducation more legitimacy. And that in turn inevitably undermined the urgency with which the pleas for public funding were greeted. For whatever mix of reasons, in any case, public funding for separate girls' schools was not forthcoming, and more and more parents turned to the grammar schools to complete their daughters' education.

But why, one might ask, were girls allowed to attend a school that, in principle at least, was a boys' classical school? The answer here is simple. Most grammar school trustees and teachers could not afford to turn away fee-paying and grant-generating pupils, even if those pupils were girls. And if local trustees opted to admit girls, who was to stop them? Before 1853 the schools were utterly unsupervised by any superior authority. After that they were the responsibility of the Education Office, and from the beginning Ryerson had made clear his opposition to girls attending the grammar schools. Though exceptions might have to be made in special cases, he told one correspondent in 1855, "it could not be sanctioned as a general rule."[123] Before the mid-sixties, however, he lacked the power to impose his views on local people. Thus, from the 1840s to the middle 1860s, trustees, teachers, and parents turned the grammar school into any kind of school that suited them. A few schools remained exclusively male and exclusively classical. But most made room for girls, offering them a range of English studies, and often Latin as well, along with a modicum of French as a bow in the direction of the accomplishments curriculum of the traditional girls' schools.

Until the late 1860s, it must be emphasized, it is rare to find anyone arguing in favour of coeducation as such. Almost without exception, contemporaries assumed that, in the best of all possible worlds, girls and boys would be educated apart, even if the exigencies of the moment made it impossible. Indeed it was probably the very existence of the gap between theory and practice that allowed such a major change in the way middle-class girls were educated to go almost entirely unremarked. By 1865, 30 or 40 per cent of total grammar school enrolments consisted of girls, and in many schools they already constituted 50 per cent of enrolments. Yet there was almost no public discussion of the issue over the two previous decades, and certainly no defence of coeducation as a principle. People knew what *should* be done, and lived with a necessary compromise until it could be done. Meanwhile, of course, people became accustomed to the habits born of exigency. As the number of girls in the grammar schools grew, they became more and more important to the economic prosperity of the schools.

Moreover, as parents increasingly used the grammar schools, local private schools found it harder to survive, and as they closed their doors, there were fewer educational options still.[124] That, in turn, increased the stake local people had in their grammar schools. And thus when Ryerson tried to exclude the girls in the mid-sixties, he found himself up against a potent political coalition indeed.

ALONG WITH BROADENING PURPOSES and a new clientele, there was also a major structural change in the organization of schooling in the decades around mid-century: the emergence of the *union* common and grammar school. As we have already suggested, a number of *de facto* union schools had been established in the 1840s when grammar school trustees allowed the grant to be used to subsidize the salaries, or supplement the level of teaching, in the common schools. But these sorts of arrangements had no legal grounding until the early fifties when revisions to the school acts permitted the formation of union boards of common and grammar school trustees, who could, in turn, establish union schools. In most years between 1853 and 1866, roughly half the grammar schools were union schools. They were not, however, distributed randomly throughout urban Upper Canada. Of the five cities in 1861, only Hamilton had a union school. Fourteen town schools were united but eighteen were not. In the villages, there were twice as many union as non-union schools, and in non-incorporated places the figure rises to 68 per cent.[125] There was, in other words, a significant tendency for unions to be more common in Upper Canada's smaller urban communities. But what accounts for this pattern?

It was not, it must be said at the outset, an arrangement preferred by many people. Indeed there is good evidence to suggest that many grammar school trustees objected to such unions and did what they could to avoid entering into one. One reason was that in non-union schools a modicum of social segregation could be preserved, something that was impossible in a union school. Certainly it was taken for granted by contemporaries that in the larger towns and cities the grammar school was intended for the superior education of the middle classes, and there are occasional comments to suggest that when common and grammar schools were united, some parents withdrew their children for social reasons and sent them elsewhere.[126] As well, there were recurring complaints that in union schools, where the master dealt with large numbers of children in the English branches, advanced classical instruction suffered neglect, and consequently boys were inadequately prepared for professional and university matriculation examinations.[127]

Non-union schools, however, also existed because grammar school trustees had no choice in the matter. Lacking resources which they themselves could tap, they often had to go cap in hand to common school boards, begging for space in the new central and ward schools or for some other arrangement that would give the grammar school security and permanency. As often as not, however, they were rebuffed by the common school trustees, sometimes due to a history of competition and antagonism between the two boards, but more often, it seems, because of legal and political difficulties. The common school board in Hamilton, for example, argued in 1856 that there was in principle a strong case for creating a city grammar school united with the common schools; but as the law stood,

the two Boards are amenable not only to different constituencies, but are selected on principles so different that the one is calculated to reflect one class of sentiments, and the other another, and opposite class, which, in our opinion, has been the real cause of the antagonism between the two Boards here. Our Common Schools are Free, and are sustained, of course, by the Municipality. The principle of Free Schools, we think, vitally important; this principle could not, however, be adopted to a United School open to the entire County.

... The Law does not confer on the United Board the same powers of levying and raising money on the County, as on the City, and they would be in danger of having to bear a disproportionate share of the burden.[128]

Unions, in sum, were not necessarily a solution preferred by grammar school trustees and were not always welcomed by common school boards either.

Whatever people's preferences, however, it was financial circumstances that determined whether or not a school would remain independent. By far the most striking difference between union and non-union schools was that the latter had substantially more income than the former.[129] Of the thirty-eight non-union schools in 1861, no less than twenty were senior grammar schools – recipients of the £100 (in 1861, $400) bounty dating back to the act of 1807. Most of these schools were also located in large towns where there was significant demand for classics so that they benefited from the average attendance rule and from the revenue generated by fees. All but five of the other non-union schools were in favoured financial circumstances as well, receiving a substantial grant from the local town council or from the county. It was one or all of these sources of revenue – the £100 bounty, larger revenues from fees, or a local grant – that enabled the non-union grammar schools to remain independent of the common school system.

Independence, however, did not mean that most schools could afford to restrict their work to classical instruction. Even a large and successful school like the Toronto grammar school, with a hundred boys by the middle 1860s and four instructors, offered both classical and commercial streams, and taught not only advanced subjects but the elementary branches as well.[130] Moreover, Toronto was one of the few schools – Galt and Barrie were other examples – that could afford to turn away girls. In other words, the relative wealth of the non-union school rarely relieved it from the necessity of serving a variety of purposes and a mixed clientele.

For those grammar schools which lacked the advantages of size or large grants, a union with the local common school held out two important prospects. First, it provided a reasonably secure source of recruits. The grammar school master might have only a handful of pupils who wanted instruction in the classics but in a united school he might also inherit the senior English and commercial pupils – pupils who would otherwise be taught in a local private school or in a common school that would, in effect, compete with him for students and fees. [131] More important, union gave the grammar school trustees access to the financial resources of the common school board – money for salaries, for suitable accommodation, supplies, and equipment, all paid for by the taxpayer. [132]

For the common school trustees, union promised some important advantages as well. The pressure to provide advanced teaching in the common schools meant trustees had to hire more expensive teachers. Union offered them a teacher who was, minimally, a university matriculant, but more commonly a university graduate, and who could, therefore, competently teach all of the higher branches, classics included, and who also brought with him a government grant that did not require matching local funds. As the Port Hope common school board put it in 1850, "we have also been considering to have a Higher School in connection with a Grammar School … The cost and support of the Higher School would not fall wholly on the town, as aid towards the erection of a Grammar School, and towards the master's salary, can be obtained from the grant." [133] When amalgamation took place in Belleville, the trustees were able to fire one of their male teachers, who had been responsible for senior classes, and they saved the costs of building a higher school since a good grammar school building already existed. [134] The effects of the depression of 1857 and the growing liabilities carried by so many Upper Canadian municipalities further encouraged amalgamations. After a full fifteen years during which the London common school board sustained its own classical department in the central school, a union took effect in 1865. The consequence, the chairman of the united board explained, was that the classical department "will still be sustained; but no longer sustained by a tax, however trifling, upon the property of our municipality." [135] A similar point was made by the editor of the *Stratford Beacon*. "The outcry has now become pretty general," he wrote in 1859,

that our Schools are managed at an extravagant expense … We see no reason why the teacher of the Grammar School should not take the situation of Principal and thus save to the town the large salary heretofore paid the teacher of the highest department of the Common School … The annual grant to the Grammar School is at present $600, which would most probably be largely augmented in consequence of an increased average attendance resulting from the union, and hence the principal's salary would cost the town almost nothing. [136]

Small communities were even more eager to lay hands on the grammar school grant. When the grammar school inspector visited the Port Rowan grammar school in 1863, he found it "merely a common school" and remarked that

the desire for the establishment of a grammar school in a place where Classical pupils are not to be had was simply a device to lighten the taxation which an exclusively common school would impose on a very small school section. The more so as I find, on inquiry, that the plan was not thought of until *after* an attempt had been ineffectually made to induce the adjoining larger school section to unite with the small Port Rowan section. [137]

The village of Scotland, in Brant County, offered a similar vista to an outraged William Ormiston who inspected the school in 1859. It was "a union school with *no pupils* either in *Latin*, Greek – French – *algebra* or *Geometry*." It had only one teacher to boot. "In such cases it would appear that application for a grammar school has been made not so much because it was needed or desired, as with a view of obtaining a portion of the monies apportioned to the grammar schools, to support the common school." [138] Supplementing local revenues, however, was not the only incentive driving grammar and common school trustees into each other's arms. The financial benefits blended synergistically with the educational advantages a graded union school could offer. No longer would one teacher have to carry boys of widely varying ages and attainments through the whole range of a classical and English education. A second teacher could now be hired to teach the senior students all of the advanced subjects, leaving the younger students to less expensive, less well educated, and increasingly, female teachers. Though at work everywhere in Upper Canada, these pressures were particularly strong in the smaller urban communities which could not afford a bevy of teachers and had to use the few they had to best advantage. The St Thomas grammar school desperately needed a master to teach the junior classes, its trustees informed the Elgin County Council in 1865: the recent union allowed the two boards to split the cost of an additional teacher and thus they had gained "what we were all along aiming at, a division of labour and economy of time and efficiency of the school; and saved the necessity of increasing the fees." [139] In Oakville the trustees had found the union "to be of great advantage and to work well. Instead of having two rival schools, we have thereby one well-organized and fully equipped establishment and we are saved the anomaly of having a grammar school master teaching the merest elements of English." [140]

Whatever the particular arrangement, however, the union school further blurred the image of the grammar and common schools as parallel institutions, the one offering a liberal, and the other an ordinary education. The tendency was, rather, for a two-tier arrangement to emerge – a junior department and a senior department, a prototype, in effect, of the elementary and secondary schools of the future. But the image of the grammar school was blurred in other ways as well. In a union school girls were present as a matter of course. So indeed were large numbers of boys studying only English subjects, and small children learning the rudiments. In many cases, moreover, the internal organization of the union turned classics into a "senior" subject like mathematics and the fifth book, and gave primacy in the early grades to English studies. One way or another, in any case, classics tended to become simply "a department of the school." The following letter, written to Ryerson in 1859, nicely catches the difference between a "classical school" and a school that also teaches classics. Though the common school in question was the London central school, the transition in the role of classics was already under way in the union schools as well.

Permit me to inquire if the course of juvenile studies at the principal common school in this city includes that of the Languages – Latin, Greek and French and if it is necessary a child should be of a particular age – or must have acquired more than a fair knowledge of writing, reading and the first rules of arithmetic before being considered eligible for the study of the languages in question. My reason in asking is this – I have two boys, respectively 7 and 9 years of age now attending the grammar school here – both are in Latin – but I am informed ... that if I send them to the Central Common School here they would not on account of their age being insufficient be classed with the Latin scholars of the Free School. I am well taxed for the common schools ... and I am dubious of sending my boys without being assured of the course of their learning being continued from where they are now learning – and the saving of $40 a year which I now pay in addition to the tax is a consideration to me. [141]

Finally, while the shifts taking place in the organization of the curriculum within the union school are important to our argument, no less important is the bald fact that half of all the grammar schools, and nearly 70 per cent of all those in Upper Canada's incorporated and unincorporated villages, were union schools. The very existence of so many union boards and union schools gradually accustomed people – especially the people in Upper Canada's small urban communities – to the notion that such schools were in the natural order of things.

During the 1850s, then, developments originating in the 1840s, and some of them even earlier, were consolidated into fixed patterns of educational provision. The lack of either firm government direction or adequate financial resources exposed the grammar schools, union and non-union alike, to the full force of local markets for schooling. In a few cases, charismatic leadership or a large pool of local recruits allowed the grammar school to retain its character as a classical school. In other cases, where the number of classical pupils was small, the grammar schools were in reality common schools – though often flourishing ones, with large numbers of advanced scholars, taught by an unusually well qualified master. Other schools fell somewhere in between, depending on local demand, on the options available within a community, and on the size of the clientele. Generally, however, the Upper Canadian grammar school became more closely allied to the common school system, more diverse in its clientele, and more comprehensive in its function – an institution that served as a classical school, commercial academy, and ladies' finishing school all at the same time. They were not the kind of institutions Ryerson and his inspectors thought they should be, as some of their comments quoted in this chapter make clear. During the 1840s and 1850s, nonetheless, *ad hoc* institutional arrangements and practices arrived at by local people bereft of central direction gradually hardened into established customs and entrenched interests. For twenty years or more there had been no King in Israel but every man did that which was right in his own eyes. When, in the 1860s, Egerton Ryerson finally turned his intellect and energies to the reform of the grammar schools, he would face a formidable legacy.

CHAPTER SIX

Teachers, Pupils, and Pedagogy: Inside the World of the Grammar School, 1855–70

While the preceding chapter offers an account of the development of the Upper Canadian grammar school in the decades before Confederation, it tells us very little about the character of the schools themselves. What did the schools actually look like? Who were the teachers? How was instruction organized? What sorts of young people attended the schools? How long did they stay and what did they study? The failure to penetrate the "black box" of the school is one of the more pointed criticisms directed at the work of educational historians. To try to reconstruct the daily reality of a social institution like the school is, nevertheless, always a difficult thing to do, for the evidence about teachers, clientele, or classroom organization is sometimes scattered or hard to retrieve, and commonly doesn't exist at all. For most of the nineteenth century very few Ontario school registers, for either the common or the grammar schools, have survived, and the few that do exist rarely provide more than a fragmentary record. Thus most studies of school attendance have relied on the manuscript census alone. While these studies are important, they cannot answer the same sorts of questions as a school register. For example, the census cannot discriminate between parents who sent children to one sort of school rather than another, and it provides no information on length or regularity of school attendance. Thus the grammar school registers for the years 1855 to 1867 are an especially valuable resource in understanding the particular function of the grammar schools in Upper Canadian society.

We will return to the registers in the second part of this chapter, but we want to begin with our second source, the inspectors' annual reports on each school, which also date from 1855. These will form the basis for our comments about the state of the schools in the years around 1860. Until the mid-1870s, when they become largely statistical, the written reports on each school are full of illuminating and acute insights, and provide a unique, if never entirely complete or satisfactory, means of getting inside the schoolhouse door.

Obviously, the reports must be used with some caution. Though the inspectors were hand-picked, knowledgeable, and dedicated men, until 1864 they were only part-time officials. In a few short weeks they had to visit every grammar school in their jurisdiction – a task often involving gruelling days of travel to get to remote villages. Once there, an inspector had only a few hours, or, at the most, a day or so at the largest schools, to observe the students being put through their paces, inspect the physical conditions of the school, assess the expertise of the teacher, and examine the pupils himself on as much of the prescribed program as he could manage, before he travelled on. Moreover, because of their other responsibilities the inspectors often paid their brief visits to the schools at unpromising times – during winter, for example, when storms might greatly reduce attendance, or at harvest time, when many students at small rural and village schools were out in the fields. Under these conditions, it is doubtful whether an inspector, even with the best of intentions, could acquire more than a quick and hurried impression of the school.

They also brought their biases with them. Their mandate was to enforce the teaching of the prescribed grammar school program, in an approved manner, to "genuine" grammar school pupils; to boys, that is, studying classics. Not only were the inspectors quick to recognize undeniably bad schools in which little was taught and that poorly, but they also castigated schools that served one or another non-traditional purpose – teaching common school pupils their three Rs, for example. In sum, the inspectors' reports are a valuable source, perhaps the best we have, on the schools. But we also need to "read through" their biases rather than accept their assessments uncritically. So long as this is kept in mind, however, the reports offer us a treasure-trove of information. The printed tables in the *Annual Reports* give us vital but barebones profiles of the finances, numbers of pupils, subjects taught, and the like. The inspectors' reports, with their pithy descriptions of classroom conditions, comments on pupils' performances, and assessments of teachers' personalities, capture the flavour of the schools in a way the figures can never do. If the inspectors disapproved of what they found, for example, their comments might still be revealing: "The classes in Mathematics do not do ... well – indeed I do not regard the system of teaching – which is almost entirely with the book and slate and without the Blackboard, as likely to prove successful. Very few of the pupils could explain the processes employed in the solution of his problem and few even seemed thoroughly to understand the definitions."[1] And their candid appraisals often captured the feel of the place:

One who expects to find an air of cultivation about a Grammar School would be disappointed with the school at Welland. A large proportion of the pupils are grown up lads, distinguished rather by a certain rude heartiness than by any special refinement of manner. The younger children are for the most part rough little cubs, who however are not disrespectful: possibly having an eye to the rod which Mr Hodgson, the owner of a vigorous arm, told me that he uses "when necessary." But, with all its want of cultivation, I rather liked the school. A great deal of real work is done in it. One branch – the French – is utterly unsatisfactory ... But, in the other branches, the work of instruction appeared to be well performed – not indeed in a high style, but with energy, and with a fair measure of fruit of the ordinary kind.[2]

What, then, was the grammar school of 1860 like? The inspectors began by commenting on the physical structure – much of it, they thought, inferior. As a model, they had the kind of schools portrayed in the architectural articles published in the *Journal of Education for Upper Canada*: diagrams, descriptions, and pictures of multi-room, multi-storey buildings with proper grounds, fences, outhouses, cellars, gates, and sidewalks.[3] The inspectors occasionally found such schools in the real world; for example, Chatham in 1855 drew high praise:

The building is large, two stories high – built of brick with a small dome and cupola, and presents a very handsome front. It is set on a plot of land containing about 2½ acres a little east of the town ... The house is large enough to accommodate 100 pupils, large recitation rooms being furnished upstairs ... The grounds are well fenced, and divided into a playground and garden.[4]

But most schoolhouses fell sadly short of the ideal. In the same year as the inspector praised Chatham, he recorded a more typical mixed review of Beamsville grammar school. "The schoolhouse is situated on a rising ground just above the village, and presents a very pleasant aspect. It is a good new handsome building, painted white with Green window blinds ... [but] there is neither fence, shed, shrub nor tree, nor outhouse of any kind upon the premises – and unless something be done soon, the house itself will fall into a dilapidated state."[5] And in Goderich, the inspector reported indignantly that the school premises were

rented from a tavern of which they are part of the upper storey; the only entrance is by steps from the back yard of the tavern, a dirty place ... the young females attending the school ... are liable to witness the offensive practices incident to such places – of course there is no back accommodation for the school and I am surprised that any decent parents would send daughters there.[6]

Throughout the period, old buildings were under repair and new ones being erected, so that the physical plant visibly improved in a number of places. The establishment of a union school often required a new building to accommodate the enlarged number of pupils, and these were sometimes models of civic architecture erected by proud townspeople. In 1859, for example, the union school at Simcoe acquired what Inspector Ormiston described as "the finest School Building in the Western District" – "a large, elegant, commodious and well furnished house" containing two large halls and many classrooms.[7] Two years later Ormiston reported that

a most marked and gratifying improvement is made every year in the accommodations ... old Houses are repaired and refitted, or new ones are built of a superior character ... Not a few Houses are now enclosed by a neat, well painted Fence; Wells, Sheds, Water Closets, and Play-Grounds provided, and the Grounds tastefully laid out and planted with Flowers, Shrubs, and Trees, or neatly covered with green sod ... In some cases still, however, there is much need of immediate improvement; the Houses are unsuitable, inconvenient, and ill adapted to the purposes to which they are applied, and a few of the Schools are kept in rented premises, temporarily fitted up.[8]

The physical condition of the schoolhouse, however, often bore no relationship to the quality of the instruction given in it or to the importance or size of the community it was situated in. Toronto grammar school in particular was housed for years in an unusually run-down, small building, though its scholarship received good reviews.[9] The Ottawa, Brockville, St Thomas, and London school buildings languished in disgraceful condition, though they housed the senior grammar schools of their respective counties.[10] At St Thomas, "the crowded and overheated state of the room is in summer so great as to endanger both the health of the Teacher and pupils – in Winter it is so draughty and cold in some parts of the room (whilst it is too hot in other parts nearer the stove) that it is totally unfit for the use for which it is occupied."[11]

There was also considerable variation in the type and quality of the furnishings and in the physical layout of the schoolrooms. In the 1850s especially, many schoolrooms were of the sort described by Robertson in 1855: "there are six desks and seats along the walls; a table partly a chest, a double desk in the middle of the room."[12] The Toronto grammar school made do with "long, backless seats, and long movable desks, scantily supplied with maps, and without any apparatus. The blackboards are very small. The rooms are warmed by stoves, and sufficiently ventilated through many a gaping chink."[13] In the early 1860s the Brockville grammar school was housed in a rented building formerly used as a store whose "counters still standing serve as desks," with "long low benches around the wall with a few chairs the only seats." The only teaching aids consisted of "a few maps, a small blackboard and a large Globe constructed by the Headmaster."[14]

Like the buildings themselves, however, furnishings gradually improved. Many of the older schools acquired better equipment through "one-time" grants from their municipal councils. And as trustees paid off the capital debt on a new building they could afford to invest in better equipment more nearly resembling the contemporary ideal of a properly equipped school, such as the Perth union school: "the apparatus consists of Blackboards, Object lessons, Holbrook's apparatus, Large maps, 2 Globes, a Box of Geological specimens, and a box of Chemical Instruments."[15] By 1865, almost all schools had blackboards, and most had maps and globes, but little else in the way of apparatus.[16]

Schools, of course, reflected the quality of their teachers, and the physical structure in some ways was less important than a capable master. The teachers were generally highly educated for their time: in 1855, 60 per cent of them had university degrees acquired from various English, Irish, American, and Canadian colleges. Many of them were clergymen. And they were nearly always men. The few female assistants we know of were in fact the common school teachers in a union school, who taught the common school program.

As might be expected, the inspectors' assessments of teachers' talents and character were mixed. Teachers generally received modest praise as "a laborious, zealous and faithful body of men" who discharged their duties in an adequate enough fashion.[17] If they were, as a group, not particularly inspiring, they were also generally perceived as being reasonable and kind. Despite the occasional heavy-handed master, wrote one inspector, "the rod is rarely resorted to for correction, and the modes of chastisement are commonly judicious, ... consisting mainly in detention, or the loss of position in the class, with marks of the Master's disapproval."[18] A few teachers received accolades as "gentlemen who would do honour to any profession, as they certainly sustain and elevate the character of their own," but there were always others who were condemned outright as unqualified and incompetent.[19] Much the same range of opinion is found in students' memoirs. Amongst the grammar school masters there were revered mentors – Tassie is one example – and, on the other hand, tyrants and misfits. G.H. Kenney, who later became a Methodist minister, never forgot one of the latter type encountered at the Oakville grammar school. The son of a rural blacksmith, Kenney had persuaded his father to pay his board for two years' study in Oakville so that he might better his chances in life. When he arrived there, however, he found a school that was

in a very bad condition ... The principal though a man of thorough education was not able to control the school. He was addicted to drink and would frequently be so overcome with drink that he would go to sleep in his chair and the schollars [sic] would turn out and play till they got tired, and often when they came in again, he would be still asleep in his chair. He was of little use when he was awake for he allowed them to do as they liked about study or anything else they pleased. They would chase one another up and down the school room and scuffle and carry on, so that those who would study could not. I would often go home sick and discouraged and [with] half a mind to leave the school.

Finally damage had been done to the School furniture and the state of the school became so notorious that the Trustees saw that they would have to interfere. So they caused a letter to be written, and sent the Secretary Treasurer to the school, read this letter and see what he could do to remedy the existing state of things. In the course of his address he said ... that they had the best school building but the worst school in the county.[20]

The inspectors' reports suggest that such extreme cases, though not unknown, were relatively rare. More commonly the inspectors were exercised by the high levels of transiency they encountered. Indeed, one of their perennial complaints was that salaries were so low that "comparatively few men of talent and spirit enter the profession ... it serves in their eyes merely as a convenient stepping stone to something better."[21] Small schools in rural locations seemed especially prone to be saddled with a series of bad teachers and high rates of turnover.[22] It is also true, on the other hand, that of all grammar school teachers listed in the *Annual Report* in 1861, about 30 per cent had been at the same school for five years or more. Considering that the number of schools was expanding, and that career teachers moved from school to school but stayed in the profession, this figure suggests not only a fair degree of stability but that teaching had its attractions as well. Salaries might be low but they were not necessarily lower than those of local Anglican or Presbyterian clergymen, and, as educated men, grammar school teachers could claim to belong to the respectable classes in Upper Canadian society. Then as now, moreover, teaching offered forms of compensation that other white collar occupations lacked. When inquiring of a friend about his chances of becoming a grammar school teacher in one small town, a senior railway clerk gave the following reason for seeking such an appointment: "The Rail Road employment is incessant from ½ past 5 o'clock AM till 7 o'clock PM – no holy days, no intermissions – on – on – on – like a locomotive."[23]

One last characteristic feature of mid-century teachers was that they were not yet unequivocally public servants, just as their schools were not yet exclusively identified as belonging to the public domain. In extreme cases, the "school" was located in the teacher's own home and operated essentially as a private-venture school. The Rev. Horatio N. Phillips taught for years at Niagara in what amounted to a private school: it was held in a wing of his own house, filled with his boarders, neglected by the public trustees, and according to the inspector "the furniture and building are of a primitive description and both are the property of the Headmaster."[24] If not physically in the master's house, the school might still resemble a private home because the master treated it as an extension of one. In one case, Inspector Cockburn noted, the master's mother, "an old woman, was seated in the school before the younger children, and was busy knitting all the time." The inspector stigmatized this school as "very miserable ... a common school in fact," but other schools, well run and reputable, shared the same blurring of public and private image.[25] Under the Rev. William Checkley, Barrie grammar school was "very much a private enterprise"; half the pupils boarded with the headmaster.[26] And like a private-venture school, when the headmaster left, the school might lose its students. At Kingston in 1862, for example, after a dispute with the board of trustees, the head took with him "over 50 of the most promising pupils" when he resigned to start his own private school.[27]

THE PHYSICAL STRUCTURE of the schools and the characteristics of the teaching force are relatively easy to describe. But what actually went on in the classrooms? What subjects were taught? How was the school-day organized or children grouped? On these sorts of matters the evidence is much thinner and in many cases we must draw inferences from recalcitrant or ambiguous sources.

It is important at the outset to grasp the scale of the operation. Though it is now an archaism, the word "school" was still used by contemporaries to refer not so much to a building as to a teacher and his or her pupils. Thus one might have two schools within the same building: a grammar school in one room, and a common school in another. This in itself tells us that by modern standards, the typical grammar school was very small indeed. There was, of course, a wide range in size: for example, from Toronto's 132 students, or St Catharines with 90, all the way down to tiny operations like Lindsay, with 16 on the roll, or Wardsville, with 27. But the overall average enrolment was only 55 students and since fewer students than those on the roll actually attended at any one time, most "schools" were no larger than a present-day "class." The task of teaching these pupils, however, was not eased by the small numbers involved. Two-thirds of the schools had only one teacher; of the rest, all but five had only two. Since students were at different levels in a number of subjects, the average grammar school teacher had his hands full, and the schools themselves more closely resembled the one-room rural schools of the early twentieth century than those of today.[28]

The published statistics give us a rough idea of enrolment by subject in these small schools. The official program of studies included classics, English, French, mathematics, geography, history, physical science, and "miscellaneous" subjects like drawing, bookkeeping, and vocal music.[29] In 1861 over 80 per cent of students took some branch of English, arithmetic, geography, history, and writing. Within these subject divisions, it is possible to separate the beginners from more advanced scholars. For example, about a third of those in arithmetic were taking the "first four rules of Arithmetic, Reduction and Fractions," while most studied the "Higher Rules of Arithmetic." Among other advanced mathematical subjects, Euclid was studied by a third of all students; almost half of all students also took algebra. Similarly, 53 per cent of all students took Latin; over half of these were at the most elementary level, in Arnold's First Book, while somewhere around a fifth or less of the Latin enrolments were in the more advanced studies of Caesar, Virgil, or Horace. Over half of all students took some form of science, while 20 per cent were enrolled in bookkeeping and 11 per cent in mensuration and surveying. These provincial totals hide a good deal of variation. Some schools had high enrolments in subjects like classics and higher mathematics, while others with large total enrolments numbered only a handful in those subjects. However, almost all schools had a considerable range and variety of enrolment by subject in the fifties and sixties.

Given the size of the schools and the range of the curriculum, how then were schools actually organized? In contrast to the late twentieth century, when in so many respects all schools are pretty much alike, in the years around 1860 no standardized form of school organization had yet emerged. Big schools differed from small schools and, indeed, from each other. And union and non-union schools, big or small, might differ again. A handful of non-union grammar schools were large, multi-teacher schools. Toronto, Barrie, and Galt each employed several specialist masters to teach their boys in separate departments, usually comprising classics, mathematics, English, French, drawing, and writing. In large union schools, the grammar school department itself might have more than one teacher, each of whom would specialize in a particular subject of the curriculum.[30] Such schools would have a number of rooms to accommodate separate classes, and were usually equipped with a variety of teaching aids. Unlike other, smaller grammar schools of the time, they probably resembled, in organization and physical structure, the sort of high school plant we are familiar with from a more modern era.

Large union schools were organized in more variable ways because they had to accommodate both advanced and rudimentary studies. The grammar and common schools usually came to share not only a building, but also some common timetabling determined by the headmaster (who might be either the former grammar school headmaster or, more often, the former common school head, an appointment that led in some cases to disputes over authority and "interference" in each other's sphere).[31] One form of organization left the grammar school master primarily responsible for classical and other subjects found exclusively on the grammar school program of studies, such as French and advanced mathematics, and he would teach only those subjects, and only to pupils enrolled in the classical program.

But for other senior subjects on the common school curriculum, the same students would move to the common school teacher. In 1859 the editor of the *Perth Courier* described this arrangement in the following way, remarking that Perth's union school was being reorganized on "the Hamilton system." The grammar school teacher was to "take charge of the classical department of the School. Pupils from any of the [other] departments, at the request of the parents, can study the Classics in the Grammar School department, while pursuing their other studies in the Common School. The school will be made *in fact* what it is in name, a public school, the classics being simply a department of the school."[32] The rules of the Oakville union school specified that "in the Grammar and Senior [common school] departments the system of interchanging shall be adopted to a certain extent – that is, pupils in either department who may wish to take up any particular study pursued in the other, shall be allowed to do so at the discretion of the teacher."[33] At Brantford, the common school principal and grammar school master divided the curriculum down the middle: the former took the intermediate classes in classics and the higher English branches, while the latter taught the highest and lowest students in classics, and junior English and mathematics to the common school students.[34] In other cases the grammar school master would take the classical pupils, along with all those in the higher English subjects, while his assistant would look after all of the junior pupils.[35]

Sometimes the sex of the student determined the division of labour. At Bowmanville in 1864, the girls in the most advanced division of the common school were excluded from the grammar school department, but as the headmaster explained, they were at the same academic level as the boys he taught in the grammar school, and some took geometry and algebra with him, "mixing and reciting occasionally in all the branches with the boys of my own division." And his boys sometimes went to the girls' room for instruction by their teacher, the female assistant to the headmaster.[36] In Ingersoll, the advanced girls took not only higher mathematics, but Latin, in the grammar school department, while learning all other subjects in their own common school division; the boys in the grammar school department went to the girls' teacher for French.[37]

The organization of one-teacher schools was, of course, simplicity itself: he taught everything to everybody. Such schools, "crowded with children at all stages of advancement," never satisfied the inspectors, though they recognized that there were few alternatives when grammar schools had been located "amid a sparse rural population."[38] A handful of descriptions survive of teaching in the small grammar schools, and invariably they reveal the difficult organizational demands placed on one teacher faced with a large number of students at many levels. His time was spent in taking up, one after the other, all the subjects of the prescribed curriculum. One such timetable, that of Queen's University school (not a grant-aided school but similar to them in all other respects), gives the following routine: on Mondays and Thursdays, the headmaster took scripture reading for fifteen minutes, followed by dictation for thirty minutes, Virgil for another half hour, and Caesar for twenty minutes; he then examined in Latin Grammar for twenty minutes. Meanwhile, his assistant took the junior class in English reading. The day continued with classes in Greek grammar, junior Euclid, and senior English grammar, usually in half-hour classes, while the assistant taught such junior subjects as writing and arithmetic. On Tuesdays, Wednesdays, and Fridays, other subjects were taken up in the same manner.[39] Davies' school at Cornwall, a highly praised school in 1861, was similarly organized: Mondays to Thursdays were divided into half-hour periods, taken in turn, on each subject of the grammar school program, from Latin v and Greek iv down to junior 1st History and Writing. Fridays were given over to review of the "subjects read during the week," and on the last Friday of the month, parents were "requested to be present, when there will be recitations and reading of original compositions."[40]

In one rare case, an inspector has left us a description of the daily routine in the grammar school department at Hamilton:

After the opening of school, Mr Buchan was engaged till 9:45 a.m. in hearing a boy read Lucian. The lesson had been pretty well learned, and the examination of the pupil was very well conducted on the Master's part. During this time, the other children present were learning their lessons at their seats in an orderly way – some being busy with Geography, some with Arithmetic, some with Arnold. A few minutes were next spent by Mr Buchan in giving out lessons in English and writing, and in answering questions which some of the boys put to him. At 9:55 a.m., a large class in Arnold (present, 16 boys and 4 girls) was called up and examined in the Grammar. The special subject was the formation of the participles of the Latin verb. The subject was gone into very minutely ... The examination of two other classes occupied the remainder of the time till 12 o'clock.[41]

It is clear that reliance on seat-work, and on the text itself, was crucial to this classroom; the teacher could manage only a few pupils at a time, examining them in a particular book in a particular subject, while the rest worked at their places. "Class" work in the modern sense, with a large group of pupils of roughly the same age and attainments, all receiving instruction at the same time, was impossible if a few pupils were in one book and a few in another, with a teacher stretched to cover all his many charges. The teacher's role became, then, one of examiner on the set text, which pupils worked up on their own. Indeed, the inspectors frequently deprecated "too much dependence on text books and on the words of the book in giving and answering questions," or "slavish adherence to the words, illustrations and examples of the Textbook."[42] But given the needs of many pupils and many subjects, it is difficult to see what else could have been expected. Students studied the texts and repeated its words to the master when he examined them; the better masters tried to elicit thoughtful answers and spark interest in their students, but more conventional teachers relied on memorization alone.[43]

One of the results of this system was the proliferation in the number of "classes" seen by a teacher during the day and organized as separate groups of students. In Perth union school, for example, the board of school trustees reduced lesson times from three-quarters of an hour to half an hour, "as this would enable teachers to teach a greater number of Classes and bring all the pupils taught by them ... more frequently under their direct instruction, and also allow the introduction of some branches crowded out by the three-quarter hour arrangement ... each pupil would be instructed by the Principal or Assistant Teacher, at least one class, during each meeting of the School." As a result, the principal taught eighteen different classes, his assistant taught seventeen, and every pupil had at least one lesson with a teacher every morning and afternoon.[44] In St Thomas in 1864, one teacher coped with thirteen different classes ranging in size from forty-eight in spelling and dictation (that is, the whole school) to eight in Caesar, prompting the board chairman to comment that "there are too many classes and too many branches and not time enough devoted to any of them, to the entire exclusion of Geography, simply because the Teacher cannot otherwise subdivide the time and do justice to all the students attending the School."[45]

The number of classes expanded not only for pedagogical reasons but because of parental and student wishes. Sometimes students attended for only one or two subjects, to finish their education or to pick up a subject they needed for the different matriculation or teachers' examinations. Even when students took a full program, they followed no set pattern of subjects. Instead of the prescribed curriculum, each student took what amounted to an individualized course:

no regular curriculum of studies is observed, but it is left entirely to the whim or fancy of the pupil or parent to determine which particular subject each will study. Accordingly one boy may take a little Latin and Arithmetic, conceiving himself to be perfect in English and the other branches, while another regards English as the great indispensable, and neglects the Classics altogether. The natural result of these options is that the master, instead of teaching his school in classes, is forced to fritter away his time in devoting five minutes to this particular pupil and ten minutes to another.[46]

Even when the textbooks were the same, the pupils studying them might be kept in separate groups because of their different goals. In Brantford, the inspector found the two most advanced boys in Greek reading separately "though so nearly at the same stage"; when he asked why there were two classes with one boy each, the headmaster replied that "they were reading with different objects in view."[47] In these circumstances it was impossible to impose a coherent program or to organize students into a few manageable classes or grades. Inevitably, the curriculum was a patchwork of individualized studies corresponding to the requirements of matriculation boards, the pedagogical demands of the classroom, and the broad age range and curricular interests of the students.

We are well aware that these last few paragraphs amount to little else than tantalizing glimpses into the pedagogical practices of the schools. We would dearly like to know more. But however unfortunate, the meagre evidence that survives allows us to pry open this portion of the black box only so much and no more.

THOUGH THE INSPECTORS' REPORTS and other Education Office files provide us with some useful insights into the character of the Upper Canadian grammar schools, they do not offer any answers to yet another set of questions. Who actually used the grammar schools? Which children in the community attended them and for what purposes? What distinguished their families from others in the same community who did not use these schools? And what patterns characterized the school attendance of grammar school boys and girls? For answers to these questions we can exploit the evidence available in the grammar school registers, which list the names of all students along with their monthly attendance records for each half year from 1855 to 1867.[48] Linking them to the 1861 manuscript census and other sources makes it possible to identify not only the sex and age of the students themselves but also their family backgrounds. And by comparing these sources to the records of non-grammar school users we can examine the ways in which grammar school children and their parents differed from parents and children who used other schools, or, indeed, used no school at all.

In 1861 there were eighty-six grammar schools with some 4700 students; over 70 per cent of these schools were located in cities, towns, or villages – that is, in urban localities as defined by the census.[49] From these urban schools we have selected for analysis five schools located in southwestern Ontario: the grammar schools of Brantford, Sarnia, Simcoe, Stratford, and Strathroy. The largest town, Brantford, had a population of 6251 (but at that, it was only half the size of London, the regional metropolis and the smallest of Upper Canada's cities); Strathroy, our smallest community, had just 751 inhabitants.[50] The availability of sources and ease of research access were important factors in choosing southwestern Ontario as a base: as well as school registers, we needed good census and assessment records, and runs of city or county directories, newspapers, and other documents. Apart from these considerations, it was also a matter of how many schools and how large a community base we could examine. In the end, we deliberately chose five quite disparate schools in communities ranging from a tiny hamlet to a large town, exhibiting a wide variety of social and economic features, and representing the diversity of schools and communities we are mainly concerned with in this book. To analyse communities like Strathroy means that we are dealing at times with rather small numbers for the purposes of statistical analysis. Much of our argument, however, focuses on the educational needs and political pressures emanating from such places, and the vast majority of schools were located in communities like Strathroy or Stratford; indeed, nearly a third were located in even smaller communities. Thus we cannot afford to neglect them.

Like the grammar schools in the rest of the province, the schools in our five towns drew their clientele mainly from the townsfolk. Some 70 per cent of grammar school students in 1861 lived in the municipality in which their school was located.[51] The proportion of students resident in the five towns ranged from a high of 95 per cent in Brantford to 60 per cent in Strathroy; the overall average was 78 per cent. The two extremes are probably explained by the size of the towns: Brantford could fill the grammar school with town scholars, and there were in any case two rural grammar schools nearby, while Strathroy drew a disproportionate number of students from outside the tiny village. The school reports of all but Strathroy indicate the presence of private schools in the towns in 1861: Brantford had nine of them, Stratford four, and the other communities two each. Thus there were educational alternatives to either the common or the grammar schools in most of our communities. All but Simcoe were railway towns, moreover, and that meant, for those who could afford boarding and tuition fees, relatively easy access to private schools in other communities. And for people in Strathroy, it was a relatively short train ride to the day schools of neighbouring London.

Our analysis of these schools draws primarily on three sources: the manuscript census and the assessment rolls for 1861, and the grammar school registers. Since the registers constitute a consecutive half-yearly record of school attendance over a period of thirteen years, while the other documents yield information for a single point in time, we have applied two distinct linkage procedures. First, we have collected information on all those families who sent children to the grammar school in 1861 by linking the school, census, and assessment records of that year alone. At the same time we also collected census and assessment information on all other families with children between the ages of ten and twenty whom they could have sent to the grammar school, but chose not to. In other words, we have tried to pinpoint a "target population" consisting of the actual and potential grammar school users of the community – a selection, we would argue, that more accurately captures the meaning of the choices made about education than do comparisons to a total population, most of whom had no children eligible for grammar school in the first place. The target population thus consists of all families with children aged ten to twenty living at home – in 1861 in our five communities, some 1372 families (see table 6.1).[52]

For the purposes of analysis we divided this target population into three groups. The first of these we term the "grammar school users" – those families who, according to the registers, sent children to the grammar school. Our second group consists of those who had at least one child recorded on the census as "attending school during the year" but whose name did not appear on the grammar school register. These were children, in other words, enrolled in a local common or private school, or a school in some other community, but not, in any case, in the grammar school. We designated these families as "other school users." The third group consists of those whose children did not attend school according to either census or register, and we have labelled them the "non-school users."[53] Lest this terminology become confusing in the pages that follow, the reader is reminded here that our "users" and "non-users" are household heads or parents and *not* the children themselves. The result of linking the 1861 records of these three groups is a convenient cross-section of school attendance patterns at one particular moment in time – and at a moment, moreover, when the grammar schools had already had several decades of development within their local environments, but were as yet relatively untouched by changing Education Department policies.

A second linkage procedure enriches the snapshot in two ways. First, we traced the school careers of the 1861 student cohort through the entire run of registers in order to examine such things as the length of time these pupils actually attended school. At the same time, we added new students to our pool by linking to the 1861 census, and thus to their families, those students whose names do not appear on the 1861 registers but do appear in other years. This procedure accomplishes two ends: first, it recaptures for the school record the boys and girls who attended grammar school in other years than 1861, but who would have been missed in the analysis of a single year, and second, it changes the proportions of "grammar school" and "other school" families by significantly enlarging the number of those families in 1861 who in fact used the grammar school for their children's education at any time in the thirteen years for which we have school records (see table 6.1). This longitudinal record, it must be emphasized, is not a picture of the community, or even the target population, *at any other time than 1861*; rather, in connecting the extended school-going behaviour of family members to their families' records from a single year, the image is now a more comprehensive and, we argue, a more accurate representation of the educational choices made by the 1861 families.

Table 6.1
Schooling Choices of Household Heads

	All families		School-using Families	
	N	%	N	%
1861 Household heads whose children went in 1861 to:				
Grammar school	139	10	139	15
Other schools	807	59	807	85
No schools	426	31	–	–
Total	1372	100%	946	100%
1861 Household heads whose children went in 1855–67[a] to:				
Grammar school	312	23	312	33

Notes   [a]Percentages for the period 1855–67 were obtained by linking families on the 1861 census to
their children's names on the entire run of registers, and are valid only for the grammar school
families. See appendix B for a more complete description of our methods and problems.
Sources   Manuscript census, 1861; AO, RG2, G1B.

One other comment on our methodology is pertinent here. There are now
a number of studies of teenage school attendance in nineteenth-century
Canada and elsewhere, and we have paid close attention to their findings
in thinking through our own work. It is important to keep in mind, however,
that this chapter is not a study of teenage school attendance generally, but
rather an attempt to illuminate why some young people were sent to a
particular kind of school. Thus our questions are different from those posed
in most other studies of the phenomenon, and concomitantly, our analysis
in this chapter does not address many important questions raised elsewhere
about teenage attendance or include detailed comparisons with other studies.

OVER TWO-THIRDS of the 1861 families with children aged ten to twenty
sent at least one child to some kind of school in that year. Most of these
children, we assume, would have attended the local common school. But
it is important to remember that there were other alternatives to the grammar
or common school and that the census does not give us any indication of
which kind of school a pupil attended. Thus we also assume that many
children of more prosperous parents would not be sent to the common school
but to a local private school, to one of the denominational college schools,
or to Upper Canada College.

As table 6.1 indicates, 15 per cent of the families who patronized any
school at all sent at least one child to grammar school in 1861. This figure

is low enough to accord with the view that the grammar school catered to a small and highly select portion of the community. But if we track down all the children of census families who ever used the grammar school between 1855 and 1867 we get a dramatically different result. Nearly a third of all these 1861 household heads sent one or more of their children to the grammar school over this thirteen-year period. The Upper Canadian grammar school was, in other words, the school of a minority, but that minority was a substantial one. These figures alone, we suggest, go a long way to explain why local resistance to the Ryersonian "reformation" of the grammar schools would be so vociferous, and so effective. By the early sixties the grammar schools had already sunk deep roots in their communities and had touched the lives of many parents and their children.

Support for the schools was also broadly based, encompassing those from a great variety of religious and ethnic backgrounds. Over 70 per cent of our family heads were British-born, and nearly a third were Anglican.[54] Given the familiarity of the grammar school as an institution to English immigrants and its Anglican bias at home, it is perhaps not surprising to find that English-born adherents of the Church of England formed both the largest ethnic/religious component of the schools' clientele (numbering thirty-five household heads) and also the most overrepresented (by some 10 per cent) compared to their distribution in the population. Together with Scottish Presbyterians they accounted for nearly 40 per cent of grammar school patrons but only 26 per cent of our target population as a whole.[55] When, however, we examine the ethnic/religious background of the 1861 household heads whose children attended in other years as well, the picture changes significantly. Scottish Presbyterians and English Anglicans comprised only 30 per cent of all grammar school parents, and the latter group was very little overrepresented (at 2 per cent). The other grammar school families were headed by men or women with a variety of religious affiliations and birthplaces: Irish Anglicans, Upper Canadian – born or English Methodists, American Baptists, and others.[56] Thus, despite the charges occasionally levelled at the grammar schools for being the schools of a sect or a clique, our five schools, at least, were not. Their religious and ethnic composition was broadly based and roughly congruent with the target population as a whole.

No such congruence existed when it came to wealth, however. Overall, grammar school users were significantly better off than their peers, and this fact alone helps to explain why they could devote so much time and money to the prolonged education of their children. As table 6.2 shows, in almost every community the proportion of grammar school parents in each economic sector of the population rose as the degree of wealth increased (overall, from 5 per cent of all those ranked as poor to 24 per cent of the wealthy), unlike

Table 6.2
School Choice of Household Heads by Economic Rank, 1861

	Economic Rank[a]					
	Poor		Middling		Wealthy	
School Choice	N	%[b]	N	%	N	%
All towns:						
Grammar school	22	5	66	15	53	24
Other schools	277	68	248	56	107	49
No schools	110	27	129	29	57	26
Total	409	100	443	100	217	99
Brantford						
Grammar school	6	3	20	9	13	12
Other schools	155	71	134	60	67	61
No schools	56	26	71	32	30	27
Total	217	100	225	101	110	100
Sarnia						
Grammar school	2	4	9	18	6	25
Other schools	36	75	34	69	13	54
No schools	10	21	6	12	5	21
Total	48	100	49	99	24	100
Simcoe						
Grammar school	5	9	18	23	13	41
Other schools	30	57	36	46	11	34
No schools	18	34	24	31	8	25
Total	53	100	78	100	32	100
Stratford						
Grammar school	3	4	5	7	11	31
Other schools	42	63	37	49	9	25
No schools	22	33	34	45	16	44
Total	67	100	76	101	36	100
Strathroy						
Grammar school	–	–	6	27	2	18
Other schools	15	71	10	45	7	64
No schools	6	29	6	27	2	18
Total	21	100	22	99	11	100

Notes   [a]Wealth categories are based on assessed wealth as follows: poor, percentiles 1–39; middling, percentiles 40–79; wealthy, percentiles 80–100. See Michael B. Katz, "Social Structure in Hamilton, Ontario," in *Nineteenth-Century Cities; Essays in the New Urban History*, ed. S. Thernstrom and R. Sennett (New Haven: Yale University Press 1969), 211–16; David G. Burley, "The Businessmen of Brantford, Ontario: Self-Employment in a Mid-Nineteenth-Century Town" (Ph. D. diss., McMaster University 1983), appendix III.
[b]Percentages in this and all tables in chapter 6 may not total 100 because of rounding.
Sources   Manuscript census, 1861; assessment rolls, 1861.

Table 6.3
Economic Rank of Household Heads, 1861

	Grammar school		Other schools		No schools	
	N	%	N	%	N	%
Poor[a]	22	16	277	44	110	37
Middling	66	47	248	39	129	44
Wealthy	53	38	107	17	57	19
Total	141		632		296	

Note   [a]Poor, percentiles 1–39; middling, 40–79; wealthy, 80–100.
Sources   Manuscript census, 1861; assessment rolls, 1861.

those who patronized other schools (68 per cent of all poor, but decreasing to 49 per cent of the wealthy). Thus in terms of a preference for particular kinds of schooling there was a clear tendency for the choice of a grammar school education to be associated with greater wealth.[57] Moreover, as table 6.3 demonstrates, 38 per cent of grammar school families but only 17 per cent and 19 per cent respectively of the other school users and non-school users were wealthy. Conversely, nearly half of the grammar school families belonged to the middling economic sector of their communities, whereas the latter groups were concentrated to a much greater extent among the poor. It is true that some 16 per cent of grammar school users are classed as "poor," indicating the wide range of wealth among them. Nevertheless, most grammar school users clearly enjoyed a comfortable material position, superior to that of comparable families.

The fact that significant numbers of grammar school users were poor or of middling wealth, however, indicates that wealth alone is not enough to explain which parents sent their children to grammar school. When we group our target population by occupation we find that merchants, professionals, and white collar workers were all overrepresented among grammar school users – in particular, professionals were more than double their normal distribution (table 6.4).[58] On the other hand, artisans and manufacturers did not send their children to grammar school in proportion to their numbers in the general population. Labourers, semi-skilled, and unskilled workers were even more underrepresented; indeed, as far as we can judge from the linkages we were able to make, the children of such workers were never present in more than token numbers. The lack of a certain minimum of material resources was probably a crucial factor in accounting for their absence, since prolonged education of the children would have meant foregoing income which their families may have counted on. However, cultural backgrounds and aspirations may have mattered too. For example, female household heads, most of whom were widows assessed at low amounts of wealth, or

Table 6.4
Occupations of Household Heads, 1861

	All Household Heads		Grammar School Users				Other School Users		Non-School Users	
	1861		1861		1855–67[a]		1861		1861	
	N	%	N	%	N	%	N	%	N	%
Merchants, dealers	201	15	32	23	60	19	105	13	64	15
Professionals, government officials	95	7	22	16	42	14	44	6	29	7
White collar workers	91	7	18	13	32	10	45	6	28	7
Artisans, manufacturers	466	34	33	24	95	30	296	37	137	32
Labourers, semi- & unskilled workers	280	20	3	2	17	5	179	22	98	23
Farmers[b]	34	3	3	2	15	5	24	3	7	2
Gentlemen	30	2	8	6	13	4	14	2	8	2
Female household heads	133	10	17	12	31	10	73	9	43	10
Outside the labour force[c]	42	3	3	2	7	2	27	3	12	3
Totals	1372		139		312		807		426	

Notes   [a]The percentage of 1861 families who used the grammar school over the period 1855–67. See note a, table 6.1.

[b]A few people listed "farmer" as their occupation, although they lived in town.

[c]No occupation or no classifiable occupation.

Sources   Manuscript census, 1861; AO, RG2, G1B.

not assessed at all, invested in a grammar school education despite having to support themselves and their families. Mrs Captain Fuller sent her two sons to Simcoe grammar school; each is recorded on the 1855 register, and one attended until 1861. Yet Mrs Fuller had five daughters to educate as well, and in an effort to support herself, had opened a Ladies' Academy in 1859 which, however, failed within the year.[59] Several other widows in the same town sent their children to the grammar school, despite their material circumstances.[60]

When we take into account all those 1861 families who used the grammar schools over the entire thirteen-year period, the percentages for all occupational categories came closer to their distribution in the general population – an indication that almost all groups in these communities were using the local grammar schools more nearly in proportion to their distribution generally. However, the same pattern of under- or overrepresentation still tended to prevail. Labourers' children seldom entered the grammar school. Professionals and government officials were the most overrepresented group, with white collar workers and merchants close behind. Thus, whether taken at

Table 6.5
Schooling Choices by Occupation and Economic Rank: 1861 Household Heads,
Selected Occupations

	Poor		Middling		Wealthy	
	N	%	N	%	N	%
Merchants & dealers						
Grammar school	1	8	7	9	21	25
Other schools	8	62	40	53	44	52
No schools	4	31	28	37	20	24
Professionals, government officials						
Grammar school	1	11	9	24	11	28
Other schools	6	67	17	46	16	40
No schools	2	22	11	30	13	33
White collar workers						
Grammar school	1	6	13	28	1	10
Other schools	12	71	18	39	5	50
No schools	4	24	15	33	4	40
Artisans & manufacturers						
Grammar school	5	3	20	10	6	14
Other schools	104	71	126	62	26	59
No schools	37	25	56	28	12	27

Sources   Manuscript census, 1861; assessment rolls, 1861.

one point in time or over an extended period, a household head's occupation bore significantly on whether he or she would choose to send children to the grammar school.

An examination of the interaction of occupation and wealth adds new dimensions to the question. The reader may remember that table 6.2 showed the aggregate number of school users within each wealth category, and suggested that the choice of a grammar school education was associated with greater wealth. Table 6.5 illustrates the same thing, except that this time the preference ranking takes account of both wealth and occupation. The numbers are small but suggestive. The proportion of those who chose the grammar school for their children rose uniformly in almost all occupational categories as wealth increased. Thus the degree of wealth would appear to be a significant factor for all families regardless of occupational category. It is instructive, nonetheless, to look again at the differences between occupational groups. Rich merchants, middling and wealthy professionals, and white collar workers of middling prosperity all exhibited roughly the same schooling preferences – about a quarter of each group chose the grammar school. However, within each economic sector, professionals tended to invest in a grammar school education at least as much as, and in most categories more than, any other occupational group. When we adjust

Table 6.6
Occupation and Economic Rank: Household Heads, 1861

| | Choosing | | | |
| | Grammar School | | Other Schools | |
	N	%	N	%
Merchants, dealers				
Poor[a]	1	3	8	9
Middling	7	24	40	44
Wealthy	21	72	44	48
Professionals, government officials				
Poor	1	5	6	15
Middling	9	43	17	44
Wealthy	11	52	16	41
White Collar				
Poor	1	7	12	34
Middling	13	87	18	52
Wealthy	1	7	5	14
Artisans, manufacturers				
Poor	5	16	104	41
Middling	20	65	126	49
Wealthy	6	19	26	10

Note   [a]Poor, percentiles 1–39; middling, 40–79; wealthy, 80–100.
Sources   Manuscript census, 1861; assessment rolls, 1861.

for the effects of wealth, in other words, we still find professionals over-represented in the grammar school.

The resultant distribution bears out this preference ranking (table 6.6). Among grammar school users, the wealthiest were the merchants, almost three-quarters of whom were in the top two deciles of assessed wealth. Nearly half the professionals patronizing the grammar school, on the other hand, fell below that rank, as did most of the white collar workers; these families were as likely to have moderate as extreme wealth. And those artisans or manufacturers who patronized the grammar school tended to be in the middle ranks of economic life as well.[61] It is also the case that among their patrons the grammar schools counted poor widows as well as artisans and manufacturers, and in the latter case as many very poor as very rich parents.

Going to grammar school, then, depended significantly on having parents who had enough of an economic surplus to invest some of it in education, and pupils were more likely to attend if parents were well off. But a father's occupation mattered too. Different family strategies, as we argued in an earlier chapter, based on different "grids of inheritance," led to high use by some occupational groups and low use by others, independent of income.

Table 6.7
Occupations of Household Heads and Average Number of Children in Their Families

	Grammar School		Other Schools	
	ANC[a]	N[b]	ANC	N
All cases	4.8	135	4.1	752
Merchants & dealers	5.6	32	3.8	99
Professionals, government officials	5.0	22	3.5	43
White collar workers	4.6	17	4.1	42
Artisans, manufacturers	4.5	33	4.2	289
Labourers, semi- & unskilled workers	3.0	3	4.3	173
Farmers	7.0	3	5.3	22
Gentlemen	5.3	8	3.9	14
Female household heads	3.8	17	3.4	69

Notes   [a]Average number of children in the family.
             [b]Number of household heads.
Sources   Manuscript census, 1861; AO, RG2, GI B, 1855–67.

Schooling was one form of patrimony, like farms, a business, or an apprenticeship and a set of tools. It was also a way of providing for children who would not inherit the family business. There was nothing uniquely Upper Canadian about this pattern, moreover. As we have already said, professional and other white collar occupations were massively overrepresented in similar sorts of schools throughout the English-speaking world and beyond.[62]

But what led these parents to choose the grammar school in the first place? Why not opt for a local private school or patronize a boarding school in another community? We can begin to answer this question by considering the relationship between family size and grammar school attendance. No matter what their economic rank or occupational category, our grammar school families had one thing in common: they all had large families to educate. And this alone, we suggest, goes far to explain why the grammar school, offering cheap, accessible, superior education, appealed to them.[63]

Overall, grammar school families in the five towns had an average of 4.8 children. In contrast, families using other schools had an average of 4.1 children.[64] Subdividing these groups by the occupation or wealth of the household head is suggestive, although, again, the numbers are small. Whatever the occupational category, the effect of family size tended to predominate. Indeed, families in the first two occupational groups who chose the grammar school were considerably larger than those who chose other schools (see table 6.7). Merchants had an average of 5.6 and 3.8 children respec-

Table 6.8
Wealth of Household Heads and Average Number of Children in Their Families

Occupations and Wealth[a]	Grammar School		Other Schools	
	ANC[b]	N[c]	ANC	N
All cases				
Poor/middling[d]	4.5	73	4.2	508
Wealthy	5.5	45	4.2	104
Total	4.9	118	4.2	612
Merchants & dealers				
Poor/middling	5.8	8	3.5	46
Wealthy	5.5	21	4.2	42
Professionals, government officials				
Poor/middling	4.0	9	3.6	22
Wealthy	5.8	11	2.7	7
White collar workers				
Poor/middling	4.8	14	4.4	28
Wealthy	5.0	1	2.4	5
Artisans, manufacturers				
Poor/middling	4.7	25	4.2	225
Wealthy	4.7	6	5.2	26
Female household heads				
Poor/middling	3.9	8	3.4	36
Wealthy	–	–	4.0	1

Notes   [a]Selected occupations
[b]Average number of children in the family
[c]Number of household heads
[d]Poor/middling: assessed wealth in percentiles 1–79; wealthy: in percentiles 80–100.
Sources   Manuscript census, 1861; assessment rolls, 1861.

tively; professionals, 5 and 3.5 children respectively. Moreover, whatever their economic rank, families who sent their children to grammar school were almost always larger than those who used other schools (table 6.8). Grammar school families, in other words, had more children to educate than others, and while they might be wealthier as well, their resources would only stretch so far. The local common school might be considered undesirable, or in the case of the union schools, might provide only an elementary education. But to send several children to a private day school, or a distant boarding school, was to invest too much of the family's income in education. Thus the local grammar school offered an attractive alternative. Only in the case of a handful of wealthy artisans and manufacturers who had large families was the relationship reversed, and other schools selected for their older children. They may, of course, have used private schools. But given the general underrepresentation of these occupations in the grammar schools, they may simply have kept their children in the common schools instead.

To reiterate, then, family size apparently played an important role for nearly *all* occupational groups in their decision to use the grammar schools. Within occupations, at whatever level of wealth, those who used the grammar school almost always had more children to educate than those who chose other schools. Such a generally consistent pattern across occupations and across levels of wealth suggests that those who used the grammar school were heavily influenced in their choice by having more children to educate than those who used other schools. Families who were both wealthy and large would choose the grammar school in preference to other sorts of schooling; families who were small and wealthy, by contrast, used other schools – probably, we suspect, the more costly, and socially segregated, private schools. Family strategies in 1861, as at other times, were shaped by the interplay of material necessity and social values, economic reality and parental aspirations; but family size played a significant part as well.

A closely related point concerns the number of brothers and sisters who attended grammar school.[65] Out of 300 families with several children, 44 per cent (131 "sibling families") sent more than one child, and these siblings constituted 64 per cent of all students over the period 1855 to 1867 (table 6.9).[66] In other words, about two-fifths of the families who would use these schools at one time or another provided two-thirds of the students.[67] In the smallest place, Strathroy, that percentage rose to 65 per cent of parents with several children, and these sibling families contributed 80 per cent of the school's pupils – perhaps not surprisingly, in a tiny village with a union school and no alternatives such as private schools.[68] Indeed, the rate of sibling usage dropped, in reverse relationship to the size of the town, to its lowest point in Brantford, where only 33 per cent of families sent just over half the students. Brantford, of course, was the largest town by far, with nine private schools reported in 1861, making alternative choices of schooling or employment available to families with many children.

These links between population size and the rate of sibling usage again draw attention to a central theme in this book. In larger communities, parents had choices and alternatives to the grammar school. But in places like Strathroy, and in so many other small communities where the majority of grammar schools were located, the grammar school was an essential institution for all those who sought a superior education. There simply was no alternative. Thus it was people living in small communities who would feel most threatened by the changes Ryerson would introduce in the decade after 1865.

There are also links between family size and the rate of sibling usage. Over the thirteen-year period, among families with more than one child, those sending several to the grammar school had an average of 5.8 chil-

Table 6.9
Occupations of Grammar School Families, 1855–67

	Families Sending One Child[a]		Families Sending More Than One Child	
	N	%	N	%
All families	169	56	131	44
Selected occupations:				
Merchants, dealers	35	57	26	43
Professionals, government officials	19	49	20	51
White collar workers	14	48	15	52
Artisans, manufacturers	55	60	36	40

Note   [a]Excluding families having only one child.
Sources   Manuscript census, 1861; AO, RG2, G1B, 1855–67.

dren.[69] The average number of children in families sending just one child out of several was only 4.4. Not only did grammar school families tend to be larger, in other words, but parents who had to provide for larger numbers of children tended to invest in a grammar school education for several of them. There were, however, definite and consistent limits to this investment. In Brantford and Stratford, which account for half our sibling population, one-student families had an average of 4.3 and 4.4 children respectively – smaller than sibling families in either town. But of the sibling families, those who sent 50 per cent or more of their children were considerably smaller than those who sent fewer than half. Brantford families who sent more than half averaged 4.9 children, and 6.8 children if they sent fewer. In Stratford, the comparable figures were 5.5 and 6.2. In fact, in all five towns, the families who sent more than half their children to grammar school were smaller than those who sent fewer than half. A family might choose a grammar school education for more than one child, in other words, but there were still constraints on how many it could afford to send, and parents of a large family may have found it difficult to offer all their children a grammar school education.[70]

The occupational status of the household head also seems to have been reflected in the degree to which families would send more than one child. More than half the professionals, government officials, and white collar workers enrolled several of their children, compared to 44 per cent of all families (table 6.9). We have already noted that these occupational sectors were overrepresented among grammar school users; they were also, it appears, more likely to take advantage of prolonged education for more than one child. Without a business or a farm, advanced education represented the only legacy they had to pass on to their children.

What, then, can be said of the heads of households who sent children to the grammar schools in 1861? In our five communities at least, they constituted a large minority of all those with teenage children, they were roughly representative of the religious and ethnic mix in the towns, but they were considerably more prosperous than their peers. They were drawn from a wide variety of occupations but most of them were middle class. Those in certain occupational categories, like professionals and other white collar workers, used the school intensively, sending many of their children to it. And above all, they were parents who had large families and needed access to relatively inexpensive day schools which, nevertheless, offered a superior education.

But what of the students themselves? Which children did parents send to the school? How long and how regularly did their children attend? What were the differences in school attendance patterns between boys and girls, and how did their family backgrounds influence their school careers?

For much of the nineteenth century, we suggested in an earlier chapter, not even the middle classes assumed that all their children would receive a prolonged education. Thus it is not surprising to find that even the wealthy grammar school users did not send all their boys or girls to the grammar school. Nor is it surprising, given the "grid of inheritance," to find that merchants and farmers sent far fewer of their boys than did professionals, other white collar workers, and female heads of households (table 6.10). Equally striking is the fact that several groups sent well over half their boys; professionals led the way in this respect, whether they were of middling economic rank or wealthy. Moreover, as parental wealth increased, these groups – particularly professionals and white collar workers – tended to provide an even larger number of their sons with a grammar school education. Parents were much less inclined, on the other hand, to send their daughters, nor is there such an obvious occupational influence. Girls from every sort of background had similar schooling experiences; from a fifth to a third of the girls in a family attended grammar school, whatever their parent's occupation. Boys needed a patrimony; girls, in the main, needed matrimony. And that stark fact is reflected in the attendance patterns of the era.

During the years between 1855 and 1867, the total number of girls in our five schools rose from a quarter to over a third of all students.[71] But while girls increasingly formed a significant part of the school population, this does not mean that boys and girls were a homogeneous group. One important difference between them was their ages. In the five towns as a whole, girls and boys attending grammar school in 1861 had the same median age of fourteen, but on average, boys were younger (table 6.11).[72] There was also

Table 6.10
Students Who Attended Grammar School, 1855–67, as Percentage of All Children in Family

	Boys		Girls	
	N	%	N	%
Merchants, dealers	67	43	48	32
Professionals, government officials	60	63	23	25
White collar workers	37	55	14	22
Artisans, manufacturers	76	36	71	32
Farmers	14	37	13	28
Gentlemen	18	52	10	29
Female household heads	30	53	21	30

Sources   Manuscript census, 1861; AO, RG2, G1B, 1855–67.

a wider age span among the boys. In almost every school there were more boys at either end of the ten- to twenty-year-old scale, whereas girls fell into a smaller age range. What we may be seeing in these age differences is the combined effect of the classical curriculum and the different purposes of advanced education for boys and girls. Boys were supposed to begin the study of classics at a relatively young age and so would enter the grammar school as early as possible, but some would also enter it in their late teens to complete preparation for a higher teacher's certificate. The education of girls was more concentrated, perhaps because they were completing only their English studies in preparation for a teaching certificate or, simply, acquiring a touch of finish before leaving school.

It is also useful to compare the ages of both boys and girls in the grammar school to those of other school attenders (table 6.11). There was, in the first place, an enormous overlap in the ages of the two groups. Considerable numbers of older students attended other schools – far more, in fact, than the grammar school. But what these figures do not reveal, and what we cannot tell from the census information, is their level of schooling. Robert Anderson remarks of Scottish schooling in the mid-nineteenth century that "it was not uncommon ... to prolong elementary education until 14 or even 15, and since this was most marked in rural and especially Highland counties, it reflected the persistence of preindustrial traditions rather than the progress of new aspirations."[73] The same may well have been true of Upper Canada. The census figures show only that some older students attended school; probably most of the teenagers we have identified from the census as attending schools other than the grammar school were attending the common schools, although there is no proof even of that without school registers. But there is no reason to assume that teenagers attending other schools were

Table 6.11
Ages of Students, 1861

Age	Grammar Schools				Other Schools			
	Male		Female		Male		Female	
	N	%[a]	N	%[a]	N	%[a]	N	%[a]
10	14	(11)	2	(4)	129	(20)	159	(23)
11	10	(19)	2	(8)	120	(39)	86	(36)
12	16	(32)	7	(21)	103	(55)	128	(55)
13	19	(48)	4	(28)	80	(68)	95	(69)
14	18	(63)	14	(55)	70	(79)	65	(78)
15	16	(76)	10	(74)	56	(88)	54	(86)
16	17	(90)	7	(87)	29	(92)	38	(92)
17	6	(95)	4	(94)	22	(96)	35	(97)
18	3	(98)	2	(98)	10	(98)	11	(98)
19	2	(99)	–	–	10	(99)	7	(99)
20	1	(100)	1	(100)	6	(100)	3	(100)
Total	122		53		635		681	
Median	14		14		12		12	
Mean	13.7		14.3		12.7		12.7	

Note   [a]Cumulative percentages

Sources   Manuscript census, 1861: AO, RG2, G1B, 1861.

all doing advanced work. They may well have been reading in the second or third book, or doing other elementary work. The relationship between age and grade, indeed, remained loose long after the 1860s. Analysing the registers of the Hess Street Public School in Hamilton during the early 1890s, Ian Davey writes that "even though age-grading was supposedly a characteristic of the centralized school system from its inception forty years before, it was not operating effectively in 1890. Although most of the children in kindergarten were, as we would expect, between five and seven, the widest divergence occurred among children in the first three grades of the primary school. Children in these grades were as young as four and as old as fourteen."[74]

Table 6.11 also shows, however, that even for the age group of ten to twenty, grammar school students were considerably older, on the average, than students at other schools. Over half of the other school-goers of both sexes were between ten and twelve, whereas grammar school pupils, in contrast, tended towards the middle teens. Though the grammar school was not yet the only, or even the chief, school for all older children, it was already a school catering primarily to that constituency.

The school registers not only allow us to identify those who attended the grammar schools in the years around 1861 but also provide us with the opportunity to study students' patterns of attendance. One way of doing this is to calculate the total length of time a student attended school – something we term a "persistence" rate. Since we had traced our grammar school students through all the registers, we had a record of the number of years each individual spent at grammar school, as well as the length and frequency of "breaks" from school, which were arbitrarily defined as absences for more than half a year (or more than one full term). The persistence record thus enables us to compare the duration and continuity of boys' and girls' school careers as well as to relate these to their family backgrounds.

There were both similarities and differences in the persistence rates of girls and boys. A large number of students of both sexes took no breaks from school at all. That is, 72 per cent of boys and 70 per cent of girls attended grammar school for consecutive terms throughout their entire school careers. This fact in itself would suggest a certain purposefulness to their schooling: most students, of either sex, did not have lengthy absences from school. But in other ways, boys and girls were quite different in their patterns of persistence. For all students, the median length of their entire school careers (excluding breaks) was 1.5 years.[75] But the mean length of schooling for boys was 2.5 years, while that for girls was only 1.7 years. This aggregate differential was repeated in each one of our grammar schools. Male students, furthermore, had a much greater range of persistence: they attended up to a total of nine years, while almost all females persisted no longer than five. On the whole, then, measured in terms of their persistence, boys received a more intensive and prolonged education.

When we attempt to relate persistence to sex, occupation, and wealth, our numbers in any one category are small enough to make our conclusions, at best, tentative. But they are suggestive nonetheless. There appear to have been important variations in the persistence patterns among boys from families in different occupational categories (table 6.12). Boys from some families, especially those headed by professionals, white collar workers, or gentlemen, were much more likely than others to have a record of long attendance coupled with few long absences from school. The sons of professionals and white collar workers, for example, stayed for a median 2.5 years, and among those boys who did drop out for a term or more, white collar workers' sons had the lowest rate of absence. These boys were the most serious attenders of all. Only the sons of gentlemen, half of whom stayed for three years, were more persistent in terms of their total schooling; but as they took far more breaks than any other boys, their record was vitiated by the erratic quality of their long-term attendance. For most of these sons of wealthy men, advanced education was not a necessary pre-

Table 6.12
Persistence of Grammar School Students by Parental Occupation, 1855–67

| | Students | | | |
| | Male | | Female | |
Parental Occupation	N	%	N	%
Merchants, dealers				
< = median persistence[a]	33	49	28	56
> median persistence	34	51	22	44
No breaks from school[b]		80%		62%
Professionals, government officials				
< = median persistence	23	35	15	60
> median persistence	43	65	10	40
No breaks from school		70%		76%
White collar workers				
< = median persistence	12	32	9	60
> median persistence	25	68	6	40
No breaks from school		68%		73%
Artisans, manufacturers				
< = median persistence	43	56	42	59
> median persistence	34	44	29	41
No breaks from school		70%		70%
Labourers, semi- & unskilled workers				
< = median persistence	11	79	10	71
> median persistence	3	21	4	29
No breaks from school		87%		86%
Farmers				
< = median persistence	8	57	11	79
> median persistence	6	43	3	21
No breaks from school		80%		71%
Gentlemen				
< = median persistence	6	32	7	58
> median persistence	13	68	5	42
No breaks from school		65%		61%
Female household heads				
< = median persistence	11	37	11	52
> median persistence	19	63	10	48
No breaks from school		69%		68%

Notes   [a]Persistence is defined as the total length of time a student attended school. The median of persistence is the mid-point for all cases, including both boys and girls.
[b]"Breaks from school" are defined as absences for more than one term.

Sources   Manuscript census, 1861; AO, RG2, G1B, 1855–67.

requisite to making a living; moreover, the sporadic establishment of private schools may well account for their erratic grammar school careers.

Whatever ambitions they might harbour for their sons, however, parents in all occupational sectors were alike in tending to send their daughters for a short period of time. Regardless of parental occupation, indeed, girls' persistence remained almost uniform at 1.5 years. Where their persistence was less than this, the reason is readily apparent. The daughters of the few labourers who used the grammar school were not likely to attend for long. Few in number, and generally from poor families, they were an anomaly to begin with. The daughters of gentlemen were even less likely to attend for long, but since their fathers were almost all well off, the brevity of their stay suggests other possibilities: they needed advanced schooling for vocational reasons less than many other girls, for example, and perhaps they tended to take advantage of the grammar school only when private schools were unavailable. The pattern of long-term absences also strengthens the impression that the occupational category of their family had much to do with how girls attended school. Professionals' daughters took few breaks of more than a term, as did white collar workers' girls; merchants' and gentlemen's daughters, however, were the most sporadic attenders in this respect of any female students.[76]

Boys' and girls' persistence also exhibited different patterns depending on the wealth of their families. Only 10 per cent of boys came from poor families, while 18 per cent of girls fell into this category (table 6.13). Moreover, the level of wealth made little difference to a girl's chances of remaining longer at school. At every economic level, more girls than not attended for a shorter period of time. However, boys from wealthier families tended to remain longer at school, up to a median of 2.5 years for the better-off. Thus both wealth and parental occupation played less of a role in the persistence of girls than of boys, for whom these factors made considerable difference.

Besides giving us some insight into the length of students' school careers, the school registers also allow us to examine patterns of daily attendance during the school year. As was the case with common school students of the period, large numbers of grammar school pupils missed many school days, and this was a source of constant complaint by the grammar school inspectors and other Education Office officials.[77] Historians have also taken note of the high level of irregular attendance and have sometimes interpreted it as indifference or resistance to schooling itself. The phenomenon needs to be understood in context, however. In the historical literature a comparison is usually made between those students attending 100 days in the year or less, and the rest. Thus, for example, we find that over half of all children attending common schools in Ontario between 1856 and 1871 went for 100

Table 6.13
Persistence of Grammar School Students by Parental Wealth, 1855–67

	Students			
	Male		Female	
Parental Wealth	N	%	N	%
Poor				
< = median persistence[a]	17	59	22	63
> median persistence	12	41	13	37
Middling				
< = median persistence	60	43	51	61
> median persistence	79	57	33	39
Wealthy				
< = median persistence	51	42	46	61
> median persistence	71	58	30	39
Total	290		195	

Note [a]See note a, table 6.12.
Sources Manuscript census, 1861; AO, RG2, G1B, 1855–67; assessment rolls, 1861.

days or less out of the total school year, and this is interpreted as an indication of very low attendance.[78] By modern standards, however, the total number of days in the school year was inordinately high. In 1861 the common school year consisted of 244 days, a length which was intended to accommodate different groups of students who habitually attended, in the rural areas at least, at different seasons of the year. By way of contrast, in the 1980s there were only 185 days in the public school year. And by the time one deducts days lost due to bad weather, illness, and other factors, the average student's daily attendance is less than that. Thus the fact that large numbers of pupils attended 100 days or less in 1861 seems considerably less significant. The same argument holds true for the grammar school year, which in 1861 was over 200 days long. For the sake of easy comparison to common school records, we too will use the 100-day marker. Our calculations, nonetheless, should also be interpreted in the light of more modest modern expectations. There is, as well, another consideration which tempers the importance of irregularity. As we have seen in the first part of this chapter, contemporary pedagogical techniques were such that much of the teacher's time was occupied in examining individual students, while the rest did seat-work on set books. Thus, in a system organized around "individual progress" rather than the lock-step instruction of a whole class, the consequences of missing many days of school were less serious than they might be now.

All that having been said, however, the fact remains that in our five towns, in grammar and common schools alike, the total number of days that pupils attended during the year fell far short of the time the schools were open. In both types of school many students were extremely irregular in their daily attendance. There were, nonetheless, differences between the patterns of attendance at the grammar and common schools. Less than one-fifth of grammar school students, but nearly 30 per cent of common school students, attended for 50 days or less. Conversely, just over half the grammar school students attended for 100 days or more in 1861, compared to 41 per cent of common school students. And a third of grammar school students attended for over three-quarters of the year, but only 22 per cent of common school students did so. Thus on the whole, grammar school students tended to be more regular in their attendance over the year.

Once again, however, these aggregate figures mask the marked differences between the sexes in grammar school attendance. Only 15 per cent of the boys attended school for less than one-quarter of the school year, whereas 28 per cent of the girls did so. At the other extreme, fully 40 per cent of the boys went to school faithfully for more than three-quarters of the year, but only 19 per cent of the girls. Girls, in other words, were much more likely to attend for shorter periods of time over the year, just as they generally had shorter school careers. Though there were variations between the different grammar schools in the percentages of low or high attenders, this gender differential was maintained in each: boys were far more regular in their attendance during the year.

Regardless of their occupational category, parents consistently sent their boys for a greater number of days during the year than their girls (table 6.14).[79] The sons of professionals and government officials were the most regular in their attendance, averaging over three-quarters of the year. White collar workers' and merchants' sons were less regular, but still attended for well over half the year. But the evidence suggests that the same occupational groups deemed regular schooling far less important for their girls. Though professionals' daughters, for example, attended school more frequently during the year than the daughters of any other occupational group, their sons averaged many more days than their daughters. White collar workers, whose sons attended on average for more than half the year, sent their daughters the most infrequently – on average, less than 50 days in the year. In fact, regardless of their parent's occupation, few girls attended much more than half the year, and most girls for much less. The more irregular attendance of girls tends to confirm the supposition that girls had fewer vocational incentives than their brothers to obtain a grammar school education, and that their families assigned higher priority to the education of a son at grammar school than to that of a daughter.

Table 6.14
Daily Attendance, 1861

| | Average Number of Days Attended | |
	Boys	Girls
a) Parental Occupations		
All Cases	127	98
Merchants & dealers	121	111
Professionals, government officials	156	119
White collar workers	128	47
Artisans & manufacturers	115	80
Gentlemen	113	81
Female household heads	114	112
b) Parental Wealth[a]		
Poor	109	100
Middling	125	81
Wealthy	136	124

Note   [a]Poor: percentiles 1–39; middling: 40–79; wealthy: 80–100.
Sources   Manuscript census, 1861: AO, RG2, G1B; assessment rolls, 1861.

The effect of a family's wealth on daily attendance was very clear in the case of boys. Overall, the wealthier the family, the more regular the attendance of its boys. Poor boys went for barely half the year; those from wealthy families, for a month longer on the average. Clearly, however, wealth and occupation were overlapping in their effects. Merchants and gentlemen were generally wealthy; the sons of both averaged more than half the year in school. But professionals, who on the whole were considerably less wealthy than either group, sent their boys the most regularly. In daily attendance as in persistence, the sons of professionals and government workers remained the most serious users of the grammar school.

The effect of parental wealth on the regularity of girls' attendance was not as clear-cut. On the average, poor girls attended for slightly more days in the year than girls from families of moderate wealth; both groups, however, were far less frequent schoolgoers than girls from wealthy families. Even if they wanted a grammar school education for their girls, then, poorer families could not afford to send them for long; only the wealthy had the means to forego a daughter's labour at home, or to indulge her in regular attendance for an advanced education. But the very poorest girls were probably in the grammar school for specific vocational reasons, such as preparing for a teacher's certificate, so that they attended more regularly than others of greater means. Despite their relative poverty, for example, the daughters of female household heads attended school for almost as many days in the year as professionals' daughters, and for much longer than gentlemen's daughters; they had to be prepared to earn a living, and there was little else in the way of legacy for them.

In 1861, in sum, the pupils who attended the grammar schools in our five towns represented only a small minority of all school pupils. But they constituted a distinct group of "serious" students. In the case of the boys especially, they had been picked from among their siblings to attend the grammar school for some specific vocational purpose. As a group they were older than other school attenders. They took few long breaks, and they missed relatively few days of school. Whether because of the extra importance to them of obtaining an education for vocational or for cultural reasons, boys from professional families were particularly overrepresented in the schools, particularly conscientious about their attendance, and were high persisters. Other middle-class boys followed in their wake.

For girls, it was a transitional period. They were the first generation of grammar school girls and, beyond preparing for teaching, they had little vocational reason to attend. Thus they were sent for shorter periods, their attendance was more erratic, and the fact that they were sent at all appears to be more idiosyncratic, wealth and occupation having less influence than it did for boys. A growing number of girls did indeed go on to get their common school teaching certificates and we know of at least one who became a teacher at the Toronto Model School and another who became a high school teacher.[80] Others undoubtedly finished their education in the grammar school and married.

The grammar schools, it bears repeating, were not merely the schools of a sect, nor were they the exclusive preserves of the wealthy. The ethnic and religious backgrounds of students were broadly based, the majority of parents were of middling wealth, and a significant minority of them were poor. A wide range of occupations was represented as well. There were labourers' children present, if only in token numbers, and a considerable number of girls and boys whose parents were poor and middling artisans and craftsmen. Thus the sons and daughters of wealthy merchants and bankers attended school with those of coopers and carters. Simcoe even had one black pupil who persisted for six years. Upper Canadians could thus congratulate themselves that their grammar schools were not the schools of a caste, but open to all who approached their doors. And congratulate themselves they did, as we shall see. In the main, nevertheless, the social composition of the grammar schools was irretrievably middle-class, and in the patterns of attendance of the students, we can divine the expectations held by middle-class parents that the schools would prepare their children for the social roles and vocations they themselves already practised.

"A Blot upon the Whole School System": The Attempt to Reform the Grammar Schools, 1853–65

In the two decades around mid-century, an era of unregulated expansion had created a variegated pattern of grant-aided grammar schools ranging from Tassie's model school at Galt, exclusively male and classical, to the union schools of Port Burwell, Vienna, or L'Orignal, hardly more than common schools, and if the inspectors are to be believed, bad ones at that. Some offered advanced classics and some did not. Some taught the three Rs and some did not. Most had girls attending but a few did not. Some had several masters, most had but one or two. Half were united with the local common school while the rest stood in not so splendid isolation from it. Almost none of the schools had the financial resources to achieve the various goals they set themselves. It was this patchwork quilt that Ryerson and his colleagues at the Education Office would set out to systematize and elevate in the watershed decade of the 1860s. As they attempted to impose on the province their own vision of a coherent and fully elaborated system of education, they would repeatedly condemn the *ad hoc* institutional arrangements that had taken root in the 1840s and 1850s. In the middle sixties, indeed, they would take decisive action to stamp them out. In turn, those with a stake in their local schools would fight vigorously to defend the institutions they had established. This struggle over the future of the grammar school was to become the central educational policy issue of the 1860s and 1870s, and the outcome would decisively shape the structure of Ontario's school system.

It was in the latter half of the 1840s that Ryerson began to consider the role of the grammar school, not only within a system of public instruction, but within the larger social system itself. Like others of his generation, Ryerson accepted the notion that differences in rank, wealth, and occupation were part of the providential order of things, constituting, as he put it in 1852, that economy of the creator, who has not only rendered various employments jointly tributary to the well-being of mankind, but has constituted men with different aptitudes for different pursuits ... Every man will be most happy, as well as most successful in the employment for which he is best fitted ... and in this diversity of human pursuits and talents, in connection with the corresponding diversity of human pursuits and wants, we recognize the Divine wisdom and benevolence.[1]

Social differences, Ryerson assumed, would inevitably be reflected in patterns of schooling. As a rule, parental wealth or occupation would determine the kind of school a child attended. "The wealthier classes," he explained in 1850, were "especially interested in the grammar school" just as "the less wealthy classes" were "specially interested in the common school."[2] A preference for social segregation, moreover, might make many parents reluctant to send their children even to a good common school, and instead, to prepare their boys for the grammar school by sending them to private schools. Social rank and patterns of schooling were, in other words, inextricably related.

It was, nonetheless, an article of faith for Ryerson, as for so many of his contemporaries, that industry and ability must be recognized and nurtured wherever it was found, and that in Upper Canada, positions of the highest rank would be open to all classes. Thus schools must not only serve the needs of particular social classes but must also be linked to each other, opening the road from primary school to the university for the talented boy regardless of his social background. "The choicest intellectual marble," as he once put it, must "be dug out of obscurity, and polished and fitted for uses the most honourable and important to the Province."[3]

In his seminal report on the organization of Upper Canadian education, written in 1846, Ryerson tried to capture this twofold conception of the social role of the schools. The colony, he wrote, should have a "gradation of schools" adapted "to the wants of the several classes of the community, and to their respective employments or professions," each one linked to the others "yet each complete in itself for the degree of education it imparts."[4] The need for schools to be linked together meant that Ryerson was not prepared to sanction a dual system of public schools organized exclusively around wealth – one system for the poor, and another closed to all but the well off. To this extent he broke with the conventions of English education that tended to assume that the common school and the grammar school were, quite simply, schools that taught two different classes. What Ryerson wanted was something more closely resembling the rural parish schools of Scotland, which, in principle at least, taught children of all social classes their letters, and also provided for the "lad of parts" to be identified and educated up to the portals of the university. While he acknowledged that large numbers of

Upper Canadian children might enter the grammar school directly from the private schools, he considered this irrelevant to the design of the public system. The basis of education in the primary schools, he wrote in 1846, "would be the same for the whole community – at least so far as public, or governmental, provisions and regulations are concerned – not interfering with private schools, or taking them into account."[5] Without a primary school linked to the higher schools of the colony, no educational ladder would exist for those of intellect and ability to climb.

It was not only these considerations of social policy that led in the direction of distinct but linked common and grammar schools, however; there was also the question of educational efficiency. A grammar school in which one master attempted to teach everything, from the rudiments of English to Latin, Greek, and mathematics, would be a school in which "no branch will be effectually taught. Those who send their children to the grammar school, either to acquire an English education, or the elements of Classical learning, will be alike disappointed," while the Grammar School Fund would be entirely wasted.[6] But the common school would be irreparably injured as well:

Pupils who are learning the first elements of an English education, are sent and admitted to the Grammar School because it is thought to be more respectable than the common school, and especially when grammar school fees are made comparatively higher to gratify this feeling, and to place the grammar school beyond the reach of the multitude. Thus does the Grammar School Fund operate to a great extent as a contribution to the rich, and in support of injurious distinctions in teaching and acquiring the elements of English education, and not to the special encouragement of the study of the elementary classics and mathematics. Thus is the common school injured in its position; and influences withdrawn from it which ought to be exerted in its behalf, and which are most important to give it ... elevation and efficiency.[7]

Throughout his career, Ryerson was to remain adamant on these two points. The particular, though not the only, task of the common school was to provide high-quality instruction in the rudiments of English. The particular, though not the only, task of the grammar school was to provide high-quality elementary classical and mathematical instruction. In Ryerson's view, however, the grammar school had been, in the past, merely the common school of the rich, poaching on the territory of the common school, and, at the same time, failing to do its own work well. From the 1840s to the 1870s Ryerson would doggedly pursue policies designed to establish the unique role of the common school as the exclusive primary school within the public system.

He did not, however, break with the conventions about the organization of education beyond the rudiments. Like most of his generation, he believed that girls and boys should be educated separately wherever possible. He took for granted, moreover, the relevance of the traditional distinction between an ordinary and a liberal education, with its complex interplay of curriculum and social class. Once pupils had advanced to the "limits of the instruction provided for all," he wrote in 1849,

> then those whose parents or guardians could no longer dispense with their services would enter life with a sound education: those whose parents might be able and disposed would proceed, some to the "Real School" to prepare for the business of a Farmer, an Architect, an Engineer, a Manufacturer, or Mechanic, others to the Grammar School to prepare for the University and the professions.[8]

The phrase "real school" was a passing fancy of Ryerson's, an anglicization of a German term for a school that offered a practical, non-classical curriculum, and he would rarely use the phrase again. But the notion of two separate but parallel institutions would be a fundamental part of his thinking for the rest of his public career. The object of the grammar school, he wrote in 1849, was "distinct and peculiar." It was the first stage "in a system of liberal studies," a school primarily devoted "to the interests of classical learning" and to preparation for the universities and the learned professions.[9] He did not mean by this, however, that the grammar school was to be merely a preparatory school. As he had said in 1846, each school was not only to be linked to others, it was also to be "complete in itself for the degree of education it imparts." Just as the lower reaches of the common school would provide all of the education most children would ever attain, so the grammar school would provide all of the liberal and classical learning most of its pupils would receive, for at a time when not even law and medicine required a university degree prior to professional training, few grammar school pupils would ever attend one of Upper Canada's colleges. It was the grammar school, in other words, which would finish the general and liberal education of most of Upper Canada's leaders and thus the grammar school could not be treated merely as a university preparatory school. "We deprecate not the importance of a Literary Collegiate University education," he had written in 1847,

> but the educational statistics of any country will prove that the education of nine young men out of ten will terminate with the grammar school. The importance of the former, therefore, in comparison to the latter, is as ten to one ... To what are we indebted but to grammar schools for the education of all our Judges in the various courts of Upper Canada ... for most of the Parliamentary Leaders of both parties in

the Legislature; and also for some of the most distinguished clergy, of the Episcopal and other churches?[10]

Similarly, the common school, though linked to the grammar school, was also to be "complete in itself." It was to be much more than a primary school alone; in its higher reaches it was "the *English College of the People*," offering not just "the a,b,c's" but the full range of higher English and commercial studies to all those who could not, or did not, aspire to a liberal education.[11] The whole point, indeed, of the supplementary Common School Act of 1847 had been to secure for urban school boards the right to levy taxes to support these higher common schools – to sustain, in Ryerson's words, not only "primary schools for children from five to eight years of age" but also a "proportionable number of Intermediate Schools for children, say from eight to eleven years of age; and one or more English High Schools, for teaching the higher branches of a thorough Mercantile Education."[12]

In the latter half of the 1840s, then, Ryerson repeatedly envisaged a dual or parallel system of schools rising above the primary grades of the common school. The grammar school would link the common school to the university, taking its pupils after they had learned the three Rs and offering the classical instruction requisite for the elements of a liberal education. The higher branches or departments of the common school, on the other hand, would complete an education preparatory to the practical pursuits of life. Only a relatively small number of young men, however, would pursue a classical education, and thus the role of the grammar school was specialized and limited. Within the system of public instruction primacy was to be accorded to the common school, which, with its elementary and higher departments, and its separate facilities for girls and boys, was the crucial institution for educating the vast majority of Upper Canada's young people.

This vision of things was not easy to reconcile with the contemporary grammar school, and initially Ryerson did not even try. Between 1850 and 1855, his first and most urgent priority was to stop the grammar schools from trespassing on ground that rightly belonged to the common school, and to articulate the two sorts of schools in such a way that they would complement rather than compete with each other. The reason why the grammar schools poached on common school territory, he believed, was that they were underfinanced. Yet the politicians persistently refused to provide the grammar schools with either increased grants or access to county property taxes. Thus Ryerson fell upon what he conceived to be an expedient solution. He would encourage the "amalgamation," or union, of grammar and common school boards, an arrangement that would allow some portion of the local assessment for common schools to be used to subsidize the local grammar school. In turn, the latter institution would become "the high school" of that particular locality. [13] It was this notion that Ryerson incorporated into both the grammar school bill of 1850 and the act of 1853. Each grammar school, as he explained, was

to fulfil the *double office* of a high English School and an elementary classical and mathematical school – a school into which pupils will be admitted from the higher classes of the common schools, and receive such an education as will fit them for mercantile and manufacturing pursuits, and the higher employments of mechanical and agricultural industry ... a school also in which many youth may be thoroughly trained in the elementary classics, mathematics and physical sciences, for admission to the University, and entrance upon professional studies. [14]

The grammar school regulations, issued in 1855, reflected the same objective. They provided for two distinct programs of study, one consisting of a set of prescribed classical and English subjects for those who sought the elements of a liberal education or who were preparing for the universities or professions, and another, separate program of English and commercial subjects which allowed a pupil "an option as to the particular subjects of his study" – a course that would provide, as the act said, "a practical English and Commercial Education." In order to prevent the grammar school from competing for pupils with the common school, Ryerson also introduced a grammar school entrance examination requiring prior competence in the three Rs. And no pupil was to be counted for grant purposes who had not already passed the entrance examination. [15]

In the middle 1850s, then, Ryerson seemed to have offered a clear definition of the role of both the grammar and the common school. The grammar school was to become a multi-purpose high school, and the common school its elementary feeder. The former would be forced to focus on senior work because the entrance examination prevented it from taking primary pupils. Though before 1866 Ryerson was unable to enforce the standards set out in the entrance examination, it was, nonetheless, an important symbolic turning point in the organization of the public school system. From that point onwards, the common school was given exclusive responsibility for the three Rs. Superior schools were to extend upwards from the common schools as a second stage, and would not be allowed to maintain their own preparatory departments, parallel to but separate from the common schools. Even though the term itself was rarely used at the time, the introduction of the entrance examination was an important first step in defining the grammar school as a "secondary" school.

By uniting with the local common schools, moreover, the grammar schools would also be relieved of their financial embarrassments and given the resources to do their own work properly. For a brief period, Ryerson was almost complacent about the efficacy of his solution to the educational and financial problems of the grammar schools. As he explained to one of the grammar school trustees in 1854,

the chief advantages of the union of a Grammar and the Common Schools of a Village or Town, are economy in school buildings and teachers, and the unity of action as well as interest in the School affairs of such village or Town – providing more certain and ample means for the support of the Grammar School, and a more efficient oversight of the interests of the common school or schools ... I do not know the number of places in which unions between boards of Grammar and Common Schools have occurred; but they are more than a dozen, and increasing every week. The tendency seems altogether in that direction, although the Grammar School Act has not yet been in force three months. The unions will probably be the rule. [16]

Ryerson's enthusiasm for the multi-purpose union grammar school was, however, short-lived, and ambivalent even then. Despite the language of both the act and regulations, which he himself had drafted, he continued to refer to the classics as "the distinguishing characteristic" of the grammar school, and to one correspondent who inquired in 1856 about the conditions for opening a grammar school he replied that the key requisite was "the number of youths in your section who may wish to study the classics – as all other subjects can be equally well-taught in a common school." [17] By the later 1850s, moreover, he was condemning union grammar and common schools outright as inimical to a sound education. [18] Equally, when he and his advisers came to draft a program of studies for the Model Grammar School, an institution established in 1857 and designed, as its name implies, "as a model for the other grammar schools," they made no provision for a distinct English course. All pupils were required to take a combined program that prescribed both classical and English subjects, despite the fact that the act of 1853 itself and the regulations of 1855 provided for separate classical and English courses. [19] Moreover the first program of studies for the common schools, issued in 1858, reinforced the idea that the grammar and common school each had distinct but parallel roles to play. The common school curriculum was to consist of three divisions, the third or highest of which included the fifth reader and such subjects as algebra, trigonometry, mensuration, bookkeeping, and natural philosophy. Thus the common schools were expected to do not only primary but advanced work as well. [20] At the same time, with the exception of classics in the grammar school and the three Rs in the common school, the official program of studies for the two schools almost entirely overlapped.

By the late 1850s, then, Ryerson had largely rejected the idea that the best vessel for higher studies was the multi-purpose high school, and had returned to his earlier preference for bifurcation – the grammar school with its classical core on the one hand, and the English high school on the other.

By the 1860s, indeed, his commitment to dualism was in full flower. As he explained to one correspondent in 1862,

the Grammar School Fund was intended to teach the elementary classics, Mathematics etc. so as to prepare pupils for the universities and professions just as the Common School Fund is designed to teach the subjects of an English education, so as to prepare pupils for ordinary employments. The English subjects taught in the Grammar Schools are the same as those taught in the Common Schools and ought not to be taken into consideration in the distribution of the Grammar School Fund. It would indeed be much better for the efficiency of the Grammar Schools if, like the Model Grammar School, no pupils were admitted into them except those who pursue the whole Grammar School course – leaving common school branches alone to be taught in the Common Schools; but as the distinction between Grammar and Common Schools was not observed in former years, the confinement of Grammar Schools to their legitimate and appropriate work could not all at once be made .[21]

By 1864, moreover, the practice of routinely moving older pupils into the grammar school department of a union school was being sharply condemned. When one grammar school master wrote to Ryerson inquiring about the legality of such a procedure, he was firmly told that

the Common School is not a preparatory school for the Grammar School except in regard to the comparatively few pupils who are seeking a *classical* in addition to a common school education, though a pupil is not admitted into the Grammar School to commence his classical studies without knowing the elements of English or Common School education; yet it by no means follows that every Common School pupil who has advanced as far in his Common School course as is necessary for admission to the Grammar School, must enter the Grammar School. If his parents wish, he is undoubtedly entitled to remain in the Common School and of course in the Common School Department of a Union Grammar and Common School, until he completes the programme of Common School Studies ... The clear intention of the Law permitting the union of Grammar and Common Schools is that neither should suffer in completeness and efficiency in consequence of such union. The Common School course of studies should be as complete in union schools, as if no such union had taken place. I do not think that any pupil in a union school, should be regarded as a Grammar School pupil (except at the request of the parent) unless he is studying subjects which the law requires to be taught in Grammar Schools (Greek, Latin, French etc.) and which it does not require to be taught in Common Schools.[22]

Equally, Ryerson unflaggingly exhorted urban boards of trustees to take full advantage of their power to create good urban English high schools – schools, as he told one leading Torontonian,

158 Inventing Secondary Education

in which should be taught the higher branches of English, Chemistry, Elements of
Natural Philosophy (especially mechanics), Mathematics, Bookkeeping, etc., so as
to qualify youth for entrance upon the various mechanical, manufacturing and other
business pursuits. The primary schools are likely to decline rather than improve
when no provision is made to complete the education commenced therein.[23]

But *why* did Ryerson prefer a provincial school system organized along
dual lines? What was wrong with a multi-purpose superior school offering
a variety of courses and streams, and catering to both boys and girls? Or
to put the question another way, what was wrong with the kind of grammar
schools that had established themselves throughout the colony in the forties
and fifties? The primary answer to these questions is simply put: the multi-
purpose grammar school was betraying the cause of classical education.

Though it is often overlooked, Ryerson was a Georgian and not a Victorian. Nearly all of the formative influences in his life – his upbringing,
his education, the most important books he read, his view of the world, the
fruits of his experience during his first thirty-five years – were all products
of a pre-Victorian world. To one extent or another, this was also true of
Ryerson's closest political allies, his senior educational advisers, and indeed,
his most formidable enemies. To cite but a few examples, the two
Macdonalds, John A. and Sandfield; George Brown; T.J. Robertson, who
was Ryerson's choice as first headmaster of the Normal School and later
the first grammar school inspector; John McCaul, the long-time head of
University College and special member, for grammar school purposes, of
the Council of Public Instruction; George Paxton Young, perhaps Ryerson's
most influential educational adviser; all of these men were born in the first
two decades of the century, and all reached maturity before Victoria's acces-
sion to the throne. On the face of it their personal and educational backgrounds might appear remarkably disparate, born as they were in Scotland,
Ireland, or Upper Canada and educated in schools ranging from the back-
woods of Norfolk and Glengarry counties to such distinguished institutions
as Edinburgh High School and Trinity College, Dublin. They all belonged
to a generation, nonetheless, for whom the study of the classical languages
and literature remained the central focus of the curriculum. Ryerson and the
two Macdonalds had attended Upper Canadian grammar schools and had
learned enough Latin to qualify for matriculation into the study of law.
Brown and Young had both studied at the Edinburgh High School which,
more than most Scottish schools, specialized in classical studies, and Young
had gone on to study classics and mathematics at the University of Edinburgh. McCaul and Robertson had attended Irish grammar schools and then
Trinity College, Dublin, where both won high honours in classical studies.
The schools these men attended, moreover, were not only dominated by

classical studies but were Georgian in another sense: they were exclusively male. The list of Ryerson's contemporaries who were shaped by such an education and who were to become influential in Upper Canadian education or politics could, of course, be extended. And there was, besides, a generation of younger men, born in the 1830s: for example, J.G. Hodgins or the future grammar school inspector William Ormiston, both of whom completed their undergraduate degrees at Victoria at a time when classical study was mandatory for matriculation and graduation; or G.R.R. Cockburn, who had won honours in classics at the University of Edinburgh, pursued his classical studies in Berlin, came to Canada as master of the Model Grammar School, served as a grammar school inspector, and then went on to become a distinguished principal of Upper Canada College.[24]

None of these men was narrowly prejudiced against the virtues of a good English education; indeed the very reverse is true, as we shall see. But inevitably they shared the view that a classical education was virtually coterminous with a liberal education, that a good educational system must among its other duties foster the study of the classical languages, and that the best means of achieving this was the kind of school they had experienced themselves. Given their backgrounds, it is not surprising that, during the decade of the 1860s, J.A. Macdonald would support Ryerson's attempts to make the Upper Canadian grammar schools more thoroughly classical and male in character; that J.S. Macdonald, as attorney-general, would rule that girls could be ejected from what must be, *a priori*, a boys' school; that G.R.R. Cockburn would draft a program for the Model Grammar School that flew in the face of the intentions of the act of 1853 and all the non-model schools of the colony; that G.P. Young or T.J. Robertson would advise abandoning the study of Latin in all but a few schools where it could be studied intensively and for prolonged periods of time. For the generation responsible for formulating educational policy in the two decades after 1850, grammar schools existed to train young men in classical learning, prepare for the learned professions, and lay the foundations of a liberal education. They might, in passing, do other things as well, but if they were not good classical schools, they were not grammar schools at all.

There remained, moreover, compelling reasons to sustain good classical schools in the two decades after mid-century. The revival of classical learning and teaching in Europe and Britain, the reform of Oxford and Cambridge in the 1850s, the primacy of the classics in the new Indian Civil Service examinations, the reinvigoration of old English grammar schools and the establishment of new foundations to form the prestigious public schools, the rise of a party of Scottish university reformers dedicated to reshaping Scottish higher education more closely along English lines – all combined to lend the classics a continuing aura of prestige.[25] Upper Canada was not isolated from these international currents, and given Ryerson's nationalism and his belief that colonial institutions must equal the best in Britain and America, it is not surprising to find him determined that Upper Canada should have high-quality classical schools as well.

As knowledge about the state of the grammar schools began to accumulate, however, it quickly became clear that the grammar schools, taken as a whole, were anything but good classical schools. As the inspectors toured the province year after year and made their reports, and as information accumulated from a variety of sources, Ryerson and his advisers became steadily more disenchanted with what they found. They also began to develop a consensus about the major causes of the problems. In the first place, the number of grammar schools was far greater than warranted by the demand for classical instruction.[26] Expansionary pressures had been allowed to run rampant since the 1840s with the consequence that there were far too many schools with no more than a handful of classical pupils, and some with none at all. In too many cases, moreover, neither the county nor the locality where the school was located would provide adequate additional funding, so that the old problem of inadequate resources remained: the schools routinely accepted any pupil who could pay the fees and taught anything fee-paying parents wished their children to study. Thus the influx of girls, and young children learning their three Rs. But as the master's time was frittered away teaching too many subjects to too many pupils of differing ages and attainments, so the quality of classical, mathematical, and higher English studies declined accordingly.

The union of grammar and common schools solved some of these problems but exacerbated others. It ensured a steady flow of recruits from the common school and it provided some greater financial security than was available to non-union schools. But it encouraged the flooding of the grammar school with ill-prepared junior pupils in order to increase the grant and thus keep local taxes down. Such pupils were taught a little Latin to meet the grant requirements but were in reality merely nominal classical scholars. In the meantime, serious classical pupils were deprived of the teacher's time and attention. Even in well-run schools, where the grammar school master was responsible only for the senior pupils, this might be the case. Of the Kincardine union school in 1864, G.P. Young wrote the following:

Besides 35 grammar school pupils proper, Mr Andrews teaches the more advanced pupils of the common school. At present only 5 of this latter class are under his care; but he has had a much larger number. For instance in the first quarter of the year, he had 23. It appears plain that a master, with 20 common school pupils to attend to, or anything like that number, cannot efficiently perform the duties of a grammar school in which there are between 30 and 40 grammar school pupils proper.[27]

As G.R.R. Cockburn pithily put it in 1860, "the pruning hook requires to be vigorously applied to these parasite grammar school unions, so that the funds frittered away ... may be devoted to the vigorous maintenance of such grammar schools as are really necessary."[28]

There were other problems with the quality of classical instruction as well. In the inspectors' view at least, the function of the grammar school was to *educate* students and not merely to prepare them for this or that matriculation examination. That was the whole point, indeed, of issuing a program of studies that all students were expected to take. But large numbers of classical students were not pursuing any sort of coherent program of liberal studies; rather, they were "cramming" for exams – taking whichever subjects and studying whichever books happened to be required by the Law Society, the Medical Board, or the ministries of the various churches. For a decade some of the strongest complaints of the grammar school inspectors were directed at this feature of the schools. Year after year they could see little improvement or increase in the numbers of advanced classical pupils; the result, as T.J. Robertson remarked, was that "very few complete the course for the university; in general the limit of their ambition is a very hurried preparation for Lawyers Hall, and the result is a miserable smattering. In fact the Lawyers Hall preparation so far as Classics is concerned seems to me a sheer loss of time."[29]

This bill of indictment against the grammar schools was reiterated by Ryerson and his associates virtually every year during the later fifties and sixties. And equally, they shared a common reform agenda. First, the grammar schools had to be given access to local taxation. This would ensure the resources for adequate accommodation and higher teachers' salaries. It would also lessen the temptation to enrol students not learning classics or to enter unions with common school boards. Secondly, existing union schools had to be broken up so that the interests of classical learning would be the central focus of the grammar school. Third, means had to be found to reduce the number of grammar schools and direct more of the Grammar School Fund to the better schools. Hence they proposed to cut off all grants to schools with less than ten classical scholars, raise the minimum amount of the fund available to counties before new schools could be established, and distribute a portion of it according to the average attendance of classical scholars.

Virtually none of these goals could be achieved under the act of 1853. A county rate for grammar schools had been repeatedly rejected by the politicians, but nothing else had been done to improve the finances of the grammar schools. Nor could Ryerson prevent the multiplication of schools, for according to the act, as soon as there was an extra $200 in its share of the Grammar School Fund, any county council could create a new school if it wished. Nor indeed could he even enforce the regulations in an effective way. His chief weapon against trustees and teachers who violated the regulations was to cut off their grant. That, however, was an extreme step which might result in closure of the school – a step Ryerson was always reluctant to take and that local and provincial politicians would probably not have tolerated.[30] Beyond that, however, he could do little but bluster and cajole.

What was needed, then, was new legislation, and thus Ryerson returned to the political arena in 1860, drafting a bill which he put before the cabinet and seeking public support for his proposals during the county school conventions of that year. Once again, however, the politicians refused to consider any form of compulsory taxation to support the grammar schools and the bill was dropped.[31] Undaunted, Ryerson decided to try again in 1863, hoping perhaps to get better results from Sandfield Macdonald's reformers than he had from J.A. Macdonald and company.

Though his draft bill of that year was somewhat crude in places, its contents are important not just because they indicate the direction he was moving in the early 1860s, but because they contain key proposals that would recur throughout the decade and beyond. First, there were new financial provisions. The county councils were to collect a rate for grammar schools in the same way they did for common schools, while cities, towns, and villages where grammar schools were located would be required to raise money to provide adequate accommodation and any additional means of support the boards of trustees might require. The grammar schools, in other words, were to be given full access to local taxation. Secondly, the schools would cease to be exclusively county institutions: the county councils were to appoint three trustees for each school, and each urban council where a grammar school was located was to appoint three more. Thus both urban and rural areas would be responsible for the support of the grammar schools and also have a voice in their administration. Next came the quality-control features of the bill: no grammar school was to receive any part of the grant unless it had ten pupils studying Latin, Greek, or French. Every grammar school which met this condition was to receive a minimum grant of $300 – an assurance that the smallest schools would be able to survive – but all apportionments above that amount were to be made according to the average daily attendance in Latin, or Greek, or French. No additional school was to be established unless the county's share of the Grammar School Fund would allow an apportionment of $300 per annum – a proposal that would raise the minimum by $100 and thus make it more difficult to open new schools.[32]

As soon as the act was put in place, Ryerson announced in the *Journal of Education*, new admission standards would also be introduced. Though the entrance examination for the classical course would remain the same so that boys could start classes at a relatively early age, the examination standard for pupils studying English subjects only would be raised substantially, requiring a far more advanced common school education than ever before. Thus the grammar school, Ryerson explained, would cease to be "a competitor with the common school, but will be a High English and Classical school."[33]

While this proposal appeared to retain the spirit of the act of 1853 by preserving the notion of the "double office" of the grammar school as a classical and higher English school, the combined weight of the bill and the new admissions regulations would have moved the grammar schools a long way towards becoming primarily classical seminaries. English pupils would not bring the school any additional revenue, since the grant was to be apportioned according to numbers in classics alone. Thus not only would English pupils find it more difficult to enter the grammar school, and thus be more likely to remain in the common school to complete their education, but trustees would also have little incentive to accommodate them.

Finally, in discussing the new regulation Ryerson used the following phraseology: "the standard of admission for *boys* studying Latin and Greek" would not be raised; "but the standard for admission of *pupils* studying English only will be raised."[34] Whether or not Ryerson intended in 1863 to exclude girls entirely from the grammar schools remains unclear. He told a correspondent after the event that "the present premier [Sandfield Macdonald] desired me to get the present Council of Public Instruction to invoke a regulation prohibiting the admission of girls to the Grammar Schools. I preferred leaving it to the Legislature to decide, when amending the Grammar School Law."[35] Though that passing comment makes it sound as if Ryerson might have wanted exclusion, his draft bill does not specify any conditions based on gender, and the inclusion of French in the average attendance clauses would appear to be a concession to the attendance of girls. As well, Ryerson and his advisers knew that the issue was sensitive and as a consequence they had been delicately skirting it for a decade, unwilling perhaps to sacrifice other goals for this one.[36] But given the wording of the proposed regulation, clearly the intent was to exclude girls from classics and probably to subject them to the higher admission standards of the English course. Thus the schools would be pushed not just towards becoming classical seminaries but would be more exclusively male preserves.

Ryerson went to Quebec to supervise personally the passage through the legislature of the grammar and separate school bills of 1863. Not surprisingly, given the politics of the era, the grammar school bill played second fiddle to the separate school question and was delayed until the politicians had secured the passage of the Scott Act. After second reading in March, the grammar school bill was sent to a special committee for review; Ryerson nevertheless was still optimistic, telling Hodgins that "I have no doubt of the bill passing."[37] It never emerged from the committee, however, and thus Ryerson lost his fourth grammar school bill in a decade. The immediate cause of its demise was the political crisis which engulfed the ministry late in the session.[38] But there were also a variety of objections that would probably have led to its defeat in any case. Complaints were lodged about tying the grant to classics and French alone, for example, and to the lack of provision for improving the education of girls.[39] Above all, there was opposition to the introduction of local assessment. Ryerson, and later Hodgins, felt that this was the decisive issue, as it had been since 1850.[40] Opinion was widespread that the grammar schools served only those who could well afford to pay for their own education, that they were gateways to well-paid professions and therefore did not deserve further subsidy from public funds, and that they were town schools of little use to the vast majority of farmers who would nonetheless be forced to pay for them if county assessment were introduced. There were even complaints that local assessment violated the rules of fairness and the eternal truths of political economy. "Let us see how the thing would operate," wrote the editor of the *Leader*:

Here are two farmers of equal means, living side by side; each has half a dozen children; all girls in the one case, and all boys in the other. The one who has the boys sends them to the grammar school, while the father of the girls contributes toward the school as much as his neighbour and derives no educational advantage from it. This thing of giving everybody everything for nothing, and making everybody else, though not a whit better able, pay for it, may be carried too far. It is a sound principle of political economy that those who enjoy an advantage should pay for it, if they are able ... Besides a thing is seldom held at true value if it costs the recipient nothing. Come easy go easy, it is as old as the hills and as true as the gospel.[41]

Ryerson's only victory in 1863 came when the government allocated enough additional funds to allow him, for the first time, to hire a full-time grammar school inspector. The job went to George Paxton Young, a Scotsman educated at the Edinburgh High School and Edinburgh University, who had taught mathematics at a leading Scottish burgh school and then become a Free Church clergyman. He emigrated to Upper Canada just before mid-century and over the next decade became a leading member of the Free Church and professor at Knox College, the church's divinity school. For years at Knox he taught the "preliminary course," the pre-divinity literary course designed to finish the general education of those candidates for the ministry who lacked the classical and other qualifications that would admit them as matriculants to University College – ideal preparation for evaluating the strengths and weaknesses of the Upper Canadian grammar schools.

Later in his career, after he had resigned as grammar school inspector, he was appointed professor of metaphysics at University College; but he would remain a powerful influence in Ontario education generally, a senior, if part-time, adviser to Ryerson and then to Ontario's first minister of education, a frequent guest speaker at the annual meetings of the Ontario Teachers' Association, member of the Council of Public Instruction in the early 1870s, and perennial chairman of the Central Committee of Examiners throughout that decade.[42] But for four years, from 1864 to 1868, he would devote all his time to the grammar schools, visiting every school twice a year and for the first time providing a thorough assessment of the state of the schools along with thoughtful recommendations for reform. Indeed his last two reports were, as Ryerson remarked, "more the reports of a School Commission on the state of the schools and suggestions for their improvement than the ordinary reports of a School Inspector."[43] Altogether it was a landmark appointment, and, aside from Ryerson himself, no one would play a greater role in shaping grammar school policy in the 1860s and 1870s.

In his first general report on the grammar schools, for the year 1864, Young reviewed the major problems other inspectors had been hammering at for years.[44] In a few crisp pages he condemned the excessive number of schools, which now stood at nearly a hundred, and remarked that "not a few of the schools, thus hastily established, are grammar schools in name, rather than reality, the work done in them being almost altogether common school work which, as a rule, would be much better performed in a well appointed common school ... Needless and contemptible grammar schools are a blot upon the whole School System." He pointed out how the grant was frittered away on such schools, diminishing the salaries of other grammar school teachers and weakening all of the better schools in the counties. Moreover, the multiplication of weak grammar schools also undermined neighbouring common schools since

where there is little or no demand for higher education the Master is obliged to occupy himself with common school subjects, and, in such circumstances, I have sometimes found the pleasant theory prevailing, that an English education is given in the grammar school of a superior kind, to what could be obtained in a mere common school. Of course there could be no more effectual way of keeping the common schools of a district in a low state than professedly to make some such provision for performing the higher part of that work which properly belongs to them.

Young went on to attack the union schools, arguing that though some were of high quality, "of nothing am I more convinced than that, as a rule, such union is undesirable": in too many cases the master had to teach both senior common school and grammar school pupils and whenever that happened the grammar school pupils were neglected, failing to receive the training in classics and mathematics that the Grammar School Fund was intended to support. He was especially critical of unions in the larger towns or cities, where he thought they were least necessary. These were, he wrote, "the natural centres of the higher education" and "therefore, in our Cities and large towns more than anywhere else, should we be careful to disconnect the grammar schools from all foreign and unnecessary adjuncts that would in any degree repress their vitality, or cramp their efficient action." Finally, he called for improved financial support. He was doubtful about the wisdom of yet another local body such as the grammar school trustees being given the right to levy a school rate, but he recommended that county councils be required to provide accommodation and a set sum annually for the support of their schools.

It was a tough report but not a savage one, and Young ended on an optimistic note that, in the light of subsequent events, seems somewhat incongruous, though it may well reflect a more judicious assessment of the state of the average grammar school than anything in the official record over the next few years. While there were indeed some thoroughly miserable schools, he wrote,

I regard these less as integral parts of the System, than as unhealthy excrescences, to be lopped off at the earliest possible opportunity. Leaving out of view schools of this sort, I do not hesitate to say that the grammar schools of Upper Canada, for as many of them as confessedly fall below the mark which it is desired that they should reach, are, as a class, not only in the promise of what they may become, but in what they actually are, at the present moment, an honour to the Country. We must not look for too much. It would be preposterous to expect, at this early period in the history of our province that its Grammar Schools generally should be able to bear comparison with the better Classical and Mathematical Schools of Great Britain and Ireland. To this, Canada does not pretend, but she has begun well, and appears to be steadily, if not rapidly progressing.

It was, however, the more pessimistic and critical passages that Ryerson, and indeed, Young himself tended to emphasize as they prepared to renew their campaign for revised grammar school legislation. In late January 1865 Ryerson wrote John A. Macdonald, explaining that "the thorough inspection of the grammar schools during the last year has brought more clearly to light than ever many abuses in connection with them and the absolute necessity of some additional legal provisions and regulations." He proposed a short bill "of three or four clauses" and an improved code of regulations, the bill to be introduced in the forthcoming session of Parliament.[45] Ryerson went to Quebec in March to shepherd the bill along, but within a few days the House prorogued because of the defeat of the cause of Confederation in New Brunswick, and the bill was deferred until summer.[46] Anxious to avoid yet another delay, however, Ryerson met with Macdonald on 7 March and convinced him to allow new regulations to be issued forthwith.[47] These had already been prepared by Ryerson and Young and were approved by the Council of Public Instruction in March, by the government in April, and published along with explanatory circulars early in May 1865.[48]

The new regulations tied funding to the average attendance of students learning Greek or Latin in any particular school and also required each school to have a minimum daily average attendance of at least ten pupils learning Latin. These conditions were to be rigorously enforced by central inspection. Moreover, the administration of the entrance exam was no longer left in the hands of the local school trustees. The initial or preliminary examination would still be carried out locally, but no pupil could be counted for grant purposes until the visit of the grammar school inspector "who shall finally examine and admit such pupils to the Grammar School." This in itself was a significant change, but one other clause was even more dramatic: "nor shall any other than pupils learning the Greek or Latin languages be admitted or continued in any Grammar School." Finally, a new program of studies was introduced consisting of a combined course of English and classical studies that banned options or partial courses.

These changes promised a veritable revolution in the schools. Since it was assumed that few girls would take Latin or Greek, girls were implicitly excluded from the grammar schools. Those boys who wanted to complete an English education without studying the classics were excluded outright. "The common school law," Ryerson explained, "amply provides for giving the best kind of a superior English education in central schools in the cities, towns and villages."[49] Small grammar schools that could not raise ten classical scholars would cease to exist and the fund would thus be expended to best advantage. Moreover, it would be expended in proportion to the number of pupils each school educated, thus rewarding the more successful and effective institutions. The prescribed course would ensure a complete education in a combined course of classical and English studies that would adequately prepare students for their future vocations.

Over the summer Ryerson and Young did what they could to defend the May regulations and the rigorous dualism they imposed on the school system. In his correspondence with local officials, Ryerson repeatedly explained that the regulations posed no threat to the availability of a good non-classical education: "boys who want a superior commercial education," he told one upset grammar school trustee, "can get it at the common schools, but are out of place in a grammar school unless they want to learn Latin and Greek, the mathematics being as well-taught to as great an extent in the best common schools as in any grammar school."[50] The August issue of the *Journal of Education for Upper Canada* carried a lengthy and pointed review of "the

Higher Schools in Prussia," emphasizing that though the *Gymnasien* and the *Real-Schulen* differed in their curricula, "they do not differ in the principles on which their respective curricula are framed: that principle being, in each case, to aim at the thorough preparation and cultivation of the mind for its future work, whatever that work may be."[51] As well, both Ryerson and Young attended the August meeting of the Ontario Teachers' Association, where Ryerson defended the changes in the grammar schools as attempts to rescue them from the "mongrel affair" they had become, while Young described the abuses he had uncovered:

In many of them he had learned that none of the pupils were in Greek, nor Latin, nor Euclid, nor English Grammar. (laughter) This, he contended, was a fraud upon the country, and should be put a stop to. Common schools should do the work of common schools, and grammar schools should be strictly confined to instructing pupils in the study of the classical education.[52]

In the larger towns and cities the new regulations do not seem to have caused much stir, presumably because Latin classes alone were enough to sustain their grammar schools. But there was consternation in smaller communities. Girls would be excluded from the schools. So would boys taking only English, or mathematics, or commercial subjects. Villages that could not provide an average attendance of ten classical pupils would lose their schools altogether. The regulations, in other words, threatened to destroy the whole fabric of superior education outside the larger towns and cities.

Those people with a stake in the schools did not suffer their loss in silence. Small-town newspaper editors condemned the regulations categorically.[53] Protests poured into the Education Office from trustees, teachers, and parents who lived in the smaller Upper Canadian communities. The chairman of the board of the Newmarket grammar school summed up two of the chief complaints succinctly: "I was thrown into perfect consternation on reading your Official Circular," he wrote Ryerson;

It appears to me to be going back to the *Dark Ages* when nothing was taught but classics; as to myself I am a man quite in love with the classics, consequently all my sympathies and prejudices are on that side but although no mathematician myself I cannot shut my eyes to the fact, that Mathematical Science is every year becoming more thought of and more important, and certainly ought to be placed upon the same level with the classics in the grammar schools; it certainly is in England ...

You have never taken any notice of girls attending the grammar schools, they were never intended to be instituted for girls, nevertheless their attendance has always been allowed or winked at; in the country such permission is the greatest possible boon. Take for instance Newmarket – a dozen Young Ladies get an excellent education at our Grammar School, which they could not obtain elsewhere; there is no

Ladies School here worth anything and none of the parents could afford to send them to expensive schools in Toronto.[54]

A like sense of grievance was expressed by a resident of Lanark. The local grammar school, he informed Ryerson, could not raise an average of ten classical pupils and if the new regulations were enforced the school would have to be closed. There was, he added, "a very general feeling of disappointment here at the prospect of losing the Grammar School – the opinion being on every hand that the new Regulations will favour the Grammar Schools in the cities and larger towns at the expense and to the unfair detriment of education in the smaller towns and villages."[55]

Ryerson, however, was not the only recipient of complaints. Teachers, parents, and trustees made their sentiments known to the politicians as well. For example, the grammar school teacher at Belleville warned his MP that the new regulations were unfair:

Ample provision should of course be made for the classics; but is the Council of Public Instruction not going too far in requiring all Grammar School pupils to study Latin and Greek? All boys are not fitted by nature for the study of the Classics. Should the regulations referred to be enforced, there is reason to fear, that even in the case of many Grammar Schools of the first class, the attendance will be reduced to a mere handful ... It seems hard for instance that a young man wishing to attend a Grammar School in order to acquire the mathematics, with a view to his becoming a surveyor or engineer, should be excluded because he will not consent to give large portions of his time also to Greek and Latin. Girls too who in several Grammar Schools are pursuing with great advantage to themselves the high or English branches, will have to leave ... Better I think to let the law stand as at present as regards the division of pupils but enforce it strictly.[56]

The opposition also made itself heard at the Teachers' Association meeting. Though Ryerson and Young received some support from city teachers, and also from some common school teachers who objected to their senior classes being depleted by transfers to the grammar schools, the majority carried motions regretting the exclusive emphasis on the classics and the exclusion of girls.[57]

By the time Parliament reconvened in late August 1865, it was clear that compromises would have to be made. There were widespread objections from MPs over the exclusion of all but classical pupils.[58] Ryerson himself had already conceded that the outcry against the exclusion of girls would have to be propitiated.[59] Moreover, without some modification of the regulations, the grammar school bill, left over from the previous session, would have no chance of passage through the House. Thus Ryerson and his advisers set out to preserve what they could of the May regulations and, at the same time, to win support for a bill which, if less than perfect, would still provide the statutory authority they needed to complete the reformation of the grammar schools.

This time, Ryerson was successful, notwithstanding the opposition he had aroused over the summer. Though its passage was not smooth, and amendments had to be accepted, the bill, unlike so many of its predecessors, did indeed become law. In part this was probably due to the fact that Hodgins stayed in Quebec to advise ministers and to argue the case with ordinary MPs, something Ryerson believed to be crucial in school matters.[60] But what was more important, the supervision of educational issues had been assigned to William McDougall, an influential member of the cabinet. In the past, no minister had had a particular commitment to, or responsibility for, education, and thus it was easy for school bills to get lost in the shuffle of events. McDougall, who described himself to Hodgins as "virtually Minister of Education," was prepared to push the bill hard, even when some of his cabinet colleagues would have been happier to leave it to the new legislature of Ontario.[61] McDougall also had the political skills to ensure its passage. He made it clear, on the one hand, to Hodgins (and through him to Ryerson back in Toronto) that the May regulations were insupportable, and, on the other, struck "an understanding … with members of the Legislature" that if they supported the bill, the regulations would indeed be modified to take account of girls, and of boys who didn't enrol in the classics.[62] Clever tactics accompanied astute compromises. "The Bill passed the second reading at 3 AM," Hodgins told Ryerson, and after its passage McDougall had winked at Hodgins in the corridor, remarking that he "knew this was the time to take them so as to get the Bill through without discussion."[63] After it was all over, Ryerson recognized McDougall's crucial role, thanking him publicly in the pages of the *Journal of Education*.[64] Indeed it may have been this event more than anything else which convinced Ryerson that Education, like other departments of government, needed a political head, an idea he had adamantly opposed earlier in his career but one he would begin to advocate regularly in the near future.

The bill, which became the Grammar School Amendment Act of 1865, accomplished three important ends.[65] First, it transferred some control for the administration of the schools from the county councils to the incorporated urban areas. In the five cities, the schools were to be entirely the responsibility of trustees appointed by the city councils alone. Everywhere else the county council and the council of the incorporated town or village where the school was located each appointed three trustees. Thus the urban communities where the schools were actually located, and where most of the pupils lived, gained some say for the first time in how the schools were run. More important, however, new financial provisions for the support of the grammar school were introduced. The act required that a sum matching at least half the sum apportioned to each school from the Grammar School Fund was to be raised from local sources. It did not specify that the sum had to be raised by a school rate. There continued to be too much opposition for that, and, indeed, even this clause met stiff criticism from many MPS. Moreover, if a rate was to be imposed, it need not be levied on the entire county but only against the town or township where the grammar school was located. What the clause did do, however, was to require the county (or city) councils to raise funds by one means or another – if not by a rate, then from the Clergy Reserve Fund, or from the general fund of the municipality, or from some other source. Though not nearly as strong as the clause in the bill of 1863, then, it constituted a major breakthrough, for local councils were now, for the first time, required to assume financial responsibility for their grammar schools.

Finally, the act created the conditions through which Ryerson and Young hoped to exercise quality control over the schools. It gave legislative sanction to apportion the grant on the basis of daily average attendance of pupils "in the programme of studies prescribed by law," and it specified that no new grammar schools were to be established unless the Grammar School Fund was sufficient to allow an apportionment of $300 to each new school without diminishing the amount available to other schools – $100 above the minimum set in 1853. Not only would this make it more difficult for councils to authorize new schools, but together with the local contribution it would guarantee even the smallest schools a total of $450, exclusive of fees, for teachers' salaries. The average attendance clause gave Ryerson statutory authority for something he had desperately sought since the later 1850s,[66] and, incidentally, finally eliminated the additional grant to senior grammar schools, the last legacy of the Public School Act of 1807.

And what had Ryerson and his colleagues sacrificed to get their act? The most important compromise was, not surprisingly, over the classics. The bill had originally restricted the apportionment to average attendance in Latin or Greek alone, but Hodgins warned Ryerson early in September that this clause was entirely unacceptable.[67] Both men were nervous about depending entirely on average attendance without any subject restrictions, however, and for good reason. If the average attendance of girls and boys studying only English subjects was allowed to count for the grant, there would be no assurance that classical studies would be given priority in most grammar schools. One alternative canvassed by Hodgins was to add payment by results to the clause so that, along with average attendance, the grant might be distributed according to proficiency in the higher subject as measured by examinations by the inspectorate. Ryerson was apparently tempted; they had both discussed the subject with the Rev. James Fraser during the latter's tour of North America in 1865 for the English Schools Inquiry Commission and they had been impressed with his testimony about the success of the scheme in England. But the idea was dropped, apparently because it was unworkable without at least three full-time inspectors and there was no promise of additional funds for that purpose.[68] Thus they settled for the average attendance clause alone and the hope that they could stiffen its effectiveness by judiciously drafted regulations.

The new regulations, prepared by Ryerson and Young, were issued in November 1865.[69] The provision in the May regulations that required each school to have an average attendance of at least ten pupils in classics was saved, thereby guaranteeing a minimum classical threshold below which no school could fall. In place of a single prescribed program, however, two courses of study were introduced. The first was, as in May, the classical program, combining Latin, Greek, mathematics, and English subjects. The second course, called "the English programme," was designed for "pupils desiring to become surveyors, or to study for matriculation in the University of Toronto as students in Civil Engineering, or to study the higher English branches and French without taking Latin or Greek." The average attendance figure, crucial to determining the amount of a school's grant, would be calculated from the number of students enrolled in these two programs.

Both of these programs of study were intended for boys alone. Girls were not allowed, under any circumstances, to enrol in the English program. They were not explicitly excluded from the classical program, but it was assumed that if they entered it they would substitute French for classics. Thus they would have a place to complete an English education and to begin the study of French. They could not, however, be counted as either classical or English students for the purposes of the grant unless they actually took Latin.

The November regulations also changed the grammar school entrance standard for the first time since 1855. Drawing on an idea he had first proposed in 1863, Ryerson introduced two different standards, one for the classical and another for the English program. The standard for the classical program was set slightly lower than the old standard, at a point just short of completion of the first division of the common school – in other words, it required a boy to complete the rudiments of English literacy but little more. Once again the traditional justifications underpinning the grammar school as a distinct and separate institution were presented: the entrance examination had been made easier than before, said Ryerson,

as it is the universal opinion of good educators that boys in order to become proficient classical scholars must begin at an early age, which would be impossible if they were previously required to go through an extended course of Common School work. The Common Schools have an ample field in the instruction of the vast number of children for whom classical learning is not required.[70]

The entrance standard for the English program, on the other hand, was set very high, at least as high as the end of the second division of common school studies. And again the familiar justification:

A great drawback to the advancement of the common schools, especially in rural villages, has been the facility with which some of the so called grammar schools could interfere with and even reduce the standard of education below that of an ordinary common school. Under the new act, however, the grammar school standard of education will be definitely fixed and uniformly maintained in all the schools; while the efforts of the Department can now be directed without hindrance to raising the standard of the common schools, so that both classes of schools will be enabled to do their own work. [71]

Girls, it should be added, were to be subjected to the second, higher standard when they enrolled in the partial classical program that substituted French for Latin and Greek, yet another wrinkle in the attempt to make it as difficult as possible for girls to attend the grammar schools. [72]

Finally, one other innovation was considered to be of crucial importance in policing the system. Since 1853 the entrance examination had been conducted by the headmaster of the school itself. As of November 1865, pupils could be admitted to the grammar school by the headmaster on a preliminary basis only. On his first visit each year the grammar school inspector was to "finally examine and admit all pupils to the Grammar Schools," and no pupil could be counted towards the grant without passing this final examination. For the first time, in other words, the central authority had real power to direct the development of the grammar schools: prescribed programs from which there could be no deviation; average and minimum attendance rules that gave an advantage to classics; and a full-time inspector to enforce the act and regulations.

Ryerson claimed that the November regulations were a compromise, but this was more than a little disingenuous. [73] Forced to give up his cherished notion of the grammar school as solely a classical school, he gave away as little else as possible. Entry to the classical program was set very low so as to pose no impediment to classical studies by boys. They were allowed to enter the grammar school immediately after they had learned their three Rs and Ryerson expected this transition to take place by age ten. [74] The English program was, however, fenced in with restrictions. In public, Ryerson always asserted that the grammar schools were not only classical but "English high schools." [75] The entry standard to the English program, however, was set prohibitively high for most pupils, while at the same time he continued to insist that the proper place for non-classical pupils to complete their education was in the upper divisions of the common school. In private, on occasion, he was more forthright. "The English Course of Studies in the

Grammar School," he told a correspondent in 1867, "was not designed as a finishing course of studies for Common School education but was specially urged upon the Council of Public Instruction and the Government and was designed to enable young men to prepare themselves for becoming Surveyors and Civil Engineers without pursuing Classical Studies." Students who did not wish to embark on the study of the classics, he added, had a legal right to complete all of the studies of the common school program in the common school itself, and it was the duty of common school trustees to provide them with the opportunity to do so.[76]

Ryerson, then, made the fewest possible concessions. Small, weak schools would still disappear for they could not raise the required ten classical pupils. The grant would still be concentrated on the largest schools with high average attendance. The attendance of girls would diminish, since trustees and teachers had little incentive to encourage them unless they were enrolled in Latin – something that Ryerson and Young assumed few sensible parents would permit. The high entrance standard for the English program would discourage boys not interested in pursuing classical studies. Thus the primacy of the classical course would be preserved in the grammar schools and the common schools would not be robbed of their more advanced English students. For the moment at least, it appeared as though Ryerson had finally achieved the goals he had sought for nearly a decade.

CHAPTER EIGHT

The Revenge of the "Parasite Grammar Schools," 1866–69

Armed with the new powers they had acquired under the act and regulations of 1865, Ryerson and Young set out with as much dispatch as possible to impose order and direction on the grammar schools. During the autumn of 1865 and throughout 1866, Young visited all of the grammar schools, administering the final entrance examination and then carrying out a more general inspection of each school. According to his own account he examined "about 2000 children individually" in 1865, and the numbers must have been much the same the next year.[1] In both years Young routinely failed 20, 30 or even 50 per cent of the youngsters he examined, thus massively reducing the number of pupils local trustees could claim for their share of the grant. By autumn 1866, the point had been made: the percentage of failures dropped off sharply as headmasters began to conduct their own preliminary examinations more diligently or began, at least, to "prep" their new pupils more carefully for the inspector's visit. Perhaps for the first time, Ryerson could legitimately claim that pupils learning only the three Rs had been eliminated from the grammar schools.[2]

Young's impact did not stop there, however. He assessed the quality of the physical plant and checked to ensure that authorized texts were being used, that the school had the minimum number of required pupils, that the prescribed program was being followed, and that the long list of other objectives set out in his instructions was being met.[3] In those cases where he judged improvement necessary he might issue his own warnings, but for serious offences he usually alerted the Education Office as well. Ryerson and Hodgins, in turn, sent out letters that implicitly or explicitly threatened to cut off the grant unless trustees took steps to remedy the defects Young had identified. The Renfrew trustees, for example, were bluntly told that the average attendance in classics was only 6½ and their schoolhouse totally inadequate. "Unless satisfactory measures are immediately taken to improve the state of the school," Ryerson wrote, "it will lose its right to participate in the grant of 1866." Within a week the trustees wrote back "in haste" to say that attendance "is now in excess of the required number and they hoped to improve accommodation very soon."[4] To teachers confronted by students who wanted to study only one or two subjects, Hodgins explained that such optionalized studies would "let in again all the disorder which the programme and regulations are designed to remedy. Such exceptions therefore are not permitted unless in special cases when recommended by the inspector."[5] To those who wanted to organize their union schools so that pupils were automatically transferred to the grammar school for their higher subjects, Ryerson was no less firm. Parents had the right, he replied, to demand that the full common school program be offered in the common school itself. "However desirable it may be," he told one trustee,

that the youth of your town should be as highly educated as possible, the law will not compel the attendance of any pupil in the Grammar School Department, either for the classical or non-classical course. The occupation for which a lad is destined may very properly influence a parent in holding the opinion that the thorough grounding in the Elementary English will be better for his son than a year or two attempting new objects which will not perhaps be so important in his intended career.[6]

Initially, then, the aggressive assertion of central policy, along with thorough inspection, won the Education Office a number of victories. Accommodation appeared to be improving. The prescribed program of studies was increasingly followed. Above all, an effective entrance examination had been put in place. Given the history of the grammar schools, this was no small achievement, and the reports written during 1866 by both Ryerson and Young reflect a spirit of cautious optimism and the conviction that the schools were finally responding to the firm slap of government.

Their optimism, however, was to be short-lived. Not only did some of their own policies backfire, producing results just the opposite of what they had intended, but it proved far more difficult to uproot established practices and local arrangements than Ryerson or Young had ever imagined. Local people vigorously resisted the transformation of their schools, first by subverting the intent of the act and regulations, and then by vociferous and public opposition to the very principles embedded in official policy. Within three short years, indeed, the new departure of 1865 was a shambles, and Ryerson and Young had conceded its defeat.

To begin with, the attempt to eliminate the union grammar and common schools turned into a fiasco. Indeed, though the process was somewhat circuitous, the act of 1865 actually *promoted* the movement to form union schools. The new legislation, it will be remembered, required grammar school trustees to raise half the amount of the government grant from some local source. One of the chief reasons for this clause had been to increase the financial independence of the grammar schools and thus to render unions with the local common school less necessary.[7] County councils, however, routinely refused to levy a grammar school rate on their rural constituents, leaving the local contribution to be raised by the community in which the school was actually located. At the same time, rising failure rates at the entrance examination reduced the number of grammar school pupils and thereby reduced the size of the government grant. As a result many non-union schools came under increasing financial pressure and some of the smaller schools were threatened with closure. But that eventuality, in turn, would have increased the pressure on common school trustees to provide more in the way of advanced instruction in the common school itself at increased expense to the local taxpayer.

The solution to both these problems, in local eyes at least, was a union of boards and schools. By this means grammar school trustees would gain access to the common school rate and thus meet the terms of the act, which required some form of local financial support as a condition of receiving the government grant. Once in possession of the grant, moreover, the joint board could use it to subsidize the costs of all the superior education the community might need. Both the grammar and common school boards, in other words, had always had something to gain by union, but because local funding was now a precondition for receiving the grant, the incentives to union were even stronger. Since the locality was going to be taxed for its grammar school in any case, there seemed to be no good reason not to unite the schools. The consequence was that despite a continuing stream of condemnation heaped on the union schools by Ryerson and Young, the number of unions actually increased from just over one-half in 1865 to two-thirds of all grammar schools in 1869. Indeed, by this means even the smallest and weakest schools managed to survive and thus thwart the intent of official policy to close them down.[8]

A disaster of equal proportions was caused by the restrictive conditions imposed on the English program of studies. In their determination to transform the grammar schools into classical schools for boys, Ryerson and Young had not only excluded girls from the English program but had set its entry standards so high, and made the program itself so advanced and specialized, that nobody enrolled in it at all. "From the first," Young wrote in 1866,

I was satisfied that there was no real demand ... for such a course of study as this curriculum for boys and the event has proved the correctness of my opinion. In the Grammar Schools – more than 80 in number – in which ... I have examined pupils with a view to their admission ... 7 boys in all have come forward to be examined for the course of higher English, French, and Mathematics; and of these only three have passed the prescribed entrance examination.[9]

Whatever the "correctness" of his opinion, Young's smug dismissal of the English program overlooked the fact that its failure was having a devastating, and certainly unintended, effect on enrolment patterns within the grammar schools. Boys did not select the English program. Girls could not enter it at all and could, indeed, earn grant money only if they took the full classical course. In other words, only enrolments in Latin offered any source of grant revenue. The results were predictable, and introduced an enlivening moment of farce into Ryerson's normally sober-sided administration of the school system. Determined to extract the largest possible grant, or in many cases to save a small school from extinction, trustees encouraged and in a few instances forced all pupils, both boys and girls, to take Latin. In union schools especially, Young reported, mass promotions to the grammar school had taken place: in St Mary's, for example, "the entire upper division of the Common School had recently been elevated by the Trustees to the status of Grammar School pupils."[10] In Brockville, the principal of the central school complained, the trustees had insisted on promoting everyone who could pass the entrance examination "as such pupils in the Common School do not probably augment the government money to the school *one* dollar per head, whereas such pupils in their proper place in the Grammar School would augment the income of the Grammar School probably at least *thirty dollars* per head."[11]

Boys who had no intention of pursuing Latin long enough to benefit from it were routinely enrolled in the classical program, reported Young; but far more critical, so were masses of girls. Owen Sound was typical:

In the early part of the year, the study of Latin was confined to boys; before my second visit, a large number of girls had commenced Latin. I cannot believe that this was owing to any sudden persuasion, on the part of parents, that it would be a good thing for their daughters to become classical scholars. I have no doubt that the movement has been produced solely by a consideration of the fact, that, when girls take Latin, the school receives a pecuniary benefit.[12]

In Wardsville, Young remarked, all the girls in the school were enrolled in Latin:

as the number of boys in the school had become very small, pressure seems to have been brought to bear on the girls to get them to take Latin, to save the school from perishing ... I could not resist the feeling that for these girls to be learning Latin was an utter waste of time.[13]

There was nothing illegal about enrolling girls in Latin, as Ryerson repeatedly acknowledged. He had, of course, intended girls to substitute French for classics, in which case they would not count for grant purposes, but neither the act nor the regulations actually prevented girls from taking the full classical program and thus earning their share of the grant.[14] In early 1866 before the influx was fully apparent, Ryerson was cautious about condemning the presence of girls. By the autumn, however, the opposition from the Education Office was undisguised and adamant. "It is not the intention of the Grammar School Law and Regulations to encourage the attendance of girls in the Grammar Schools," Hodgins told one headmaster; "you are not advised to instruct girls in the classical course as it is not adapted for them, and it is probable that in the future the attendance of such pupils will not be reckoned."[15]

It was, perhaps, a fine irony that Ryerson had finally achieved near-universal enrolment in Latin but only in a form that outraged his sense of good practice and propriety. Because he was away in Europe from November 1866, nothing was done about the situation till his return in May 1867. Then, in what can only be described as a panic measure, the Education Office announced that the forthcoming grant would be based on a calculation which made two girls studying Latin the equivalent of one boy. Ryerson was never more explicit about his own conception of the grammar school than in his justification for this bizarre innovation.

It is the received opinion of all educationists – with very few exceptions ... that their [girls' and boys'] more advanced education should be continued separately. The plan on which all private educational efforts for the higher branches are conducted shows this to be the feeling of the community.

The Council of Public Instruction in framing a programme of studies for Grammar Schools has acted upon the principle that these were boys schools ... But the courses of study adopted, one classical, and one for high English and Mathematical Studies, in order that they may be the best fitted for maturing the intellect of boys, and preparing them to enter the Universities and professions of life, are for that very reason, not at all adapted for girls ... Any course of study which would attempt to be equally excellent for the higher education of boys and girls, would be simply caricatures for either. It therefore becomes advisable to discourage the present unusual attendance of girls at grammar schools.[16]

The new rule only exacerbated the situation, however. The number of boys and girls in "qualifying Latin" continued to multiply, as did the number of union schools. Early in 1867 Young wrote a pessimistic review of the situation and by October an increasingly shrill Ryerson asked the attorney-general, Sandfield Macdonald, for an opinion as to whether girls had any legal right whatsoever to attend the grammar schools.[17] It took Macdonald six months to formulate an answer, but in May 1868 he replied that his personal views were "exactly in accordance" with Ryerson's on the "impropriety of permitting girls to be received in Grammar Schools." His interpretation of the intent of the grammar school law was, moreover, that "boys only should be admitted to these schools and that consequently the Grammar School Fund was intended for the classical, mathematical and higher English education of boys."[18]

Immediately, Ryerson announced that the grant would be apportioned solely on the basis of boys' attendance.[19] Strictly speaking, this did not altogether exclude girls, for under the regulations they could still enrol in the partial course, substituting French for Latin. But it did mean that trustees and teachers would have little incentive to provide instruction for them, since the girls generated no revenue beyond their tuition fees. Whatever the technicalities, in other words, the intent was to eliminate, as much as possible, the attendance of girls in the grammar schools.

Even as they introduced the prohibition on girls, however, Ryerson and Young were already privately conceding that the policies of 1865 had failed. For his part Young had drafted two highly critical but perceptive assessments of the state of the schools – assessments which, though not actually published until late 1868, constituted his annual reports for 1866 and 1867.[20] Throughout his inspectorate Ryerson had always encouraged Young to visit the common schools in towns where the grammar schools were located and especially those where the two schools were united. Thus Young's reports are not simply reviews of the grammar schools but are, rather, surveys of the general state of higher studies in urban Upper Canada.

The tendencies he had observed in the schools, Young wrote in 1867, had led to the degradation of both the common school and the grammar school. Particularly in the union schools, the result of the average attendance rule was that "boys and girls alike are, as soon as they have got the merest smattering of English Grammar, driven like sheep into the Grammar School, and put into Latin in order to swell the roll of Grammar School pupils." The purpose of the common school, Young continued, was "to furnish a good English and general education to those desiring it." But how could this be accomplished "when the machinery of the union is managed in such a way as systematically to empty the Common Schools of all moderately advanced pupils, male and female, and therefore to leave only very elementary work to be done by the Common Schools?" He had heard it said that the degradation of the common school department was counterbalanced by the facilities available in the grammar school department; but this notion made a decent English education conditional on the study of Latin. "Such an idea, when nakedly put, must be felt to be monstrous." The common schools could be seen in two ways: as "having a complete and independent work of their own to perform, namely to impart a good English education to those desiring it," or "as institutions designed to prepare pupils for the Grammar Schools. It will not be denied," he presumed, "that the former of these offices is incomparably the more important of the two." And yet in too many schools the common school department had ceased altogether to offer "the upper parts of what may be called a fair Common School programme. I look upon this," he concluded,

as an excessive evil. I have such a sense of the importance of maintaining a high standard of education in the Common Schools, that, rather than see them degraded … I would be willing that all the Grammar Schools in the country should perish. I protest against making the Common Schools, in all above the most primary classes, mere hotbeds to force forward seedlings for the classical field.

Lest this be construed as an attack on classics *per se*, Young emphasized in his report for 1867 that he considered classics an indispensable part of liberal education, and he reviewed at some length the case for classical studies recently expounded by J.S. Mill. But the benefits of classics could only be purchased by prolonged study and that was precisely the problem. Most of Upper Canada's Latin pupils "have no object in prosecuting a classical course of study," and their "circumstances and views in life render it perfectly certain that they will never become classical scholars in any proper sense of the expression." For them, it was nothing but a waste of time and they "ought not to be compelled or induced to enter on the study of Latin." Nominal Latin, moreover, corrupted and degraded the grammar school itself, encouraging no more than study of the rudiments and a "false show" of classical learning. And this was especially true in those schools located in small villages where there was no demand for Latin and where it was taught solely to obtain the grant.

For girls, Latin was not only a waste of time but a destructive diversion of energies as well. There was no doubt, said Young, that girls were as capable as boys of learning Latin, but that was not the point. A smattering of Latin "while it is a miserable education for either boys or girls, is especially miserable for the latter." Girls would never find Latin "of practical benefit to them in life" and no less important, it would swallow up "the principal opportunity of intellectual cultivation which they are ever likely to possess." Boys, he continued,

who obtain no culture at school may, perhaps, if their minds are of a vigorous order, gather a considerable measure of it afterwards in their intercourse with the world. But the sphere of women is more retired than that of men. Hence, if girls leave school without the beginnings of culture, there is the greatest danger of their remaining uncultivated all their lives. What a pity, then, that so many of our Grammar School girls should be sacrificed on the altars of the classical Divinities … What a benefit it would be, to girls even more than boys, if the pretence of Latin … were swept away as rubbish, and the ground cleared for the introduction of something worthy of the name of education.

Young's assessment, in sum, was that existing arrangements – above all, the provisions for union schools and the average attendance in Latin rule – undermined the viability of either good common or grammar schools, and in the process left what he estimated to be about 75 per cent of all youngsters without the facilities to complete a good English education. What Upper Canada had was the worst of both worlds – neither high classical seminaries nor good higher English schools. But what was to be done? To put the education system "into a right condition," he wrote, "it is not enough that an end be put to the unnecessary study of Latin; a thorough reformation must be made in the teaching of English." What Upper Canada needed, in fact, was "an organization of a different sort of school from either the Grammar Schools or the existing Common Schools." Extending the curriculum of the common school upwards to provide a solid basis in the elements of an English education was the first requisite. Children under thirteen years of age who were intended for classical studies might need something more than the common school so that they could begin Latin early, but for the rest, they

have no educational wants which the Common Schools, properly conducted, are not fitted to supply. For children of 13 and upwards, who have already obtained such an Education as may be got in good Common Schools, it would, I think, be well to establish English High Schools: – a designation which I borrow from the United States, though unfortunately, I have only a vague idea of what the High Schools in the United States are.

Young went on, nevertheless, to outline a minimum curriculum of English studies, morality, physical science, history, mathematics, and French, and concluded that the establishment of such high schools "either through a development of our Common School system, or through a modification of our Grammar School system, or partly in one way and partly in the other ... would be one of the greatest services that could be rendered in the Province."

By the time Young's two reports were published in late 1868, he had already resigned as grammar school inspector and had accepted a chair at University College, Toronto. In his own annual report, Ryerson expressed regret at Young's resignation and heaped accolades on his efforts as inspector. He also agreed with Young's pessimistic assessment of the state of the schools, referring to the "perversion of the grammar schools," their "failure as superior schools," the moral dangers of "educating large boys and girls together," the irrelevance of classics for girls and for most boys, and the damage the grammar schools did to neighbouring common schools. Ryerson, indeed, concluded with an unqualified condemnation: the large majority of grammar schools, he wrote, "are little better than useless as

Classical Schools, as High English Schools, even as Elementary English schools."[21]

It was not only Young and Ryerson who believed that the grammar schools had been perverted, however. So indeed did many people who had a direct stake in the grammar schools, though their reasoning took a different course. In their view it was official policy itself that had led to the "degradation" and "perversion" of their schools. As the short-lived but effective revolt against the May regulations of 1865 had demonstrated, what Ryerson described as the *reform* of the grammar school was, to local people, an assault on established institutions that were serving them well. From the late 1850s onwards, in effect, Ryerson had been trying to undo the *ad hoc* arrangements and practices that had taken root in the two previous decades and to impose on the province a radically different kind of institution. Protests against his grammar school policies had been muted before the mid-sixties because, however much the Education Office might bluster, it lacked the power to enforce its will: local people simply ignored the inspectors' directives or complied with them in nominal ways. From 1865, however, as official policy began to operate more effectively and threatened to impose unwelcome changes on the schools, trustees, teachers, and other voices of local opinion had to learn to defend their traditional practices actively and aggressively against the incursions of the central authority.

In part they did this, as we have already suggested, by subverting the intent of the new law – by enrolling their girls and boys in qualifying Latin, for example, or by establishing preparatory classes in the common school where pupils were coached for the entrance examination and the inspector's visit. They also began to marshal a variety of ideas and arguments that could be used to attack Education Office policies, and to mount an articulate defence of their own way of doing things. The overlap between the common and grammar school programs of study is a case in point. In Ryerson's view, the grammar and common schools were intended to be two distinct, parallel institutions, and thus it was perfectly reasonable that the subjects of study in the second and third divisions of the common school should be identical to those prescribed for the junior forms of the grammar school, the only exception being that the grammar school also offered classics and French. In most smaller communities, however, with but one building and one or two teachers, it was impossible to separate the two programs. In a one-teacher school, for example, it might be possible to maintain one combined class for senior arithmetic consisting of both common and grammar school pupils; but given all of the teacher's other responsibilities, two distinct classes were out of the question. Similarly in two-teacher schools, "common sense" dictated a division of labour that assigned the common school teacher to the junior pupils while the better-educated grammar school master taught the higher subjects to all of the senior pupils regardless of whether they were formally classified as grammar or common school pupils.

Ryerson and his inspectors, however, had repeatedly condemned such arrangements, and from 1865, attempted to put a stop to the integration of the two classes of pupils. In response, trustees and teachers mounted the verbal barricades in defence of local practices by attacking the "absurdities" of trying to maintain two distinct programs in the first place. In a perceptive and passionate letter written in 1865 to G.P. Young, for example, James Cameron, the master of the Drummondville grammar school, remarked that he could not even imagine that the two programs had been drafted by the same board. Rather

it would seem as if they emanated from hostile Boards, determined that the one Institution should flourish only on the ruins of the other ... the Common Schools are required to do *all the work* of the Grammar School in the *higher* classes of English, and leave untouched only Latin, Greek and French, and yet the Grammar School is compelled to receive Pupils fit only for the *2nd Division* of the Common School! How can *collision* be avoided? The fact is, that Pupils, with rare exceptions, never come from the Common School until they have gone through the 2nd and 3rd forms ... It is true, that a *few* families object to exposing their children to the promiscuous company of a Common School; and *these* usually send their children to the Grammar School *as soon as* they come up to its *low* standard. These Pupils are *very few* in comparison with those who are drafted from the Common Schools. What are we to do with the *latter*, coming fully prepared for the *most advanced* classes in all the English branches? They want Latin, or French, and some of the *finishing* subjects such as Mathematics, –History,– Philosophy, insofar as the Grammar School courses can carry them. Am I to put them in *Latin* and confine them to the ABC of the other branches belonging to the *first* form?! Am I to restrain them from French till the *3rd year*? ... As things now stand, the two Institutions are forced into *constant* and *fratricidal* collision ... As the Programme stands, it is simply *impossible* to do the work of the Grammar School *properly* with *one* master. The Expense will, in most cases, prove an *effectual* barrier to the appointment of a Master for the *Preparatory* department, embracing at least the first two forms. The simple remedy to all this seems to me to be, the *raising* of the Grammar School *standard*. Let the Common School be, as it should be, *preparatory* to the Grammar School; and prescribe for the Grammar School *exclusively* the Classics, French, and higher branches of a solid and liberal education fitted for all who do not aspire to the learned Professions.[22]

Here was an argument that was at once a defence of existing practice, a critique of official policy, and a proposal for an alternative way of doing things. Juxtaposed against an impractical model of parallel programs and schools was a more efficient and cheaper system where the common school became an elementary school and served as a feeder to a reformed grammar school that would specialize exclusively in higher studies.

As Cameron made clear elsewhere in his letter, he at least understood the rationale behind the dual organization of schools even if he considered it unworkable. To many laymen, however, it was simply unintelligible, and when confronted by the attempt to impose it on the province in the later 1860s, they made their incomprehension palpable. "If the Central School teaches precisely the same studies as the Grammar School," wrote the editor of the *Brantford Expositor* in 1868, "and carries them *equally* or *nearly as far*, and if as reported the Central School rather *hinders* than promotes the transfer of pupils to the Grammar School, Cui Bono? of supporting two rival institutions."[23] The editor of the *London Free Press* supported the union of the grammar and central schools for the same reason. The city now had "two institutions, endowed from the same funds, sustained by the same community, and teaching the same course"; among its other advantages, union would allow the reduction of two staff members, saving more than $1100 a year, while at the same time introducing a proper system of "correct classification."[24]

It was not just the idea of distinct programs or schools that generated debate. Ryerson's scheme of tying grants exclusively to enrolments in classical studies also forced people to articulate alternative conceptions of the function of the grammar school. By the later 1850s the grammar schools, especially those in smaller communities, were already heavily involved in preparing pupils for a variety of occupations that did not require classics, such as clerical work or common school teaching.[25] Yet if Ryerson had his way, pupils who took only higher English subjects would not count for grant purposes. As the Streetsville grammar school trustees had complained as early as 1858, the rule was "unfair, especially to grammar schools in villages, where the attendance of classical pupils is in general comparatively small." In many cases, they continued, parents sought an education "in the English and French languages, and also in the sciences, superior to what they can receive in the common school." But because their children did not attend the local common school, they didn't count for the common school grant, and unless they enrolled in Latin they didn't count for the grammar school grant. Thus the entire village was penalized by the attempt to maintain the grammar school as a primarily classical institution.[26] The same argument was put in an acerbic note to Ryerson from the Colborne board of grammar school trustees. The classical requirement was, they insisted, unjust to the "large number studying Mathematics, English and Natural Science" alone.

The board would beg to submit that the Grammar Schools are emphatically the Peoples Colleges and should not by such restrictions ... be cut off from funds ...

The Grammar Schools are (or should be at least) for the benefit of the masses – and that the restrictions, if any, should relate to the higher branches of an English education, embracing Agricultural Chemistry, the Natural Sciences, the Higher Mathematics, and the Latin if you please (until such time at least that professional men will learn their mother tongue sufficiently to enable them to adopt English phraseology instead of the dead languages). These are the branches which will necessarily interest the great majority of our youth and the general diffusion of which will have the greatest tendency to elevate the Agricultural, Mechanical, Commercial, and I may say, professional population of our fair Province.[27]

Similar complaints were to be heard over and over again in the years after 1865: the conditions of the grant simply bore no relationship to the actual work of the schools and the educational arrangements of local communities.

This growing volume of criticism drew additional support from the fact that on some critical issues, Ryerson's policies were just plain muddled or contradictory. For example, the act of 1853 and the attendant regulations both made provision for two programs of study in the grammar schools, one of which did not require pupils to study classics. Yet despite the apparent intent of the law, Ryerson persistently attempted to tie funding to classical enrolments alone. Similarly, whatever his strictures about union schools, it was Ryerson himself who had encouraged them and who, indeed, had drafted the legislation that made them possible. Ryerson and Young bewailed the "degradation" of the common schools; yet the standard of entry to the grammar school had been set so low, and the per capita grant for grammar school pupils set so much higher than for common school pupils, that union boards of trustees found it almost impossible to resist the temptation to transfer, at the first opportunity, as many pupils as possible to the grammar school department. And why would urban common school trustees opt to create an English high school paid for by local taxes and common school grants, when they could have a grammar school teacher subsidized from the grammar school funds alone?

Above all there was the apparent irrationality of regulations that allowed the admission of girls for certain parts of the grammar school program but would not allow them to be counted for grant purposes unless they took Latin. The new grammar school bill made no provision for girls, an irate correspondent to the *Globe* wrote in 1865, "unless they adopt a course of study designed especially to prepare boys for law, medicine or matriculation in arts ... No one thinks this course of study suited to the wants of girls ... What reasonable answer can be given to the question why should girls be compelled to study Sallust or the love ditties of Horace?" But according to the law, he continued, they must. "Have not girls a right to a part of the Grammar School Fund ... and have they not a right also to the benefits of a system of superior education, which is in harmony with ... the sphere in which they are likely to move?"[28] The Rev. George Blair, headmaster of the Bowmanville Grammar School, voiced similar objections. In his most recent report, he said, he had listed the girls as belonging to the grammar school department even though they were not enrolled in Latin:

They are essentially a part of the same division studying French and the higher English branches, some of them studying Geometry and Algebra with myself, and mixing and reciting occasionally in all the branches with the boys of my own division. Sometimes my boys go to Miss Kyle's class-room, sometimes Miss Kyle's girls come to mine. In fact they are to all intents and purposes members of one and the same division; and I do not see how, on any correct principle of classification or of common sense, I can return the boys as in the Grammar School and the young ladies as in the Common School. In reality I think the latter average higher in attainment than those boys under my own immediate charge who do not study the classics. The classics are now only a comparatively small part of a thorough university education and I do not see why they alone should constitute the exclusive criterion of the Grammar School Department – especially as I know that in other Grammar Schools girls are returned as pupils and *are* pupils.[29]

In Ryerson's view, of course, Blair had no business encouraging the presence of girls in the first place because they simply didn't belong in grammar schools. But it was on this point, above all else, that Ryerson was most at odds with trustees, teachers, and parents alike. By the mid-sixties, girls constituted 40 or 50 per cent of grammar school enrolments and many parents had come to depend on the schools to provide all of the superior education their daughters would ever get. The country grammar schools, moreover, had already established themselves as important centres for preparing girls for the common school teachers' examinations. As one correspondent put it in the *Norfolk Messenger*, "should the new rules remain in force, the County of Norfolk will be deprived of what has virtually been a training school for female teachers, and many young ladies who might otherwise secure for themselves the honourable position of teacher, will be prevented from doing so."[30] Given the importance of the grammar schools in the education of girls by the second half of the 1860s, it is not surprising that the attempt to exclude them provoked outrage amongst local people, and, more than any other issue, mobilized the opposition to Education Office policies.

It was not that trustees, parents, and teachers had been uniformly converted to coeducation while the Education Office had not. During the late 1860s and early 1870s Upper Canadian public opinion was divided on the issue, and the preference for segregation remained strong.[31] Ryerson's exclusionary policies, nevertheless, produced one new element hitherto almost entirely absent in Upper Canada. Arguments began to be heard offering a positive defence of coeducation. Speaking before the teachers' association in 1868, for example, its president, William McCabe, quoted British and American sources that refuted the two major charges against coeducation, its moral dangers and the unsuitability of a common curriculum for boys and girls. Women, McCabe said, "have an equal right with young men to a liberal education" and thus it was time to put aside the "superficial and flimsy" aspects of the accomplishments curriculum. Teaching boys and girls together increased the diligence of the boys, "while the greater depth of the boys tells on the girls." A mixed school, moreover, "produces an enormous improvement in purity, both of boys and girls; it is difficult to say which most; because girls schools are, on the whole, rather worse than boys schools in this respect."[32] Our point here, it bears repeating, is not that such views had come to be generally accepted, for that was not the case. If some editors and educators supported coeducation, others emphatically did not.[33] What is important is that coeducation in the grammar schools now had advocates as well as opponents. For the first time it was being promoted not just as a legitimate educational arrangement but as an even *better* one than the segregation of the sexes.

The more traditional defence of coeducation, however, remained the one most often heard in the late 1860s. For the Clinton grammar school trustees, the principle of the thing was irrelevant; for most people living in small communities, there was no alternative. "We have not thought it necessary," they explained to Ryerson in 1868, "to enter into the general question whether girls and boys of the age of those who usually attend Grammar Schools should, or should not, be taught together, because, as has been before observed, if girls are excluded from the Grammar Schools, they will for the most part be sent back to be taught with Boys of the same age in the Common Schools."[34] The same point was made in the legislature by Dr William McGill. "Many girls," he said, "were now getting a good education in Grammar Schools, which they could not possibly get otherwise. Separate High Schools for the education of girls, could not, in the circumstances of our Country, be at all generally established."[35]

The Clinton trustees also pointed to another gored ox. To refuse to count girls for grant purposes was to penalize the teacher by diminishing his salary – a "result so contrary to the views which you have always urged in regard to the salaries of teachers ... that we cannot believe that the Regulation which produces it will continue to receive your approval."[36] Not surprisingly, the most vocal proponents of coeducation were the grammar school teachers themselves. Each year between 1865 and 1868 the grammar school masters saw to it that the Ontario Teachers' Association passed strong resolutions condemning the exclusion of girls. The OTA debates on the subject routinely referred to the harm exclusion did to girls and the benefits they could reap from the solid teaching available in the grammar schools. But William Tassie was probably close to the mark when he said at the annual meeting of 1868 that "they would not hear the co-education of the sexes so fully advocated if it were not for the money. He knew of many men who were advocating the admission of girls who would not send their own daughters."[37]

The grammar school masters were, no doubt, motivated by self-interest in the matter, as not only Tassie but Ryerson was wont to point out.[38] The same might be said of the small-town trustees as they fought to preserve their schools. In speaking out against Education Office policies, however, they were also building their own case for a grammar school that served broader purposes than classical studies alone. Indeed, as the gap between official policy and local realities widened during the later 1860s, alternative ways of thinking about the organization of education became not only more common but more persuasive. Educational efficiency might be better served by a division of labour based simply on pupils' ages rather than on distinctions between English and classical instruction. For both economic and educational reasons, the grammar school might better be conceived as the senior department of a village school rather than as an institution paralleling the local common school. *Faute de mieux* there was no good reason why the local grammar school shouldn't provide a suitable education for girls, or for boys who did not require classics. First articulated in the form of protests against Ryerson's policy initiatives, questions and arguments such as these were to become staple components of an alternative approach to the organization of education during the conflicts that developed in the decade after 1865.

Critics of Ryerson's policies could also draw upon the corpus of contemporary political thought. Though it was the particular property of nineteenth-century liberalism, the idea that careers must be open to talent and ability regardless of social origin was widely shared across the political spectrum. No less widely shared was the corollary that public investment in education was justified precisely because education was a powerful engine for identifying talent and giving it a fair field of opportunity. In the two decades after mid-century these ideas were already conventional components of public discourse in Upper Canada, routinely incorporated into ceremonial speeches, newspaper editorials, and political platforms. George Brown, for example, articulated this shared rhetoric when, in a defence of the rich endowments held by the University of Toronto, he remarked that he "hoped to see the day" when "the young man of any rank who shows talent, should have the means placed at his disposal to elevate himself to any position to which the acquirements of knowledge can bring him."[39] And Adam Wilson, the mayor of Toronto, was merely reiterating the mythic history invented by nineteenth-century liberalism when he told an audience in 1860 that

the older persons whom he now addressed would recollect the blessing of education was in their young days chiefly conferred on those favored classes who were able to purchase this valuable acquisition. As it was now, however, in this country, education was open to all, no matter of what rank those seeking it belonged, or what means they possessed ... The foundation of the whole massive and substantial structure was the Common School. All rested upon it – rising gradually from it to the Grammar School and college, and then to the University, where the pupils finished with honors and degrees.[40]

At annual prize-givings and public examinations, much was made of labourers' sons or "coloured" children who had won school awards, for such examples vindicated the self-image of a society where "the son of the humblest citizen may rise to the highest station."[41] The reality, of course, was something else again, as any number of historians have demonstrated. But that did not render impotent the rhetoric itself. In any age, shared convictions about social ideals, and the public oratory which taps into them, are powerful weapons and operate independently of social reality. And in any case, these were convictions that gained credence from the proofs provided by exceptional examples: in Simcoe or Stratford, bankers' sons and lawyers' daughters did indeed attend grammar school with children of poor artisans and "coloured" labourers, even if it was a token number of them.

The benchmark of an open system of education was not, in any case, measured by the number of labourers' children who attended grammar school or university. Demands for greater access tended, as the quotation from Adam Wilson makes clear, to be put in apposition to the special privileges of wealth or birth. Equal opportunity would be secured so long as the rich and the powerful were not allowed to sequester all of the advantages of a higher education for themselves. Thus phrases such as "the son of the humblest citizen" were elastic notions that easily encompassed the children of ordinary farmers, clerks, teachers, or others of limited means and no connections or "interest." By yet another extension they might include all kinds of middling people who had no patrimony to offer their children other than a prolonged education. The rhetoric of merit and a career open to talent, in other words, had a substantial political constituency, made up of those parents of small means throughout urban Upper Canada, and an even broader social group in the smaller communities, who depended on local, subsidized forms of public education to provide for their sons and daughters.[42]

As much as anyone else, Egerton Ryerson was committed to the principle that public education must cultivate the talents of individuals regardless of their wealth or social origins. Indeed, he had, from the beginning, tried to ensure that the common school was linked to the grammar school and the grammar school, in turn, to the university. Especially after 1865, nonetheless, his grammar school policies posed a threat to accessibility in several respects. The attempt to restrict the work of the schools to the classical program threatened to cut off opportunities for the higher English education of both boys and girls. The attack on union schools and the attempt to sharpen the separation of programs of study restricted the options available to pupils, forcing them to choose at a relatively young age between the classical and English programs, and every year thereafter making it more difficult to shift from one program to the other. Above all, there was the issue of the small country school. To Ryerson and Young it seemed obvious that the grammar school grant should be concentrated on fewer, better institutions. Schools which could not stand their tests of efficiency did not, in their opinion, deserve to survive. To many parents and trustees, however, this was a formula designed to deprive their children of access to any form of superior education. However imperfect the quality of instruction might be, even in a one-teacher school, opportunities would exist to obtain a modicum of classical studies, or finish the English education of a boy or girl. Nor were local people alone in this view. As John McCaul put it to the select committee on education early in 1869, every grammar school should continue to offer the classics: to restrict the teaching of Latin and Greek to the larger schools alone "would be depriving the sons of men in humble circumstances of their chances of attaining to the highest position as scholars."[43] What Ryerson proposed to do, in sum, not only struck at people's pocketbooks, and their hopes for their children, but challenged the political convictions of the commercial and professional middle class, the very group that saw itself as the vanguard in freeing society from the bonds of unearned privilege and closed corporations.

For most of his career, Ryerson had faced little articulate opposition to his policies, and most of what there was lacked the intellectual force to match the vigour of his rhetoric or the breadth of his reading and experience. In public at least, Ryerson had had it mostly his own way for twenty years. After 1865, however, this ceased to be the case. Ryerson's attempts to reform the old grammar schools forced people to articulate a case against Education Office policies and spurred more intense public discussion about the future of superior education in Ontario than there had ever been before. The public defence of local interests and established practices, and the political rhetoric of opportunity and accessibility, both contributed to the construction of alternative visions of that future. Never again would Ryerson and his advisers have the kind of free hand in the shaping of educational policy that they had had in the past.

The revolt against the May regulations of 1865 had been the first proof of this. But it turned out to be a mere skirmish compared to the storm that was to break upon Ryerson in the latter half of 1868. The imposition of a strict entrance examination and the mass failures that accompanied it, the pressures Ryerson and Young brought to bear on teachers and trustees to improve accommodation or to adhere to the prescribed program, the discounting of girls to half the per-pupil grant, and other irritants besides had together created deep-seated and widespread discontent over grammar school policy by the spring of 1868. The exclusion of girls in May of that year was the last straw. For the second time in four years, Ryerson's grammar school policies were widely condemned by newspaper editors, correspondents, and at public meetings organized by grammar school trustees and local grammar school supporters generally. In the village of Scotland, for example, what the editor of the *Brantford Expositor* described as a "large and influential" meeting heard Ryerson described as a dictator, his exclusionary tactics flayed, and a motion carried condemning his policies as "unjust and impolitic as having a tendency to lower the standard of womanhood, and as being a deep layered plan to do away with the Grammar Schools in country places, and confine the benefits of a superior education to cities and towns." The meeting concluded with an agreement that the legislature was to be petitioned for changes in the regulations.[44] The legislature, indeed, was bombarded during the autumn of 1868 with petitions expressing similar sentiments.[45] From Farmersville, for example, came the plea that there was an urgent demand for the higher education of youth of both sexes not only in towns and cities but also "in convenient centers in Counties." The petition went on to assert that it was

a matter of injustice to enrich those schools which educate boys only, at the expense of those who deem it right to educate Boys and Girls together. That the programme now enforced does not carry out the obvious intentions of the statute ... That there is pressing need for the instruction of the large class who do not intend to proceed to the University in the elements of modern science, and in higher English.[46]

In early August 1868, other influential voices made themselves heard. The Ontario Teachers' Association, which had generally taken a moderate and conciliatory stand since 1865, now came out foursquare against the policy of the Education Office. In his presidential speech, William McCabe, the headmaster of the Oshawa grammar school, launched a long and swingeing attack on Ryerson's proposals to create different schools for classical, English, and commercial studies, and for boys and girls. Indeed, using tactics worthy of Ryerson himself, McCabe ransacked the European and American educational literature to demonstrate that the recommendations in Ryerson's European *Report* constituted anything but sound or acceptable policy.[47]

One man's opinion, even in a presidential address, might not have been damaging; but in fact the OTA went on to pass unanimously a series of resolutions that condemned without qualification the thrust of educational policy from 1865 through to spring 1868. The exclusion of girls was described, among other things, as "contrary to the wishes of the great majority of the people amongst whom these schools are situated, as is evidenced by the fact that 96 out of 104 such schools admitted girls last year." Another motion called for the revision of the program of studies to give more prominence to science and other non-classical studies, and to make Greek optional. And the summary resolution urged "that the wisest policy would be, not to establish separate high schools, or commercial schools for either sex, but to increase the efficiency of the grammar schools by affording greater facilities for giving instruction in them in the additional studies indicated above." Finally, a committee was struck to lobby the politicians on the views expressed by the association.[48]

Faced with the growing opposition to a broad range of his policies during the summer and fall of 1868 and convinced in any case that the act and regulations of 1865 had failed to effect their purpose, Ryerson prepared remedial legislation that was put before the House in November 1868. By that time, however, it was too late to retrieve control of the momentum of events. Led by Edward Blake inside the legislature, and outside by George Brown in the editorial columns of the *Globe*, a loose coalition of old reformers and young liberals, who had long nursed a variety of grievances against Ryerson's political and educational policies, launched an all-out assault on his far-flung educational empire, and they were only too happy to add to their arsenal the complaints of teachers and trustees against his grammar school policies. As usual Ryerson gave as good as he got rhetorically, but he lost some key political battles along the way. The grammar school bill had to be withdrawn because it was being amended to death, as was an important common school bill.[49] Ryerson was hauled before a select committee on education and questioned thoroughly, and sometimes aggressively, by his political enemies. He became embroiled in the fight over the elimination of government grants to the denominational universities, and his active participation on the side of the churches strained his relations with the government and provided his opponents with more fodder. And finally, in January 1869, the premier, Sandfield Macdonald, bowed to continuing pressure inside and outside the legislature and assured the House that until educational issues generally were sorted out, girls would be admitted to the grammar schools.[50]

By the spring of 1869, the administration of grammar school policy had descended into near chaos. Assuming new legislation would follow shortly, the Education Office ceased to enforce any particular policy vigorously.[51] There were conflicting interpretations of what subjects girls could take to be eligible for the grant, and a flood of correspondence from grammar school teachers and trustees asking how to proceed in the matter.[52] Boards that had, in 1868, restricted the admission of girls, or in some cases actually closed down their "Ladies' Department" and dismissed the female teacher,[53] reversed themselves and scrambled for the financial windfall girls now represented. The new grammar school inspector, J.G.D. Mackenzie, vividly described the effects in his report for 1869. As a result of the change in policy, he wrote,

the "new-born rage for Latin" burst forth with redoubled vehemence, and large numbers of Girls were promptly herded into "Arnold," or the Introductory Book. The phrase "qualifying Latin" is well understood at present in the Schools, and, I need hardly say, is not taken to mean qualifying for higher stages of Classical study, for advanced intellectual culture, or for the active duties of life. During the past year Girls have risen in the educational market ... During the latter half of the past year there have been 1,472 names of "Girls on the Roll"; of these 850 were reported to me as being in Latin ... How many of these shall we set down to "qualifying" Latin? How much of sound, substantial, practical English has been sacrificed to this "qualifying" Latin? And how much longer are we to endure a system which specially rewards some of our poorest Schools with the increased Grant of Money, in proportion to the relentless energy with which unhappy Girl-conscripts are pressed into the Introductory Book.[54]

By early 1869, in sum, the policies that Ryerson and his advisers had pursued for a decade or more lay in tatters. In his own view at least, Ontario still lacked good classical schools, good superior schools for girls, and good English high schools for boys. "There are with us," he wrote, comparing Ontario's provision for superior education to that of Europe and the cities of the eastern United States,

not even high Central schools for both sexes; there is only the dead level of the common ward school; there is no High English School to teach the higher branches of English, including the elements of Natural History, Chemistry, and Philosophy, and the proper subjects of a Commercial Education; much less is there a High School for girls, embracing a curriculum of studies required for imparting a sound education for females. Our grammar schools do not supply this desideratum.[55]

In his testimony before the Select Committee on Education in 1869 he reiterated this assessment, admitting that his twin policies of creating higher common schools on the one hand, and classical grammar schools on the other, had failed. He had always thought, he said, that there were far more grammar schools than "the wants of the country required for Classical instruction. And I thought that the Act of 1865 would reduce the number of schools, and add to the efficiency of those that remained. That was my expectation," he continued, "but it was not fulfilled. The weaker schools, which I supposed would be closed up, held on with surprising tenacity. My intention was to make them classical schools, but I could not succeed." What had actually happened was that trustees had "impaired the efficiency and standing of the grammar schools by the introduction of a large number of girls to study Classics, in order to swell the attendance and thereby obtain larger means of support." Similarly with the policy he had pursued since 1847 of encouraging boards of common school trustees to establish their own high schools. "I did suppose that the Trustees would establish High English Schools in the different towns and cities of Canada, as in the United States. But they did not do so, and we were not able to bring sufficient influence to bear to induce them to do so."[56]

For Ryerson this was an unusually forthright admission of failure. It did not mean, however, that he was prepared to give up his project of an improved system of superior education. Indeed he had already incorporated a new approach to the problem in his grammar school bill of late autumn 1868 and he would pursue it vigorously until his retirement in 1876. Around him, however, the world was changing. New men and new ideas had emerged in the 1860s, and his own conception of the proper order of things would be fiercely contested throughout the rest of his public career.

CHAPTER NINE

Ryerson in Retreat: The Politics of Education, 1868–76

"It is wise to anticipate what is inevitable."[1] Ryerson had penned that aphorism at the outset of his career as chief superintendent of education, and just as it had directed his course of action on other important occasions, so it would again during the crisis of the late 1860s. Confronted by the rising tide of opposition to his grammar school policies, he was now prepared to bend to the political winds by formulating proposals that would conform more closely to local sentiments and to the views of his critics in the legislature and the press. But he still intended to preserve some of his most cherished objectives for superior education. This new approach was incorporated in three grammar school bills submitted to the legislature in late 1868, 1869, and 1870, which, though they differed in detail, were substantially the same.[2]

In the bill that went before the House in November 1868, Ryerson proposed to transfer all those grammar schools located in incorporated urban areas to the control of the common school boards of trustees. For those schools in non-incorporated places, the county councils were given the power to create school districts out of one or more townships and villages; all provisions of the school acts for incorporated areas would then apply to these schools as well. The boards were to be entirely elective, and would have the power to finance the grammar schools in the same way as the common schools: they would, in other words, be required to raise, through local property taxes, at least as much as the amount of the government grant for grammar schools and would have the power to raise more if they saw fit.

The name "grammar school" was to be changed to "high school" and the curriculum was to provide "the higher branches of an English education, and the Latin and Greek languages, to Pupils whose parents and guardians may desire it," according to a program of studies laid down by the Council of Public Instruction. The Grammar School Fund was to be applied to the support of the new high schools but all high schools had to have a minimum average daily attendance of twenty pupils. Each school above that minimum would receive a grant of at least $300 and not more than $1000 according to average attendance and the number of days it was open.

In some respects, the bill incorporated provisions Ryerson had sought several times before in earlier legislative proposals. The schools, for example, were to be uncoupled from unsympathetic county councils, dominated as they were by the representatives of rural townships, and would become instead exclusively urban institutions under the control of the towns and villages that supplied most of the pupils. Local funding was not only to come from local property taxation but the amount raised was to equal the government grant. Trustees were to be elected rather than appointed by municipal councils. None of these things was entirely new in 1868.[3] What was new were the proposals relating to the program of studies. In both the acts of 1853 and 1865, all grammar schools had been required to offer classical and other subjects up to the standard set for matriculation at the University of Toronto. The grammar schools, moreover, had been intended as schools for boys alone. In 1868, however, the matriculation clause was excised, and the attempt to turn all the grammar schools into classical schools was abandoned. Instead, the schools were to become higher English schools designed to complete the education of boys and girls alike. For the first time, moreover, classics were to be made optional: no school would be required to offer Latin and Greek unless parents demanded them.

This was indeed a major departure from the objectives that had traditionally guided official policy. Ryerson had failed to turn the grammar schools into classical institutions. He had failed to persuade local common school trustees to create their own English high schools for either boys or girls. He now proposed a new solution to both problems. The grammar schools were to be converted into high schools focusing primarily on English studies, and the Grammar School Fund was to be used to stimulate local support for higher studies in English as well as classics, for girls as well as boys. Thus the bill was designed to respond to the pressures exerted by local people for a more variegated form of superior education than official policy had previously allowed.

The new bill had another advantage as well. With the high schools in the hands of locally elected trustees, and with classics optional, Ryerson himself would no longer be saddled with the unenviable task of imposing unwelcome rules upon recalcitrant communities. While he would continue to influence the rules of the game by regulating the conditions for the grant, no locality had to have a classical school; no locality had to adopt prescribed courses it did not want. Ryerson would, in other words, be back on his preferred ground – as the source of stimulus for local initiative rather than policeman of an unenforceable law.

Because the grant was no longer to be tied to classics, Ryerson and other Education Office spokesmen assumed that the effect of the bill would be to "banish classics almost entirely from the majority of high schools ... If this should happen," Paxton Young explained in a speech to the Ontario Teachers' Association, "it would not be a misfortune," for teachers could then turn their full attention to English and scientific instruction, "a genuine and important work which they were not doing previously."[4] What would then emerge would be a two-tiered hierarchy amongst the high schools: those which taught no classics at all but concentrated exclusively on English studies alone, and those which operated primarily as English high schools but which also contained a classical department – an option that would ensure that even in smaller communities access to university and professional education was available to the handful of local boys who might seek it out.

There was also to be a third tier, however, and this was perhaps the most innovative clause in the 1868 bill.[5] Though Ryerson was now prepared to concede that not all grammar schools could or should be classical schools, he was not about to give up his dream of establishing high classical seminaries in the province. Since the high schools were about to be "thrown open to girls, and provision ... made in them for giving a purely English education apart from classics," he explained, "it was thought desirable to prevent the possible extinction, in our educational system, of a purely Classical School, which should serve as a proper link between the public school and the University."[6] Thus was born the collegiate institute. Any high school, the final clause of the 1868 bill read, with four masters and at least seventy male pupils could be named a collegiate institute and receive a special grant of $750 per annum. Whether or not to establish a collegiate institute was left entirely up to the local community. No one was going to impose a classical school where it was not wanted. But only a few communities could ever meet the conditions: schools with four teachers and seventy pupils of any kind, let alone seventy boys enrolled in classics, were rare indeed in the province. These few schools, nevertheless, would offer a classical education of the highest quality. As Ryerson would explain his scheme to the Select Committee on Education early in 1869,

in the infant state of the country, and with their very limited means of support, you cannot expect that all the Grammar Schools can be equally efficient. In the scheme of Collegiate Institutes, it is designed to give encouragement to those places where there is local enterprize and intelligence, and liberality sufficient to erect the Buildings, and to provide Masters to the number of four, of sufficient merit and reputation to gather Pupils round them, – Boys engaged in Classical Studies to the number of 70. Under such circumstances, it is proposed that the liberality of the City, or Town, where such an Institution may be established, shall receive further encouragement, and by such a union of ability and means, of course more efficient Institutions would be established.

Query. – In your opinion, does Upper Canada College represent something like what you propose?
Answer. – Yes ... [7]

The inspiration for the idea of the collegiate institute remains unclear. The province-wide reputation of Upper Canada College, the rising prestige of the great English public schools, and the success of new private schools like Trinity College School or Hellmuth College all may have played a part in giving shape to the plan. So most probably did the German *gymnasien* and the French *lycée*, public-sector classical schools that Ryerson had long admired and that he had recently praised in his report on his European tour of 1866–67.[8] As for the specific standard of four masters and seventy pupils, it was apparently based on Tassie's school at Galt, which, throughout the period, was often seen as the archetypical public-sector, classical grammar school.[9]

The term "collegiate institute" is also of uncertain origin, though similar phraseology was commonly used in the period. The words "college" and "collegiate" had already acquired a variety of overlapping connotations that included residential rather than day schools, a level of education superior to ordinary schools, and linkages to the universities.[10] Eton, to take a classic example, was a "college," not merely a school, and all sorts of colonial institutions followed suit, not just Upper Canada College but, for example, the Wesleyan Female College, or Hellmuth College. The latter, indeed, had originally been called the London Collegiate Institute. Moreover, the two most common generic terms for institutions offering a broad range of preparatory and undergraduate education were "collegiate institution" and "collegiate institute." Similarly, preparatory schools, as a category, were often called "collegiate schools," especially if the reference was to boarding schools that offered higher classical studies.[11] The terminology was, in other words, simply part of the conventional usage of the age, and the reason why Ryerson selected "collegiate institute" rather than one of the other variants was probably a matter of convenience or personal taste.[12]

Whatever the origins of the name, the idea was clearly to create, within the public sector, large, male, classical schools endowed with special grants in order to sustain high levels of classical and mathematical instruction, preparatory to matriculation to the universities and professional education. There is also some indication that boarding facilities were considered as possible appendages to the schools.[13] The intent was, in any case, to keep the number of collegiates small. Ryerson had first thought in terms of only four collegiates, and then of a maximum of ten;[14] Paxton Young estimated that no more than a dozen would be necessary. The collegiates were also to be sharply differentiated from the much larger number of high schools. The purpose of these special schools, Young explained, was to do "the same substantial work" as Upper Canada College. "They should be a class of institutions," he added, "essentially different from ordinary High Schools."[15] The same sort of differentiation was emphasized by the new grammar school inspector, the Rev. J.G.D. Mackenzie. Though some high schools might continue to offer Latin as an option, he wrote in 1869, "we shall look chiefly to the Universities and to our Collegiate Institutes ... to advance the interests of superior education."[16]

Ryerson and his advisers, then, had not abandoned the notion that the epitome of a liberal or superior education was an immersion in the classics, or that special institutions were necessary to ensure the promotion of classical instruction. Nor had they abandoned their conviction that there was a program of studies peculiarly suitable for boys (and implicitly a different one for girls). What they had done in 1868 was to reconceptualize the institutional organization of the higher schools. The parallel structure of classical and English schools would continue to characterize Upper Canadian education, but the dichotomy would no longer consist of the distinction between the grammar schools, on the one hand, and the common schools, on the other. Instead they proposed to convert the grammar school itself into two differentiated institutions: the classical collegiate institute and the English high school.

IF RYERSON BELIEVED that his new proposals for the reform of the grammar schools would be enough to quiet local fears or bank the fires of political opposition, he was disabused soon enough of any such notions. The experience of the years 1865 to 1868 had made his critics chary of any legislation that left large discretionary powers in the hands of the Education Office. In the press and the legislature there were repeated demands that the word "pupils" be changed to "boys and girls" so that there could be no conceivable doubt about the right of girls to attend the high schools.[17] In order to mark the schools indelibly as multi-purpose institutions, moreover, his critics insisted on unequivocal assurances that English, modern languages, science, and commercial subjects would all have a status equal to classics.[18] Mistrust of Ryerson's intentions went deep enough, indeed, that some of his opponents in the legislature called for the publication of his proposed regulations *before* any new act passed – "a proposition," Ryerson protested in a typically overblown way, "without precedent in Canada, or any other Country, and absurd in itself."[19] One private member's grammar school bill went much further, and provides an instructive example of the paranoia Ryerson had engendered. In an attempt to limit Ryerson's discretionary powers as much as possible it specified that

no Regulation shall be made prescribing the number of pupils to be required for a School, or for pursuing any special branch of study; nor shall any difficult qualifications be required for admission of classical and non-classical students. And no School shall be deprived of its due apportionment ... for any irregularity, except by order of the Lieutenant Governor-in-Council, made after due notice to the Board of Trustees of such School, and reasonable opportunity given for amending such alleged irregularity.[20]

Along with the evident suspicion that Ryerson would once more attempt to use the regulations to circumvent the intent of the legislature, there was also a good deal of unease and disagreement about various substantive changes proposed in the bill. The board of directors of the Ontario Teachers' Association, reflecting the views of several influential grammar school masters, approved the establishment of the collegiate institutes, though they went on to remark that the standards for the institutes should be reduced to three masters and sixty pupils; otherwise "the prospect of any High School being able to benefit by this provision would become remote."[21] There were, on the other hand, a number of grammar school masters who expressed their opposition to the principle of special classical schools as such, fearing that they would provide the justification for the extinction of classical instruction everywhere except in the collegiates.[22] Opinion was split as well over the elective principle for grammar school trustees. Some people, Ryerson included, felt that local financial support would never be forthcoming until the schools were run by trustees elected by local taxpayers. But there were also complaints that the elective principle would eliminate the highly educated and respectable men who had hitherto been appointed as trustees, replacing them with the ill-educated, the ignorant, and the demagogue.[23]

The financial clauses of the bill drew criticism too. Fears were expressed in the newspapers about the minimum average daily attendance requirement on the grounds that it would result in the closure of small schools. Similarly it was said that the minimum grant of $300 was so low as to encourage the same outcome.[24] Both trustees and teachers, moreover, found the financial provisions of the bill unsettling. In the view of the Grammar School Masters' Association, for example, the changes would only make things worse. The proposal to shift the main source of financial support from the county councils to the villages and towns would simply increase the burden on "already overtaxed municipalities," while the county councils "which, as a class, rank among the wealthiest of our Municipal Corporations, ... contribute towards educational funds a sum at present very trifling in amount, and annually decreasing relative to the increasing wealth of the country."[25] Most schools, the association report added, were union schools and thus had access to the rates already, while the proposed changes would only "have the effect of forcing a union, where such a measure is at present regarded as unnecessary, and where it will doubtless be distasteful."[26] Not even the requirement that localities must raise an amount equal to the grammar school grant met with approbation. One knowledgeable correspondent to the *Globe* argued that many small communities which barely managed to raise one-half the amount of the grant, as required by the act of 1865, would refuse to raise the full amount, with the result that their schools would be closed. [27]

The volume and variety of criticism brought against the bill during the legislative session of 1868–69 resulted in so many amendments that its intent was seriously compromised, and on Ryerson's advice it was withdrawn by the premier. In late 1869, it was reintroduced but once again it was subjected to a torrent of criticism inside and outside the House, and once again it was withdrawn. The following year Ryerson incorporated a revised version of the bill in an omnibus piece of legislation that also introduced major changes in the Common School Act. [28] The new combined grammar and common school bill was introduced in the House in the autumn of 1870.

Recognizing that further concessions were necessary, Ryerson had modified many of those clauses in the 1868 bill that had drawn the most fire from his critics. The high schools were still to be placed under the control of the boards of common school trustees, but up to four additional high school trustees could be appointed by the municipal council. Additional subjects were specified: the high schools would now offer "the higher branches of an English and Commercial education, including the Natural Sciences, with special reference to agriculture, and also the Latin, Greek, French and German languages to those pupils whose parents or guardians may desire it." The minimum number of students required for a collegiate institute was reduced from seventy to sixty. Finally, the clause requiring a minimum average attendance of twenty pupils was excised and replaced by a new formula for calculating the grant based on a combination of average attendance, the length of time the school was kept open, and "proficiency in the various branches of study" – a phrase designed to provide for the distribution of the grant, in part at least, on the basis of payment by educational results. Under this new formula a small school might receive no more than the minimum grant specified in the act, but even with fewer than twenty pupils it would not be closed.

Ryerson may well have believed that all this was compromise enough, but once again he was to be proved wrong. Little record survives of the motives or political manoeuvring that resulted in the further modification of several of the key high school clauses of the bill, perhaps because public interest was focused on its more controversial common school clauses, above all the proposals to make the common schools tuition-free and to introduce compulsory attendance. But for whatever reasons, there were some substantial changes made in the high school clauses, designed to address the major complaints of the previous five years. For one thing, the politicians nailed open the doors of the high schools (though not those of the collegiate institutes) to pupils of both sexes by changing Ryerson's sexless "pupils" to "male and female pupils." The list of modern subjects was left as Ryerson had written it, but a rider was attached that gave the Council of Public Instruction the power "to exempt any High School, which shall not have sufficient funds to provide the necessary qualified teachers, from the obligation to teach the French and German languages." The effect of this qualifier was to protect small schools by limiting Ryerson's power to make regulations tying the grant to instruction in subjects that might require more than one or two teachers. For similar reasons, the minimum grant was raised from $300 to $400 – a gift to the smallest schools.

No less important, however, the legislature backed away from the proposal to transfer control of the high schools to elected, urban boards of common school trustees. The name of the boards was changed from grammar to high school boards, but other than that, no modifications were made to the act of 1865: except for the cities which appointed their own, half the trustees of each high school would continue to be appointed by the council of the town where the school was located, and half by the county council. When the school was located in an unseparated village, the county council appointed all six trustees.

The politicians also modified Ryerson's long-standing proposal to have local councils raise an amount equal to the government grant. The minimum amount to be raised was left at one-half that amount. The legislature then added a clause that required municipal councils in cities and towns to raise, at the request of the high school boards, additional amounts for the support of the high schools. The rural townships were, however, exempted from that provision: schools in unseparated villages had a right to receive an amount equal to half the basic grant from county funds, but any additional amount could be levied only on the high school district itself, which normally included only the village where the school was located.[29] These arrangements, in other words, represented a delicate political balancing act between the financial needs of the schools and the long-standing conviction of the rural population that the grammar school was an urban institution and should be treated as such.

IN THIS MUCH-AMENDED FORM, Ryerson's grammar school bill of 1868 became the high school clauses of the Schools Improvement Act of 1871. For the third time in twenty years, Ryerson had rewritten the school legislation in an attempt to find the right formula for integrating the various kinds of higher studies in the public system of education. Yet the central questions of the 1850s still remained to be resolved: what was to be the role of the grammar school within the school system and what was to be its relationship with the common school? The act of 1871 had changed the names of both institutions to high school and public school respectively, and indicated, in a general way, what subjects the high school was to offer. But it did little to specify the range or organization of the high school curriculum, or spell out how it was to be articulated with the public school. Though Ryerson had been forced to make a wide variety of concessions on these matters during the later 1860s, his own long-standing conviction about the role of both the grammar and common schools had remained unshaken. Compromises there had been, and these would inevitably be reflected in the regulations for the new act. He was determined, nonetheless, to preserve what he could of his own vision, and if possible, indeed, to win back ground conceded in the political battles of the previous five years.

Ryerson's first priority in drafting the new regulations was to reassert the primacy of the common school within the public education system. In an attempt to ensure the largest possible grant for their schools, Ryerson wrote in 1871, trustees and teachers "had virtually merged the Grammar into the Common School, with the nominal addition in most cases, of only a little Latin and Greek. The object of the High School Sections of the new Act is to put an end to this anomalous state of things, and to prescribe for each class of schools its own legitimate work."[30] The "legitimate work" of the common schools, he had always maintained, should not be confined to the three Rs but extended far beyond that, encompassing all of the education necessary for "the ordinary employments and duties of life."[31] This meant, in turn, that the common school must offer not just the rudiments but more advanced instruction in all aspects of a sound English, scientific, and commercial education. Ever since mid-century, he contended, the official program of studies had encouraged the common schools to develop their curriculum in this direction, placing few limits on the subjects or levels of instruction they might provide. But most common schools had been content to offer only a "very meagre" curriculum, "extending for practical purposes very little, and in many cases not at all, beyond what has been termed the three Rs."[32]

The time had now come to remedy the situation, however. "Our school law," Ryerson wrote, "wisely lays down the principle that every youth in the land is entitled, not only to a sound practical Education in the three great essentials of English Education, – Reading, Writing, and Arithmetic – but ... [also in] such other elementary subjects as the advanced intelligence of the present day prescribes as the essential minimum of Public School Education."[33] With this end in view he introduced, for the first time, a *prescribed* program of studies for all common schools, including not only the three Rs but also the work contained in all five English readers, natural and physical science, geography and history, lessons in civil government, bookkeeping, and the elements of algebra and geometry.[34] Because such subjects constituted "an essential minimum," no subject in the prescribed curriculum could be omitted in any school. The new program of studies even laid down the sequence in which subjects were to be taught and the levels of learning to be attained in each subject before promotion through the six successive classes was allowed. Despite the proliferation of compulsory subjects, Ryerson believed nonetheless that the new program could be "thoroughly mastered by Pupils of ordinary capacity and diligence within thirteen years of age."[35]

The change of name, from common to public school, symbolized the intent behind Ryerson's new program of studies. Though he routinely referred to all of the grant-aided schools and colleges of the province as parts of the "public" system of instruction, he had from the beginning envisaged the common schools as "public" in a special sense. Their task was to provide the common core of knowledge essential to all future citizens of Ontario. Thus they had a central role to play in the public life of the province in a way that other schools and colleges did not. With the new program of 1871, then, Ryerson was attempting to convert the common school into what he believed it should be – not merely a place where the rudiments were taught but a school which provided the public with that minimum of knowledge essential to the private and public life of the nation. J.A. McLellan, one of the new high school inspectors, caught Ryerson's intentions nicely in his own attempt to define the purpose of the public school. Its great object, McLellan wrote in 1872, "is not only to place within the reach of all a course of education sufficiently extensive and thorough for all the ordinary pursuits of life, but to create a national intelligence which shall be effective in national progress."[36]

But if this was the role of the new "public school," what, then, was the role of the high school? Because the modern high school was still being constructed piecemeal out of older institutions and ways of thinking, there was a good deal of ambiguity about its particular tasks and its relationship to the public school. However, a passage written in the early 1870s by the high school inspectors helps clarify official thinking about the different roles of the two kinds of school.

The *raison d'être* of the High School System is entirely different from that of the Public School System. The object of the latter is to provide for every child of sound mind the means of obtaining a minimum amount of knowledge and mental training; the object of the former is to provide for a comparatively small fraction of the population the elements of a liberal culture. The Public Schools exist to sow intelligence widely, the High Schools to plough deeply a small portion of mental soil. The all-important aim of the former is to reach every child; the all-important aim of the latter is to combine thorough training with breadth of mental vision. In the former case the number of the pupils instructed should be mainly regarded by the community, in the latter, the quality of the instruction. The quality of the instruction given in the Public Schools and the numbers attending the High Schools are not in themselves unimportant matters, but their relative importance is different in the two classes of Schools.

We conceive, therefore, that while a rapid increase in the number of High Schools, and in the numbers attending them, are not perhaps at present desirable, it is desirable that the instruction given should reach the highest attainable point of excellence. In the High Schools are being educated, it is to be presumed, the leading men of the next generation, its Clergymen, its Lawyers, its Doctors, its Editors, the men who are to make Farming a Science, its Engineers and Machinists, its prominent Manufacturers and Merchants, and its Teachers. It is important that they at least as the advisers and guides of the future should receive a wide culture and know what thoroughness is. [37]

Ryerson provided his own parallel definition in his preamble to the new program of studies. The purpose of the high school, he wrote, was to teach classics, modern languages, and mathematics in order to prepare for the professions and for university matriculation; and "to complete a good English education, by educating Pupils not only for Commercial, Manufacturing and Agricultural pursuits, but for fulfilling with efficiency, honour and usefulness, the duties of Municipal Councillors, Legislators, and various Public Officers in the service of the Country." [38]

For both Ryerson and his advisers, then, the high school was to be a school for a small number of young people. It was to offer them the elements at least of a liberal education. And it was to provide an education for leadership in economic and political life. It was not, however, simply the upward extension or second stage of a unified system of education. Embedded in the act of 1871 was the principle that had animated all of Ryerson's earlier legislation and that, indeed, harked back to Georgian conceptions of the organization of schooling: the grammar school and the common school, or to use the new terminology, the high school and the public school, would serve distinct if somewhat overlapping purposes and would, in the main at least, serve different clienteles.

Though the public school and the high school had their own distinct purposes, there was never any question that they were also to be linked together. But how were the links to be fashioned, and at what point would the transfer from one institution to the other take place? Here again, Ryerson's proposals were virtually identical to those of 1865. First, the programs of study were to be articulated in such a way that the curriculum of the public school, however complete in itself, also prepared pupils for entry to the high school. Secondly, to ensure that each institution remained true to its own vocation and did not trespass on the proper work of the other, there was to be a high school entrance examination that all pupils had to pass before they could be counted towards the high school grant. [39] The examination was to be conducted, as in the past, by a local committee of examiners, but the standards were to be set by the Council of Public Instruction and enforced by the high school inspectors.

The different requirements of classical and English studies, however, continued to pose difficulties for the integration of the two institutions. During the late 1860s and early 1870s, Ryerson often claimed to be converted to the view that classics should be commenced only after a sound English education had been attained.[40] Still, he found it difficult to break free of traditional views to the contrary, and there were pressures from the masters of some of the larger high schools, particularly from those like William Tassie who saw themselves in competition with the private schools, to ensure that they could continue to receive boys for classical instruction at a relatively early age.[41] Thus the new regulations maintained the principle of setting two different entrance standards, one for English and the other for classical studies.

Ryerson intended to set the entry standard for the English program at a very high level, almost certainly at the completion of the fifth or sixth class of the public school program.[42] As in 1865, in other words, English studies in the high school were to be accessible only after the full program of studies in the public school had been completed. Any other alternative, Ryerson believed, would undermine the primacy of the public school and threaten to reduce it to a mere elementary feeder of the high school. The classical standard, however, was set much lower. Students intending to study Latin could transfer to the high school at the end of the fourth class, a point that coincided with the completion of half the fourth reader. Indeed, the mathematical standard was set even lower, at the end of the third class.[43] This, however, meant that the high school program had to overlap the instruction of the public school: classical pupils in the high school had to be taught the English and mathematics their peers learned in the fifth and sixth classes. Ryerson and his advisers do not appear to have been troubled by this overlap in 1870 or early 1871, probably because they still assumed that many, or even most, high schools would cease to offer classical instruction, in which case the duplication of subjects would be restricted to places with a collegiate institute or an unusually large high school. The introduction of these dual entrance standards, however, testifies to the continuing influence of the traditional dichotomy between classical and English studies in shaping the act and regulations of 1871.

The new regulations are also a testimony to Ryerson's continuing antipathy to loosely structured programs of study, to small schools, and to coeducation. As in 1865, the regulations of 1871 introduced two rigidly segregated programs of study, one termed "classical" and the other "English." Pupils had to enrol in one or the other, there were virtually no options to choose from, and the two programs were to be kept separate and distinct. The study of

English formed a cornerstone of both programs, but other than that, classics, modern languages, and mathematics dominated the classical program, while the English program concentrated more on science, practical mathematics, and commercial subjects.[44]

In Ryerson's view the main justification for organizing the curriculum in this fashion was its educative value. The aim was to provide a focused and coherent pattern of studies rather than a jumble of options driven by short-term vocational goals or the preferences of parents or pupils. During the hearings of the select committee on the universities in 1860 he had passionately condemned the optionalization of the curriculum at University College and, in the process, laid out his grounds for imposing a coherent program of studies on schools and colleges alike. "It is not the object of Collegiate, any more than of common school, education to minister to individual tastes and whims," he told the committee, "nor to deal out snatches of knowledge on various subjects; but to develop and discipline the powers of the mind, by a common course of application and exercise, sanctioned by the experience of ages, and for which Utopian experimenters have found no substitutes, any more than they have found a substitute for the ordinary food and exercise requisite for physical development and discipline. It is only, therefore, when the foundation, common to all, is broadly and deeply laid, and at an advanced stage of the Collegiate Course, that Options are admitted and the essential subjects are not to be abandoned during any part of the Course, and least of all, at the end of the first year."[45]

There was, then, an educational principle at the heart of Ryerson's commitment to a prescribed program of studies for the high schools. But the particular way in which the programs were organized served other objectives as well. Delivering two tightly organized programs of study was not beyond the capacities of the collegiate institutes or the larger high schools. But it would be difficult in the small schools with only two or three teachers, and impossible in one-teacher schools. Thus small schools could be forced to abandon classical instruction and concentrate their efforts on the English program. To ensure that this happened, moreover, French and German were included in the classical program, making it almost inevitable that more than two teachers would be required to offer competent instruction in classics, modern languages, and science and mathematics. All of the evidence from the late 1860s points to the conclusion that the legislature intended to protect and encourage the country high schools; nor did the politicians intend to abolish Latin instruction in any high school but simply to make it optional. Ryerson's new program regulations, however, appear to have been drafted in such a way as to force small communities to pursue one of three choices: to invest more money in their high schools, to restrict their teaching to English subjects only, or to close down their high schools entirely. Beyond that, Ryerson attempted to abolish the one-teacher schools altogether by requiring, as a condition of the grant, that all schools have a minimum of two teachers.[46] Regardless of the wishes of the legislature, in other words, Ryerson was continuing his attack on the small high school in the regulations of 1871.

Again, the act guaranteed that girls could no longer be excluded from the high schools. But while all of the official rhetoric acknowledged that the schools were now open to girls, the program of studies was hardly designed to encourage their presence. French, for example, was available only if they also took classics and three mathematical subjects. Indeed they were exempted from geometry in the English but not in the classical program. The English program, on the other hand, was not literary but practical and biased towards preparing boys for commercial vocations. Thus girls were forced into science, linear drawing, commercial arithmetic, mensuration, and bookkeeping but excluded from taking French. It may have been that in some fundamental way Ryerson simply didn't know how to draft a curriculum suitable for a school attended by both sexes; still, the regulations of 1871 do look as though they were deliberately constructed to persuade parents not to send their girls to the public high schools.

It was also Ryerson's intention, we have suggested, to set the entry standard to the English program at or near the completion of the public school program of studies. Had Ryerson succeeded in doing this it would have been a major blow to the smaller high schools, for it would have robbed them of all but the handful of pupils seeking a classical or very advanced English education. But he was forced to retreat on this point even before the regulations were published. The experience of the 1860s had alerted people to the fact that relatively few pupils could meet the high standard Ryerson proposed to set, which meant, in turn, that fewer pupils would qualify for the grant. As a result, in Ryerson's own words, "constant pressure was brought to bear on the Council of Public Instruction," and thus "the Chief Superintendent, against his better judgement, consented to lower the standard to a point between the 3rd and 4th (out of 6) Classes of the Public School."[47] In the final version of the regulations, the standard was actually set at the completion of page 244 of the fourth reader, a point that marked the end of the fourth class. Except for the lowered standard in mathematics required for the classical program, then, the entry requirement for both programs was now the same.

The result of reducing the standard for entrance to the English program to that of the classical program was the creation of a major curricular anomaly. If all students were to be promoted to high school out of the fourth class, then the curriculum of the high school would have to be altered to include the work covered in the fifth and sixth classes of the public school. It was one thing to concede this necessity in what Ryerson thought would be the special and restricted case of the classical program, and quite another to allow all high schools to teach what was intended to be public school work. Inevitably this would put the high school and the public school in direct competition with each other. The only other alternative was to reduce the work of the public school by two full classes, something Ryerson was not even prepared to consider. The outcome was that in the new regulations of 1871, the programs of study for the two different schools were allowed to overlap. "We have the singular fact presented to us," Ryerson commented in disgust, "that both Public and High Schools are doing substantially the same work as laid down for the 4th (in part), 5th and 6th classes of the Public Schools, and for the 1st, 2nd, and 3rd Classes of the High Schools!"[48]

What Ryerson feared most about this arrangement was that local boards would refuse to duplicate classes and instead would amalgamate their schools, allowing the high school to gobble up all but the elementary classes of the public school. In 1871, however, he probably believed he could keep this problem under control by astute use of the regulations and his other administrative powers. Not only did the regulations require all public schools to offer the entire program of studies, for example, but they also gave parents the right to keep their children in the public school for the full six classes. Boards, in other words, could not abolish the senior public school grades, nor could they force parents to transfer their children to the high school. "It is quite at the option of the parents ... of Pupils," the regulation read, "whether they shall enter the High School, or not, before they complete the whole Programme of Studies in the Public School."[49] Beyond that, the Education Office began to formulate plans to implement the clauses in the act that provided for the allocation of part of the grant through "payment by educational results." If the grant could be heavily weighted towards successful teaching in the higher forms of the high school, so the reasoning went, the teachers and trustees would have little incentive to push children out of the public school and into the high school. Based as it was on the regular visits by the high school inspectors, however, the first scheme to apply payment by results foundered on the workload it would have imposed on the two inspectors. Without the appointment of additional inspectors it appeared unworkable and was put off until that event.[50]

Ryerson's other tool for preserving the integrity of the public school was the high school entrance examination. Almost immediately upon the passage of the act, he instructed the high school inspectors to impose tougher standards during their re-examination of pupils admitted on a preliminary basis by the local committee. As a result, many more candidates were failed in 1871 than in the two previous years, encouraging teachers to keep pupils in the public school longer than otherwise might have been the case.[51] The inspectors, nonetheless, were convinced by the end of 1871 that there was far too much variation between schools in promotion standards and that, generally, standards were being set too low. Their solution to both these problems was a uniform written examination, set by the Education Office and, though marked locally, subject to re-evaluation by the inspectors themselves. In mid-1872, Ryerson circularized the high school boards, making this procedure mandatory and, for good measure, raising the pass level to 75 per cent.[52]

By this point, however, all of Ryerson's policies had fallen hostage to the conflict being fought out with Edward Blake, the new Liberal premier.[53] Years of antagonism between the two men boiled over in 1872 into a series of confrontations involving politics, educational policy, and personal slights and insults.[54] Ryerson was now seventy years old, in ill health, in debt and thus unable to resign, and too often cranky and petulant. Blake was contemptuous of Ryerson personally and dismissive in public of his abilities and achievements. As the younger man and the political leader of the province, Blake revealed a streak of mean-spiritedness which even at this remove does not serve his reputation well. It is a mistake, nonetheless, to dismiss the *contretemps* of 1872 as merely personal. From the administration of J.S. Macdonald onwards, successive ministries were determined to regularize the procedures of the Education Office, to impose financial accountability on it, and above all to exercise a firm hand in educational policymaking. Thus Blake was not alone in his efforts to bring Ryerson to heel. No less important, educational policy itself had, from the late 1860s onwards, become a matter of public debate and Ryerson's voice, though still pre-eminent, was no longer the only one to be heard. Ryerson nonetheless remained surprisingly unresponsive to these changes in the political climate. Intent on completing his life's work, he continued to pursue policies which flew in the face of public opinion and which, in the case of some of the regulations of 1871, came perilously close to contradicting the expressed intent of the legislature and of the statute itself.

It all caught up with him in 1872. There had been growing protests from disparate quarters over a number of issues such as the new standards of school accommodation required by the regulations, his insistence that all high schools hire at least two teachers, the future of the book depository, and other controversial innovations besides. Then came the new entrance regulations of 1872. The promotion standard was set too high, critics claimed, and the result would be a dramatic decrease in enrolments and grants. Pupils were "utterly unaccustomed to written questions" and would fail even though they might pass equally demanding oral examinations. By insisting on the use of examination papers drafted by the high school inspectors, the Education Office had usurped the powers given to local examiners in the act of 1871. Complaints such as these, combined with the wider conflict between the government and the Education Office, prompted Blake to issue a circular to local boards announcing the suspension of all regulations relating to high school admissions.[55] Not only that, but without any consultation with Ryerson or the Council of Public Instruction, the government set out its own views about what might constitute a reasonable standard of admission: "It is desirable," the circular suggested, "that the utmost facility should be afforded to the admission of Pupils to the High Schools, consistent with their showing that amount of previous training, without which it is improbable that they could obtain any advantages from the further prosecution of their Studies in the High School."[56] Not surprisingly perhaps, given the vagueness of this new standard, many high school boards leaped at the opportunity to augment their share of the grant. Helpless to expel the "swarms of ill-trained Pupils" who flooded into the schools, the high school inspectors could do little more than bemoan the renewed "degradation" of the high and public schools alike.[57]

Blake's term as premier proved to be a short one. He resigned in late 1872 and was succeeded by Oliver Mowat, a man no less determined to be his own master but more conciliatory and adept at applying liberal amounts of soft sawder to assuage Ryerson's prickly sensitivities. Convinced in particular by J.A. McLellan's school-by-school review of the consequences of suspending the admissions regulations, as well as by the more general arguments put forward by the Council of Public Instruction, Mowat allowed Ryerson to restore some degree of central control over the entrance examination in early 1873, though he insisted that the pass mark be lowered to 50 per cent and that the papers drafted by the high school inspectors be "recommendatory only."[58] As it turned out, however, only a handful of boards opted to use their own papers, and, thus convinced that further centralization would not provoke a political outcry, Mowat guided new legislation through the House which gave statutory sanction to Ryerson's proposals of mid-1872. The local examiners would continue to conduct the high school entrance examination but were required to use papers drafted by the high school inspectors, and to submit pupils' written answers to the Education Office for final confirmation of the marks assigned.[59]

Mowat sustained Ryerson in other things as well. Despite growing criticism about the inflexibility of the dual program of studies, it was preserved without any changes in the revised regulations of 1873. The government, moreover, finally accepted the long-standing contention of Ryerson and his advisers that union schools constituted a blight upon the land: new unions were banned in the School Act of 1874, though the law did not go so far as to abolish existing ones.[60] And no less important, Mowat permitted the restoration of the two-teacher rule which had also been suspended by Blake in 1872. Ryerson and his inspectors, from G.P. Young onwards, had always been convinced that no single teacher could cope with all the subjects and levels of instruction contained in the grammar school curriculum, and this was even more true, they believed, after 1871. Though many exceptions would be made in order to avoid penalizing small schools and poor com-

munities, the inclusion of the two-teacher regulation in 1873 set a minimum
standard for the establishment and maintenance of a high school for years
to come.[61]

As Ryerson moved towards retirement in 1876, then, he seemed to be
ending his public career with a string of successes, finally achieving many
of the goals he had set for the reorganization of higher studies in the 1860s.
And that, indeed, appeared to be a view widely shared amongst the politicians, newspaper editors, and policymakers alike. In what was almost
certainly intended as a peroration marking the end of the Ryerson years, the
high school inspectors prefaced their report for 1875 with a brief review of
the achievements of the previous decade. "Many of the questions," they
wrote, "which, for years past, have served as the texts of the Annual Reports
on the state of the High Schools, have been provisionally, perhaps, finally
settled. If ever they crop up now, they are mere ghosts of what they were."
Drawing on G.P. Young's report of 1866, the inspectors referred to the
multiplication of union schools, the degradation of the public and high
schools "due to the draft of unprepared pupils," the "evil consequences"
of compulsory Latin, and several other recurring themes besides. "How
completely the condition of the High Schools has been altered," they concluded, "may be inferred from the fact that all the evil tendencies complained
of by Mr Young have been checked, and all of his proposals substantially
adopted."[62]

There was, of course, a good deal of truth in this assessment. Both Ryerson
and Young could point with pride to any one of a large number of their
proposals which had become provincial policy. And yet in some fundamental
respects what had developed under Ryerson's tutelage was something quite
different from what he had intended. From the beginning of his career as
superintendent he had believed that Upper Canada's system of public instruction must be organized according to two central principles. One of these
was the primacy of the common school. The other was the differentiation
of superior education by curriculum and gender. Despite his best efforts,
however, both had been problematic from the beginning, and during the
decade of the 1870s they steadily lost ground. Even as Ryerson reaped the
encomiums of thirty years of public service, the gap between his own vision
of how things should be and the schools as they actually were was already
too wide ever to be closed.

CHAPTER TEN

The "Degradation" of the Public School

The common school, Ryerson had always insisted, must be more than just a primary school. It must offer not only the rudiments of learning, however important they might be, but a complete English education as well, advanced enough to finish the education of all but the small number of children who would attend a classical or ladies' school. He had first articulated this expansive vision of the common school in his inaugural report of 1846, had reiterated it in 1858 in his first program of studies for common schools, and, in 1871, had incorporated it into the prescribed curriculum for public schools. For Ryerson, in other words, the primacy of the common or public school was a fundamental part of his thinking about the way in which schooling was to be organized in Upper Canada. Nor was it an idiosyncratic *idée fixe*. Its roots lay in pre-Victorian distinctions between ordinary and liberal education and in overlapping assumptions about the relationship between education and social class. It was a conviction shared by many trustees, teachers, and local inspectors throughout the entire period, and it remained official policy well after Ryerson had retired. [1]

It was, nonetheless, a chimera. The overlapping programs of studies written into the regulations in 1871 – fifth and sixth classes in the public school, first and second forms in the high school – pitted the two institutions against each other in direct competition for students. Year by year, throughout the 1870s, the high schools gained ground at the expense of the public schools. The number of senior classes and pupils in the public schools dwindled while the grip of the high schools on them tightened steadily. By the early 1880s, indeed, Ryerson's worst fears had been realized. The common or public school had lost any claim it might ever have made to primacy within the system and had largely been reduced to an elementary feeder to the high school. The reasons for this shift are various, reflecting both the unintended consequences of official policy and the educational imperatives of local boards, teachers, parents, and county inspectors. But however explained, the "degradation" of the public school proceeded relentlessly.

Perhaps the most important factor in undermining the primacy of the public school was the differential in the high school and public school grants. In 1871 the legislature raised the high school grant from $57,000 to $70,000 annually. Additionally, the new act required local municipalities to raise at least half that amount, or $35,000, making a minimum amount of $105,000 to be distributed on the basis of average attendance and payment by educational results. But so long as no workable scheme of payment by results could be agreed upon, average attendance was the crucial determinant of how much a high school would receive. In 1871 Ryerson estimated that by this gauge each high school pupil earned a school board between $25 and $30. As the number of high school pupils rose over the next few years, the value of the grant declined to about $16 per pupil in 1875. Even this lesser amount, however, stood in stark contrast to the value of a public school pupil, which in either year amounted to a paltry $1.00.[2]

If, as Ryerson had originally intended, the high schools and collegiate institutes had trained only classical pupils or those in English studies who had already completed the full public school program, this differential might have had little impact on enrolment patterns. But the decision to lower the entrance standard for both programs to the fourth class of the public school was fatal to any hope of preserving the public school program intact. Even if they wished to, local boards, and especially union boards, could hardly resist the temptation, or the demands from local taxpayers, to press pupils into the high school at the earliest possible moment. And such pressures could not help but increase with the economic depression of the middle 1870s. The smaller high schools had especially strong incentives to keep their entrance standards as low as the inspectors would tolerate, for the smaller the number of students, the greater the risk that the schools would not survive at all. The comment of the local public school inspector about the effects of the Omemee high school on the public schools in nearby Emily township is typical. They were, he reported in 1873, not in an efficient state, due mainly "to the low standard of admission at Omemee High School. Scholars have been admitted who should have attended the public schools at least another year, and thereby pupils, Teachers and Trustees have been deceived and led to think that scholars were better qualified than they actually were."[3] Equally, public school boards had powerful incentives to establish a high school in order to reap grant revenues and lower the cost of local education to the taxpayers. In Almonte, a new high school was formed, the visiting inspector noted, "by discharging one of the Public School teachers, and erecting the highest division [of the public school] into a High School, and now three Public School teachers, one man and two young girls, are trying to do the work of at least five teachers."[4]

As well, many high school boards abolished tuition fees, hoping by this means to attract large numbers of students who might otherwise be kept in the senior grades of the public school; by 1872, indeed, 74 of the 104 high schools were tuition-free, while most of the rest charged merely nominal fees.[5] The logic of the situation was such that not even large communities, with well-established school systems, could resist the pressure to transfer pupils as soon as they could pass the entrance examination. By 1873, for example, Hamilton had adopted this policy holus-bolus. At the last entrance exam, the high school inspector explained, "several divisions [i.e. classes] of the Central School were admitted to the Collegiate Institute." Three of these classes never actually darkened the door of the collegiate, remaining in the central school to be taught the overlapping senior subjects by public school teachers. But they were registered as high school pupils "simply because the grant *per capita* to pupils in a High School is much greater than to pupils in a Public School."[6] The way in which pupils "have, in some places, been rushed into the High Schools," clucked the editor of the *Brantford Expositor*,

has become almost a scandal. In many places the trustees of the Public Schools, unlike the trustees of ours, have taken a practical view of the matter and have pushed up into the High School scores of pupils wholly unqualified – enough for them to know the more pupils the greater the government money. Towns of one-fourth the population of Brantford have been for years drawing double the money we have drawn simply because they have had double the average attendance.[7]

Despite the advantages bestowed by the grant differential, the financial position of most high schools, especially the small country schools, remained precarious until the later 1870s. Tuition fees aside, there were three sources of funds to support the high schools. One was the legislative grant. Another was the contribution from the county, which had to raise an amount equal to at least half the legislative grant. The third source was taxation levied by the high school board on the property within each high school district. Outside of cities and the large incorporated towns, it was the duty of the county council to create these districts. Ever reluctant to impose high school taxes on farm folk, however, the councils tended to create high school districts encompassing urban communities alone, or at least including only a village plus its contiguous townships. Large parts of most counties were not included in any high school district and were not, therefore, liable to be taxed by any high school board.[8] Because the counties were required to raise an amount equal to half the legislative grant, however, county pupils who lived outside a high school district still had the right to attend a local high school without paying tuition fees, or, at least, paying no higher fees than village children. Thus the villages and small towns, under financial pressures themselves, were left to build and maintain a school and impose on their own residents whatever additional rate was required to keep the school going. Since the grant to country high schools could be quite small, a village might well be forced to choose between taxing itself heavily or closing the school. To impose tuition fees was no solution either, since fees might drive pupils away and thus lower the per pupil grant. Overall then, small urban communities bore more than their fair share of maintaining a high school, or so at least their school boards and municipal councils believed. In Kemptville "fully one-third of the students come from beyond the corporation," the headmaster of the local high school complained, "and yet neither the County nor any part of it contributes either to the school or the teachers' salaries. Over and above the local [County] and legislative grants fully $300 are to be made up. The village itself pays this and still allows a free school. The taxes here are over 3¢ in the dollar and in the townships around not 8 mills."[9]

As the number of high school pupils began to rise in the middle 1870s, complaints such as this multiplied. The villages and towns of rural Ontario bore the burden of subsidizing the education of wealthy farmers' sons and daughters, and at the same time the costs of maintaining a local school were, on a per capita basis, far higher than in the cities. Should such injustices persist, warned a memorial to the legislature from the boards of trustees of twelve small high schools in eastern Ontario, "the benefits of Higher Education must inevitably be confined to Cities and Towns."[10] The county councils, dominated by township representatives, remained unsympathetic: when the village of Meaford sought to establish a high school, for example, the county threatened to redraw the boundaries of the high school district in order to exclude the farm properties in nearby townships.[11]

Traditionally, provincial politicians had shrunk from any measure that would have taxed farmers for urban high schools. But as the complaints from unhappy villagers multiplied, and as the number of children from rural townships climbed steadily in the 1870s, due in large part at least to higher standards required for teacher certification, and perhaps due as well to the needs of farm families to provide for their sons and daughters in new ways, the government was persuaded that remedial measures were necessary.[12] Early in 1877, Adam Crooks, the new minister of education, explained to the House that while government appropriations to high schools had risen massively during the 1870s, the attitude of too many county councils had been one of "extreme parsimony"; this despite the fact that "the whole benefit is not derived by the town or village in which the school is placed, but that the surrounding country is [also] deriving substantial benefits."[13] Thus the law was to be changed to ensure justice for all. Councils could no longer carve parts of a county into high school districts. Instead the whole of the county must constitute one or more districts, thus making all inhabitants liable for high school taxes. But more important, counties were now required to raise an amount equal not just to half the legislative grant, as had been the case since 1865, but equal to the full amount – something Ryerson had been proposing for twenty years.[14]

The new legislation did not right all the wrongs of financing the high school. Towns and villages remained responsible for building schools and maintaining them, while so long as the grant remained tied to average attendance, imposing tuition fees to offset costs merely invoked the law of diminishing returns. Complaints about the inequities between urban and rural contributions would continue well into the next century.[15] The revised act of 1877, nevertheless, contained one signal accomplishment. It finally secured for superior education the kind of tax support the common schools had had since 1841. While this undoubtedly benefited all high schools, it was the salvation of the small-town high schools, enabling even village schools to improve their physical plant and hire additional teachers. By 1880 all but one or two schools complied with the two-teacher regulation, while the average number of teachers per school stood at three.[16] The incentive to maintain free high schools, meanwhile, remained in place: there was little to be gained by imposing tuition fees if the effect was to exclude pupils and thereby lower the grant. Thus by 1880, 75 of the 105 high schools were free to residents.[17] The new legislation of 1877, however, compounded the advantage the grant differential gave the high school over the public school. For the first time the high school could compete in terms of physical plant and equipment, areas where the public school had always had an edge, and aside from such things as books and supplies, it was no more expensive for individuals than the local public school.

The accumulating advantages won by the high school were not, of course, designed deliberately to undermine the primacy of the public school. Throughout the 1870s the intent of official policy was to maintain the teaching of the higher subjects in the public schools and to encourage transfer to the high school only after the fifth and sixth classes had been completed. Though the compromises forced upon Ryerson in 1870–71 had lowered the entrance standard and allowed the two programs of study to overlap, the Education Office had, from the beginning, another regulatory device at its disposal to act as a counterweight to the low standard of the entrance exam in controlling the flow of pupils into the high schools. A portion of the grant, in the words of the act of 1871, was to be distributed according to "proficiency in the various branches of study." In common parlance this meant "payment by results."

Payment by results had been applied to elementary education in England in the early 1860s and had very quickly caught the fancy of a variety of Upper Canadian editors, politicians, and schoolmen. An editorial in the *Globe*, for example, described the scheme in glowing terms as one which would ensure that government grants "will be exactly proportional to the results achieved." The writer then went on to quote approvingly Robert Lowe's now infamous aphorism that "under the new system there will be either efficiency or economy, while under the present system there is neither."[18] The idea had also attracted the attention of Ryerson and Young, who saw it as a means of improving the grammar schools by tying part of the grant to the quality of teaching in classics and higher English subjects. They had apparently held discussions on the subject with the Rev. James Fraser, a visiting English school commissioner, and from his first report in 1864 onwards, Young himself was particularly persistent in promoting the idea.[19] The effect of distributing the grant solely by average attendance, Young would write in 1871, had been "to empty into the Grammar Schools all the upper Classes of the Common Schools ... The Common Schools were degraded by having almost all their Pupils ... drained off as soon as the children were able to parse a single English Sentence; and the Grammar Schools were crowded with Boys and Girls for whom the Grammar School Course of Study was not adapted." The only solution was to make the grant dependent "not on numbers alone, but on results likewise. To speak mathematically," Young concluded, the size of the grant "should be a function of the two variable quantities, the number of Pupils in attendance, and the character of the instruction imparted."[20]

The problem was that the English version of the scheme depended on intensive site visits by an inspector, and neither in 1865 nor in 1871 was the Ontario government prepared to underwrite the salaries of the additional staff needed to do the job properly. Yet the issue was urgent because the low standard set for the entrance examination in the regulations of 1871 meant that the "emptying" of the senior public school classes would inevitably continue if no countermeasures were taken. The solution, put forward in its final form by the high school inspectors, gradually emerged during 1873 and 1874 and was approved by the Council of Public Instruction in May 1875.[21]

The new scheme retained the fixed sum of $400 automatically given to all schools – a guarantee that even the smallest schools would be assured of a minimum level of income. As before, a part of the grant was also to be given for average daily attendance, but the rate was set at an amount equal to the public school grant. For the first time, in other words, the high schools would earn no more than the public schools from attendance alone. Yet another portion of the grant was to be awarded on the basis of the inspectors' assessment of such things as accommodation, equipment, and general efficiency. But the most innovative part of the scheme was the introduction of an "intermediate examination" to be drafted by the department and administered to all pupils at the end of the second form. Only those who passed this exam would be allowed to enter the third form. A portion of the grant would then be allocated on the basis of average attendance in the third and fourth forms.

On the face of it, the idea was ingenious. The Gordian knot of grammar school finance was to be cut by the joint operation of two province-wide written examinations, both administered by the Education Office. The entrance exam already maintained minimum entry standards that were at the same time set low enough so that even the smallest high school would not be starved of pupils and a share of the grant. But with the reduced rate for average attendance in the lower forms, and the premium derived from en-rolling students in the upper forms, the better high schools would have every incentive to concentrate their efforts on their senior students, leaving the junior pupils to finish the fifth and sixth classes of the public school before transferring to the advanced forms of the high school. Small country schools, in sum, would survive; larger schools would be rewarded for high-quality advanced work; and the degradation of the public school would be halted. The plan went into operation in 1876 and following the first round of examinations in the summer of that year the high school inspectors reported that they could see improvement: the adoption of payment by results, they wrote, "has differentiated more clearly the functions of the High Schools from those of the Public Schools, and has also lessened the difficulties arising from the overlapping of the High and Public School Courses of Study."[22] By late 1877 they were well pleased with themselves. The solution they had "ventured to recommend to Council has been beneficial in a marked degree," not only in distributing the grant "in a more equitable manner as regards the merits of the several schools, but in imparting a stimulus to higher education throughout the Province, and in making that education better suited to the wants of the general community."[23]

Though they are not alone in this, it is a common conceit amongst ed-ucational administrators that vexing educational problems can be ameliorated by the application of more efficient machinery and more minute regulations. Their best intentions, consequently, often come to naught. So it was in the case of Ontario's experiment with payment by results. The Intermediate examination was, in the first place, an administrative device – it existed to channel money in some directions and not others. The results mattered a great deal to trustees and to teachers, but for students and parents, an obvious question arose: of what use was it to write this new examination? Initially at least, the answer was, none at all, for it provided a pupil with no qual-ification for anything beyond admission to third form. For their part, teachers were reluctant to exclude senior pupils who might well be preparing for "real" examinations – those which qualified them for matriculation in law or medicine or the universities. Such students were often unavailable for the Intermediate in any case since it was scheduled at the same time as several matriculation exams. For other pupils, not intending to continue into third form, there was no incentive to write the Intermediate at all. And they didn't. Late in 1876 the ministry had to issue a circular warning that no pupils could be counted towards the grant unless they had passed the ex-amination, nor could such students remain in the school unless registered in the lower forms. Thus, according to regulation 8, "absence from the examination precludes a pupil from again being admitted to the school except as therein provided."[24] High school boards, understandably exercised about the grant, took to suspending pupils for skipping the examination.[25] And John Seath, an activist headmaster and rising star in the province's educational firmament, condemned ministry arrangements in a speech to the Ontario Teachers' Association, pointing to the impossible dilemma posed by the Intermediate: the teacher

must either do injustice to his pupil, by interference with his course of study, and so likely drive him away, or do injustice to his employers, by conniving at a loss of government aid, not to speak of the injury he will himself sustain. The trouble arises from the fact, that while the strongest possible inducement is held out to the master to prepare candidates for the "Intermediate," there is, in a great many instances, no reason why the pupil should attach any significance to it. There can be no justification in placing the teacher at the mercy of the pupils and their friends.[26]

Some of these problems were obviated in 1878 when the Intermediate was linked to teacher certification; and students gradually became accustomed to the fact that, useful or not, it had to be written in order to gain access to upper school. Teachers and their allies, however, were not so easily placated. In language that would recur for almost a century thereafter with reference to one provincial examination after another, until every last one was abolished, the Intermediate was condemned as "degrading" to the profession of teaching. Men, one observer asserted, "who are capable of holding the position of teachers in our Collegiate Institutes and High Schools are worthy of being entrusted with the performance of their work."[27] The examination, it was said, fostered pressure and cram, directed the efforts of pupils and teachers alike to subjects and parts of subjects easiest to memorize and to test, and promoted an undignified rivalry among schools.[28] The *Educational Monthly*, a new journal devoted to Ontario education, kept up a barrage of criticism of the ministry because of the deleterious effects the examination was having on the high schools and by 1880 even two of the three high school inspectors were critical of its educational effects.[29]

The cry of the countryside, moreover, was heard once more. Payment by examination results gave all the advantages to the city schools. One or two teachers in a village school, no matter how devoted, could never hope to prepare their scholars for competition with the products of the large urban high schools. The country schools "are thus impoverished, despoiled of the legitimate credit for their work, shorn of the glory which should have adorned their brows."[30]

The Intermediate was also difficult to administer. In the initial years, mass cheating was widespread and caused public scandal and bureaucratic embarrassment.[31] As the number of students writing the examination grew, it became difficult to have the papers marked within a reasonable time. And besides everything else, it was, as one critic pointed out in the *Globe*, a terribly expensive way of dividing up a legislative grant.[32] The examination had to be printed and distributed; proctors had to be paid; high school boards had to arrange for space to be available and had to provide answer papers; and the papers had to be marked by special examiners.[33] Local administrative costs and a rising number of candidates reduced the value of the grant, complained the Clinton trustees in 1880, from $36 to $3 per pupil in five years.[34] One of the high school inspectors agreed: he hoped the minister would soon take some action in the matter, he wrote in a private report, "as the Intermediate examination now costs nearly as much or more than the revenue it brings."[35] By 1882 the minister and his advisers were also convinced that the scheme was causing more trouble than it was worth and they prepared to abandon it.[36] The Intermediate examination itself was kept in place until 1885, but it ceased to be an arbiter of how the grant was to be distributed and became instead, like the high school entrance examination, a gatekeeper guarding the passage from one level of the system to the next.

For the internal history of the high school the short-lived experiment with payment by results is of limited significance. But its consequence for the relationship between the high and public school was important. Once again the men from the ministry had tried and failed to prevent the degradation of the public school by forcing the high school to focus on those studies not included in the public school program. The failure of the scheme meant that, as before, there was nothing but the high school entrance examination to protect the public school from the depredations of high school trustees or teachers in search of pupils and grants. Big urban schools could afford to refuse entrance to those who were minimally prepared and sometimes did. But for most schools, the failure of payment by results ensured that the differential in grants and the increased revenues arising from the act of 1877 worked in an unqualified way to the advantage of the high school in the competition for pupils and, no less important, in the competition to secure control over those subjects just beyond the rudiments of learning.

The high school had two other advantages as well. First, the educational and social *cachet* of the high school encouraged many parents to transfer their children from the public schools at the earliest possible moment. The high schools, of course, had more highly educated teachers, a factor undoubtedly important to some parents. "As the special subjects of the 5th and 6th classes are taught in the High School," the Perth County public school inspector remarked in 1871, "I imagine that these subjects will rarely be taught in the public schools, at least in a town, in which, as is the case with Stratford, a High School is in efficient operation and is taught by a gentleman of acknowledged ability."[37] It was not simply a matter of educational quality, however, as J.G. Hodgins explained to an American audience in the mid-1870s. Along with "parental ambition," he said, "it also involved somewhat of a social question, and is therefore the more embarrassing," a rare official acknowledgment of the continuing preference among parents for the social segregation of their children, which in this instance manifested itself in the early transfer of children into the high school.[38]

Secondly, there was the growing utility of the high school. Until the late 1870s, the high school had no special niche in the educational marketplace. It was, of course, not entirely without advantages: compared to the private schools, it was local and cheap; compared to the public school, it offered a variety of pre-vocational subjects such as classics or mathematics, and it might offer a degree of social exclusivity not available in the local public school. But it had no singular magnet to attract students to it. Between 1878 and 1880, however, that situation was to be dramatically changed – not, however, because of some historical *deus ex machina* such as the increasing relevance of superior education to an emerging urban, industrial society, but because of a bureaucratic decision to shift the main burden of teacher certification to the high schools.

Though the rules governing teacher certification, like so many other aspects of the system, had been revamped following the act of 1871, the minimum academic qualifications for the lowest level of certification, known as the third-class certificate, were set at about the end of the fourth class of the public school, and virtually no professional training was provided for candidates applying for that certificate. The academic standards for first- and second-class certificates were substantially higher and students were also required to attend the Normal School. But to go to Toronto (or by the mid-seventies, to Ottawa) for Normal School training was an expensive option for students and as a consequence the number of teachers holding only third-class certificates multiplied rapidly during the middle seventies, with no proportional increase in the number of those holding higher qualifications. By 1877 the ministry concluded that the province had a surplus of ill-educated, ill-trained teachers, and it was ready to raise substantially the levels of both professional and non-professional training.[39]

For third-class certificates this was simply a matter of pushing up the "non-professional" or academic qualifications and introducing a new system of professional training through the creation of a network of county Model Schools. For first- and second-class certificates the problem was more complicated. In the past these certificates had required several sessions at the Normal School, where students received both academic and professional training. Not only was this method of certification expensive for the individual, but the per capita costs to the province were high – substantially higher for example than the cost of educating high school pupils. While the ministry was eager to increase the number of higher certificates, it was not prepared to fund a massive expansion of the existing Normal School program. And thus, following a pattern already establishing itself in the United States, the ministry hived off academic work from professional training, making the latter the exclusive task of the Normal School and assigning the former to the high schools. Between 1878 and 1880 the Intermediate examination became the minimum non-professional qualification for the second-class, and then for the third-class, certificate. As a final step, in 1880 even the academic training for the first-class certificate was transferred from the Normal School to the high schools.[40]

The impact of this shift was enormous. For at least twenty years the high school had played a growing role in preparing candidates for the teachers' examinations – the inspectors' reports and a wide variety of other sources record the growing tendency for students who wanted a teaching certificate to transfer to the high school for a year or two before they wrote their qualifying examination.[41] Until 1878, nonetheless, this was entirely voluntary. Standards were low enough that academic preparation for second- and especially third-class certificates could just as well be carried on in any common school that offered competent instruction in the fourth and fifth classes. After 1878, however, it was increasingly necessary to attend a high school, since not all of the subjects of the Intermediate were taught in the public schools and most public school teachers themselves lacked the education to prepare pupils for that examination. One immediate consequence was a remarkable increase in high school enrolments. These had been climbing steadily during the 1870s at around 6 per cent a year; in 1878, however, enrolments grew by over 14 per cent, and increased by that much again in 1879.[42] Whatever the other uses of a high school education, the transfer of responsibility for the non-professional training of teachers to the high school was a crucial element in securing its future role within the Ontario educational system. Indeed it transformed the high school into a giant teacher-training machine; by the late 1870s it was estimated that somewhere between a third and a half of all high school students were preparing for teaching certificates.[43] It was, moreover, of critical importance to the country schools, which had led such a precarious existence for so long. Rural youngsters who might otherwise have finished their general education in the common schools and then entered directly into teaching now had no choice but to make the trek to the village or small-town high school for at least a year or two, ensuring that even the smallest, weakest high school had a role that the public school could not perform.

It was more than a matter of numbers, however. The transfer of academic preparation to the high schools secured them a degree of "popular sympathy," as one observer put it, that they had traditionally lacked.[44] The transfer, John Seath explained in 1879, had given the high schools

a claim on public support that in many places is the strongest argument for municipal generosity. Their claims on other grounds are no doubt equally cogent, but this is one in which the case of an efficient school comes home to the most economical councillor.

No less important, it brought the local high and public schools more closely together. "The Public School Master of the future will have been the High School student, and we may look for the complete extinction of an antagonism which still lingers in some localities."[45]

While the links between the high and public school might indeed have been tightened, the price was the further subordination of the public school. As large numbers of its senior pupils were drawn away to the high school, the viability of its senior classes decreased and the focus of attention inevitably shifted increasingly to the junior grades and pupils. The chief task of the public school was rapidly becoming not to complete a good English education but to prepare youngsters to complete that education elsewhere.

The weight of our argument thus far has fallen on those forces that pulled pupils into the high school. But there were also a variety of pressures *pushing* senior pupils out of the public schools. One of these was the simple fact of overcrowding in the public school. As public school enrolments began to climb in the early 1870s, due in part at least to the introduction of compulsory education, there were increasing pressures on the available classroom space in existing schools. In London, for example, the schools were so crowded that senior pupils, according to the editor of the *London Advertiser*, "willing or unwilling ... have to pass into the High School as soon as they acquire such a smattering of education as will bring them up to the standard prescribed for admission."[46] As in the 1860s, moreover, there was a good deal of complaint that the overlapping curricula of the schools defied common sense and should therefore be eliminated regardless of the dictates of the official program. "The work of the 5th and 6th classes corresponds almost exactly with that laid down for the first and second forms of High Schools," one bemused high school teacher wrote in 1875. "As far as pupils individually are concerned, it does not matter one iota where they go over the work laid down in the programme for those classes. Why the Council of Public Instruction has caused the programme of the two classes of schools to overlap is more than I have been able to determine."[47] For similar reasons, the Port Hope Board of Public School Trustees petitioned the Education Office in 1876, begging to be allowed to abolish their fifth and sixth classes, and at the end of the decade the Oshawa trustees informed Hodgins that they were about to make it compulsory for pupils to transfer to the high school at the end of the fourth class.[48] In public, the ministry firmly rejected all such initiatives, reiterating that boards were required to maintain fifth and sixth classes and parents had a legal right to keep their children in the public schools for senior work.[49] Many boards, nonetheless, simply allowed the senior classes to lapse: by 1880, for example, less than half the incorporated towns had fifth classes and only 10 per cent had sixth classes.[50] And in private at least, even senior ministry officials had doubts. In 1874 a new high school inspector remarked in passing that the existence of overlapping fifth classes and first forms in one small town "raises the question whether two schools should be supported by public money to do the same work in the same place."[51]

In the townships the decline of fifth and sixth classes occurred for somewhat different reasons. Most rural schools had but one teacher and her attention was necessarily focused on the majority of youngsters, who were concentrated in the first three classes. If she had time left over it would be spent with the fourth class, preparing them for the entrance. She could cope with little else. In most country schools, as one public school inspector pointed out, "the number of classes under charge of one teacher prevents the bestowal of the time necessary to ensure even reasonable proficiency; hence the [senior] class is nearly insignificant in numbers and nominal in rank."[52] Many rural teachers, moreover, held only third-class certificates, which limited their ability to instruct senior pupils. "So long as our teachers are unable to take at least a Second Class Certificate," said one observer, "we may look in vain for 5th and 6th class pupils."[53]

But even where teachers were competent to handle senior classes, the reformation of the rural schools being carried out by the new public school inspectorate tended to de-emphasize the importance of fifth- and sixth-class work. The first generation of inspectors, who were generally required to hold first-class certificates, and who had often learned their craft in the graded schools of the towns and cities, saw their mandate as one of replacing the irregular practices of the rural schools with order and regularity.[54] Among other things this meant a massive program of reclassification of pupils downwards in order to correct what the inspectors saw as the haphazard promotion policies common in rural schools. "Imperfect classification" was blamed on teacher error or ignorance, on parental pressure, or, as one inspector remarked, on the fact that "scholars have been known to promote themselves in the interval of changing teachers."[55] Throughout the seventies, inspectors attempted to organize country pupils into groups that advanced uniformly, subject by subject, grade by grade, through their school careers. In short, they tried to bring the graded city school to the countryside.

The process of reclassification pressed forward the decapitation of the public school. Among their other objections to traditional modes of promotion and classification, inspectors charged that senior students were often advanced in one or two subjects but very weak in others. Some inspectors claimed that pupils had been promoted with inadequate preparation even in reading and arithmetic; J.J. Wadsworth reported that in Norfolk County many senior pupils "had exactly the same knowledge of words that parrots have."[56] Therefore one of the first results of reclassification was the demotion of large numbers of students to junior grades and the consequent shrinkage of enrolments in the fifth and sixth classes.

The success of the high school entrance examination played a part in the decline of the senior public school classes as well. Though the examination was originally designed with very limited purposes in mind – to ensure that public school pupils who wished to enter high school were properly qualified, and to prevent the high school from encroaching on the primary work of the public schools – the "entrance" gradually came to be a major influence on the entire public school program. Teachers, concentrating their efforts on the first half of the program of studies, saw it as the upward limit of their capacities and the crowning achievement of their efforts. Public school inspectors and editorial writers saw it as the supreme test of the efficiency of the local public schools and the means by which schools could be ranked and compared. For pupils and parents it gained significance as a school-leaving examination, the entrance certificate awarded for a pass being coveted even when pupils had no intention of going on to high school.[57] For all these reasons, and without any prior intent, the entrance examination gradually came to be seen as the symbolic terminal point of the public school, while senior work increasingly seemed less integral to its purpose or a legitimate part of its task.[58]

Once such opinions had become commonplace, it was but a short step to enshrining them in law. Between 1877 and 1882 a series of revisions in the program of studies introduced more flexibility and allowed local teachers and trustees more control over the curriculum of their schools.[59] Embedded in this process was the gradual marginalization of senior work in the public schools. The regulations of 1871 had outlined a set of prescriptions which, however suited to the big graded schools of the cities and towns, were utterly impractical for the vast majority of Ontario schools. As one public school inspector remarked in 1873, it was "the almost unanimous verdict of the Teachers after prolonged trial ... that these models cannot be strictly followed in rural Schools. Some of the best and most diligent Teachers have, after twelve months' experience, been compelled to make wide variations."[60] Such complaints were heard repeatedly during the middle seventies but nothing was done until after Ryerson's retirement in 1876. The next year, however, a revised program was issued containing significant modifications. On the face of it, the Ryersonian program remained intact, for there were to be six classes, the last two, as before, overlapping the work of the high school. In principle all six classes remained mandatory. In fact, the regulations made it clear that teachers, trustees, and inspectors might modify the program to fit the circumstances of their localities. In 1879 trustees were given more discretionary powers over the curriculum and the emphasis in ministry reports began to focus more and more on teaching the "essentials" to the great bulk of public school pupils concentrated in the first three classes rather than the "secondary" subjects to the small number of "clever" pupils in the fifth and sixth classes.[61] Yet another revision of the regulations in 1882 went even further. There were still six classes listed in the program, but now, for the first time, it was divided into two parts, one covering classes one to four, and the other, five and six. Part I was labelled "elementary" and part II "secondary." Trustees were further instructed that "the subjects in the Course are not to be taken as obligatory upon all Public School Boards ... without discrimination, but only so far as, in their judgement, the circumstances will allow."

The final step was taken in 1885. New regulations abolished the sixth class and specified that "trustees are recommended not to form a fifth class in the public school in any city, town, or incorporated village, where a High School is situated."[62] In the same year, John Seath, now elevated to the high school inspectorate, remarked that "for very many pupils, the High School Entrance Examination is a 'leaving examination' and in very few public schools has a fifth class been established. The High School Entrance Examination practically, therefore, defines the superior limit of the Public School course."[63] Two years later the minister of education, George Ross, pronounced the epitaph for Ryerson's expansive vision of the public school program. The fourth class, Ross wrote, "may be said to be the limit of the ordinary Public School course. For advanced pupils, to whom a High School is not accessible, a more extended course of study is provided, corresponding to the First Form in a High School; many of the best schools in the Province, however, confine themselves exclusively to the work of the four forms."[64]

The transition from the Ryersonian vision of the public school to the elementary school of the 1880s was not without its critics. Some leading public school teachers and inspectors, for example, repeatedly condemned it as inimical to the status of public school teachers themselves, and because it rushed pupils into the high schools at too early an age, educationally unsound as well.[65] The "degradation" of the public school was also condemned because it interfered with the promotion of equality of educational opportunity. City high schools, and especially the collegiate institutes, were the most likely schools to charge tuition fees; indeed, at a time when most of the province's high schools were tuition-free, only about 40 per cent of the collegiate institutes were free to residents.[66] The consequence was described by the public school inspector for Brant County. "During the last ten years," he wrote of Brantford in 1879,

our principal aim here has been to train up pupils for the High School Entrance Exams. The result has undoubtedly been beneficial to the Collegiate Institute, but whether or not it has been so to our Public Schools, is open to debate. A number of those who pass the examination every half-year, decline to enter, their parents probably being unable to supply them with the necessary fees and books. These remain often in the first division of the Central School and go over the work again that they had just finished. To remedy this evil a Sixth Class might be formed for more extended and higher instruction in English, science and mathematics.[67]

In a society that was overwhelmingly rural, inequities of access caused by geography tended to be of particular concern. In the midst of a long speech given in 1884 on the ills of the school system, George Grant, the principal of Queen's University, posed the following question: how shall "the poorest child in any part of the country ... be enabled, if he has brains, to come into contact with the best teachers in the country? Does our system accomplish that? No, it does not." The problem, Grant continued, was that Ontario had no equivalent to the Scottish parish schools where boys could be prepared for university and still live at home. In Ontario, he said, "the boy must go to a High School. But that is out of the question for thousands. It is as expensive to board five miles from home as five hundred ... Besides, those who can afford to go to High School cannot afford to stay long. They thus get a smattering, and are miserably prepared for college."[68]

Whatever the pertinence of these criticisms, however, for all the reasons we have reviewed in this chapter, the provision of senior work in the public schools declined precipitously during the 1870s. In 1869, the year before the new act, 17 per cent of common school pupils had been enrolled in the fifth reader. In 1871, 14 per cent were enrolled in the fifth and sixth classes. By 1881 the figure was 3.3 per cent (see general table 6). During the same decade, high school enrolment rose from 7500 pupils to just under 13,000. The vast bulk of these pupils, moreover, were concentrated in the first two forms. Even as late as 1883, four-fifths of the students were enrolled in the two lower forms of the high school – the very forms that duplicated the work of the senior classes of the public school.[69]

At its higher reaches, the high school remained primarily a preparatory school for the universities and the professions, thus retaining elements of the distinctive and specialist role Ryerson had assigned it. But in the two decades after 1871 it began to acquire the outlines of another role as well. As the public school withdrew from senior work, the high school absorbed the second part of the mandate Ryerson had given the public school – to provide not only the rudiments but to finish the English education of the majority of young people.

This shift, however, had a paradoxical effect. While the high school absorbed the senior curriculum of the public school, it made no provision for actually offering that curriculum to the majority of the public school pupils. For decades the door to the high school was barred by a rigorous entrance examination and the high school itself considered to be a highly selective institution. The public school had, in effect been cut off at the knees and left with no program of studies to offer older pupils, most of whom could not or would not attend a high school. This curious lacuna would remain in place until the middle decades of the twentieth century, when the introduction of a unified intermediate curriculum, extending from grades 7 to 10, and the enforcement of the compulsory school-leaving age of sixteen, recreated the notion of a common school for all pupils which included senior studies and not just the rudiments alone. Perhaps it did not matter much in any case, since in the 1870s or 1880s, universal education hardly extended beyond the third class, only a relative few staying on to complete the fourth class and fewer still attempting the entrance examination.

By the 1870s, nonetheless, the model for the future was in place. The overlap between the two programs of study had virtually been eliminated and the boundary lines between the high and public schools had been stabilized. The public school now prepared for entrance to the high school, and not only were the two programs of study articulated but, conceptually at least, they were part of a single curricular whole, the one incomplete without the other. By the standards of Ryerson's expansive vision at least, the public school had been "degraded" to a primary school, and even in the few cases where it did "secondary" work, it was implicitly an inferior if necessary form of secondary education suitable only for those pupils, as George Ross put it, "to whom a high school is not accessible."

CHAPTER ELEVEN

Reshaping the High School Curriculum

Just as the primacy of the public school was steadily undermined during the 1870s, so indeed was that other principle which had informed Ryerson's vision: the differentiation of superior education by gender and by the curricula appropriate to a liberal and ordinary education. In the first case, this demanded separate schools for girls and boys, and, in the second, distinct programs of study; but one way or another such differentiation had been a fundamental goal for Ryerson from the time he had been appointed superintendent of education. Here again, however, he was never able to translate official policy into educational practice. In the 1870s, as in the 1860s, long-established patterns of educational provision proved obdurate against Ryerson's best efforts to change them, while new currents of opinion arose to challenge the legitimacy of his own pedagogical prescriptions. As a result, even as Ryerson prepared to retire from office, the pattern of superior education taking shape in the province was far different from the one he had sought for nearly thirty years.

In all of their plans to rewrite the act and regulations of 1865, Ryerson and his advisers had assumed that there was only a very limited demand for classical instruction and thus that once the yoke of qualifying Latin was removed, many high schools, especially country schools, would abandon Latin altogether and concentrate their resources on English subjects alone. It was this conviction that underpinned their recommendations in 1871 that each high school conform to one of three categories: the collegiate institute, with its primary emphasis on advanced classical work; the large high school, which though it focused on English studies might offer some classical instruction if demand warranted it; and the majority of schools, including all of the smaller ones, which would offer instruction only in the English program. So seriously was this scheme taken, indeed, that the regulations of 1871 made it very difficult to offer both the classical and English programs in small country schools.[1]

From the outset, however, the schools refused to be moulded into this tripartite pattern. In their report for 1871, the high school inspectors had already been forced to concede that "the abandonment of classical study has been by no means as general as might have been anticipated."[2] Not surprisingly, total enrolments in Latin declined considerably once it ceased to be linked to the grant. But it continued to be taught, even in the smallest schools. Not just in 1871 but throughout the decade *every* high school in the province reported pupils enrolled in Latin. And virtually 90 per cent of the schools had at least a handful of pupils enrolled in Greek.[3] To the inspectors, the explanation seemed simple enough: "the greater difficulties of the English programme, with its larger quantum of science" encouraged pupils to enrol in the classical program instead.[4] There may have been an element of truth in this, particularly in light of the fact that only by enrolling in the classical program could girls take French and also avoid a stiff dose of commercially oriented subjects. But classics remained a *sine qua non* for matriculation into law, medicine, and the universities, and thus there was continuing demand for classical instruction not just in a handful of cities, where the prestigious collegiates might be located, but in places like Aylmer, Arnprior, and Almonte as well. And Latin presumably remained attractive to parents and students for another reason too: even a smattering of classics bestowed a sheen of culture and liberal learning. Whatever the regulations or the official program of studies might say, then, classics refused to disappear, even in the smallest and weakest of country schools. And thus the organization of the high schools according to whether they did or did not offer classical instruction became one more lost cause.

Yet another casualty was the prescribed program of studies itself. In 1871, as in 1865, Ryerson had tried to ensure that the high school curriculum was organized into tightly structured, clearly focused groupings of subjects that would provide students with a coherent course of study. The regulations set out two such courses, classical and English, each with its own set of prescribed subjects. Each course was to be kept distinct from the other, and, in the words of the regulation itself, "no departure from the prescribed Programme is allowable."[5] Virtually all schools, as we have just suggested, provided instruction in Latin and Greek. But, large or small, they were under a variety of other pressures as well – to offer bookkeeping or telegraphy to budding clerks, trigonometry and mensuration to apprentice engineers, or the full range of required subjects to those preparing for the second- and third-class teachers' certificates. Even two or three teachers in a school could not teach all of these subjects, at several different levels, and still maintain two entirely separate courses of study. From the beginning, then, and especially in the country and small-town schools, the prescribed program of study proved utterly unworkable. After three years of visiting the schools, the high school inspectors provided a bleak assessment of its future. The program assumed, they told Ryerson in 1873, that every School possesses the requisite number of Teachers for the prescribed subjects, and that all the Pupils in the respective courses are willing, or can be persuaded, to take all the subjects prescribed for them. To state these assumptions is, to any one acquainted with the circumstances of the High Schools, to refute them ...

The rigid inelasticity of the Programme renders it as a Provincial scheme, unsuitable to the varied states of society that are to be found among the people of this Province.

Nor was it their conclusion alone, they continued. "The verdict of the Masters in regard to the present Programme of Studies is singularly unanimous." When teachers were asked if the program was observed in their schools, they replied in one of three ways: "1st. 'We try to'; 2nd, 'We don't pretend to'; 3rd, 'As far as practicable'; all of which, being interpreted, resolve themselves into this, that the Programme, is practically, inoperative, so far as controlling and shaping the Course of Study in the High School is concerned."[6] Summing up the problems in the following year, the inspectors were no less blunt. "It has been found that the formal distinction between the English and Classical Course cannot in practice be maintained; that the sharp division into four Forms cannot be effected; and that too many subjects and too many classes have to be carried on concurrently."[7]

Such criticisms as these constituted a direct attack on Ryerson's own long-standing convictions and on policies he himself had drafted and advocated; it is an index of his faltering leadership during the mid-seventies that they should be published at all by his subordinates in the Education Department's annual reports. They reflect nonetheless an internal shift in the same direction: Ryerson was now increasingly seeking advice from his inspectors, whereas only a few years earlier, they would have turned to him.[8] Even before he retired, indeed, he acquiesced in a major revision of the high school curriculum that entirely overturned the principles embedded in the regulations of 1865 and 1871, and that challenged all of his convictions about a well-ordered program of studies.

The occasion for the rewriting of the program was provided by the decision to use a written examination as the basis for payment by results.[9] Such an examination required a common core of subjects that all pupils had studied. Too many subjects would prove unmanageable, while different subjects, written by pupils enrolled in two different programs, would not provide uniform criteria for distributing the grant. The fact that the existing program was unworkable was, in itself, enough to justify revision, the inspectors argued, but the imperatives of introducing payment by results made it urgent. Thus the inspectors recommended the abolition of both the classical and English courses and also the four existing forms or grades. The program of studies was to be divided instead into two parts: lower school and upper school. The Intermediate examination would mark the completion of the former and give access to the latter. The number of subjects to be taught in the lower school would be reduced, while headmaster and trustees would be given the right to decide the year or term in which particular subjects were offered. The list of prescribed or compulsory subjects, moreover, was to be substantially reduced. All lower school students would be required to take English, history and geography, and mathematics (including arithmetic, algebra, and geometry). Students would then choose one or more additional subjects from modern languages (French and German); ancient languages (Latin and Greek); physical sciences (natural philosophy and chemistry); and bookkeeping. In the Upper School a similar pattern was to be followed unless a student was preparing for a particular matriculation examination, in which case he was required "to take only the subjects prescribed for such examination." Headmasters, moreover, were allowed to offer only those subjects at upper school level that they believed their staff competent to teach. Though the actual groupings of subjects were modified somewhat, the inspectors' program recommendations were adopted by the Council of Public Instruction in the spring of 1875, and came into effect in 1876.[10]

The new program contained some radical innovations. All pupils, regardless of their choice of options, were to be tested on the core subjects by the Intermediate examination.[11] This alone gave English, geography and history, and mathematics an unprecedented pre-eminence in the high school curriculum. Latin, on the other hand, was dethroned, taking its place as one subject amongst equals in the list of options. And in place of a prescribed *course* of study, students took a common core, and then selected those options which suited their taste and vocational destination. In the upper school, virtually all prescription was abandoned.

To anyone accustomed to Ryersonian notions about a coherent, focused course of study, the revised program of 1876 constituted a veritable revolution. The curriculum shibboleths of the past, above all the pre-eminence of the classics, and the distinction between a liberal and an ordinary English education, had been decisively rejected. Though these changes were the immediate product of some pressing administrative problems, their magnitude cannot be explained by the exigencies of the moment. What gave them legitimacy and their own internal coherence was a much broader and long-term shift in nineteenth-century thought about what constituted the curriculum of a liberal education.

Throughout the nineteenth century, the primary goal of education, superior or otherwise, was the acquisition of "mental culture" by means of "mental discipline." These were the two key phrases in a theory of learning associated with the doctrines of faculty psychology, the dominant explanation of the constitution of the human mind. According to faculty psychology, the mind consisted of a series of discrete faculties that matured in response to particular sorts of training or cultivation. One conventional analogy was to the development of the body through the exercise of different groups of muscles. A second metaphor was gardening. Teachers tilled or cultivated the pupil's mind with the aim of encouraging the growth of various moral and mental powers. The teacher's task was, for example, to ensure that the faculty of memory was exercised, the moral faculties stimulated, the will disciplined, the reasoning powers improved, and the capacity for understanding strengthened. [12]

Certain school subjects, so the argument went, were especially efficacious in promoting the growth of the mind. According to the high school inspectors in 1872, for example, the various branches of mathematics

cultivate and develop ... the powers of memory, abstraction and generalization, – that they familiarize the mind with the forms of strict logical inference, and impart habits of accuracy in the use of language, caution in the admission of premises, ingenuity in analysis and comparison, and powers of continuity of thought, – and are, therefore, entitled to a prominent place in every system of liberal education. [13]

Other core subjects had similar effects on the development of mind, and once the various faculties had matured, the powers acquired through education could be brought to bear, or transferred, to all of the experiences and challenges an individual might confront throughout life.

Though there was always some ambiguity in the matter, it is important to emphasize that "mental culture" did not, as modern usage might suggest, refer to the mastery of a particular set of facts, or a body of ideas. Rather a mind was "cultured" in the same sense as the word is used in the term "cultured pearls." It was a *quality* of mind, or a set of moral and mental attributes, that one acquired through cultivation. [14] Throughout the nineteenth century this interpretation was pervasive and fundamental. A college, Ryerson told his students at Victoria in 1842, was not so much "the storehouse of *general knowledge*" but rather "the School of *mental discipline*," and a collegiate education

is that regular apprenticeship of the mind which develops and harmoniously matures its latent faculties and directs their skillful application to the varied and noblest objects of human pursuit. The wealth of general knowledge is an acquisition subsequent to the servitude of apprenticeship, and is the fruit of its culture. And as the regularly taught and accomplished mechanic possesses by his skill a tenfold power over that of the untaught labourer ... so the natural strength of mind is variously multiplied by scholastic discipline. [15]

In his inaugural address at Queen's College in 1860, the new principal, Rev. William Leitch, made the same point in his description of the goals of a liberal education.

It ought not to be forgotten that the most valuable result of a College education is the mental culture rather than the technical acquirements of learning. No doubt a knowledge of Latin, Greek, Mathematics, Moral and Natural Philosophy has its special uses, which ought not to be overlooked, but in a course of liberal education, the great object to be aimed at is the cultivation of the mental powers. We are to look, not so much to the Knowledge itself as to the power of acquiring Knowledge. The technical branches of learning are the mere scaffolding, the training of the faculties is the solid structure. The scaffolding may be removed; a man may, in after life, forget his College learning, but his labour has not been lost, if there remain the solid and enduring result of a sound judgement, steady application and a refined taste, in short, the capability of excelling whatever his pursuits in life may be ... Men may, amidst the pressure of professional avocations, lay aside, though not wisely, the Knowledge they acquired at College, but they cannot, if distinction is to be gained, dispense with those mental habits and tastes which a College training conferred.[16]

Late in the century precisely the same point was made by George Ross, the minister of education. An acquaintance with scientific facts was, he said, "undoubtedly of practical value ... but the main reason for the introduction of the study of Science in our schools is the mental discipline to be obtained therefrom. The training of the reasoning powers and the acquisition of the scientific habit of mind are objects with special reference to which the methods of instruction should be chosen, and these will also be the main objects of the examination papers."[17]

   Mental culture, then, was central to the educational enterprise throughout the nineteenth century. But what subjects were best for cultivating students' minds? Or to borrow the phraseology of George Grant, yet another principal of Queen's, which subjects were "of the highest gymnastic value"?[18] The Georgian inheritance offered a clear answer to that question. Along with mathematics, classics were the paramount subjects in training and furnishing the mind. "The experience of long centuries," William Leitch explained, "has shown that, for general mental culture, there is no means to be compared to the study in early life of the ancient Classic Languages. Not only the Memory, but the judgment, logical accuracy of thought, and the exercise of a fine taste are necessarily brought into requisition."[19] So persuasive was this idea, especially before mid-century, that Ryerson's explanation in 1842 of the curriculum at Victoria College contained this telling preamble: "the admission of an English Department of Language, Science and Literature into a Collegiate Institution, may, I am aware, be regarded as a novelty or innovation."[20] Such subjects as English and science might be taught as regular and important parts of the curriculum in grammar schools and colleges but their place was generally acknowledged as subordinate to the literature and language of Greece and Rome. Nor did such convictions simply fade away in the second half of the century. Even some of the most avid proponents of English and scientific studies in the high schools and colleges remained convinced of the unique efficacy of classics. Paxton Young, for example, was no isolated voice when in the later 1860s he remarked that "the languages and literature of Greece and Rome are the most perfect of all educational instruments."[21] It was this same conviction that underpinned Ryerson's determination to sustain high classical seminaries and that made classical study a prerequisite for matriculation into the colleges and for the study of medicine and law. Classics might be pre-eminent as they were in the English tradition, or one indispensable element of general studies as they were in the Scottish tradition, but one way or another, they were considered essential in the acquisition of mental culture and would remain so throughout the nineteenth century.

During the middle decades of the century, nonetheless, there was growing pressure to modify the traditional hierarchy of subjects to take account of new knowledge and to accommodate the utilitarian demands of a new age. Occasionally these demands were couched in the language of philistinism, condemning the classics as pretentious obscurantism and mere relics of the dark ages: "the human race," said one editor, "would be no better fed or clothed if every man and woman in the world were a classical scholar."[22] This was not, however, an opinion shared by most influential Upper Canadians, and especially not by those in charge of the colony's educational institutions. They held no animosity towards the classics, but they also believed that a variety of new subjects needed to be accommodated in the curriculum along *with* classics. What justifications were there for the addition of science and modern languages to the college curriculum? John McCaul, the head of University College, spoke for many others when, in 1857, he answered that question in the following way:

The answer is plain and obvious. Within the last few years, their development has been so remarkable, or their utility has been so generally recognized, that they can no longer be ignored as essential parts of a liberal education. Is there one whom I address, who is not persuaded that it is of the utmost importance, that our graduates should not leave our halls in utter ignorance of such subjects as Chemistry, Zoology and Botany, Mineralogy and Geology – strangers to even the leading characteristics of this globe, on which we dwell; of this air, which we breathe; of this light, whereby we see; of the countless myriads of animated existences, which flourish and die around us?

Again, can any one, who is at all observant of the features of the age in which we are living, question the expediency of having our students at least initiated in foreign modern tongues, and well versed in the use of their own language? Time was when Science and Literature chose the Latin language as their appropriate vehicle. But how many learned treatises and discussions are there now written in the vernacular of each country, and what immense stores of valuable knowledge are hidden from the view of those, who have not made some progress in this important department of education?[23]

But how could the addition of these new subjects be reconciled with the crucial role of classics in promoting the acquisition of mental culture and discipline? "In the past, new [mental] faculties had always been created to take care of new subjects or methods," Sheldon Rothblatt remarks, "but eventually the absurdity of this procedure was recognized."[24] Increasingly after 1850 the answer was that classics had no exclusive claim to cultivate these powers. English or history, French or science could also train the mind, and do it as well as Latin or Greek. Though the name of Thomas Huxley is most often associated with this argument, it was also being propagated at the same time in British North America by the likes of J.W. Dawson of McGill, Daniel Wilson of University College, Toronto, and many other local commentators on education.[25] "For ages," wrote J.G.D. Mackenzie in 1869, "our language, with all its beauty and strength; our literature, with its unsurpassed wealth of intellectual treasure, was made to move in the train of classical learning." But in recent years, he added, "the culture of the Mother-tongue" had been accorded its rightful place in education.[26] "The development of the higher nature, the intellectual quickening, and the refinement of taste," the high school inspectors explained in 1874, "are the natural fruits of an attentive perusal of the Masterpieces of our Literature ... The culture offered by the study of the Physical sciences," they continued, "though not so rich in the ethical element as that derived from the study of literature and history, is nevertheless valuable. The reverence for truth, ... the conviction for the necessity of patience in investigation, and for caution in coming to conclusions, the appreciation of the beauty and the method of the universe ... must render a Scientific Course, properly conducted, an important means for developing the character and faculties of a human being."[27]

Not only did modern subjects train the mind, but they also had one important virtue that classics lacked: direct applicability to the tasks of everyday life. Most schoolmen agreed that a liberal education, whatever its particular content, was the most useful form of education a student could acquire, because, by training the full mental and moral powers of the mind, it equipped the student with the most important intellectual tools he needed in adult life. There was, in other words, nothing merely ornamental about a thorough training in classics or mathematics, history or science. But the enthusiasts for the modern subjects were prepared to push the argument further. Latin might train the mind, they contended, but so did French, and the latter was more useful for doing business in Montreal; Greek might cultivate the faculties, but so did science, while the former built no bridges and revealed no mineral wealth. In his testimony before the University Commission in 1860, Daniel Wilson put the case this way: not only could subjects like modern languages, natural sciences, and mathematics "no less thoroughly train [the student's] mind" than classics, but they deserved priority because they "will supply him in many cases, with far more useful acquirements for the future course he is to pursue."[28] Thus by the 1860s, influential figures in Upper Canada and abroad were contending not only that modern subjects could discipline the mind as well as Latin or Greek, but that they were, at one and the same time, more directly applicable to the everyday issues of life.

This happy marriage of culture and utility would become one of the conventional educational clichés of the late nineteenth century. Mathematics was to be valued and taught "both as a means of intellectual discipline and as a necessary element in material progress."[29] Science was "an agent of liberal culture no less than of material progress."[30] The faculties were "strengthened and sharpened as much by engineering or any other practical study, carried on thoroughly and systematically, as by the study of classics or mathematics."[31] And beyond all that, the modern subjects were easier to sell to the majority of parents mainly concerned with seeing their children get on in life. "To many it is useless to recommend a subject on the ground that it is an admirable instrument of mental culture," J.A. McLellan commented in 1872. "They want their children to learn something *useful*."[32] On that score alone, the appeal of modern subjects over classics was obvious to school and college administrators concerned to secure the popularity of their institutions in the public mind.

But if there were now a score of subjects, all of which cultivated the mind, how could the demands of breadth and depth be reconciled? Specialization would invite excessive narrowness, inconsonant with the meaning of a liberal education, while exposure to all the important subjects would invite superficiality. The solution, as John McCaul explained in 1857, lay in a system of core plus options.

It is certain that the extent and accuracy of attainment must be most materially diminished, if seven or eight subjects of study be compressed into that period of time, which was formerly barely sufficient for four or five, and equal attention be required to be paid to each throughout the course. The only practical solution of the problem is to be found in the system, which has been adopted in this University and College, whereby, whilst each student is required to possess at least an elementary knowledge of each subject prescribed in the course, he is at liberty, within certain restrictions, to select those departments for which he has a special aptitude, or which are most useful, with a view to his future occupation in life. This system, after much consideration and prolonged discussion, was introduced in this University, in 1854. According to the plan, which was then brought into operation, the student after one year's study of a fixed course, was at liberty to select between the Greek and Latin languages, or the English and French or German, and between Mathematics or the Natural Sciences.[33]

Three years later in his defence of the new arts program at University College, John Langton made the same point. The subjects "which are now considered essential to a liberal education" had become so numerous that if a student tried to take them all, mere superficiality would be the outcome. "A respectable acquaintance with all of them should be possessed by everyone who has passed through a university; and this is provided for by making them all compulsory in some part of the course. But if any student had exhibited a decided taste and capacity for any special study ... he is permitted ... to confine himself more and more to the particular subjects in which he has distinguished himself."[34]

During the late 1850s and early 1860s, there were those, Ryerson included, who were appalled by the introduction of options and the proliferation of modern subjects at University College, and charges of declining standards at the provincial university formed one of the central issues in the testimony before the University Commission in 1860.[35] What the university reformers had accomplished, however, was to integrate modern subjects within the traditional rhetoric of a liberal education, and to reconcile, however precariously, the goal of mental culture with the rising pressures of vocationalism. Ryerson's solution might have been more coherent in its approach. But his preference for tightly packaged bundles of prescribed courses was also dependent on the preservation of what was becoming an outmoded and invidious distinction between an ordinary and a liberal education. It forced students, moreover, to engage in prolonged study of some subjects that they did not like or that were irrelevant for their future occupations. As Daniel Wilson was wont to point out, the combination of core plus options provided the best of all possible worlds. It exposed students to each of the central subjects of a liberal education. It allowed more intensive pursuit of one or two subjects and therefore the kind of depth traditionally associated with the cultivation of the mind. And it could be knitted to preparation for a variety of professions. Unlike aristocratic England, Wilson would say, "in Canada at least education must be practical." And thus, he continued, when a student sought advice on the courses to pursue following his freshman year, a professor might ask, "what is your object in life? If you intended to be a medical man drop your Greek and Latin and go on with the Natural Sciences and Modern Languages ... If the young man intends to become a Theological student ... then we say go on with your Classics, your Moral Science ... If a Land Surveyor, devote your chief attention to your Mathematics, Geology and Mineralogy."[36]

Inevitably such advice put less emphasis on the pursuit of classical studies in the undergraduate curriculum. Men like Wilson, Langton, or McCaul were not proposing to abandon classical studies. No less than Ryerson or Young, they believed classics to be an indispensable part of a liberal education, as indeed, the reformed curriculum at University College made clear: students not only continued to need Latin for matriculation but it was a required course in their first year. And that would not change for decades. Classics, nonetheless, became less important in the overall curriculum of the university and less central to its purposes.

There were, moreover, more radical implications to many of the arguments we have been canvassing than cautious moderates like McCaul might have been willing to admit. And these tended to have more impact at the lower levels of the education system, including the grammar and high schools, than they did on the undergraduate curriculum. If, for example, Latin was only one of several equally worthwhile subjects, all of which trained the mind equally well, was it necessary to learn Latin at all? Raising that question exposed to scrutiny a critical weakness in classical pedagogy. As we have repeatedly noted, most educationists agreed that if boys were to reap the full benefits of a classical education they needed to begin the study of Latin and Greek at an early age and pursue their studies for a lengthy period. Yet most observers also conceded that only a handful of Upper Canadian boys could afford to stay in school that long. Why, then, should most boys study any Latin at any time? During the 1860s, this line of argument became more commonly heard, especially with respect to the curriculum of the schools. A *Globe* editorial of 1865, for example, reiterated the conventional view that the "real value of any system of education must be determined principally by a consideration of its fitness to develop the capacities of the mind." Nor did the writer challenge the value of the classics in achieving that end; indeed he urged the study of Latin "wherever possible." But the key question, he continued, was whether

with the limited time our youth have at their command, and for all the practical purpose of life, it is not better to forgo the study of Latin and Greek in preference to an intimate acquaintance with modern languages, natural history and physical science ... and whether there will not be more real pleasure and profit, both now and hereafter, in being able to understand and discourse upon, and apply the properties of matter ... and the laws of the heavenly bodies ... than in the recollection of the fables of heathen mythology, or in the ability to construe correctly a Greek tragedy or a piece of Roman history?[37]

The challenge to the pre-eminent place of classics, moreover, was easily extended to the classical school itself. If many subjects were equally worthwhile, a school that took boys at an early age and focused primarily on the classics was, *pari passu*, less necessary. If other subjects were important and also trained the mind, Latin could be given less time and attention. It might, indeed, be started at a later age, converting it in effect into a senior subject to be begun at the same time as other senior subjects. Reinforcing this notion was a shift in opinion that began to take place in the later sixties about the optimum time to begin classical studies. Influential voices such as the English Schools Inquiry Commission began to express the view that a good English education ought to be acquired *before* beginning Latin, a view that was shared in some quarters at least in Ontario.[38] But if this idea was pedagogically sound, then there was little need for a school that overlapped the common school in order to provide concurrent elementary classical and English studies.

The case for converting Latin into a senior subject was all the more persuasive since the University of Toronto had, in the late 1850s, substantially lowered its matriculation standard in classics in an effort to link the university more effectively to the majority of the province's grammar schools and enable more boys to make the transition from grammar school to university.[39] The simple fact of the matter, in other words, was that it took less training in Latin to meet matriculation standards in the 1860s than had been the case before.

No less relevant, if options were a legitimate educational innovation at the provincial university, why not in the provincial grammar schools? Within the framework of a core curriculum, why should students not be able to choose whether they pursued the ancient languages or science, or French and German? In what was increasingly a typical expression of majority opinion, a grammar school headmaster, speaking to his colleagues at their annual meeting late in 1869, pulled together the various threads of the argument as follows.

He was not one of those who wished to throw the classics overboard, but he believed the teachers should be permitted to educate pupils to a certain stage in English branches, and afterward put them into classics. Up to the age of 12 or 14 he believed a boy should be confined to the English branches only. At that age the Latin grammar could be placed in his hands, and his mind would be so developed that he could proceed without difficulty in the classics. At that age too, a boy's future course was likely to be marked out for him. If he were to be a mechanic he could be trained in mathematics; if he were to be sent to the University, he could be taught the classics and higher mathematics. He believed the system of putting boys into classics at a tender age was like making Sunday a day of confinement in church, and only tended to make him dread the subject with which he was crammed.[40]

By the early 1870s, a decade of debate had produced a broad consensus about the need to modernize the curriculum of a liberal education. Mental culture and mental discipline were to remain the animating purpose of the grammar schools as of the universities. And classics were to maintain a place near the centre of the curriculum for all those who intended to pursue their education beyond the early years of the grammar school. On that point there was near-unanimous agreement with J.S. Mill, who had recently declared in a widely admired address that Latin and Greek were essential to the education "of all who are not obliged by their circumstances to discontinue their scholastic studies at a very early age."[41] At the same time, however, classics were being subtly discounted in three important ways. There was, in the first place, a growing habit of including classics in the generic category "literature," which allowed commentators to attribute the same disciplinary or cultural advantages to the study of the modern languages, especially English, as to Latin and Greek.[42] Moreover, once people agreed that it was not necessary to begin Latin at an early age, it tended to be relegated, in a double sense, to a "secondary" language: one that was not as essential to learn as English, and one that needn't be begun until after a proper foundation in English had been laid.

Finally, Latin and Greek lost their exclusive claim to be the definitive studies of a liberal education. Science, English, and modern languages took a place within the charmed circle of studies that could discipline and culture the mind. Indeed, for the majority of students, who would not prolong their studies beyond the grammar school, it was now asserted that the modern subjects actually offered disciplinary advantages that classics lacked. And if that were the case, then the optionalization of the curriculum was not merely a vulgar concession to the utilitarian spirit of the age but an essential pedagogical imperative.

Arguments over the content of the curriculum rarely arranged themselves in tidy dichotomies. With a few exceptions it was not a case of ancients versus moderns, or Ryerson and his advisers versus a coalition of enlightened opponents. Rather the debates were almost always about balance and emphasis. Ryerson himself, after all, had long been a vigorous advocate of a more prominent role for English and science, as had Paxton Young. Both men, indeed, had been at the forefront of promoting these subjects in the 1860s and early 1870s. Yet on one crucial issue a fundamental change had taken place, rendering Ryerson's curriculum policies of 1871 indefensible. The disciplinary value that modern subjects had now acquired meant that the Georgian distinction between an ordinary and a liberal education ceased to be a legitimate principle around which institutions or programs of study could be organized. Ryerson, however, remained wedded to that principle long after it had ceased to command the intellectual allegiance of educated public opinion, and even of his own inspectors. And thus in the mid-1870s, as his grip on policymaking began to relax, the dual program of studies, classical and English, was abandoned, to be replaced by something more consonant with majority opinion. The curriculum was now to be structured by a combination of core plus options. Students would be required to take an essential core of subjects, within which the study of English would hold a pre-eminent place, and then to select from a list of options those subjects that suited their tastes or vocational destinations.

There was nothing definitive about the new program of studies issued in 1876, and repeated revisions would take place in the 1880s and beyond. The size of the core would wax and wane. Fierce debates would recur over the inclusion of particular subjects, and they would be shuffled from core to options and back again. The bias of the core would oscillate between the discipline of the mind and the practical needs of everyday life. But the principle of organizing the high school curriculum around a combination of core plus options would last for decades to come.

In the wake of this long discussion about the curricular ferment of the age, one might plausibly ask an additional question: what about the girls? What impact did their presence in the high school have on the construction of the high school program of studies during the 1870s? With the exception of the exclusionary years of 1866–68, the rise in the proportion of female enrolments that had begun about mid-century had continued throughout the 1860s and into the early 1870s. By 1874, it stood at about 45 to 50 per cent and it would remain there into the 1880s.[43] In the first half of the 1870s a few schools, probably all collegiates, may have excluded girls. By 1880, however, every school in the province had its share of female students.[44] From 1871 onwards, then, there was no question that girls constituted a significant segment of the school population.

Their right to be there, moreover, was no longer contested. The act of 1871 secured them a place in the high school as a matter of law, and after that no one ever proposed to turn the clock back. Not everyone approved, and in the first half of the 1870s a few leading schoolmen, including one high school inspector, were openly hostile.[45] Yet 1874 appears to have been the last year when the issue – a perennial one since 1865 – was debated at the annual meeting of the Ontario Teachers' Association. Dissidents may have continued to grumble, but the legislation of 1871 had made coeducation a *fait accompli*, and there were, as well, a growing number of voices willing to testify to its moral and intellectual virtues. "The two sexes now attend the same common schools, high schools and collegiate institutes," said George Grant in 1879, "and no one dreams of there being anything improper in their doing so."[46]

This does not mean, it must be said once again, that the principle of coeducation met with universal approbation. The multiplication of girls' boarding and day schools in the seventies and eighties demonstrates that some parents continued to opt for segregated schooling, and there were always those prepared to make the case that it was a preferable arrangement for those who could afford it.[47] But that was the crux of the matter, as it always had been. Coeducation was inevitable, as the principal of a leading private school put it in 1884, "because it is practically the only hope that multitudes [of girls] can ever have of securing the higher education."[48] In

the 1880s, indeed, the arguments against mixed high schools virtually disappeared, though the debate over coeducation itself did not, breaking out
afresh over the question of where to locate university-level education for
women within the University of Toronto. The same factors, however, that
had been primarily responsible for integrating male and female education
in the common and high schools influenced the outcome in the case of
University College: in 1884, despite some vociferous opposition from university authorities and other pundits, the legislature voted on the grounds
of economy against establishing a separate women's college, and directed
University College to go coeducational instead.[49] From that point onwards,
the public school system of education in Ontario, from elementary school
to university, was formally coeducational.

Girls, then, were to be taught in the same buildings as boys. But *what*
were they to be taught? Conventional habits of thought throughout the
nineteenth century had prescribed a distinct curriculum for the superior
education of girls, and thus one might expect the debate over the high school
curriculum to focus, at least in part, on their particular needs. If the schools
were to be required to teach classics and commercial subjects, those traditional studies for boys, why not a regulation requiring trustees to purchase
pianos, or offer fancy needlework, ornamental drawing, and the other accomplishments that traditionally formed part of a girl's education? As one
critic of a common curriculum put it succinctly in 1879,

the higher education of boys has in view not simply a liberal culture, but specially
a preparation for some one or other of the learned professions, such as the teacher,
clergyman, lawyer or physician. For these ends the university and high school
curricula are purposely adapted, and are the stepping stones to a position which
secures subsistence and promises wealth and honour. But to the girl these professions
are, for the most part, forbidden. Why should she, therefore, be required to pursue
courses of study which offer little or no reward, and are not adapted to her special
wants? Her proper sphere is social and family life – not however, the narrow domestic
life sometimes assigned her, but one that is wider far, and touches a great variety
of human interests. For these ends a wider range of acquirement and accomplishment
is needful than that which any special profession demands.[50]

There were in fact a handful of high schools that did indeed buy pianos
or teach other accomplishments in the early 1870s. But it appears to have
been unusual.[51] In the main, girls not only selected their subjects from the
same list as did boys, but in the smaller schools particularly they also studied
the same subjects, including, in many cases, Latin and mathematics.[52] At
the level of provincial policymaking, moreover, there was never any sustained discussion about framing a curriculum especially suited to female
high school students. The reasons for this deserve consideration.

In the first place, and this is particularly pertinent in the early 1870s, the shape of the future was seen through the prism of the past. The observable fact that half the pupils were now girls carried far less weight in conceptualizing the curriculum than the embedded conviction that the high school was a grammar school and that a grammar school was, *au fond*, a school for boys. Girls were not intended to be grammar school pupils, said the past; they were there because of economic exigencies and would, as a matter of course, be removed to their own schools once public and private wealth allowed. The unselfconscious language of one headmaster, writing about the purpose of the high schools in the *Canadian Monthly* in 1873, is revealing. The high school was a vital institution, he argued, because "it is of importance that every lad who has the ability to profit by a superior education" should be able to obtain it; because every local community will benefit from the presence of "a body of highly cultivated men"; because the province must produce its own "clergymen, lawyers, medical men and teachers, who must be trained in the High School. The boys educated in our High Schools will, as men, be the natural leaders of the communities in which they reside."[53] In a passing comment made in the same year, the high school inspectors wrote in a similar vein. "In the High School are being educated, it is to be presumed, the leading men of the next generation, its Clergymen, its Lawyers, its Doctors, its Editors, the men who are to make Farming a Science, its Engineers and Machinists, its Prominent Manufacturers and Merchants, and its Teachers."[54] Everyone, the reader will notice, but its Mothers. Aside from anything else, it took time to modify inherited categories of thought that reduced girls to an untoward presence in a school meant for boys, and thus rendered them invisible when curriculum issues arose.

During the first half of the 1870s, moreover, the unexamined assumptions of the past were reinforced by the actual intent of official policy. The grant for the collegiate institutes was tied to the average attendance of "boys." The classical program was proclaimed to be a course designed for boys. The list of compulsory subjects in either program made almost no concessions to girls, requiring them to take classics, linear drawing, commercial arithmetic, or other subjects tied to boys' vocations. So long as these provisions survived in the act and regulations they could not help but encourage curriculum policy to focus on the education of boys rather than girls. When schoolmen did address the question of a suitable curriculum for girls, however, they produced a remarkable transmutation. While one might have expected them to reconceptualize the curriculum in the light of the rising number of girls in the grammar schools, what actually happened was the reverse. Girls were reconceptualized to fit the curriculum.

Throughout the first half of the nineteenth century there had always been some debate about the nature of women's minds and the education best suited to them. Depending on which authority one consulted, their minds might be inferior, or simply different, from men's, and their education might demand more intellectual training and fewer accomplishments or *vice versa*. But it was almost universally assumed that beyond the limits of a common English education, the schooling of boys and girls would be different, and that in turn reflected not just the separate spheres that they might occupy in adult life, but the differences in their mental propensities and capacities. Though there had always been ambiguities and exceptions, the pedagogical language of a liberal education had been indelibly masculine in tone and content. Mental culture and the rigorous disciplining of the mind through classics and mathematics, science and literature, was a form of education peculiarly appropriate for men, and only incidentally for women, if at all.

Beginning in the 1860s, however, these doctrines came under attack from a variety of sources including newspaper editors committed to women's rights, clergymen involved in one or another aspect of the superior education of women, and above all, grammar school headmasters provoked to mount the barricades in defence of the right of girls to attend their schools. The notion that women were less intellectually able than men was commonly rejected on the grounds that personal experience or the innovations of the modern age had shown it to be false. The "University examinations of England, the Colleges examinations in the United States, and our own everyday experience," wrote the editor of the *Brantford Expositor* in 1868, revealed "that the female mind is not inferior in comprehensive ability to that of the male."[55] In response to Ryerson's initial attempt to exclude girls in 1865, Archibald McCallum, the principal of the Hamilton public schools, replied that "the girls were capable of taking up the same studies as the boys, and of pursuing them equally as well, or better."[56] Allied to this was the attack on the accomplishments curriculum itself, which, as one editor put it, merely invited "superficiality," or, in the words of a high school headmaster, encouraged girls to become "accomplished nonentities, better qualified for such engagements and pursuits as fashion and frivolity stamp with their approval than those requiring serious intellectual effort."[57] What girls needed instead, the critics maintained, was mental culture and discipline, the kind of qualities their brothers absorbed from the rigours of studying literature and science.[58]

Arguments such as these were to become increasingly common in the late 1860s and 1870s. Not only were they heard in the debate over the grammar schools; they also began to be canvassed at least as early as 1869, in speeches about the need to give women access to higher education.[59] But perhaps the best single example of the way each of these arguments was interwoven into a coherent whole is provided by a speech given in 1879 by G.M. Grant.[60] "The popular idea of a girl's school," he said, was that "any lady, especially if she be a widow not so well off as she once was, can keep a boarding school, and if she brings in teachers to give instruction in French, drawing, deportment, and fancy-work, what more is wanted? Scraps of history and science may be thrown in, but as to the systematic study of anything, or methods of study, or mental training, it is seldom dreamed of. Why should it, if insipidity of mind, and apathetic elegance of manner be considered more valuable?" Such an education, however, did no justice to women themselves, nor did it equip them for the challenges of the age, at home or abroad. "What kind of mental training should be given to women?" Grant then asked. To answer that, one must first establish the true aim of all education, which was, he continued,

not to store the mind with facts, but to train the mind itself ... That is a good education which enables us to look at things in the clear light of reasoned thought ... Education should guarantee not merely the possession of truth ... but the knowledge of how to proceed so as to attain truth ... Now it has always been thought a matter of the last importance to give such an education to men ... The whole structure of our magnificent educational system has always had this in view.

But, he then asked, do women need such an education as this? "Unless mind in women is something essentially different from what it is in men, that is, unless they do not possess minds at all, there can be no hesitation as to the answer." Indeed, he added ominously, "there are physiological reasons to show that women require a sound mental training more imperatively than men; and that therefore no obstacles should be placed in the way of those who are struggling to obtain its advantages."

Like other advocates of such views, Grant was no rigorous egalitarian in matters relating to the sexes. He was perfectly content, for example, to see a college curriculum provide special options for women: "a thorough knowledge of music, for instance, might stand for Greek or senior mathematics." He assumed that women would find regular attendance at classes difficult; thus he emphasized that it was generally unnecessary in any case, it being "sufficient if actual attendance is given from two-thirds to four-fifths of the session." And though he was not at all opposed to the expansion of vocations for women, that was not the primary aim of their education. "What need of a woman learning Greek or Mathematics?" he asked rhetorically. "Her end and aim is marriage; her kingdom a happy home ... Exactly so; and just because her relation to men is so close, just because her sphere is so important to man's highest welfare, is she not entitled to the best that education can do for her? Because of her relation to man, and because of what she is herself, a thorough mental training is due to girls."

Our own argument here, it bears repeating, is not about the liberation of women from the stereotypical confines of Victorian thought. It is, rather, about the means by which girls were integrated into a curriculum originally intended for boys. Economic realities delivered the girls to the schoolhouse door, but their presence could not be legitimized without a theory that justified a common curriculum for both boys and girls. The advocates of intellectual equality and mental culture provided that theory and, in the process, took the first halting steps toward the notion of "a sexless intelligence."[61] At the same time it relieved policymakers of having to think about girls *qua* girls or about how the grammar school and its curriculum might be accommodated to their special circumstances or educational traditions. Girls, in effect, were made honorary boys, and adapted to the existing curriculum, not the other way around.

The integration of girls was, in any case, a relatively undramatic process because large parts of the traditional girls' curriculum paralleled or overlapped the boys'. As we have already suggested in a previous chapter, such subjects as English, arithmetic, history, and geography had always been taught to both sexes. And as English became the foundational subject in the high school curriculum during the early 1870s, it became easier still to accommodate girls. Thus the transition was more of a shift in emphasis than the wholesale imposition of something new – a shift away from one portion of the girls' curriculum, the accomplishments, and towards a greater emphasis on more purely academic subjects. Moreover, for some families, obtaining both sorts of instruction remained possible. A correspondent to the *Canada School Journal* claimed that "many girls finished their entire scholastic education" at the local high school and then were sent away "to boarding schools in cities to obtain those accomplishments and those social advantages which such schools offered."[62] And for the rest, if the high schools failed to offer much in the way of instrumental music, art, or "fancy work," there was at least that other staple of the accomplishments curriculum, French. "By far the greater portion of pupils who have taken up French are girls," the inspectors reported in 1871:

It is gratifying to observe this growing taste amongst our Girls for a graceful and elegant language, so peculiarly a woman's study and accomplishment as French is. It is to be hoped that such works as the "History of Charles XII" and Corneille's Tragedy, "Horace," will come to the aid of a high and pure English literature, in fortifying the minds of our young women against the many publications of the day, that are calculated to turn the minds of young people, and to destroy the charities and joys of the Christian Home.[63]

Finally, there was the effect of women's vocations. During the 1870s, the separate spheres of men and women began to blur a little at the edges, as middle-class women trickled into the labour market, some driven to it by "the superfluity of women," a problem much remarked upon in Ontario during the 1870s as it was elsewhere,[64] and others motivated by their own ambitions or discontent with their lot at home. The intrepid Elizabeth Smith was a good example of the latter category. "Like increasing numbers of middle-class girls," writes Veronica Strong-Boag, "Elizabeth ... rejected the option of remaining passively at home for a suitable mate to turn up. Without spurning marriage as a future alternative, she embarked on a search for economic independence and satisfying employment."[65] Elizabeth and a handful of others eventually became doctors. Some with more modest ambitions or talents tested the waters of clerical work. But the overwhelming majority became public school teachers, which is primarily why the matter is relevant to our argument here.

In the second half of the seventies, as we noted in the previous chapter, the academic training required for even a third-class certificate increasingly shifted to the high schools and turned them into machines for stamping out newly minted teachers. Estimates in the late seventies set the number of high school students preparing for certificates at anywhere from a third to a half of total enrolment, and while no figures exist on this point, it must be assumed that large numbers of these students were girls. The qualifications for girls were, however, virtually identical to those for boys. From 1871 onwards, there were no differences whatsoever in the qualifications required of men and women for a third-class certificate, and only minor ones for the second- and first-class certificates. As of 1877, indeed, even the minor differences required for the second-class certificate – the number of books of Euclid a student was expected to master – disappeared.[66] Thus as the high school began to be tied into an expanding credentialling system, and above all, to teachers' certificates, girls and boys increasingly were required to study the same subjects and write the same examinations. This too loosened the hold of the accomplishments curriculum on the education of girls and, concomitantly, encouraged the integration of girls into the curriculum of the high school.

For a number of reasons, then, the curriculum of the high school changed little in response to the influx of middle-class girls. Perhaps their largest impact was simply to reinforce the growing primacy of non-classical studies: in the years between 1872 and 1875 they most commonly enrolled in the English course, helping to make it substantially larger than the classical course.[67] In a similar fashion, they helped drive up enrolments in those subjects required for the various non-professional examinations for teaching certificates, subjects such as English composition and literature, arithmetic and elementary mathematics, history and geography.[68] They were not alone in this, however, for as the experience of the sixties had shown, many parents were seeking a superior education in English and commercial subjects for their boys and would not enrol them in Latin once it ceased to be compulsory.

Ryerson, of course, had intended none of this. No enemy of the superior education of girls, he nevertheless had looked forward to the day when they would attend their own schools and be taught a curriculum appropriate to woman's peculiar nature and duties in life. During the 1860s and early 1870s, however, these hopes grew ever dimmer. As the skirmishes of the later 1860s demonstrated, he had few allies in the political arena to sustain his policies on girls' education. Indeed it was the politicians themselves who insisted that the right of girls to attend the grammar schools be explicitly recognized in the act of 1871. As for the distinct curriculum, its fate was sealed by shifts in educational theory. As the goal of mental culture was extended to include girls, as the traditional disciplinary subjects were deemed appropriate for girls to study, and as the accomplishments were denigrated and dismissed as trivial, the intellectual props of the accomplishments curriculum were undermined, and the way cleared to extend the boys' curriculum to girls as well. In sum, the exigencies of economics, politics, and intellectual fashion all conspired to undermine the Ryersonian version of what constituted an appropriate education for Ontario's daughters.

THE EARLY EIGHTIES would see the death of yet one more of Ryerson's progeny. When, in the 1860s, he had failed to turn all of the grammar schools into good classical schools, Ryerson, as we have already seen, invented the collegiate institute to promote advanced classical instruction for those boys preparing for the universities and professions. The relevant provisions of the act of 1871 specified that to obtain collegiate institute status a school must have four masters and sixty male pupils enrolled in Latin. In return it would receive a substantial bonus of $750 a year in addition to the grants that all other high schools were entitled to – grants for average attendance, Intermediate examination passes and upper school enrolment, quality of equipment, and the like.

On paper at least, the collegiate institutes proved eminently successful in promoting classical instruction. At the end of the 1870s the thirteen collegiates taught about as many classical pupils as the rest of the ninety-one high schools put together.[69] Yet many critics of the collegiates, including, most tellingly, the high school inspectors themselves, were convinced that far too many of their classical students were merely beginners, recruited into the rudiments of Latin in order to retain the special grant, a phenomenon that evoked a recrudescence of the complaints of the 1860s about schools full of pupils enrolled in "qualifying Latin."[70] The additional grant to the collegiates "has not had the effect of developing a class of schools specially devoted to the ancient classics," one of the high school inspectors wrote in 1879. "The object was foreign to the genius of the country, and therefore has not been attained. But it would be wrong to infer that the grant has been without good effects."[71] What it had achieved, he said, was to enable the collegiates to attract good teachers and pay them well. It was, moreover, one of several advantages that turned the collegiates into schools superior to most other high schools. They were generally located in the larger towns and cities, which gave them a strong municipal tax base and a pool of pupils large enough to ensure the collegiates of a healthy share of that part of the legislative grant based on average attendance. They could also count on larger than average upper school grants for the same reason. Altogether these resources meant that the collegiates could hire more teachers than most other high schools, could recruit more qualified teachers, could obtain specialists for most subjects, and could afford well-equipped classrooms. The collegiates had become, by the end of the seventies, not so much distinctive classical seminaries as superior high schools offering high-quality instruction in all of the subjects on the course of studies.

But their advantages also made them easy targets. During the 1870s local municipalities increased their spending for high schools substantially, but there was no equivalent increase in the legislative grant, which remained roughly stable throughout the decade. As a consequence the share of expenditure for high schools borne by the province dropped from almost 40 per cent in 1872 to just below 20 per cent in 1878.[72] Hard-pressed municipalities pressured local boards to reduce both their capital and operating expenses, while government insisted that more of the costs of education should be raised by local taxpayers, who directly benefited from the schools. Not surprisingly, there was a growing volume of complaints to the effect that financial stringency was "crushing the life out of our High Schools."[73] The headmasters' association petitioned the legislature to transfer the endowment belonging to Upper Canada College to the high schools, school boards called on the government to increase the grant, and there were other remedies suggested besides.[74] Among them was the abolition of the special bonus of $750 to each collegiate institute.

The collegiate bonus provoked complaints for a variety of reasons. Many towns had large high schools with new buildings, several teachers, and upper schools as substantial as those of the smaller collegiates. But their schools had fewer than sixty boys in Latin and were thus ineligible for the collegiate bonus. Smaller communities, on the other hand, complained that the bonus simply rewarded those towns that were already rich, at a time when village schools and village taxpayers were hard-pressed to find the resources to provide an adequate education for their own young people. Beyond the financial issues however, there were also growing complaints about the premium given to the ancient languages and the discrimination against girls entailed in the collegiate bonus.[75]

In 1879 and 1880, criticism of the collegiate bonus was confined to the reports of the high school inspectors, the Ontario Teachers' Association, and the pages of the educational press. But early in 1881, it spilled over into the legislature when George Ross, a rising star in the Liberal party, an experienced teacher, and future minister of education, introduced a motion to abolish the collegiate grant. In his speech he pulled together all the criticisms that had been heard in the previous years. It was, he said, "an unjust discrimination against the great majority of High Schools in favour of those in the large centres of population, which are least in need of special aid," and which "would be superior schools irrespective of any legislative grant." By placing a premium on the study of Latin it "gives an undue prominence to a branch of study not practical in its tendencies and opposed to the progressive spirit of modern education." And it "unjustly discriminates against females either as teachers or pupils … If Latin was necessary for boys, then was it not also for girls?"[76]

Other members of the House concurred with Ross' sentiments but opposed abolition of the grant as such, arguing that it would damage what were widely conceded to be good schools without substantially aiding others. Ross then withdrew his motion, but it precipitated action nonetheless. Adam Crooks, the minister, invited both the high school inspectors and the high school section of the Ontario Teachers' Association to confer on the matter and make recommendations to him. Their advice was that the special grant should be maintained but that the terms should be changed entirely, tying it not to Latin or to boys but to the stimulation of superior instruction in the course of studies generally.[77] This advice conformed to Crooks' own sentiments, and in 1882 regulations were put in place which made the grant conditional upon three things: suitable buildings and grounds; laboratory facilities for the proper teaching of chemistry; and at least four masters "each of whom shall be specially qualified to give instruction in one of the following departments: – English, Classics, Mathematics, Natural Science, and Modern Languages; the teaching staff being such as to provide the means of thorough instruction in all of the departments mentioned."[78]

With the remodelling of the collegiate institutes, the Ryersonian era in the history of Ontario's secondary schools comes to a definitive end. They had been intended as a last bastion for classical studies by males, and their design was founded on a conception of a liberal education belonging to an earlier era. Implicitly at least, they also symbolized the ideal of a separate and different education appropriate for girls. The fate of Ryerson's collegiates went hand in hand with the ideas that sustained it. For nearly a century after 1871 the designation "collegiate institute" would be a coveted mark of academic distinction in Ontario education. After 1882, however, it was only the name, and not the substance, that was left of Ryerson's legacy.

CHAPTER TWELVE

Defining the Upper Boundaries of the High School

By the end of the 1870s, the boundary between the public school and the high school had largely been defined and the former reduced to a feeder for the latter. What had still to be determined, however, was the nature of the relationship between the high schools and those institutions which provided higher education in Ontario – the universities and professional associations. Before the 1880s, the boundaries between the two levels of education had yet to be defined, the academic responsibilities of each had not been clearly delineated, and efficient mechanisms for articulating the schools with higher education had not yet been established. Until these things were accomplished, the upper limits of the high school, and thus the meaning of secondary education itself, would remain uncertain.

By the 1850s Upper Canada already had several universities, each entirely independent of the rest. The University of Toronto was a secularized successor to the Anglican-dominated University of King's College, the colony's first chartered university. Heavily funded by government grants and an endowment of Crown lands dating back to the 1790s, the "provincial university," as it was often called, was an examining and not a teaching institution. Like its model, the University of London, it offered no direct instruction but was limited to regulating programs of study, setting examinations, and awarding degrees to students enrolled in any college affiliated with it. Only one college, however, was actually affiliated: the non-denominational University College, the sole beneficiary of the university's wealth and a dominant influence in its policies.

Upper Canada's other universities were all products of denominational enthusiasm. Queen's University, for example, was founded and run by the Church of Scotland, Trinity by the Anglicans, Victoria by the Wesleyan Methodists. In the pre-Confederation era these three church colleges survived on small government grants and vigorous denominational fundraising, coveting all the while the riches bestowed on University College. Other, mostly smaller, denominations limited their ambitions to founding theological seminaries. The Free [Presbyterian] Church, for example, established Knox College to train its clergy after the disruption within the Church of Scotland denied it access to Queen's. Located in Toronto, Knox used the facilities of University College to complete the general education of its ministerial candidates. Other denominations pursued a similar course, though as the years went by, and the numbers and wealth of their congregations grew, most lusted after a full university charter as well.

At one time or another all of the universities established one or more professional faculties to complement their arts programs. But one of the crucial differences between higher education then and now was that professional training more commonly took place outside the university than within it. The Church of England and the Church of Scotland required their ministerial candidates to have arts degrees and to attend post-graduate theological schools, but several other large denominations, such as the Methodists, neither required an arts degree nor had established theological seminaries. [1] By the mid-sixties, though not before, medical students were required to attend medical schools, but these were not necessarily affiliated with a university, and the students were not required or expected to have any preliminary university education – they entered their medical training directly from the grammar school or its equivalent. [2] Lawyers were not required to have a university degree or attend a law school, their training being carried out entirely by apprenticeship methods. [3] Grammar school teachers were expected to be arts graduates and were required, minimally, to be arts matriculants, but there was no professional school at which they were trained. [4] Land surveyors, an important occupational group in the colony, were trained entirely by apprenticeship. [5]

In order to qualify as a student in one of the universities or professions, an individual wrote a matriculation, or entrance, examination. These were examinations set by each university, or by the Medical Board, the Law Society, or some other professional association that had the power not only to license practitioners in a particular field but to establish educational programs for, and control entry to, professional training. In the mid-nineteenth century, however, there was no common matriculation standard that all candidates were expected to attain before they entered higher education. Each institution established its own standards and these were almost invariably *sui generis*. To cite an example drawn from but one point in time, in 1857 matriculation at Queen's required examination in elementary classics and mathematics, and nothing else. At Victoria, however, students were examined in classics, mathematics, natural philosophy, English grammar, and geography. The two universities, moreover, tested their candidates on different mathematics and classics textbooks, and required different readings from classical authors. The law society's matriculation examination was set at a higher standard than either Queen's or Victoria demanded, requiring substantially more mathematics (three books of Euclid rather than one), along with English history, modern geography, and the first and third books of Horace, readings different from those assigned by either Queen's or Victoria. The matriculation examination in surveying required no classics at all but demanded far more mathematics than required by either university or by the Law Society, testing students in geometry, trigonometry, mensuration of superficies, and the use of logarithms. Matriculation standards at the University of Toronto were different again, as indeed were those set out by the Medical Board.[6]

The effect of this plethora of matriculation standards was to fragment the curriculum of the grammar school and leave it with no clearly defined upper limit. There was, of course, an official program of studies written into the regulations of 1855. But there was no incentive to take all of the subjects included in the program because most of them had no relevance to students' vocational goals. The result was that beyond the elementary level, where all pupils might be introduced to Latin and mathematics, the grammar school consisted of a set of discrete classes organized around the subjects or set books required for this or that particular matriculation examination. There was, in other words, no course of studies in the modern sense, where a group of pupils pursued several subjects concurrently for four or five years at increasing levels of difficulty. Nor was there a common terminal point that could serve as a symbolic culmination of the program of studies and thus define the boundary between the work belonging to the grammar school and that appropriate to other institutions in the way that grade 13, and the uniform departmental examinations, crowned the work of the Ontario high school for much of the twentieth century.

Not only did matriculation standards vary enormously, they were also set low, reaching downwards to include levels of work that would now be classified as secondary or even senior elementary work, and thus much of the university curriculum overlapped the official program of studies set out for the grammar schools.[7] The universities and professional associations not only contributed to the fragmentation of the grammar school curriculum, but they also duplicated large parts of it.

One common explanation for low matriculation standards was the absolute shortage of qualified university students in mid-century Upper Canada. And there is some truth in this. Until the 1860s, most of the population lived beyond easy reach of either private or grant-aided schools capable of preparing students for matriculation, the grammar schools themselves were relatively scarce, and in some cases their work was limited to no more than elementary classics, English, and arithmetic.[8] Yet colleges like Queen's and Victoria, both of which teetered on the brink of collapse in these years, could ill afford to turn away any fee-paying student, however ill qualified he might be. And clergymen had to be recruited and educated to meet pressing denominational needs even if their previous education did not measure up to the standards set at home in Britain. High matriculation standards, in other words, posed a direct threat to the survival of the denominational colleges, and even to the future of the denominations themselves.

The shortage of qualified applicants was not the only reason for low matriculation standards, however. Not only in Upper Canada but in much of the rest of the English-speaking world, "secondary" education was not yet a distinctive sector, in the modern sense, within a three-tiered system of education. Nor, indeed, were the universities exclusively "tertiary" institutions. As we have already seen, it was common for Upper Canadian universities to operate preparatory departments – to link themselves, in effect, directly to the elementary schools of the colony. Similar arrangements existed elsewhere, in parts of the United States, in the arrangements of the new civic universities of England, and above all in Scotland where, in Robert Anderson's words, the long-standing

underdevelopment of secondary education encouraged the most distinctive feature of Scottish education, the direct relationship between the parish schools and the universities. The parish schoolmasters taught the so-called "university subjects" – Latin, mathematics, and perhaps Greek – and the universities came down to meet the parish schools by admitting boys at 15 or even younger and by providing elementary instruction in the "junior classes" which began the college course. Some Latin was essential for university entry, but the Greek junior class began with the alphabet ... Functions which in other countries were reserved for secondary schools were in Scotland performed both by the parish schools and by the universities themselves.[9]

Thus the low matriculation standards of their own institutions struck many Upper Canadians as neither anomalous nor merely due to the exigencies of a frontier society. Rather it was an arrangement sanctioned by the practice of the venerable universities of Scotland and of forward-looking institutions elsewhere. From the time of their establishment, the curriculum at Queen's and Victoria had overlapped the work of the grammar school. The exact extent of the overlap is hard to gauge before 1855 when the first official grammar school program was issued, but from then on comparisons between the program and university calendars give us some indication of the amount of duplication involved. In 1855, for example, Queen's matriculation standards in classics were set somewhere between the second and third forms of the official grammar school program, while the standard in arithmetic was no more than that demanded in the senior grades of a good common school.

In 1857, the studies prescribed for freshmen and sophomores at Victoria substantially duplicated those of the third, fourth, and fifth forms of the grammar school.

Throughout its short history, on the other hand, King's College had always maintained a far higher standard of studies. Influenced perhaps by the example of Oxford and Cambridge, but most immediately by the higher levels of training available at Upper Canada College where a sixth and seventh form provided students with very advanced preparatory work in classics, King's had a matriculation standard far above the other colleges and, indeed, far above the preparatory capacities of most grammar schools. [10] A relatively high standard was continued at Trinity, the Anglican successor to King's College, and initially at the new University of Toronto. At the latter institution, however, it soon came under vigorous attack, especially from an influential trio of Scotsmen operating both inside and outside the university: G.P. Young, in charge of "preliminary" or pre-divinity studies at Knox; George Brown, editor of the *Globe*; and Daniel Wilson, the new professor of history and English literature at University College. In a series of slashing letters published in the *Globe* in 1854, Young pointed out that virtually the only place where boys could obtain preparatory training for the matriculation examinations at the University of Toronto was Upper Canada College. But, he argued, University College was not established merely to service Toronto or Upper Canada College "and in the province generally no such facilities exist for forming accurate and superior classical scholars" of the standard demanded at University College.

The system, therefore, pursued at University College is unsuited to the circumstances and to the interests of the country ... The immediate result of this unsuitableness is, that comparatively few of the class for whom a national college ought to be available, ever think of matriculating. Young men, anxious to become respectable classical scholars, but not yet very thoroughly accomplished in Latin and Greek ... find upon inquiry, that they would get no good at University College, and of course ... they make some other arrangement. [11]

Young was particularly concerned about his pre-divinity students, who, he said, "come for the most part from rural districts where educational advantages are few and they belong ... to the poorer rather than the wealthier division of society." They could not afford to finish their education at Upper Canada College nor were they prepared enough to benefit from the advanced instruction in classics at University College. This, Young argued, was a ridiculous situation, since no object of a national university was more important than training divinity students. Such students, he concluded, "have a right to demand that the Provincial College be placed on such a footing that after they have acquired respectable knowledge of the Latin and Greek languages ... they may avail themselves of it for remedying the unavoidable defects of their previous education and making greater proficiency." What was needed, in sum, was "a total alteration in the System of Classical Instruction" at University College.[12]

During the 1850s arguments such as these carried the day in the university senate and led to major reforms in the undergraduate curriculum. In 1854 a full year was added to the program of study, increasing it from three to four years in order to take better account of the educational backgrounds of matriculants. Borrowing from Scottish precedent, moreover, a "classical tutor" was hired "to take in hand," as the *Globe* put it, "those students chiefly coming from the country districts, where as yet good grammar schools are wanting, and starting them from a much lower point than the regular University scheme contemplates ... supplementing the deficiencies of the country schools." It was, Brown added in a swipe at Oxbridge, a "wise resolution to follow the model of old institutions so far only as they prove themselves adapted to the wants of this young and vigorous country."[13] The Scottish presence was also no doubt influential in giving modern subjects a greater role in the curriculum and in introducing optionalization – innovations we have discussed in an earlier chapter.

No less important, in 1857 the Senate substantially reduced the matriculation standard, bringing it down to the ordinary level of teaching to be found in most of the colony's grammar schools.[14] The university authorities were roundly criticized for this before the University Committee in 1860 by the supporters of the denominational colleges, including Egerton Ryerson. But as Daniel Wilson argued, it was a victory for common sense and equal opportunity. "If the University and College are to be for the benefit of the people at large, there can be no gap, or interval, between the Grammar Schools and the University. The Grammar Schools train the youth up to the point at which the University receives them, and are we to adopt a standard for Matriculation placed at a point which these Grammar Schools cannot reach?" If the old matriculation standard had been maintained, Wilson continued,

we might just as well have nailed up the University door ... But ... our decision has been, that, if our true aim is to elevate the education of the whole Province, we must provide a Matriculation adapted to the specific capacities of the Grammar Schools. Any other System, while pretending to elevate education, must either have restricted its whole advantages to a favoured and wealthy few; or been a mere deceptive paper programme.[15]

Unable to stand alone without losing students to the other colleges, Trinity followed suit, lowering its own matriculation, as its provost put it, "to meet the general system of the Country."[16]

The result of these curricular changes was that by the late 1850s all of Upper Canada's colleges were engaged in teaching subjects at levels that massively overlapped the official grammar school program. As had been the case at Queen's and Victoria since the 1840s, the freshman year at University College now largely duplicated the work of the third, fourth, and fifth forms of the program. One of the things that most outraged Ryerson about the revision of the University of Toronto curriculum was the extent of the overlap. "Looking at the outline of the subjects of the History Course in the University Calendar," he told the University Committee, "it is very clear that the subjects comprehended in the course of History and English Literature are embraced in the Grammar School Course. These subjects are taught in the Grammar Schools, and from the same textbooks."[17] Indeed the work of the university even overlapped that of the common schools: when in 1861 the first-year students at University College studied algebra, their textbook was Colenso's Algebra; the same text was used by students in the grammar schools and in the common schools as well.[18]

The effect of low matriculation standards on the grammar schools was to aggravate the existing shortage of senior pupils, and thus to narrow the pedagogical range of the grammar school curriculum. Only a relative handful of Upper Canadians ever prepared themselves for the universities and professions, but they constituted the only group of students likely to stay on in the grammar school much beyond the rudiments of a classical education. The grammar schools, however, had to compete for such students with the college schools, with a variety of private schools, and, indeed, with the universities themselves. In his important thesis on Upper Canadian university students, David Keane demonstrates that some 43 per cent of all matriculants in the 1840s left by the end of their freshman year, and if that figure is even roughly typical for the 1850s, then in both decades the universities were offering virtually the same curriculum as the senior forms of the grammar schools, but no more, to large numbers of arts matriculants.[19] In many cases, moreover, the grammar schools had no great cost advantages over the universities. Fees were relatively low at Queen's and Victoria, and University College with its endowed wealth was virtually tuition-free for all matriculants.[20] And if boarding costs had to be paid, there was, after all, not much difference between the expense of attending a distant college or a distant grammar school. The "low state" of the grammar schools, that constant refrain in the official record during the 1850s and early 1860s, was probably due as much to this as to anything else. Unable to hold, or to attract, the few senior students there were, grammar school masters inevitably had to look elsewhere for students and revenues, including the teaching of boys and girls in the elements of the three Rs.

The multiplicity of examination standards exacerbated this situation. Grammar school masters, especially those in one-teacher schools, often found it difficult to prepare students for all of the various matriculation examinations and, at the same time, meet their other responsibilities as well. Thus students were tempted to leave the grammar school in order to finish their preparatory education elsewhere – at Upper Canada College, for example, or the preparatory schools attached to Victoria or Queen's, or indeed with a "crammer," a label which sounds faintly disreputable to twentieth-century ears but which was a common and eminently rational Victorian response to the plethora of idiosyncratic matriculation examinations. The crammers were clergymen, barristers, and other perfectly respectable gentlemen who, to supplement income or tide themselves over between employments, would offer to "prep" or "cram" a student for a particular examination. The practice was common enough that even students who had the advantage of an excellent grammar school education might finish their preliminary education this way. Amongst them, for example, was Ryerson's son, who had received most of his education at Upper Canada College. Charley, Ryerson told his daughter Sophie in 1866, and "the eldest son of Chief Justice Richards are reading Latin and Mathematics together, with a Private Tutor, with a view to admission to the Law Society."[21] In cases such as these, the grammar school provided an elementary or first stage of a preparatory education while the private tutor finished the job, acting as intermediary between school and higher education. Whether the student completed preparatory work in one of the college schools or with a crammer, in any case, or matriculated directly into the universities, low matriculation standards, along with the multiplicity of examinations, tended to denude the grammar schools of their senior pupils, leaving the work of the grammar school largely restricted to the more elementary parts of the curriculum.

The universities overlapped the work of the grammar schools in yet another way – through the admission of large numbers of "non-matriculants"; students, that is, who were allowed to enrol in one or more university courses but who, for one reason or another, did not sit the matriculation examination and who were therefore not entitled to proceed to degrees unless they passed an equivalent examination at some point in their studies.[22] Since this category of student is almost unknown now, it is important to emphasize that they constituted a major segment of the student population in the mid-nineteenth-century universities. David Keane found that most students at Queen's were matriculants; but a large minority of arts students at Victoria, the University of Toronto, and University College entered as non-matriculated students.[23] Before the 1860s, the number of non-matriculated exceeded the matriculated: "for example," Keane notes, "from 1854 to 1859, non-matriculated students comprised, on average, 70 percent of the annual enrolment at University College."[24] At Victoria in the 1840s, only 16 per cent of students were matriculants. Given these kinds of figures, one is left asking whether Victoria should be treated as a university at all, or as a large preparatory school with a few associated undergraduates.[25] But in any case, aside from Keane's thesis there is ample published evidence to support his conclusions, since the universities were expected to produce annual statistics in return for small government grants that they received throughout our period. To cite but two examples, at University College in 1858–59 there were 63 matriculated and 105 non-matriculated students.[26] And in 1856, Victoria had 33 matriculated students and 196 in preparatory courses. By way of explanation, the principal of Victoria commented that "the number of Matriculated Students is small in comparison with the whole attendance, but we would call attention to the fact, that many of those set down in the Preparatory Course, though not properly matriculated, are nevertheless pursuing University studies in certain departments, and correspond to what are called 'occasional students' in other Universities."[27]

One might well ask, in passing, why there were so many non-matriculants in the Upper Canadian universities. One reason was that country pupils who did not have easy access to a nearby grammar school might be sent directly to a college school or enrolled as non-matriculants to prepare for eventual matriculation.[28] Beyond that, individuals might seek out this or that college-level course for particular vocational purposes without wanting or needing a full program. Again, many non-matriculants at University College were completing their preparation for theological studies. The [Presbyterian] Free Church, for example, routinely required its ministerial candidates to raise their preliminary education to at least undergraduate levels before beginning theological studies. Thus throughout our period it maintained a preparatory department at Knox College for students without a grammar school education, and sent those who were more advanced to University College even if they were not qualified to matriculate in arts.[29] And finally, at a time when only a few occupations required a diploma and indeed when educational qualifications of any sort were a major prerequisite for only a small number of occupations, many students never bothered to matriculate as they had no need for the educational certificates associated with matriculation and graduation.

But if students could attend the universities without having to matriculate, and if they could opt to become regular students during their university studies, then what relevance had the senior levels of the grammar school? The latter could hardly claim to be the crucial gatekeeper for higher education if the university itself routinely allowed students to bypass it. In this respect the universities were direct competitors, attracting students some of whom at least might otherwise have attended the local grammar school.

Lest our argument thus far be misunderstood, it is important to emphasize that the problem was not that the universities had suddenly "invaded" territory that properly belonged to the grammar school, nor that the collegiate preparatory schools or crammers were attempting to poach on the grammar school's historic prerogatives. Our point is just the opposite. At mid-century the grammar school had yet to appropriate a piece of pedagogical terrain that it could clearly call its own. In a general way, its job was to prepare pupils for higher education – that had always been understood. But it had no exclusive claim to a particular portion of the curriculum, the terminal point of the grammar school remained uncertain, and the extent to which the universities and other institutions would also be involved in relatively elementary instruction was still unsettled.

At mid-century, indeed, it was not even clear that the grammar school was destined to assume full responsibility for preparing students for matriculation. A variety of alternatives presented themselves and some were potential competitors for the niche in the system that offered the final stages of preparatory work. Until at least the 1860s, for example, Upper Canada College was sporadically visualized as "the" preparatory institution for the provincial university, taking boys from the local grammar schools and finishing their preparation for the matriculation examinations. Testifying before the University Commission in 1860, Ryerson himself remarked that the main justification for the existence of Upper Canada College was that "it was intended especially as a feeder to the Provincial University College; that it was designed to take up our youth at a stage when they had advanced beyond the competency of ordinary Grammar Schools, and gather them there for the special purpose of preparing for the Provincial University. Why else is it," he asked, "that £3000 or £6000 per annum has been given to Upper Canada College, and from £50 to £200 only to each of the Grammar Schools, except that the College had work to do superior to that of the Grammar Schools?"[30]

Though no formal steps were ever taken to give the college this intermediate role, there is no question that, until at least the 1860s, it operated in that way, sending a steady stream of boys to King's and then University College. So indeed did the preparatory schools attached to Victoria and Queen's. As David Keane has shown, these three schools alone produced 60 per cent of all matriculants to the universities in the 1840s. Formally or not, the college preparatory schools effectively operated at mid-century as the key institutions in preparing pupils directly for matriculation. And the pattern would persist: in 1860, for example, only eight of forty-four arts students at Queen's had completed their preparatory education in one of the grant-aided grammar schools.[31]

Between mid-century and the early 1880s, nonetheless, a number of interrelated developments began to define the boundaries between the schools and the universities, to provide a sharper focus for the work of both, and to make the preparatory work of the grammar schools more essential to the universities. The rapid multiplication of the grammar schools in the two decades after 1850 made the rudiments of a classical and mathematical education more available throughout the province and thus gradually reduced the need for remedial institutions such as the grammar school course at Knox, or the classical tutor at University College. It also reduced parents' dependence on the college preparatory schools. A steady, if unspectacular, rise in university enrolments had its effect as well. Not only did absolute numbers grow – at University College, for example, enrolments increased from 110 to 282 between 1854 and 1863 – but even more important, the balance between matriculated and non-matriculated students shifted dramatically. The former had constituted only a third of enrolments at University College in 1854. By 1863 they were in a substantial majority and that trend would persist, until by the early 1880s nearly all students were matriculants, pursuing the full course prescribed by the university for the degree of BA.[32]

In the middle 1860s, moreover, rising enrolments in the universities, and concern about overcrowding in the professions, led both universities and professional associations to push up their matriculation standards. A major overhaul of the undergraduate program at the University of Toronto raised matriculation to a point at which students had to pursue most subjects at a level equivalent to the fourth or fifth forms of the official grammar school program. The university also introduced a dual set of matriculation standards – one for "junior" and the other for "senior matriculation."[33] The latter allowed a student to complete the equivalent of first-year university studies at his local grammar school and then sit the senior matriculation examination that led directly into sophomore studies. The Law Society revised its entry standards upwards in 1864, and in 1866 the Medical Council did likewise, including, for the first time, Greek as a prerequisite for medical studies.[34]

In one way or another, each of these changes redounded to the advantage of the grammar schools. As matriculation became routine, the senior work of the grammar schools became more pertinent to the student's vocational goals. As matriculation standards rose, it became necessary to stay in school longer. A nodding acquaintance with elementary classics or mathematics would no longer ensure matriculation in medicine, law, or arts at Queen's or the University of Toronto. Students were now compelled to pursue more advanced work in matriculation subjects, and, as they did so, the relevance of a grammar school education to individual ambitions and to the well-being of local communities became more palpable.

Higher matriculation standards, however, did nothing to mitigate the problems created by the variety of standards that existed. If anything, indeed, they made the situation worse, for the higher the standard, the more room there was for diversity in subjects and readings. A modicum of Latin, for example, had always sufficed for medicine, and that in turn was enough for Victoria or Queen's as well. But after 1866, medical students needed more advanced work not only in Latin but also in Greek, and for the latter, the Medical Board assigned a passage from St John's Gospel, a reading no other matriculation examination demanded.[35]

If preparing students for matriculation had been the only responsibility of the grammar schools, the variety of requirements imposed by the universities and professional associations might not have become such a burden, for the actual number of matriculants remained small – until the 1870s they never amounted to more than a hundred a year, and even in the late 1870s, when we have figures for both university and professional matriculants, they still numbered fewer than a thousand annually.[36] But this was not the only, or even the main, responsibility of the grammar schools. During the 1860s and 1870s, their total number of pupils tripled, rising from about 4500 to nearly 13,000, of whom aspiring matriculants were a mere drop in the bucket. At the same time the purposes of the schools broadened substantially. With the failure of Ryerson's policy initiatives of 1865, the notion of a single-purpose grammar school devoted to preparing boys for the learned professions breathed its last gasp. After that, teachers were expected to provide an education in English, science, and commercial studies for boys, and a suitable education for girls, as well as to prepare boys for matriculation. Increasingly they were also expected to prepare students of both sexes for teachers' examinations and certificates. In sum, more pupils were to be taught more subjects, and more examinations and certificates were to be prepared for.

Not surprisingly, then, the continuing burden of preparing students for a variety of matriculation standards provoked a growing volume of complaints from high school masters and ministry officials. In 1872, for example, one high school inspector noted that St Catharines Collegiate had three pupils in Latin preparing for a major scholarship examination and one preparing for the Law Society, which altogether involved two different Latin classes for four pupils. In Greek there was one pupil in each of three classes. Three more boys were preparing for surveyors' examinations while the same number of druggists' assistants attended three hours a week for lessons in experimental chemistry. The multiplication of small matriculation classes in this manner meant, among other things, that "classes in English Grammar, Arithmetic etc ... are too large, in fact like large Divisions in Public Schools." Altogether, he concluded, the school was not well classified. There were "too few teachers and too many different classes (each small). There ought to be 8 teachers instead of four."[37] In the little village of Scotland the story was the same: there were too many classes and yet "this can hardly be avoided in any school that attempted to do High School work – some of the pupils preparing for teachers' examinations, others, for matriculation ... hence there must be a large number of classes, no matter how small the number (comparatively) on the roll."[38] Summing it up in 1876, the high school inspectors agreed that it was essential to diminish

the labour which the Masters are forced to undergo, in consequence of the diversity of requirements on the part of the Examiners for the different professions. In the same school there may be Pupils preparing for the Law Society, for the Medical Council, for the University, and for Teachers' Certificates. In each of these cases a different Preparatory Course is prescribed, and to meet the wants of candidates the Master is compelled to multiply Classes to such an extent as to interfere seriously with the general work of the school.[39]

The solution, sought by the department and by the Grammar School Masters' Association with increasing fervour from the late 1860s onwards, was the unification and standardization of the different matriculation examinations so that they would jibe with the regular program of the schools. Typically, a resolution of the Ontario Teachers' Association in 1874 stated

that since the great diversity of books in the same subjects prescribed for entrance into our various Colleges and Professions causes much unnecessary work to the teachers in our High Schools, and puts the Candidates to considerable expense, the High School Section of the Ontario Association would respectfully and strongly urge upon the governing bodies of the various Colleges and learned Societies the desirability of having, as far as possible, uniformity in the books and subjects of examination. – Carried.[40]

The arguments did not all work in favour of a common standard, however. The universities and professional associations were independent corporations and guarded their prerogatives jealously, all the more so in the case of medicine and law, where the connection between control over their own matriculation standards and control over the numbers entering the professions was clearly understood. But beyond that, unification was difficult because matriculation examinations served two distinctly different purposes. John Langton put it this way in 1860. Matriculation in medicine

stands upon an entirely different footing from Matriculation in Arts. The object of a matriculation Examination in Arts is to show that a student is sufficiently far advanced to go on with his studies in a prescribed course. The object of a Matriculation examination in Medicine is to ascertain whether he has finished his studies in those departments in which he will never be examined again.[41]

Langton's distinction applied more widely as well, for matriculation into medicine was like entering law or writing the examination for a higher teaching certificate. These were tests of a general education completed, and students were expected to be more sophisticated and knowledgeable than was necessary for matriculants in arts. Thus it was difficult for contemporaries to see how a single examination could serve both purposes satisfactorily. Unification also demanded a common list of subjects, but this too caused difficulties, for different institutions wanted their students to have different combinations of subjects. The University of Toronto, for example, resolutely resisted making science a matriculation subject for arts throughout the 1870s, but the Medical Council had included it from 1866 as did the university's faculty of medicine.

The universities and professional associations, for their part, made demands that the high schools simply could not meet. When in 1881 the Medical Council required aspiring matriculants to take three out of four of the optional subjects listed in the high school program, one headmaster complained bitterly in the pages of the *Canada Lancet* that it was

out of the question to expect that the great majority of High Schools can, under such circumstances, undertake to prepare candidates for the examination prescribed. The ... classes in these schools are so arranged that instruction in the optional subjects is to a great extent simultaneous. While one portion of the class ... is engaged with a Latin lesson, those who do not take Latin may be occupied with Natural Philosophy, while still another division may be under the charge of another master studying German or French.

Attempting to meet the council's extraordinary requirement would result in "the entire arrangements of any High School being completely disturbed. In fact in most schools, it would be a simple impossibility to accomplish this work." If the council really meant three out of four, he concluded, "it will be necessary for candidates to qualify themselves for this severe test by home study or private tuition."[42]

An issue such as this, moreover, raised the fundamental problem of reconciling the demands of the universities and professions for particular standards or courses with the other responsibilities of the high schools. Preparing students for matriculation was one important purpose of the high school but not the only one, and it could not be allowed to dictate the curricular priorities of the schools. The issue of how to balance the various demands on the high school curriculum – a conundrum for the high school from that day to this – was elucidated by Adam Crooks in 1877. "The subjects for ... matriculation in the provincial university," he wrote in a private memorandum to his advisers,

necessarily influence the whole direction of the studies in the High Schools, yet it must not be overlooked that probably but one in ten of High School pupils intend to matriculate. The matriculation examination should be so regulated as not to disturb the general usefulness of the High Schools in affording Higher education to the nine tenths, who are unable to proceed further, and of whom one half are probably preparing to become Public School Teachers. The University should of course require a proper standard at matriculation and especially at Senior matriculation, so as to secure that amount of grounding which will enable the student to satisfactorily overcome the subjects of a proper University course, but it appears to me that at this time of day, undue prominence should not be given to the Greek and Latin Classics, or to Mathematics, so as to diminish the importance of other Departments ... Considering also the necessary subjects in the High School Curriculum in order that these Schools may continue to fulfil their very useful work of preparing intending Public School Teachers, it is desirable that such subjects as Chemistry and natural philosophy should also appear in the University Matriculation examination (Junior and Senior). The objection that it is better that all instruction should be given in University College or some other Institution is untenable in my judgment. Opportunities now exist, and are improving, for a great deal of useful grounding in these subjects being done by the High Schools ... It appears to me that a satisfactory curriculum in the general public interest cannot be adopted for matriculation examination (Junior or Senior) in the Provincial University which does not pay due regard to the proper work which is assigned our High Schools in our educational system, and which prominently includes instruction in these subjects, which the Public School Teacher should have capacity to teach in the Public Schools. [43]

Given these different interests and expectations, it is perhaps not surprising that progress towards a common matriculation standard was slow and halting. The first steps were taken in the late sixties when, in response to a resolution passed by the Grammar School Masters' Association, Victoria, Queen's, and Trinity agreed to base their matriculation examinations on the books and subjects listed in the grammar school program. [44] This brought all of the universities in line with the University of Toronto, whose matriculation examination had, since the act of 1853, established the upper limit of grammar school work. The Medical Council did likewise, but the Law Society resisted all pleas to assimilate its examinations to the grammar school course, perhaps because of the fear that it would make law more accessible and thus encourage further overcrowding of the profession. [45] With that exception, however, there was now common ground. Each university continued to hold its own examination, and each might require somewhat different readings or subjects. But at least they had agreed that their matriculation examinations would be limited to the content prescribed in the grammar school program of studies.

The idea of a common examination was a much more radical step, for it meant that the universities and professions would not only have to agree on a single standard but would have to hand over the control and administration of the examination to some superordinate authority – a joint university examining board, for example, or the Department of Education itself. [46] Before the late 1870s this was an almost unthinkable departure and there was, in any case, no instrument that could serve as a common examination. The introduction of the Intermediate in 1877 changed all that, however. The new examination was pitched at a level that was a rough match to several of the existing matriculation examinations, and the high school masters immediately saw its potential for standardizing the course of studies by putting an end, once and for all, to the problem of preparing students for different examinations. Thus at their annual meeting in 1876 they proposed a dramatic overhaul of the matriculation system, making the Intermediate examination a substitute for *all* of the other examinations – junior matriculation at the University of Toronto, the teachers' examinations, and the matriculation examinations of the Law Society, the Medical Council, and the other universities as well. A committee was appointed and instructed to pursue the matter with the relevant authorities.[47] The Department of Education also supported the idea, and its enthusiasm grew as the bureaucrats discovered, in 1877 and 1878, that students were resisting writing the Intermediate because it served no useful purpose for them. For the department, tying the Intermediate to the matriculation and teachers' examinations would give some public purpose to an examination that existed solely as a means of distributing the legislative grant. To promote this end the minister was given statutory powers in 1877 to amalgamate the teachers' examinations with the Intermediate and also to arrange reciprocal agreements with the various universities and professions.[48]

The grand scheme proposed by the high school masters was far too radical for the 1870s. There was no common agreement about standards and the various institutions involved were reluctant to surrender their authority to an arm of government. Lobbying by the teachers and the minister, however, had some effect. In 1876, responding to "the representations made from time to time," the Legal Education Committee of the Law Society assimilated their matriculation to that of the arts matriculation at the University of Toronto, which in turn was based on the grammar school course.[49] Though neither the university nor the Law Society would accept the Intermediate in lieu of its own examinations, this at least meant that all of the universities and professional associations now based their examinations on the high school curriculum. Queen's, Victoria, and the Medical Council went further. By 1880 all three had agreed to accept the Intermediate as equivalent to their own matriculation examinations, though in each case they also required students to take additional examinations in subjects like Greek, which was not included in the Intermediate, or in more advanced Latin than the Intermediate demanded.[50]

But why, one might ask, concede even this much? What was it that convinced the universities and professional associations to strike these bargains with the state? For one reason, the high schools were now vital reservoirs of students that the universities needed to tap. At mid-century, as we noted earlier, something like 60 per cent of all matriculants came from the three collegiate schools and many more came from private schools and tutors. But David Keane has shown that by 1879–80 Ontario's university students were overwhelmingly products of the public high schools, and though the percentage was somewhat lower at University College than at other universities, by the mid-1880s even that institution drew 85 per cent of its students from the high schools, the other 15 per cent coming mainly from Upper Canada College, St Michael's, and Woodstock College.[51]

As the importance of the high schools to the universities increased, so too did the influence of the minister of education and the high school teachers' association on the admission policies of the denominational universities. As the editor of the *Canada School Journal* put it in 1878, in recent years there had been a rapid rise in the number of boys and girls preparing for the University of Toronto junior matriculation and if the other universities did not join in a common examination, Toronto "will have a virtual monopoly of intending university students."[52] Given the continuing competition for students amongst the universities, this was no idle threat: a prerequisite that could not easily be accommodated in the schools might not be taught and students lacking it would apply to institutions elsewhere.

As for the University of Toronto, it was the "provincial university," linked to government by a variety of financial and other ties that made it sensitive to pressures from the legislature and especially from the cabinet, including the minister of education. The Ontario Medical Council recognized similar political imperatives. Seeking legislative sanction on a number of fronts in the late seventies, the council was sympathetic to the idea of "grafting the system of elementary medical education upon the government system. By accepting the High School standard," one member of Council pointed out,

it would prove a mutual assistance, and it was but reasonable to expect that if the Council endorsed the Government in this matter they would be benefited in return. No one would deny that they had a perfect right to receive assistance from the Government, and they would have a better claim to it if they endorsed the government standard of teaching.[53]

There were also administrative and financial advantages to co-operation. As it was, each institution held its own examination and marked its own papers, or, in the case of law and medicine, hired examiners to do so. In medicine, for example, the examinations were held four times a year, candidates were dragged to Toronto for nearly two weeks to write all the papers involved, and there were too few examiners to mark the papers properly in the time allotted, giving rise to appeals and to complaints in the press.[54] A common examination run by the Department of Education would be written in the candidates' own high schools, marked by departmental examiners, and all the expenses paid for by the department itself. Thus, argued the editor of the *Canada Lancet* in 1880, to use the high school examinations would make the whole selection process "more satisfactory, less troublesome and expensive ... than the matriculation as at present conducted. There would in this way be a saving of expense to the [Medical] Council"; and indeed it might actually prove profitable: "the fee for registration ... might still remain as at present, viz. $10 each, so that the exchequer of the Council would sustain no loss by the arrangement, but on the contrary, a gain, by reason of the discontinuance of the present poorly paid examiners."[55]

It was these sorts of arguments that led the universities and professions steadily towards a common matriculation standard and a common examination. The developments of the late 1870s and early 1880s were no more than the first steps towards that end, and it would take more than a decade and all of George Ross' political skills as minister of education to move the various institutions towards a final settlement. By the middle nineties, nonetheless, a combined school-leaving and matriculation examination, administered by the Department of Education and set by a joint board composed of representatives from the department and the universities, had been put in place.[56] This was, of course, a far more comprehensive solution than existed in 1880, but it was not much different in principle from the more modest standardization achieved in the late seventies when the high school course became the basis for all the matriculation examinations and when some institutions at least began to accept the Intermediate as a matriculation equivalent. As one high school master put it in congratulating Victoria for adopting the Intermediate, the university had simply recognized

the fact that our various educational institutions – from primary school to the University – are parts of one system – a system of which our High Schools and Collegiate Institutes form an essential and integral part; that upon the efficiency of our primary and secondary schools very largely depends the success of our Universities; that there is no surer means of securing this efficiency than by receiving their work at its current value, thus conferring a well-merited boon on our high school teachers, and simplifying our complicated means of supplying our Universities from their natural feeders, the secondary schools of the country.[57]

During the 1870s, then, the high school began to acquire for itself a secure niche within the province's system of education. As the universities increasingly focused their efforts on matriculated students, more and more of the responsibility for preparing students for matriculation fell to the high schools. The preparatory department at Victoria, for example, which, in terms of numbers at least, had almost entirely overshadowed undergraduate work in the 1850s, was abandoned in the late 1860s and a special relationship with the Cobourg grammar school established in its stead. A decade later, after a protest against the teaching of elementary Greek launched by the headmaster of the Cobourg collegiate institute, the university senate declared that "it is both unnecessary and inexpedient for a Professor of the University to teach any class for which provision is made in the high schools of the country; and especially in the Cobourg Collegiate Institute, the recognized Preparatory Department of the college."[58] Measures such as these enabled the high school to advance its work upwards, creating in the process a course of studies that, for junior matriculation at least, extended over three or four years.[59]

The universities and the Medical Council, moreover, were not the only institutions to integrate their matriculation requirements with the high school program and examinations. In 1878 the Methodist General Conference moved in that direction, announcing that any candidate for the Methodist ministry "who may present a public school teacher's certificate of the second class, or a certificate of having passed a matriculation at any of our universities, shall not be required to be examined [by Conference examiners] on the English branches of the Preliminary Course."[60] By 1881 the Royal College of Dental Surgeons of Ontario had followed suit, allowing candidates to substitute the high school Intermediate certificate for its own examination.[61] The increasing homogeneity of matriculation standards, based upon the curriculum and examinations required by the Department of Education, not only increased the drawing power of the local high school, anchoring it firmly to the professional ambitions of young people and their families, but allowed the course of studies to assume a degree of unity and coherence impossible before. As John Seath put it in 1885, the amalgamation of examinations had remedied "what has been the most vexatious defect in our system. Formerly it was almost impossible to construct a suitable timetable, and the differences between the courses led to a most provoking waste of manpower."[62]

The boundary between the university and the high school remained imprecise in one respect. The two institutions overlapped by the equivalent of a year, for the work that constituted senior matriculation was also the work of the first year of the university. Though there were occasional complaints about the waste of money involved, and a flurry of debate in the years around 1880 about the possible abolition of one or another year, nothing came of it, and, indeed, the dual levels of matriculation would survive for decades to come.[63] In 1880, at least, the vast majority of students entered university through the junior matriculation examination. The senior matriculation was considered a "back door" means of preparation, faintly second-rate, but an avenue to be taken by those who for whatever reason had not availed themselves of the earlier opportunity to transfer to the university.[64] And David Keane's research implicitly supports contemporary comment on this point. In his examination of the 1879–80 student cohort, Keane found that those first registering in the sophomore year were, on average, not one, but more than three years older.[65] Put another way, if a student did not transfer at junior matriculation, he was likely to attend university substantially later than his peers.

Thus, though there continued to be overlap, duplication was now restricted to senior matriculation work. The university had become a "tertiary" institution, and the high school could claim a curriculum uniquely its own, stretching from the high school entrance examination to the junior matriculation. Few students actually stayed that long. But the latter examination quickly became the symbolic culmination and terminal point of high school studies, a symbol given formal recognition at the end of the eighties with the creation of the joint High School Leaving and Junior Matriculation Examination and Certificate. The developments of the sixties and seventies had left behind them a distinctly "secondary" sector in Ontario's education system.

CHAPTER THIRTEEN

The Social and Educational Limits of a High School Education

During the 1870s and 1880s, the high school began to consolidate its role in Ontario society by acquiring a secure pool of recruits and a sharper definition of its purpose. Though enrolments grew rapidly throughout the period, the high school continued to cater to a small minority of adolescents, attempting to keep the two principles of wide accessibility and rigorous selectivity in delicate balance. It promised this minority mental culture and a practical education, but its interpretation of both was circumscribed by the educational and social shibboleths of the time. These characteristics of the late-nineteenth-century high school, and the tensions embedded in them, would endure far into the twentieth century.

For decades the Upper Canadian grammar schools had suffered because there were too many schools and too few students who sought instruction in classics or the higher branches of an English education. In the two decades after 1870, however, as more students sought to qualify themselves for entry to teaching, the professions, the universities, or commercial occupations, the high schools gradually acquired a stable clientele willing to submit itself to the level of instruction they offered. Between 1872 and 1882, enrolments rose by 55 per cent, from just under 8000 to 12,400 pupils. By 1892 the number stood at 22,800, an increase over the decade of 84 per cent. Compared to overall enrolments in the public schools, of course, the actual number of high school pupils was small, amounting to no more than 4.3 per cent of all enrolments in 1891. Throughout the seventies and eighties, nonetheless, high school enrolments were growing at a far faster rate. Public school enrolments, indeed, had already begun to stabilize at levels congruent with the relevant school-age population. Sustained growth was now the preserve of the secondary school.[1]

During the two decades after 1870, moreover, the terms of access to the high school became more clearly defined. The high schools were to be open to all, regardless of social class or gender. They were to be day schools, widely dispersed geographically so that they would be easily accessible regardless of where students lived. But they were not to be schools that educated all children. Rather they were to be meritocratic institutions that admitted only a minority of adolescents and prepared them for particular purposes.

One precondition of equal access was the elimination of the "preparatory classes" in the high schools, classes that represented the last vestige of the dual system of schools so prevalent in the early nineteenth century. For most of their history, the Upper Canadian grammar schools had routinely taught young pupils the elements of an English education, including, often enough, the three Rs. After the introduction of the entrance examination in 1855, it was, strictly speaking, illegal to hold these preparatory classes, and Ryerson ceaselessly inveighed against them because they invited the grammar school to compete directly with the common schools and thus threatened the notion of a common beginning for all pupils within the public school system. Preparatory classes, nonetheless, continued to flourish. Though the record of their existence is shadowy, local people failing to report what they knew their masters did not want to hear, it is tolerably certain that preparatory classes existed in most of the grammar schools in the larger towns and cities, and in at least a few of the country schools as well.[2]

The preparatory classes survived for a number of reasons. For one thing, they offered parents who objected on social grounds to the common schools a plausible alternative to the private sector. As Paxton Young put it in 1865, if some such provision were not made, "such pupils would be compelled to go to private teachers and having once been placed under private tuition would probably continue with them when they became older, and so never enter the grammar school."[3] Beyond that there was also the long-standing conviction, still shared by many in the 1860s, that a good classical education required an early beginning. Indeed, William Tassie tried for just this reason to convince Ryerson in 1871 to allow him to maintain a preparatory school: if boys were not allowed to begin Latin at an early age in the Galt grammar school, their parents would remove them to private establishments where they could.[4] In the country schools particularly, preparatory classes also served remedial purposes, compensating for deficits in the quality of the local common schools by completing the preparation of students for the entrance examination or for the higher studies of the grammar schools.[5] And in town and country alike, whenever masters found their salaries inadequate they turned to preparatory classes as a natural way to supplement their incomes.[6]

Until the early 1870s, the preparatory classes had survived for yet another reason. For much of the period, the coercive powers of the Education Office had more bark than bite, and local teachers or trustees could afford to ignore Ryerson's huffing and puffing so long as that situation existed. By 1873, however, there were three inspectors instead of one, their visits were more regular, and control over the entrance examination had been transferred to the Education Office itself. In each case these measures made it easier for Ryerson and his aides to maintain surveillance over local activities or to enforce departmental policies. With these new weapons in hand, the Education Office moved decisively against the preparatory classes, issuing a regulation that prohibited the attendance at any high school of a pupil who had not passed the entrance examination.[7]

Almost immediately opposition to the new regulation developed. The common schools alone, it was said, could not adequately prepare pupils for the entrance examinations, and the result of abolition would be to "delete" the numbers in the high schools, thus undermining their finances.[8] The precise origin of the impetus for repeal is not clear: it may have been the high school masters, led perhaps by the influential heads of the Toronto, Kingston, and Ottawa schools, all of which had preparatory classes; it may have come from the politicians themselves. But in any event the new School Act of 1874 included a clause expressly permitting trustees to establish preparatory classes so long as they used none of the legislative or county grant to support them.[9] This did not, however, preclude trustees from levying a district rate to support such classes as long as the municipal council approved of it. The alternative means of support was tuition fees alone.

The Education Office was outraged, the high school inspectors condemning preparatory classes as "morbid growths," destroying "the harmony which should exist" between the high and public schools. "The High School with its preparatory class (for which high fees must be charged) will be regarded as a school – not for the people, but for a *class*: while the *people's* school (the Public School) will be placed in direct hostility to the High School, and cease to be what it ought to be – its legitimate feeder."[10] No less offended was a leading public school principal, Henry Dickinson. "After having introduced shakiness into a majority of the fifth and sixth classes of the Province," he said in an address to the Ontario Teachers' Association in 1875, the authorities "must needs try their hands on the third and fourth" by allowing the establishment of preparatory classes.

If the discipline or the attendance at the Public Schools be not in accordance with the preconceived ideas of certain classes of the community, their children are removed and find a too ready asylum in these preparatory classes. We thus find that, wherever found, these classes present either a sort of a *heterogeneous* mass of malcontents, or else are composed almost entirely of a few children of aristocrats, who will not allow their offspring to be contaminated with too familiar connection with the masses. This pandering to aristocracy is scarcely in harmony with the character of our institutions. If preparatory classes are a necessity to the classes supporting them, let them establish them as private institutions. The "otherwise educated" clause of the late School Act allows them the privilege; but why the Government should allow their establishment in connection with the High Schools of the Province is a mystery. They are considered by all, except this aristocratic element as unnecessary.[11]

The fears expressed in these outbursts were not, it must be emphasized, unfounded. A law had been put in place that would, in effect, permit the establishment of a dual system of elementary schools: one under the aegis of the high schools, financed by fees, or even by local taxes, and the other under the aegis of the Public School Act. The former would inevitably become the schools of the middle classes, would compete with the public schools for clientele and for scarce resources, would inherit the political advantages that inevitably accrue to the schools of the privileged, and thus would gradually be in a position to reduce the public schools to an inferior system serving only those who could afford nothing better. The modern reader may think such a scenario far-fetched. But systems organized in that fashion existed elsewhere and were at least as familiar to contemporaries as any other way of doing things. Indeed for those adults who, thirty or forty years before, had received their own education in Upper Canada, it was the conventional way for schools to be organized: grammar schools for the middle classes offering both an English and a liberal education, and common schools teaching little more than the three Rs to everybody else. Viewed from the perspective of the 1870s there was nothing inherently implausible about such an outcome.

It didn't work out that way, however. By 1880 only five out of 104 high schools reported having preparatory classes. By 1886 the number was down to three, and in 1891 none but Toronto maintained them.[12] Thus we are confronted with the paradoxical fact that the preparatory classes flourished in those years before 1874, when they were illegal, and petered out later regardless of the fact that they had received legal sanction. In 1891, in any case, and despite a petition from some Toronto parents and opposition from a few members of the legislature, George Ross carried through the House an amendment to the Education Act consigning the preparatory classes to oblivion, with the epitaph that "what had ceased to be useful might as well be abolished."[13]

There is very little hard evidence to explain the decline of the preparatory classes in the years after 1874. Our own reasoning, however, is as follows. The preparatory classes survived so long as they were financially essential to the schools, so long as significant numbers of parents objected strenuously to the social promiscuity of the common school, and so long as remedial work was necessary if grammar school standards of work were to be maintained. By the later 1870s, each of these circumstances was less pertinent. First, remedial work by the high school ceased to be necessary as the high school entrance examination increasingly became the litmus test for both successful pupils and teachers in the public schools. Secondly, large numbers of middle-class parents were increasingly willing to make use of the public schools as the primary vehicle in preparing their children for the high school entrance: by 1884, 97 per cent of all those who sat the examination had been trained in the public school, 2 per cent in a preparatory class, and less than 1 per cent in a private school.[14] And finally, growing enrolments, along with the improved provisions for school finance introduced in 1877, removed the incentives to recruit non-secondary students and, at the same time, encouraged the schools to focus their own efforts on those pupils who were pursuing distinctly secondary-level studies.

There was, however, yet another, and, we suspect, an overriding reason for the demise of the preparatory classes. To the extent that they did indeed raise the spectre of a dual system of schools divided by social class, they contravened some fundamental political and social convictions shared by most influential Ontarians. It was one thing to tolerate the survival of a handful of preparatory classes here and there; it was another thing altogether to contemplate a socially segregated school system. From John Strachan and Egerton Ryerson to Adam Crooks and George Ross, the good society was one that made room for rising talent, and the education system was expected to encourage it. To achieve this, the public schools had to be organically linked to the high schools and universities, so that bright, ambitious students, whatever their backgrounds, might easily move up each step of what George Ross felicitously described as "the great stairway of learning."[15] In Ontario, Adam Crooks had explained in a speech given in 1876, his first year as minister of education, "a pupil was able to go in the lowest class and come out at the University. Great difficulty had been found in England in arriving at a similar position, *viz*. – to allow a youth of humble origin to pass on to the highest sphere through an Educational System." But it would be "a disgrace" if "our Educational System debarred anyone from enjoying its advantages."[16] With views such as these it is unlikely that Crooks would give any encouragement to preparatory classes, and Ross evidently took some pleasure in his speech to the House advocating their abolition. There had to be ladders and stairs to climb, or stepping stones to negotiate, all common contemporary metaphors; but the ladders must have rungs, the stairways must have steps, and the stepping stones must lead to the other side. Barriers must exist, in other words, but they had to be permeable. The closed, dual system of old England could not be allowed to take root in a new country like Canada.

There may be other, more plausible reasons for the demise of the preparatory class than we have suggested, but whatever the case, it eliminated once and for all the intervention of the high school in elementary instruction, and thus defined the high school exclusively as a second stage in Ontario's system of public education. As Crooks remarked in the legislature in 1877, "the High Schools ... by one step after another, have come to occupy conspicuously a position dependent mainly on scholastic as distinguished from other considerations (Hear, Hear)."[17]

NONE OF THIS, it hardly bears saying, is intended to suggest that by the 1880s, social class had ceased to be an influence in determining who went to high school. In contrast to the years between 1855 and 1867, no one systematically collected the high school attendance registers for the later nineteenth century and thus we cannot trace the social origins of students in our five towns twenty or thirty years after 1861. The official records of the Department of Education are, however, of some help, and beyond that there is the invaluable work of Anthony Ketchum, who has located and analysed the registers of four high schools – Whitby, Elora, Arnprior, and Grimsby – for varying periods of time between the 1870s and the turn of the century.[18]

In all four of Ketchum's schools, the fathers of high school students had a wide variety of backgrounds ranging from "gentleman" to labourer. The high school was not, in other words, closed to any portion of the population. Indeed, there may well have been a significant increase in the number of working-class children in the last three decades of the nineteenth century. For our five schools in 1861 no more than 1 per cent of fathers were labourers and semi-skilled workers.[19] For Ketchum's schools the percentage stands at 12 per cent. Another 14 per cent were skilled workers. In all, a quarter of those sending children to high school came from the lower half of the socio-economic order, thus lending credence to claims that the school system offered Ontarians equality of educational opportunity. And there undoubtedly was real upward mobility by means of the school system. Skilled and unskilled workingmen may have been substantially underrepresented in the extent to which they used the high schools, but they were not a token minority.

Most of the clientele of Ketchum's high schools, however, continued to be drawn from the same classes as it had in 1861. Gentlemen and those in the major professions made up 11 per cent of high school parents between 1894 and the end of the century; a further 13 per cent were in business, the minor professions, and government service. Fourteen per cent of parents were small proprietors of one sort or another. In all, a total of 38 per cent of the parents fell into these categories. Another 36 per cent were farmers. Thus almost three-quarters of the parents were drawn from various occupations located in the top half of the social spectrum.

These findings are corroborated by another source: the statistics on parental occupations contained in the *Annual Reports* from 1894 on.[20] Here, for example, we find that in all Ontario high schools between 1894 and

1907, about 10 per cent of the fathers of high school pupils were "professionals," and together with the "commercial" and "agricultural" categories they comprised some 65 per cent of all parents.[21] In the closing years of the nineteenth century, in Ketchum's four schools, the proportion of parents in the professional, commercial, and agricultural categories ranged from 63 per cent in Arnprior, to 80 per cent in Whitby.[22] In the five southwestern Ontario high schools that we examined for 1861, as indeed in the province generally, the "middle-class" categories of professional, commercial, and agricultural occupations accounted, in 1896, for about 65 per cent of all parents.[23]

Between 1861 and the turn of the century, in sum, there were only modest changes in the social composition of high school students. The number of children from skilled and unskilled workers' families increased, and given the occupations that the high school led to, their numbers indicate a significant amount of upward social mobility. There may have been, as well, another form of mobility which tends to be overlooked – horizontal mobility as farm families, and small proprietors hurt by the reorganization of commerce, moved one or more of their children off the land and out of the shop, into the expanding sectors of urban white collar work.[24] This remains a matter of speculation; what we do know, however, is that professional fathers remained massively overrepresented in the high schools, and, to a lesser extent, so did most other middle-class occupations. The high school remained what it had been at mid-century, an essentially middle-class institution.

While it may suit neither the political left nor the right to describe the schools as institutions that promoted both social mobility *and* social reproduction, it is not as problematic a proposition as it is sometimes made to appear. "Class" and "mobility," R.W. Connell points out, are not opposed terms. "Both as a fact and a possibility, change of circumstance is an essential part of the class structure and of the class/education complex. Contrary to various shades of popular and scholarly opinion, it is a fundamental feature of schooling that it routinely produces 'upward' mobility, 'downward' mobility, and no mobility at all. The collective practices of families acknowledge this fact. They are organized by both the fear of becoming worse off, and by the possibility of promotion."[25]

Contemporaries themselves recognized the dual social functions of the high school. On the one hand, they insisted on the need for open access as we have already seen; and yet on the other hand, they took for granted that the high schools were the particular property of the middle classes. Sometimes they were even quite explicit in describing the schools that way, as for example when one editor referred, in passing, to "our middle class educational institutions, including our high schools in Ontario and the academies and schools corresponding to them in other provinces."[26] No one expected the high schools to be free of class bias. The classic formulation of equality of educational opportunity called only for open access and the allocation of places for those who proved themselves meritorious. Ontario's public schools were free and so were many of its high schools. University College was almost tuition-free. Thus, as Adam Crooks put it in 1876, "in our educational system, the poor have the same chance as the rich."[27] There was nothing inconsistent in describing the schools as middle-class institutions so long as they were not exclusively middle-class.

There are, unfortunately, virtually no sources for the later nineteenth century that help us distinguish between the social backgrounds of girls and boys, and thus we cannot make the kind of comparisons that can be made on this score in 1861. But it is possible to draw some conclusions about the level of access girls had to the high schools. By the late 1880s, the number of boys and girls enrolled in the schools was roughly equal, but when we compare students in the collegiate institutes to those in the high schools, we find that the sex ratios differ. Girls were in a slight majority in the high schools, while in the collegiate institutes they lagged behind at 47 per cent of the student population.[28] Ketchum suggests several plausible explanations for this imbalance. Industrialization created jobs that pulled boys out of high schools earlier than girls, while girls flocked into high schools to earn the certificates or skills they needed for teaching, clerical jobs and, a little later, for nursing. On the other hand, boys attended collegiate institutes in greater numbers than girls because the collegiates were better equipped to prepare pupils to meet university and professional matriculation standards.[29]

There is also evidence that girls gradually established a presence not only in the lower forms of the high schools but in the upper forms as well. The published statistics of the department do not provide breakdowns by gender for enrolments in forms or subjects, but in some years the information is available in the unpublished high school inspectors' reports. In 1878 these include a handful of references to the gender of students at each grade level, and in every case the girls were heavily concentrated in the lower forms of the school. In Brantford, for example, 49 per cent of those in form I were girls and form II was 60 per cent female; the percentages then dropped off sharply, to 37 per cent in form III, 23 per cent in IV, and only 10 per cent in the highest form. Similarly in Owen Sound, girls made up 56 per cent of the lower school student body but 33 per cent of the upper school. And in Ottawa, girls were never in the majority at any level, but they were similarly concentrated in the lower forms. We have no other conclusive evidence on the matter until fifteen years later, but by then the pattern had changed dramatically. In 1895, in a sample of nine schools, girls were in the majority in every form in three of them; very close to a majority in most of the rest, even in the upper grades; and in only one was that majority restricted to the lowest grade.[30] Thus we would suggest that the full range of high school studies had become accessible to girls in a way inconceivable a few decades earlier.

In our own day struggles over access to the schools tend to focus exclusively on gender and social class. But for most of Ontario's history, geographical access was even more at issue. The scramble to establish grammar schools in the middle decades of the nineteenth century, and the successful resistance by local people in the late 1860s against policies that would have closed many schools down, demonstrated the potent political power of the demand for access to superior education from people in small communities throughout the province. Despite persistent attempts by the department to limit the growth of small schools, the pressures to expand the schools would continue, multiplying their number from 104 during the 1870s to 120 by 1890. And as the high school inspectors remarked in the mid-seventies, the schools were "not confined to the larger centres of population; they are scattered broadcast over the country."[31] In 1891, students attending high school outside of the province's ten largest urban centres constituted over 80 per cent of all enrolments.[32]

The number of students attending the high schools from beyond the borders of the town where the school was located also grew substantially. In 1861 about 30 per cent of high school students came from outside the high school district.[33] From scattered evidence we can estimate the percentages for various years in later decades, and in almost every case the figures are higher. In 1880, for thirty-eight schools mainly in the eastern half of the province, the proportion of non-resident students rose to 37 per cent; ten years later, the published figures stood at 35 per cent for collegiate institutes, and 46 per cent for high schools.[34] "The number of pupils attending from the rural districts has largely increased," the minutes of the Ontario Teachers' Association noted in 1887, "and the work done for the townships adjacent to High Schools is much greater than in former years."[35]

By the 1880s, then, much of the rural population was within reach of a high school and a growing number of rural children were making the trip to town by road or rail to attend the schools. "Facilities for attending high school are so favorable in this county," the public school inspector for West Middlesex wrote in 1893, "that a large proportion of successful applicants can walk, or reach by conveyance or rail, and board at home."[36] In many places, nonetheless, the high schools were much less accessible. Boarding in town cost money and the nearest high school might charge tuition fees, especially to non-resident students. "Parents in rural sections," said one inspector in 1889, "are not willing, and, in many cases, are not able to send their children away from home, to a High School."[37] Thus, despite the rapid growth in the number of high schools, access remained limited and the pressures to expand it remained acute. Though the department had discouraged the establishment of fifth classes in the public schools – classes that taught the same curriculum as the first form of the high school – enrolments in fifth classes began to expand from a low in the mid-1880s of some eight thousand pupils to more than double that a decade later. There was, in other words, a demand for high school level work beyond that suggested by high school enrolments themselves: by 1896, there were some twenty-four thousand high school pupils but seventeen thousand more were enrolled in fifth classes.[38] It was these pressures in the countryside which would soon lead to the establishment of "continuation" classes and schools – public schools that offered high school work in a place too small to have a high school but where there were enough pupils to form a substantial high school class. While such developments lie beyond the scope of this study, they do indicate the pressure for geographical accessibility that continued to direct policy far into the twentieth century, and, at the same time, gave shape to conceptions about the meaning of equal opportunity itself. Indeed the earliest use of the phrase we have come across exemplifies our point: in 1881 Inspector McLellan commented, in passing, that "to give *Equality of Opportunity* to as many as possible is the grand principle which underlies our system of education, and therefore *good schools* in *many centres* has been and should continue to be the policy of the Department."[39]

On THE ONE HAND, then, there was the principle of wide accessibility, both social and geographical. But on the other, there was the principle of selectivity. The high school of the 1870s and 1880s did not exist to provide secondary education for all, a goal that in Ontario was decades away. Its responsibility was to continue the education of "the clever few," enabling some to go on to higher education and preparing others for a variety of middle-class occupations.[40] No one expected the high schools to cater to any but a small minority of adolescents. In the early 1870s, the high school inspectors estimated that the total number of pupils attending the high schools "was about one-half of one percent of the entire population" and that, they thought, was just about the right proportion for the foreseeable future: "it is not to be expected that this percentage will be either much, or rapidly increased, and it may be taken as a rough guide in estimating the probable natural and healthy attendance in the future."[41] Writing in the *Canadian Monthly*, an anonymous headmaster made a similar point in describing his own vision of the high school. It was sometimes suggested, he said, that the masses had little stake in the high schools. "It is true," he contended,

that they have no direct interest in them, that under the very best system only a very small percentage of the population can ever enter for educational purposes the doors of a High School, but yet it is not the less true that they are of immense indirect importance to the masses. Not only is it of importance that every lad who has the ability to profit by a superior education should have the means of readily obtaining it at hand; not only is it important to the general well-being of a community that it should have in it a body of highly cultivated men; not only are clergymen, lawyers, medical men, and teachers necessary, who must be trained in the High Schools but the High Schools are most advantageous in another respect, namely in giving tone to the lower schools. If the High Schools are put in a thoroughly efficient state, the elementary schools will be immensely better than they are. The boys educated in the High Schools will, as men, be the natural leaders of the communities in which they reside, and must give a tone to everything in them.[42]

However pretentious this assessment of the role of the high school might sound, the author was certainly correct in his assertion that only a small minority would ever darken its doors. In order to be admitted to high school a student had to pass the high school entrance examination, which was set at the end of the fourth class of the public school, a class largely devoted to intensive preparation for the examination itself. In the late nineteenth century, however, most pupils left school at the end of the third class, a point that roughly matched the upper limit of the age of compulsory schooling. Between 1877 and 1892 only about 17 per cent of all public school pupils enrolled in the fourth class. Thus even the pool of recruits for the high school entrance examination was small in comparison with the total school-age population. But of these, only a small minority actually sat the examination – 10 per cent in 1877 and 18 per cent in 1892. About half those candidates, in turn, failed the entrance. Between the third class of the public school and the first form of the high school, in other words, a ruthless winnowing took place. To see just what it meant in raw numbers, consider but a single cohort. In 1887 there were about 102,000 pupils enrolled in the third class. In 1888 enrolment in the fourth class was just under 80,000. Of these, 16,790 wrote the High School Entrance Examination. Just over 9000 passed the entrance. We do not know how many of those actually entered first form in 1889 because enrolments in its two subdivisions were always recorded together. But if we take total first form enrolment and divide it by two, the figure is around 7000.[43]

The decision to leave school, as we know from the work of Ian Davey and other historians, was shaped by parental circumstances; while there were all kinds of exceptions, the better-off the parent, the more likely a pupil was to stay in school into his or her teens. Thus middle-class adolescents were more likely to stay on for the fourth class, to prepare for the entrance, and to be found in the high school. There is, in other words, no reason to take Adam Crooks' assertion about equal chances for rich and poor at face value – the process of self-selection was hardly independent of students' backgrounds. And yet, since all students sat the same entrance examination, we presume that large numbers of failed candidates were children from middle-class homes, and we also know from the work of Anthony Ketchum that those who actually made it past the entrance and into high school included the sons and daughters of farmers, artisans, and mechanics. Thus the transition to high school, we suggest, can best be described as semi-independent of social class, or quasi-meritocratic.

Once students were in the high schools, there may have been some tracking by social class, though we do not know for certain that this was the case. [44] We have nothing like adequate indicators for enrolments by program until the late 1880s, and there was also massive overlap because many subjects were compulsory in both programs. About 13 per cent of students in 1888 were preparing for university or professional matriculation examinations, and another 45 per cent for one or another of the teachers' non-professional examinations. The collegiate institutes had a substantial edge in the former category but a much lower percentage of pupils preparing for the teachers' examinations, though the difference is almost entirely accounted for by the fact that large numbers of pupils were using the high schools to prepare for the third-class teachers' certificate whereas in the collegiates this was less common. [45] There were, in other words, some differences between collegiate institutes and high schools, and there were internal "streams" consisting of a common core with different options. But whether or not enrolments in the different streams were related to students' social backgrounds remains unknown.

At least until more research is done, in any case, we need to be cautious about assuming that social tracking existed in the late nineteenth-century high schools. Joel Perlmann has shown how little tracking by social class there was in Providence, Rhode Island, during the same period, and he notes that "the evolution of tracking must be understood in the context of access to secondary schooling generally ... when access was very limited, social differentiation among curricula had a different meaning than it did when access increased." There were also, Perlmann continues, "reasonably long-lasting configurations quite unlike what a single generalization about the evolution of tracking would predict, and quite unlike what in fact came into being by 1925."[46] To put it another way, the high school of the 1880s was not the high school of the mid-twentieth century, after the impact of mass secondary education and of the vocational training and progressive movements had begun to make itself felt. Or to use Fritz Ringer's terminology, the streaming that did exist in the 1880s may have been due to "horizontal segmentation" – different occupations "at roughly comparable levels in the social hierarchy" using the schools to train children for different vocational outcomes. [47]

And how did social class and intellectual ability interact as students proceeded through the high school? Once again, the sources that might be used to answer that question for Ontario's schools have yet to be located, if indeed they exist at all. For the moment at least we have nothing like the kind of definitive answers that David Labaree has been able to provide for the Central High School in Philadelphia, where full student records survive for the nineteenth century. His conclusions are suggestive nonetheless.

When one cuts through the rhetoric and looks at the way the high school actually dealt with its students, how meritocratic was it? What I find is that students obtained admission to the school through a mixture of class background and actual ability. However, once admitted, they found themselves in a model meritocracy where actual performance was the only characteristic that determined who would receive the school's valuable diploma. Therefore, although middle-class students were still the primary beneficiaries of the high school, since they constituted the majority of those admitted, the class effect was mediated through a form of meritocracy that held all students to the same rigorous academic standards.[48]

Parallel conclusions have turned up in England and elsewhere where schools similar to the late-nineteenth-century Ontario high school have been studied.[49] In any case, whether the effects of class were increasingly mitigated or not, the same winnowing out that occurred at the entrance examination took place again for those students attempting to obtain departmental certificates or pass one of the matriculation examinations. Throughout the 1880s, no more than 40 per cent of those who wrote the non-professional teachers' examination for second or third-class certificates passed.[50] In the first joint university-departmental matriculation examination, held in 1893, only 16 per cent passed.[51] Though the editors of the *Canada Lancet* considered it excessive, the examiners failed "82½%" of the candidates in medicine in 1880.[52] The late-nineteenth-century high school had indeed become a second stage in Ontario's system of public education, but it was emphatically not the second part of a system of universal education. The high school continued to have purposes more specialized than the public school, and its clientele consisted of "the clever few," or at least, that minority of children who were unusually good at passing examinations. Meritocratic ideas demanded both wide access and vigorous selectivity and the new high school reflected both these impulses, as it would continue to do until at least the 1950s.

WHATEVER THE ORIGINS of its clientele, the purpose of the high school, as our anonymous headmaster pointed out, was to prepare for certain kinds of occupations necessary to the community, and to instil "tone," or mental culture, in its students. By the 1880s, the former purpose was explicitly recognized in the organization of the curriculum. In the first form, all students took a common core of subjects, but after that they were streamed into different programs of study organized around their vocational destinations – programs leading to matriculation, to the teachers' non-professional examinations, or to preparation for commercial occupations. The various programs were by no means entirely differentiated, students normally taking several subjects in common along with the various options they were pursuing. But whatever the extent of the common core, the official program of studies was formally structured to reflect the vocational aspirations of students enrolled in the high schools.[53] It was a long way from Ryersonian notions of a common curriculum suited to all students regardless of their future occupations.

Yet the emphasis on vocationalism was not fundamentally inconsistent with the goal of mental culture that animated so much educational theory in the nineteenth century. The new subjects such as English or science that had secured a place in the high school and undergraduate curriculum in the quarter century since 1850 could train the mind as well as classics and mathematics, which meant that choices between them could be made without sacrificing the central goal of education. Programs of study, in turn, could be organized around different vocational destinations because such options were legitimate. Thus a high school education could continue to yield the values of a liberal education and, at the same time, be useful – "of actual practical value to the individual in his struggle for existence in the particular society in which his lot may be cast."[54] And as Ontario schoolmen were wont to say interminably, the high schools and universities had to provide a practical education if they were to meet the needs of a new country, and no less pertinent, continue to garner public support.

There were, however, limits to this happy marriage of culture and utility. Mental culture was not inconsistent with some forms of practical education, but it was with others. Vocationalism might include training for the professions or commerce but it did not extend to training for artisanal trades or crafts. This outcome was, of course, not due simply to the nature of things. Rather it was fashioned around the dual axis of curricular theory and social class that had always given superior education its particular character and shape.

For much of the nineteenth century, "science" was a generic term for a bundle of related but radically different sorts of activities ranging from esoteric theorizing about the structure of the universe to building better bridges and making better bulls. The same was true for science education. Until the early 1870s, science education and technical education were often treated as close to synonymous and there were only hazy distinctions between training for the workshop skills practised by artisans and training for the so-called scientific professions.[55] During the 1860s and early 1870s, moreover, there was a growing chorus of enthusiasm for technical education – for training in art and design, agriculture, engineering, metallurgy, industrial chemistry, and other similar applied sciences.[56] But it was not clear where the varieties of technical education were to be located. Physics and chemistry might belong in an arts faculty but what about applied mechanics or industrial chemistry? Did one provide for the education of engineers, chemists and metallurgists, artisans and mechanics in the same institutions or were there natural hierarchies amongst such groups that needed to be reflected in their educational institutions? Could technical education be integrated into the general school system or should it be provided in separate schools? And, indeed, what was the purpose of teaching science in the schools?

In 1870 there were contradictory answers to all these questions, and a good deal of muddle about which kind of science education belonged where. Ryerson, for example, was well aware of the arguments that science was a disciplinary subject; yet when he added it to the program of studies prescribed for public schools in 1871 he justified it on the grounds that it would be taught "in connection with the Agricultural, Mechanical and Manufacturing pursuits, and thus render practical help to these great material interests of the country."[57] Again, in his report on European education in 1868 he pointed to the need for a variety of schools – not just schools that trained for the professions but also for separate institutions that offered "practical education in connection with the different pursuits and employments of life."[58] Yet like other commentators, he also called for the injection of technical education into the existing system of public and high schools.[59] Or another example: when the School of Practical Science was established in 1873, its mandate was not only to train students in "Engineering, Mining and Manufactures" and to offer "special instruction in the different departments of Experimental science" but also to give "instruction to Artisans, Mechanics and Workmen ... in such subjects as may further their improvement in their different callings."[60] Its responsibilities, in other words, were inclusive, teaching pure and applied science and crafts skills to operatives and engineers alike.

During the 1870s and 1880s, nonetheless, technical education was systematically integrated into the existing educational and social context. We do not pretend to offer a full account of how this occurred, nor would it be pertinent to the main themes in this book. But for our purposes, two developments are important. First, the distinction between professional and liberal studies was sharpened within the University of Toronto which, in turn, helped clarify the different roles of science education for the lower schools. In the middle 1870s, for example, James Loudon, a leading scientist at the university and its future president, fought vigorously to maintain science "as part of a general system of liberal studies" within the arts program, and at the same time worked to create a separate university school of applied science that would take responsibility for practical education in engineering, mining, industrial chemistry, and the like.[61] As this distinction took root it helped to specify the different institutional locations in which science as mental culture, and science as applied art, belonged, and distinguished more clearly between the different functions of science education.

No less important, the social matrix of science education became more differentiated. Loudon, along with other advocates of a professionalized School of Practical Science, tirelessly promoted the view that the study of science, pure and applied, and the education of the artisan were entirely different enterprises. "Many persons fail to distinguish between scientific training of an Arts, or Engineering Student, on the one hand, and the education of the Artisan classes," Loudon wrote in 1875. "Where there is a large Artisan Class, I am free to admit that it is well to furnish those whose early education has been neglected with facilities for improving themselves. Such classes, however, form no necessary adjunct to a School of Science ... Under any circumstances, the Mechanics Institute is the proper place for such instruction to be given."[62] In a similar vein, the principal of the School of Practical Science remarked in 1891 that

technical education may be classified into two broad divisions, manual training and theoretical training. In a school for manual training the teachers should be expert tradesmen ... In addition, it is usual and advantageous in such schools to give a certain amount of theoretical or scientific instruction: as, however, the main work is the training of the hand, the scientific training must to a great extent be of an elementary character.

The second division of technical education is theoretical or scientific training. In a school undertaking this work it is essential that the teachers should be scientific men, thoroughly versed in the theories relating to their several departments.[63]

Parallel developments were taking place with respect to the elementary and high schools. There were those in the 1880s who advocated that distinct technical schools be established to provide an appropriate education for artisans and operatives.[64] But aside from considerations of cost, it was an impractical suggestion at a time when most working-class children left school by the end of the third public school class. It was probably that blunt reality which led the government in 1880 to transfer supervision of the mechanics institutes to the Education Department and give them the mandate "to gradually develop evening classes in studies not within the Public School course, and especially in elementary instruction for industrial purposes."[65] By 1884, indeed, George Ross saw the mechanics institutes as the chief vehicle for artisan education: "technical education for the working class," he wrote in that year, "is the application of science to industrial purposes, and it should be the chief aim of the Mechanics Institutes to aid mechanics in becoming acquainted with the branches of science which are of practical application to their various trades."[66]

The development of these modern dichotomies – pure and applied, professional and technical, theoretical and manual – which are constitutive elements in our own conceptions of how education should be organized, deserve more attention from historians than they have received thus far. What had emerged, in any case, was virtually a reconceptualization of the Georgian distinction between a liberal and an ordinary education, though the terminology was now an "academic" or a "general" versus a "technical" education. Like its predecessor, it encapsulated both curricular and social distinctions, and directed the organization of education towards two mutually exclusive tracks. "Technical education, like general education," Daniel Wilson wrote in 1887,

may be advantageously divided into three classes – primary, secondary and higher … Primary technical education is intended for boys up to the age at which they should begin their apprenticeship to their trades: there are no institutions for doing this work in the Province. Secondary technical education is that of the artisan after he has begun his apprenticeship or actual work at his trade: the only method of providing for it on an efficient and broad basis is by instituting night schools … Higher technical education is the training of engineers and chemists … The School of Practical Science … has been endeavouring … to give systematic instruction in engineering subjects.[67]

What almost no one suggested by the 1880s was that the high school itself should extend its range to incorporate applied science or technical education. Lacking any mandate that would require it to provide secondary education for all; tied to the universities not only by its program of studies and the matriculation examinations but by the loyalties and presuppositions of teachers who were, in the main, their products; serving a clientele with no stake in technical education for its own sons and daughters; and having finally acquired enough students so that it was no longer forced to shape its programs to attract new pools of recruits, the high school was able to hitch its star to science as it was taught in the undergraduate arts curriculum – "as part of a general system of liberal studies." An acquaintance "with scientific facts," said Ross in 1886,

is undoubtedly of practical value, and the High School programme recognizes this; but the main reason for the introduction of the study of Science in our schools is the mental discipline to be obtained therefrom. The training of the reasoning powers and the acquisition of the scientific habit of mind are the objects with special reference to which the methods of instruction should be chosen, and these will also be the main objects of the examination papers.[68]

The concept of mental culture, then, was elastic enough to encompass some of the new subjects pushing their way forward in the second half of the century, but not others. English, history, science, and modern languages had, by the 1880s, established their claims to a place in the curriculum alongside classics and mathematics. These were useful subjects in the sense that they could be applied directly to a task or led on to certain careers. But they were useful in an even more important way – "useful in the sense of enticing study, and forming a sufficient foundation for future building."[69] Mere utility, however, was not enough. The acquisition of marketable skills, divorced from mental culture, was not education but training, and belonged elsewhere.

There was, of course, one great exception, which brings us back to the dual axis around which the high school curriculum was built. From the early 1860s the call to introduce commercial studies in the high schools was heard and heeded. Subjects such as bookkeeping, penmanship, and phonography found their way into the high schools; commercial programs were established in individual schools; and then in 1885 the ministry introduced both a formal program of studies and a Commercial Diploma.[70] No one, at least, tried to pretend that phonography was more liberating or culturally worthwhile than woodworking. But the rapid progress of commercial studies in the high schools of the 1880s and the entire absence of trades training is a reminder that the high school curriculum was not the product simply of disinterested educational theorizing.

There were, then, close limits placed by contemporaries on the meaning of a practical or useful secondary education. It did not extend much beyond that handful of old and new subjects which claimed to provide mental culture, and which were, at the same time, free of the taint of the workshop. But it is no less true that the ideal of mental culture was circumscribed as well. Students attended high school to obtain qualifications for jobs and took those subjects required by the university and teachers' examinations. Teachers, already overburdened by the plethora of examination subjects they had to teach, neglected those subjects not required for one or another examination. During the 1880s, for example, music virtually disappeared from the schools – by 1888 it was taught in only 22 of 115 high schools – because it was not an examination subject.[71] Even science suffered. Though the newly defined disciplines of physics, chemistry, and botany were recognized by some as a legitimate part of knowledge with a just claim to a place on the high school curriculum, others disputed their importance, and these subjects fought an uphill battle to be taken seriously in the 1870s. Their neglect was due, in part at least, to the lack of proper equipment for doing experiments, the lack of teachers competent to teach science, and the lack of good text-books.[72] As early as 1874 Whitby high school had "a room furnished and fitted up for the teaching of physical science" – but it was considered an exception.[73] More commonly, schools lacked proper laboratories and eager young science masters had to make their own apparatus.[74] However, the single most important reason for the neglect of science was that until the mid-1880s it was not a matriculation requirement at the University of Toronto. As a consequence there were near-annual complaints from high school teachers about the indifference to science of all but those pupils preparing for the teachers' examinations, where it was a prerequisite.[75] Once it became a matriculation subject, on the other hand, there was a rapid rise in the standard and prevalence of science teaching and a substantial increase in school board investment in science equipment.[76] In sum, subjects were important if they were examinable, and if they were not, they were not taught.

As the new system of core plus options established itself, and as the departmental and matriculation examinations were put in place to mark off the exit points, the program of studies began to congeal into what generations of students would recognize as the curriculum of the Ontario academic high school. It had no room for trades training but did offer commercial skills. Latin remained important but was one subject amongst other important subjects. The cornerstone of the program of studies was English, subdivided into reading, orthography, grammar, composition, and literature. Everyone took English, as well as the other core subjects of history, geography, arithmetic, and algebra. Beyond that, subjects were taken to prepare for this or that examination. In the first form, for example, 79 per cent of students were enrolled in bookkeeping because it was required for the third-class non-professional teacher's certificate.[77]

The emerging academic curriculum was imposed, as we have already suggested, on boys and girls alike. In the later 1870s there is no record indicating which subjects girls actually took, but the curricular revisions of 1876 left them very little choice in any case. The vast majority of high school students were enrolled in the first two forms, and the compulsory course of studies in the lower school included English, mathematics (arithmetic, algebra, and geometry), history and geography, writing, drawing, and music. The only choice available to students of either sex was in the optional subjects – Latin, French, German, and, as a fourth option, natural philosophy, chemistry, and bookkeeping. Since this latter option was required for a teaching certificate, most students, girls and boys alike, would have taken virtually the same list of subjects.[78]

In the early 1880s there was some unease about the drift towards a common curriculum, and a modest amount of back-pedalling. In 1880 and 1881 complaints were voiced in the legislature and the educational press about girls being forced to take algebra and geometry. On the one hand, it was said, they were not good at it: "it seems the uniform opinion of headmasters," the editor of the *Canada School Journal* wrote, "that it is impossible to bring to the passing point in mathematics many girls who stand high in all other departments of their work."[79] On the other hand, these two subjects in particular, according to the minister, had "little value or application to the duties of their sex," and thus girls "might be correspondingly relieved from" studying them.[80] The result was that in 1882, algebra and Euclid (though not arithmetic) were removed from the compulsory list, and a special option for girls was introduced consisting of "French or German with, when selected by the parent, Music or Drawing." At the same time the requirements for the non-professional examinations were changed so that "any female candidate ... may substitute for Algebra, one of the subjects of French, German, Music, Botany, as she may desire." Room was also made in the list of subjects that might be taught in the high school for "Household Arts – as sewing, cooking, and Housekeeping."[81] For reasons that remain unclear, however, this latter category of subjects was swept away in 1885 along with any reference to a special female option, a situation that prevailed for the rest of the century.[82] There may well have been differences in the enrolment patterns for girls and boys in different subjects from 1882 onwards. For example, the modern tendency for most girls to take humanities and many boys to prefer mathematics and sciences may well have embedded itself in the high school curriculum in the eighties and nineties. And "household arts" would reappear in the twentieth century. But the traditional accomplishments curriculum gave its last gasp in 1882 and disappeared from the high school after that. So indeed did the notion that there were fundamental differences in the education that boys and girls should receive. In the reshaping of the curriculum that had taken place between 1871 and the mid-eighties, the boundaries between girls' and boys' subjects had become more fluid, the internal content of subjects more standardized by examination requirements, and the experience of the sexes more assimilated to each other due to the common compulsory core and to the certification requirements first in teaching, and then in other vocations.

The impact on girls of a common curriculum taken in coeducational schools remains very hard to assess. As one student of the subject notes, there is a remarkable dearth of information on the subject either in official sources or in memoirs by women themselves.[83] But it is important, we suggest, not to trivialize the magnitude of the change by focusing only on the rise of separate classes in physical education or the introduction of a Friday afternoon of home economics. In 1850, girls were educated in separate facilities and taught a distinct curriculum, which, whatever its virtues, led on to a sharply separate sphere. By the 1880s girls were taught in the same rooms as boys, took mostly the same courses, and were eligible to write most of the same qualifying examinations. The high school was one of the institutions where women in the late nineteenth century found opportunities available that had never existed before. The sexual division of labour was increasingly linked to occupations, not sex *per se*, and thus it was not girls *qua* girls who took this or that particular subject, but future teachers or nurses or university matriculants. If most of these divisions corresponded in a rough way to sexual divisions, the barriers to crossing them were far more permeable for individual girls than distinctions based exclusively on sex, and as society itself changed, they held the potential to become more permeable still.

But there were also constraints, and these represented, to borrow a phrase of Marjorie Cohen's, "the modernization of inequality."[84] The assimilation of the school experience between the sexes was carried out, at best, on unequal terms. As we have just seen, even as girls established a firm foothold in the high schools, it began to be bruited that they couldn't do mathematics, and the same would soon be said of their ability to do science. New curricular dichotomies, in other words, began to take the place of old ones, and these would limit women's access to some of the most expansive sectors of the new economy. Or consider two issues raised for English schools by Carol Dyhouse – role models and school governance.[85] In the Ontario secondary schools, the teachers were overwhelmingly male, as were the local trustees, the principal, and the educational policymakers in the ministry. Thus girls entered a male preserve and then studied a curriculum which was the traditional prerogative of boys. If access to this curriculum opened new opportunities, moreover, integrated schools also created a single hierarchy of prestige. Boys (or at least some boys) stayed in school longer, more commonly took prestigious subjects like classics, and went on more frequently to university and the professions. Girls congregated at the bottom of the hierarchy, at least until they had pushed their way up into the senior forms in the last decade of the century. Beyond that, they most commonly qualified for women's occupations. For girls, access to the new secondary schools was, at best, a mixed blessing. The separate spheres of an earlier era had disappeared, to be replaced by forms of subordination that would last far into the future.

One loss rarely mourned by the historians of women's education was the accomplishments curriculum, but perhaps it should be, at least by those concerned with the quality of the academic curriculum that replaced it. In the coeducational high school French ceased to be an "ornamental subject," a language one learned in order to converse in it, and became primarily a written language that could be crammed for an external examination. Drawing remained a school subject, but especially from the mid-1880s became more and more oriented towards industrial design.[86] Music, when it was taught at all, was group vocal music. Except for the brief period 1882–85, domestic subjects had no place in the curriculum at all. Once girls entered the coeducational high schools, then, mental culture meant for them what it meant for boys, an education which earned them vocational qualifications but which was narrowly academic and shorn of some of the real virtues of the accomplishments curriculum. Girls entered the grammar and high schools, but the peculiar sensibilities of the accomplishments curriculum did not make the transition with them and thus failed to inform the high school curriculum in its formative years. The reasons for this are not surprising, but it may, nonetheless, be one of the great missed opportunities in the history of public education.

The contrast between the high schools and the private schools for girls is instructive on this point. The number of well-financed boarding and day schools for girls had multiplied from just one or two in the 1860s to seven or eight in the mid-1880s.[87] Often richly endowed by private benefactors or subsidized by various denominations, and charging substantial tuition fees, they could, of course, afford luxuries that the public high school could not. Their educational programs, nevertheless, almost uniformly included a rich mix of both academic subjects, leading up to the university matriculation examinations, and the accomplishments as well. They gave, as one of their advocates put it, "a liberal education, embracing a knowledge of Music and the Fine Arts."[88] Few of their students, said another, took only academic subjects. "More than 90% carry side by side with the prescribed course a very liberal course in Music and Art. Many of them are also well advanced in Art studies, Drawing, Water Colours and Oil Painting."[89]

The authorities responsible for public education, it must be emphasized, never denigrated such subjects. Indeed the reverse is true. Throughout the 1870s and 1880s, schools were exhorted to offer music and art regardless of their status as examination subjects.[90] The attitude amongst some trustees and teachers that such subjects were frills, however, along with the additional costs, and the pressures against wasting time on subjects that did not count on examinations, left music, art, and other accomplishments in a shadowy curricular limbo as peripheral parts of the program of studies.

The emerging curriculum of the academic high school, in sum, circumscribed the meaning of both a liberal and a useful education. For either boys or girls, the practical skills of everyday life and the whole realm of aesthetics were ill provided for at the best, and while language and mathematical skills were highly prized, the content of such subjects tended to be shaped by the imperatives of preparing for external qualifying examinations. Writing about the curriculum of a particular high school in Australia in the same period, Gwyneth Dow makes a perceptive comment that applies just as well to the coeducational academic high school in Ontario. "In the preoccupation with scholastic excellence," she writes,

it was not just the narrow domestic curriculum that was discredited; practical activities as a whole were devalued and the highly esteemed purely academic curriculum was too often divorced from fruitful relationship with the world of practical realities, whereas each should have enriched the other. Few seemed to notice that academic studies were not only often arid but were also illiberal in that they were the vocational route to the professions: they became the apogee of utilitarianism.[91]

CHAPTER FOURTEEN

The High School in the 1880s: Changes and Continuities

Without school registers like those available for the years around 1861, we know less than we would like about the students who attended the high schools of the 1870s and 1880s. Without the written reports of the high school inspectors, we know less about the quality of the teachers or the physical layout and internal organization of the schools.[1] There is, nonetheless, a large amount of scattered information on each of these subjects that can help us compare the character of the high schools in the two decades after 1871 to the unreformed grammar schools of the fifties and early sixties.

By the 1880s, the high schools and collegiate institutes were becoming a distinct, identifiable, and sometimes impressive part of the urban landscape in city, town, and village alike. Many of them were housed in sizeable new buildings or in remodelled and improved ones, often enough on choice sites on heights of land, or in the midst of spacious grounds; they formed part of the new and imposing municipal townscape of central school, courthouse, hospital, and churches.[2] As Robert Anderson remarks of a similar surge in rebuilding the Scottish secondary schools in the nineteenth century, this refashioning of their physical presence "helped to impose the idea of the secondary school as an institution and to bring its rather blurred image into focus."[3] Similarly in Ontario, the "handsome and capacious" buildings of brick or stone edged with ornamental trimmings, the assembly rooms and "lofty" halls, "spacious" entrance steps and "grand old elms" created the image befitting an important civic institution.[4]

Lists of improvements and additions to the physical plant of the high schools appeared almost annually in the reports of the ministry through the 1870s and 1880s, while contemporaries described with pride the new buildings being erected at substantial cost.[5] One such description, of Thorold Secondary School in 1876, is typical:

The building is made of brick, the windows and doors, edgings and watertable are made of white brick, and the building itself, which is two storeys in height, is surmounted by a high roof ... the west porch having a projection for a tower and belfry; the lower storey contains a hall, library, recitation room and two classrooms; ... the second storey is divided into a hall, recitation room, and one classroom extending the whole length of the building ... The whole building is admirably lighted, the windows are frosted and can be easily raised or lowered, the ceilings are lofty ... The grounds surrounding the building ... [are] adorned with a large number of fine wide spreading elms of many years' growth. Below the terraces a fine lawn intervenes.[6]

Similar improvements were being made elsewhere. In Brantford two years later, for example, the new collegiate institute included six large classrooms, a principal's room, library, laboratory and science gallery, teachers' room and separate stairway, boys' and girls' cloak-rooms, and central examination hall in a substantial two-storey building.[7]

Not all secondary schools were caught up in the wave of rebuilding, of course, and not all local boards wanted to expend large capital sums. An inspector's complaint in 1880 about Harriston high school echoes some of the early grammar school reports, including the fact that "the two privies are quite unsuitable, being perfectly exposed to public gaze."[8] Nor was inadequate accommodation confined to smaller communities or to those in country places. The high school in Ottawa occupied an "unsightly tenement house" in the early 1870s until a reluctant city council was forced into making funds available for a better building.[9]

Sometimes local taxpayers had already made substantial contributions in the 1860s to new physical facilities that twenty years later were deteriorating or obsolete. This was the case in Peterborough, for example, where a union school, built in 1860, had at that time been described as a "commodious brick and stone structure after the Italian style, the finest school in Canada." Twenty years later, however, the high school classroom was condemned as "a badly constructed and badly ventilated basement room."[10] And Belleville earned a good report in 1874 for its "large assembly room where all the school gathers at the opening and closing of school," but in the mid-1880s was criticized for inadequate science rooms and apparatus, as well as deficient water closets, lighting, and playgrounds. The board retorted that the vacant lots next door provided "sufficient opportunity for exercise and sport."[11]

As late as the mid-eighties many high schools, like Belleville, lacked proper gymnasiums, playgrounds, and other basic amenities; as J.E. Hodgson noted in his report for 1885 on the schools in eastern Ontario, most "are fairly supplied with globes, maps, and charts, but are deficient in books of reference, apparatus for the practical teaching of natural science, and appliances for physical training."[12] The situation was not much better in the western half of the province, where, John Seath noted, only five schools had a gymnasium, and two of these were actually the school basements.[13]

Improvements in facilities would come slowly. [14] Nevertheless, looking back in 1893 over a decade as minister of education, George Ross boasted that "during the last 10 years alone, 45 High Schools of unsurpassed architectural beauty and convenience, and equipped with all modern appliances have been erected, 25 have had additions made to them and many old buildings [were] substantially repaired." [15]

As the high schools and collegiate institutes were rebuilt and expanded, the number of teachers increased as well, though not as fast as the increase in student enrolments. In 1877 the pupil/teacher ratio stood at 33, while a decade later it had climbed to over 40. Individual classes were therefore not much different in size from those of a previous generation. However, instead of an entire student body of 50 or so taking all their subjects from one teacher, as was common in 1861, the schools of 1886 had an average of nearly 150 pupils organized in several classes. There were still a few small schools with a handful of students; there were also some very large ones with two or three hundred or more. And there were many more teachers per school: the one-teacher school had disappeared by the mid-eighties, while high schools on the average had a staff of three, and collegiate institutes had seven. [16]

Building new schools and hiring more staff to teach a steadily growing number of pupils meant that the costs of education increased as well. In 1880 the average sum spent on buildings and sites came to nearly $650 per school, and 16 per cent of total expenditure went for capital investment. [17] But by far the largest proportion of high school expenditure went into teachers' salaries, and this amount was increasing as well. By the beginning of the 1880s, the amount spent to operate and maintain the average high school was nearly $4000 a year – 90 per cent more than a decade earlier. [18] And local people were shouldering more of the financial load than before. At mid-century, the legislative grant to the grammar schools provided a third to a half of their total income; by the mid-eighties, that share had dropped to one-fifth. The local taxpayers' share went up over the same period from under 20 per cent to over half of total income. [19] Rising taxes provoked protests and demands for an increase in legislative grants. [20] The ministry's response to these concerns was to recommend imposing or raising tuition fees. As George Ross argued, "the High School is the preparatory school ... devoted to qualifying young men and women for professions, by which they may become self-supporting. Would it be any hardship to require them to contribute a reasonable sum towards that education by which they are afterwards to make a livelihood?" [21]

Many boards, indeed, were doing exactly what Ross recommended. The legislative grant was tied to average attendance, but as its share of school income declined, the sheer numbers enrolled in a high school became a less important consideration in financing the school. With rising enrolments, moreover, and a secure clientele who needed the services of the high school, boards no longer had to worry that levying tuition fees would put the school at risk. Thus, beginning in the middle 1880s, the trend of the 1870s towards free high schools was gradually reversed, and by 1890 the majority of high schools charged tuition fees.[22] The percentage of total income raised in this way, however, increased little during the decade.[23] The bulk of financial support still rested with local taxpayers.

DURING THE THREE DECADES after 1861, the character of the teaching force changed in a number of ways. One significant shift was that teachers became more sharply delineated as public servants who worked in distinctively public institutions. Schools were no longer operated as part of a teacher's domestic arrangements or, indeed, as the private preserves of pedagogical entrepreneurs. Some headmasters appear to have taken a few boarders well into the 1870s, though if the number of advertisements is any indication the custom was declining. Pupils' fees went directly to the board, not to the teacher, whose income was now entirely dependent on a stated salary. Each school had its own board of local trustees who by law, if not always by inclination, were responsible for establishing policies and procedures. Though it was not impossible, it was far more difficult for disaffected teachers to resign, start a school of their own, and carry off the high school's pupils with them. Altogether, the teacher, even the influential headmaster of a leading collegiate institute, had become much more of a public employee than was the case at mid-century.

Another significant shift was that a growing number of high school teachers were women. In the mid-century grammar schools, the headmasters and almost all of the assistants had been male. The evidence is sporadic until 1890 when the department began to publish nominal lists of high school teachers, but in 1880, Inspector Marling reported that 9 per cent of the teachers in the western half of the province were women.[24] In the five grammar schools we studied intensively, 11 per cent of the teaching staff in 1885 were women.[25] And for the entire province in 1890, 63 out of 452 teachers, or 14 per cent, were women.[26] Thus the number of female teachers in the high schools seems to have been slowly but steadily rising to more than a tenth of the teaching force by the beginning of the last decade of the century. As we might expect, the collegiate institutes remained more exclusively male: in 1890, the first year for which the department published such statistics, only 11 per cent of their teachers were female, compared to 16 per cent of the high school teachers. However, the proportion of male to female teachers varied widely. Jarvis Collegiate in Toronto claimed the highest percentage, with women forming 27 per cent of its staff, while other collegiate institutes had 20 per cent or less, and some had none.[27] Since female teachers were generally paid less than men, their numbers were almost certainly related to such factors as the income of a school, as well as to the relative status of men and women teachers. But it is clear that there was at least a small and growing group of women teachers, probably concentrated in the lower grades in the high schools and in such subjects as drawing or music.[28]

Compared to their colleagues in the elementary schools, or, indeed, to society at large, high school teachers were a highly educated group of men and women. In 1890 almost all headmasters and 64 per cent of all teachers held university degrees, and of those remaining, 65 per cent held a first-class elementary school teaching certificate, the lowest category of which required completion of form III of the high school course, a standard roughly equivalent to honours junior matriculation.[29] Thus all but a handful of teachers had completed four years of high school, and a majority had also completed a university degree. In either case this represented an uncommonly high level of education in the period. There were, however, quite dramatic differences between men and women teachers. Seventy per cent of male teachers held university degrees but only 30 per cent of the women did so: a majority of the latter held one or another category of first-class certificate. Two of the women, nonetheless, held MAS, and the university women were concentrated heavily in the collegiate institutes – 53 per cent of all women graduates taught in the thirty-one collegiates, leaving the rest thinly spread throughout the other eighty-nine high schools in Ontario.

There were also important differences in the qualifications held by collegiate teachers on the one hand and high school teachers on the other. Seventy-three per cent of the former held degrees: 77 per cent of the men and 45 per cent of the women. The high schools settled for a less educated staff. Only 58 per cent of all high school teachers held degrees – 64 per cent of males and 22 per cent of females. Most of the rest held first-class certificates, but a minority held only second-class certificates and were ill equipped to cope with high school level instruction. In 1885, an inspector could remark of an assistant teacher with a second-class certificate in Newcastle that she "has to teach pupils who are reading for the same grade of certificate as she holds."[30]

In many sections of the province, in fact, the high schools were training grounds and way stations for their staff, as they had always been, and thus there were high rates of mobility among teachers. But two distinct patterns of mobility existed. On the one hand, there were many teachers who viewed the job as a temporary stepping stone to another career.[31] On the other, there were individuals who, though they frequently changed schools, remained in teaching for many years and often worked their way up to positions of importance as headmasters of prestigious collegiate institutes. To refer yet again to the 1861 grammar schools that we examined, twenty-five years later they had people with a great deal of teaching experience on their respective staffs, but whose careers had involved a high degree of mobility. Brantford's headmaster had twenty-two years of teaching experience, but only three of them at that school. His six male assistants had between three and sixteen years' experience each, but an average of only four years at Brantford. In Sarnia, the headmaster had been at the school for fourteen years, but his teaching career stretched over thirty-two. One of his female assistants had been teaching for twenty years, the last eight of which had been spent there. The other female assistant, just appointed to Sarnia school, had seven years' experience. [32]

The inspectors' reports routinely identify teachers of individual schools and thus can also be used to trace patterns of career mobility. John Seath, for example, is first recorded at one school in Brampton and then at another in Dundas, [33] before going on to become headmaster at St Catharines collegiate institute and after that, a high school inspector and eventually deputy head of the Department of Education. Similarly if we look at the teaching records of the headmasters and first assistants for the whole province in 1885, the dual theme of experience and mobility among these career teachers is quite clear. For the 203 teachers whose records were listed in the inspectors' reports, the average number of years of teaching experience was eleven. But the average length of their current appointment was less than five years. And if we consider only the headmasters, the average length of their entire careers was fifteen years – about the same as for headmasters a decade earlier. [34] There was, then, a lot of career stability among high school teachers, but also a great deal of job mobility.

From the nominal lists of teachers in the 1890 *Annual Report* we are even able to see the differences in career patterns between teachers in collegiate institutes and high schools, and between male and female teachers. Overall, 10 per cent of the workforce had spent ten or more years at the same school; fully a quarter of all teachers had been appointed for five or more years. But although men with long service at one school were equally likely to work at either sort of school, women teachers' records showed quite a difference: though the women teachers at collegiate institutes tended to stay as long as the men, only 5 per cent of females teaching in high schools had stayed for as long as five years. [35] Women teachers thus had a much higher record of instability than men.

There were various causes for the high levels of mobility among both transient and career teachers. No doubt many women teachers left to be married. As in earlier decades, moreover, some teachers were incompetent, lazy, morally reprehensible, or unsuitable for a variety of other reasons, and they seldom stayed long at any one school. At Orangeville in the early 1870s, the high school inspector noted the "frequent changes of masters. There have been five headmasters during the past twelve months. One of them is reported to have caned not only the pupils, but the trustees; another absconded, a third drank himself out of his position in a week."[36] Other teachers, as had always been the case, left their positions and teaching too, to go to university or take other jobs.[37] These teachers formed part of a permanent floating pool of transient workers. But career teachers who stayed in the profession for twenty or thirty years also had reason to move from place to place. Ambitious local boards happily hired good teachers away from other positions. "Mr James McNevin's recent experience," remarked the *Canada School Journal*, "is an illustration of the fact that trustees throughout the Province are keeping watch for the men who are most successful in raising the standard of their schools." His school at Caledonia had a record of examination passes as good as Hamilton's, and "at least two School Boards decided to secure a portion of the Caledonia leaven." Thus McNevin had accepted a new job at Walkerton High School; after only one week there, he received another offer from Ottawa collegiate institute.[38] Good teachers like McNevin could write their own ticket; the offer of another position at a higher salary could be accepted, or parlayed into a raise at the current job.[39]

Throughout the entire period the conventional explanation for high levels of transiency was that salaries were too low. Certainly they were substantially higher than the average industrial wage in the period,[40] but inspectors and teachers did not make that the basis of comparison. Rather they matched themselves against other middle-class occupations and believed themselves to be the losers. In 1862 Inspector Checkley had commented that "while a well conducted young man can earn from $500 to $600 per annum as Clerk in a Store, or some similar way, it is clearly vain to expect him to undertake the labour and expense of qualifying himself specially for an office which is far more irksome and not better paid."[41] Just over a decade later, in 1875, the three high school inspectors voiced the same complaint. "University graduates of ability," they warned,

are deterred from entering a profession in which the rewards are so small. A High School Head Master may deem himself fortunate, if, after years of successful teaching, he rises to a position, the emoluments of which are equal to half of those of the manager of the branch bank, or of ordinarily prosperous lawyers and doctors in the same place.[42]

Whether or not high school teachers were actually paid less than the average middle-class worker, they certainly had the edge on their public school colleagues. In 1885, at our five southwestern Ontario high schools, the headmasters were all paid between $1200 and $1500 a year, and their male assistants' salaries ranged from $1100 down to $400, while the few women teachers received salaries of $600 or less. At Bowmanville, the teachers received "liberal salaries" ranging from $1400 to $800; but the inspector regretted the poor salaries paid at Ingersoll, where the headmaster's income was only $1000.[43] And yet by comparison, in 1880 male public school teachers earned an average of $743 in the cities, and much less than that on the average in towns and rural areas. Women teachers in the city public schools earned only $324 on the average, and a hundred dollars less elsewhere.[44] Compared to the $740 of the average high school teacher, the salaries of almost all public school teachers were lower.[45]

Salary differentials may also account for the level of "upward mobility" amongst elementary school teachers who sought jobs in the high schools. From the early 1890s, when the department first published records of teaching experience, it is clear that many high school teachers had started in the public schools. Indeed, the *Annual Report* for 1893 stated that "the better salaries in our High Schools constantly attract first class teachers from Public School work," estimating that one-quarter of the high school teaching force fell into this category. There may have been other more persuasive reasons for the move upwards, however. Teaching in a collegiate or high school carried, in the 1880s, as it had decades earlier, a degree of prestige and public recognition no public school could match. Even if a particular teacher held only a first-class teacher's certificate, one's colleagues were university graduates, products, in the main, of the more prosperous and influential families in the community, and themselves leaders in churches, voluntary organizations, and municipal affairs. Moreover, high school teachers educated a select group of pupils destined to become the leaders of the next generation. A high school teacher's job gave him or her something less tangible than money but no less valuable as social currency, and something that couldn't be bought for cash alone: social status. The reality of this fact is recorded even in the statistical columns of the Department of Education's annual reports: one table is labelled "Number of High School Teachers": "Gentlemen" and "Ladies," while another reads "Number of Public School Teachers": "Male" and "Female."[46] The social and academic distinctions embedded in such phraseology would characterize teaching in Ontario for decades to come.

And what of the quality of instruction offered by the teachers in Ontario's new collegiates and high schools? Without the inspectors' written reports we have no means of assessing it and we do not presume to do so. There were undoubtedly, as always, the competent, the knowledgeable, and the conscientious; those who were lazy and superficial; the good disciplinarians and the poor ones; and scattered amongst them, a few treasures who would decisively influence the lives of their pupils and quicken the social and intellectual life of a small town or village.[47] At least one such teacher deserves to be recorded here. When G. Edgcumbe took up a position in Elora he received this review in a private letter from a father to his daughters written in 1875.

He is about 20 ... in school he is at home and goes to work with vim and enthusiasm. He is an ardent lover of science, a student if not an admirer of Darwin ... He is a good musician, owns a Weber piano for which he paid $650, and plays with considerable skill ... He is a good chemist, too, and paid $50 a few weeks ago for a fortnight's instruction in practical experiments along with a German professor. He is a keen student of astronomy ... and has purchased a $120 telescope. He owns a good microscope which he knows how to make useful. He has an electric machine and is thoroughly up in the use of it. He has a geological collection intelligently made. He is deep in the mysteries of the spectroscope and would like to go into the study of spectrum analysis. He has already won the good opinions of his pupils ... The literary society is revived, and every pupil in the school has to take part in the work. A Greek class is about to be formed, and six or eight will join it ... He has Mill's style of teaching – by lectures, and treats his pupils as if they were rational human beings. A class in drawing will be formed I think, and music will be introduced. Mineralogy will be taught to those who care for it, and we are already deep in blow pipes, and glass blowing.[48]

DURING THE THIRTY YEARS after 1861, growing enrolments, larger staffs, new or expanded buildings, and changing attitudes all brought important changes in the internal organization of the high schools. In the first place there was a gradual decline in attempts to organize the schools so as to prevent the intermingling of the sexes. During the sixties and early seventies many school boards had done what they could to provide for the physical separation of girls and boys. Commonly, the grammar school department in union schools included boys only, taught by the grammar school headmaster, while advanced girls were hived off to the senior girls' department of the common school, usually taken by a woman teacher. However, the separation was seldom total; the girls went to the grammar school department for "partial instruction," usually in Latin or mathematics, and the boys might equally well go to the common school department for particular subjects taught by the common school teacher.[49]

There were other strategies adopted as well to preserve a modicum of separation. At Belleville, for instance, "the only provision for the *Girls* has been made by cutting off from one of the rooms a portion by means of a partition half the height of the room."[50] Prescott was praised for its "separate staircase for the sexes" in 1874.[51] Some schools provided, at a minimum, separate entrances, and some had separate playgrounds. But in small communities especially, the financial and physical impediments to separation were enormous and the inspectors' reports of the era suggest that, increasingly, the mingling of the sexes in classrooms and corridors was the normal pattern.[52] Toronto was the exception, so much so that Inspector Hodgson found it necessary to comment in 1885 on the fact that

there are in this Institute really two schools, one for boys and another for girls, the sexes being kept apart in all their studies. In the lower forms this arrangement is unobjectionable as there are enough pupils of each sex to make classes as large as a teacher can manage with advantage; but in the advanced forms I think that teaching power might be saved by combining the sexes. In the comparatively small classes reading for University honors, for instance, it seems to me that a waste of time is involved in teaching one lesson to a class of boys at one hour, and the same lesson to a class of girls, at another ... I think that it is worth the Board's while to consider whether they are wise, in totally condemning a system (coeducation) which prevails in every other High School and Collegiate Institute in the Province, and so far as I know, with no evil results.[53]

Thus boys and girls generally sat in the same classrooms and took the same classes in high schools throughout the province. The battle for coeducation at this level was largely over, though faint echoes of its fury could still be heard. We know very little about whether lingering preferences for sexual segregation affected the internal arrangements of those classrooms, although there is some tantalizing evidence to suggest they did; in Almonte, for example, the inspector disliked "the promiscuous sitting together of young men and women in crowded classes," which suggests that some teachers may have sought to segregate the girls and boys in different sections of the room.[54] Whatever the situation with classroom arrangements, in any case, the inspectors' reports largely cease to mention the issue of coeducation in the 1880s – presumably because there was nothing remarkable about it. In fact, there is some evidence to suggest that, whatever educators might have preferred, parents thought it was silly to separate boys and girls at all. In Listowel in 1892, for example, parents objected vociferously to Inspector Seath's recommendation and the principal's ruling that the boys had to use the rear door and go to and from school separately from the girls.[55]

The gradual decline of attempts to separate girls and boys was one significant change in the internal organization of the schools. Another was the shift in the way the program of studies was delivered. Despite all the complaints in the early 1870s about the overcrowded Ryersonian program of studies, the curriculum was still said to be overcrowded in the mid-eighties. Even small schools had no choice but to offer English, history, arithmetic, algebra, French, classics, bookkeeping, drawing, music, and science, divided into three subdisciplines. The optionalization of the curriculum caused difficulties as well. As J.A. McLellan argued in 1883, in some cases the many-option system is a source of worry and perplexity to masters – causing an unnecessary increase in the number of classes, and not seldom calling for an unpleasant exertion, not of "authority" but "influence" to prevent young scholars, and their parents, from making an unwise choice of studies; in other cases where this judicious firmness on the part of masters is wanting, it works a positive injury to the schools.[56]

When "influence" was lacking, the results were predictable, as John Seath complained in 1885:

Before last July I inspected some three and even two-masters schools in which every subject on the programme was attempted ... The explanation given by the masters is that they have been driven to this course by the importunities of the candidates for the different examinations. One candidate, for instance, discovers that French exactly suits his mental capacity; another has fully made up his mind that German would be an agreeable and profitable study; while a third insists that the Science Course was designed by Providence and the Education Department for his particular case.[57]

The perennial problem of "too many classes" marked the school of the 1880s, then, as much as it had the grammar school of twenty years before. But in another way there was a profound transformation in its organization. Schoolwork and therefore "classes" in the sixties were structured around particular textbooks; individuals studied the "six books" of Euclid or the readings in Horace or Virgil required by the program of studies and by particular examinations, and an individual might form a "class" of one.[58] In the seventies the language of the inspectors still revealed their tendency to think in terms of "the three algebraists" or "the one geometrician" in a school organized by individual text and student.[59] Yet the two decades after 1870 also witnessed the slow dissolution of this older style of school organization into a newer structure based on specialized subject departments.

A large number of classes was dictated by a large number of texts; as departmental examinations were streamlined and matriculation examinations assimilated to them, the differences in examination requirements shrank and in turn enabled teachers to concentrate their efforts on fewer texts. But more important, larger schools with more pupils and staff to teach them were necessary before teachers could become specialists in one or two subjects, and teach only these to all students in the school. In the one-teacher grammar school, not only had that teacher been obliged to instruct every student in every subject, but to do so he had had to rely heavily on individualized seat-work from textbooks. Not until schools and staffs grew larger, in other words, were both class instruction and specialization by subject possible.

It took some time, however, to establish new organizational forms. Of an otherwise outstanding school, one inspector wrote in 1873 that "the organization of this school is defective. The masters do not divide the work either by subjects or by forms. In fact the pupils are not divided into forms. Many of the classes are excessively large. One class in geography numbers over 100."[60] In effect, this large school was operating much like the one-teacher grammar schools of an earlier era, each teacher having his own group of pupils for all subjects and teaching them at all levels. And in two-teacher schools, older styles of organization persisted as well. In Simcoe in 1873, for example, headmaster Dion Sullivan taught all the classics, French, and higher mathematics, while junior subjects were left to his assistant.[61] But there were also transitional patterns. Hamilton Collegiate provided an example in 1878; there, the four classes of form I each had four separate teachers, while students in forms above that level received instruction from "Department Masters," who were specialist teachers in particular subjects. In a smaller school like Goderich, the female assistant taught the first form in all subjects, but also the classes in botany and form II French; the head-master took all the rest.[62]   Gradually, however, one begins to find, in the inspectors' reports and in related sources, a more familiar arrangement. As early as 1876, the prospectus for St Catharines Collegiate listed eight dif-ferent teachers, each specializing in one or two different subject areas such as science, classics, English and mathematics, and so on.[63] By 1879 the inspectors could report that "the practice of teaching 'by departments' and of engaging teachers of proved ability for special subjects, is extending."[64] An organization much like that of the twentieth-century high school, with its combination of "home-room" teachers and subject specialists, was al-ready in place in Peterborough collegiate institute in 1879. There were five forms, each with a "teacher in charge" for administrative purposes; but each of those teachers taught his or her specialty to all forms at all levels. Mr Jeffers, the principal, taught two classes in French to girls; he also taught intermediate and university French classes, university German, and one class in chemistry, apparently to both sexes. Mr Earl taught English grammar, composition, and literature; Mr. Dixon, Algebra, Euclid, arithmetic, statics, and hydrostatics.[65] The extent of specialization still depended on the number of teachers available and the number of pupils in a school. But in stark contrast to the situation in the years around 1861, the internal organization of most of the schools of the eighties would be immediately recognizable to any twentieth-century observer.

Finally, we turn to the students themselves. Though we have already considered changes in sex ratios and the social origin of students in the thirty years after 1861, there are other important matters that deserve con-sideration. One of these is the changing age structure of our student pop-ulation. Between the 1860s and the 1890s, the overall average age of high school students changed little, remaining at around fourteen years; but this tells us little, since the average age is skewed downwards by the dispro-portionately large number of pupils in the first form. The age of entry to high school is more informative. In the thirteen-year period from 1855 to 1867, the median age of entry in our five southwestern Ontario grammar schools was, on the average, twelve years for boys and fourteen for girls. In Anthony Ketchum's four schools between 1894 and 1910, it was fourteen years for both boys and girls.[66] Girls, in other words, tended to be older in the earlier period and their entry age remained the same throughout the nineteenth century. Thus the student body aged primarily as a result of an older male population. Since this shift appears to have been under way in the early 1870s, it is most likely explained by the growing effectiveness of the entrance examination from 1866 onwards, and the decline in the belief that, if they were to benefit from classics, boys had to start studying them at an early age. Equally important, however, the range of ages also narrowed down. Between 1855 and 1867, the ages of pupils entering the grammar schools ranged from six to twenty-six. By the 1870s virtually all of the pupils under twelve had been eliminated and though we have no evidence on this point about individual older students, the inspectors increasingly reported a range of average ages for the different forms that conforms to modern notions of the appropriate ages for a secondary school population – approximately twelve to fourteen in form I, to sixteen or eighteen in form IV.[67]

Between the 1860s and the 1890s, then, the high school population became more homogeneous in age, sharpening the image of the secondary school as a school attended by teenagers alone. There was also a significant decline in the rate at which pupils dropped out of school within the first few months, testimony perhaps to the more rigorous entrance examination that winnowed out the mere dabblers with no serious purpose in attending the high schools. At our five schools between 1855 and 1867, 19 per cent of all students remained at school for less than one year. In the 1870s at Whitby, about 15 per cent of students attended for less than a year – probably, as Ketchum notes, older students who were returning for a brief period in order to complete the necessary university or professional qualifications.[68] In the later 1870s, indeed, we find a great many references in the high school inspectors' reports to the fact that at various schools, many students held teachers' certificates and had already taught school themselves; it is most likely that they had returned to upgrade their qualifications or to try for entry to higher levels of study, and would have stayed only for as long as that required.[69] But by the 1890s, in two of Ketchum's schools, the number of students who attended for less than a year dropped to 5 per cent or less of the total, while in all four schools, attendance for less than a year characterized 10 per cent of the student body by the first decade of the twentieth century.[70]

In two significant ways, however, little changed between the 1860s and the 1890s. First, the average number of days attended remained at between

55 and 65 per cent of the total days in the school year.[71] But far more important, the average length of stay in the high school remained roughly the same as well. In our five towns, the average persistence rate for all students was 2.7 years.[72] Ketchum finds that the average persistence by the 1890s was around 2 to 2½ years.[73] The apparent decrease, we suggest, is not terribly significant given the differences in schools, geographical locations, and other factors besides. But what does deserve attention is the fact that so little change took place. More pupils were going to high school by the 1890s, fewer were dropping out in the first few months, but overall they were not staying in school longer than in the 1860s, and the length of stay was not much more than two years. Provincial averages, moreover, confirm these findings. In 1888, when the first statistics on enrolment by form were published, only a tiny minority of students were in forms III and IV – about 5 per cent. Another 18 per cent were enrolled in form II. The vast majority, about 77 per cent, were in form I.[74]

Historians have sometimes suggested that the growth of high school enrolments during the late nineteenth century is a good deal less impressive than it looks at first sight because nearly all pupils were studying in the two junior forms, doing work hardly more advanced than that of the elementary school. But this is to misunderstand the function of the various forms and indeed of the high school itself. Enrolments were low in the two highest forms because for most pupils they served no useful purpose. According to the regulations of 1885, which remained in force until 1891, the fourth form prepared for senior matriculation, an examination that, as we have already suggested, was a "second best" alternative to the freshman year at the universities and that attracted only a few special categories of students. All of the teaching, professional, and junior matriculation examinations were set much lower than the requirements of fourth form work. Honours junior matriculation, a set of University of Toronto examinations written for scholarship purposes, along with the highest non-professional teachers' examinations, were taken at the end of the third form. But pass matriculation, which led directly into freshman year, was set at the end of form II. So indeed were the professional matriculation examinations and the second-class non-professional teachers' examinations. The newly created diploma for the high school commercial course demanded second-form work as well. Thus virtually all of the important matriculation and certification examinations were set no higher than the end of form II.[75] It should not surprise us, then, that in the late 1880s only 5 per cent of all high school enrolments were to be found in the two highest forms: there was little reason for any student to stay in school so long.

While only 18 per cent of all students were enrolled in form II, the significance of that figure may be gauged if one recalls that of all students who began high school in 1951, only 21 per cent entered grade 13 four years later; and of those who began in 1965, only 36 per cent entered grade 13 in 1970.[76] The percentage enrolled at the minimum grade level which gave access to the universities in 1888 was smaller than it would be in 1955 or 1970, but it was not that much smaller. And if we add up enrolments in the three highest forms, then 23 per cent of high school pupils were studying in one or another of the forms that gave direct access to the undergraduate Arts program, to professional training, and to the first and second-class teachers' certificates.[77]

Form I consisted of not one but up to *two* years of work and thus the high school experience of a majority of pupils was longer than it appears at first sight.[78] Some pupils undoubtedly left before they completed form I in order to enter commercial or other occupations where no specific examinations or certificates were required. But others would stay for the full two years in order to qualify for a third-class teacher's certificate.

The fact remains, the reader may well reply, that 77 per cent left school before, or at, the end of the first form, which meant most pupils had only a very limited exposure to the high school. Our response here is to insist on the importance of context and perspective. First, one or two years of high school was, in the late nineteenth century, substantially more education than was received by the vast majority of children, most of whom left school no later than the third class of the public school. Merely to pass the entrance and attend high school for a year or two conferred a cachet marking off a handful of pupils from their peers. But more to the point, to assess enrolment levels from the perspective of the 1980s, when the high school has been transformed into an instrument of universal secondary education, is misguided presentism. The high school of the 1880s was not a temporary way station, or a transitional form, waiting to become something else. It was a long-term institutional configuration – one indeed that would last for most of a century. As late as the mid-1950s, 62 per cent of all high school enrolments were to be found in grades 9 and 10, a remarkably small change over seven or eight decades.[79] The explanation for this degree of continuity lies, we suggest, in the fact that by the late 1880s, the Ontario high school had acquired a set of purposes that would remain substantially unchanged for decades to come. Credentialling and other occupational requirements might change the strategic exit points and thus keep this or that group of pupils in school somewhat longer. And overall, enrolments would swell with population increase and the growth of white collar occupations. But the proportion of pupils in the various grades would change only modestly until the purpose of the high school itself was revised in the latter half of the twentieth century.

As the preceding paragraphs make clear, we know a good deal about such things as students' ages, persistence rates, or the subjects they studied and the formal organization of the school. We know almost nothing about the

growth of a cohesive sense of identity about being a high school student or
of the emergence of a distinct student subculture. And only occasionally do
we get an insight into the beginnings of the extracurriculum. As early as
the 1870s we begin to hear about student literary and debating societies,
and sports clubs and activities. Much of this socializing was organized by
the schools in a conscious effort to improve the students' cultural awareness,
educational opportunities, and moral fibre. The provision of "systematic"
physical training was a way to develop not only "more useful and graceful
bodies" but "better-tempered, cooler, and more honorable characters."[80]
While regretting that more high schools did not have the proper equipment
or facilities, the inspectors also noted that sports activities were becoming
more common: "the formation of school clubs for various athletic games
has become more general than formerly," wrote one, and another noted that
in Berlin high school "some of the masters take a great interest in football,
in which game the School club takes a frequent place."[81] Inspector Hodgson
remarked that in most of the high schools "some outdoor game, such as
cricket, lacrosse, and baseball in summer, and football in the spring and
fall, is regularly played"; he added, however, that these games were for
boys only, and the girls "take no part in them, and are not supplied with
any equivalent."[82]

Student literary societies were also increasingly common. Sometimes
enthusiastic masters like Edgcumbe at Elora school inspired them,[83] and
sometimes they were the creation of the students themselves. "Toward the
close of 1874," reported headmaster George Dickson of Hamilton collegiate
institute,

some of the more advanced pupils formed a Literary and Debating Society for the
purpose of improving themselves in public speaking, reading, essay writing, and
general literature. The society rapidly increased in numbers and usefulness and is
now established on a permanent basis ... Soon after the formation of the society,
the publication of a Quarterly Journal was commenced by its members. This paper
has already reached its second volume and its literary merit has been acknowledged
by its leading contemporaries throughout the Province.

The beginnings of such extracurricular activities formed "an essential branch
of education which could not well be acquired in any other way" and marked
yet another way in which the late nineteenth-century high school began to
create an identity of its own.[84]

And what happened to these students when they left school? Did they in
fact go on to university, teaching, and the professions in the numbers pre-
dicted by the examination passes? To answer this question we have only
their *intended* occupations, grouped into four categories and listed in the
Annual Reports from 1871 on, and for the four schools that Ketchum studied,

the same information but in its original detail from the registers.[85] In 1880, students from all provincial high schools who "became occupied with agriculture" made up 16 per cent of all school-leavers. Those who intended to enter the "learned professions" comprised a slightly larger group, and those entering mercantile life, slightly larger still, at some 20 per cent in 1880. The group entering "other occupations," which included teaching, made up 41 per cent of departing students. Naturally, these percentages varied from school to school: for example, from 30 to 40 per cent of students out of Brantford, Simcoe, and Strathroy went into farming; while the "learned professions" drew anywhere from 36 per cent, at Sarnia, to none from Stratford and Simcoe. "Other occupations" took anywhere from about 40 per cent at Brantford and Strathroy, and 16 per cent from Sarnia, to none at Stratford and Simcoe.[86] When the category of "teaching" is first added to the provincial statistics, in 1888, some 28 per cent of all departing students indicated their intention to enter that occupation, while those entering the learned professions dropped to 5.9 per cent, though that was the lowest figure reported between 1871 and the turn of the century.[87]

Working from school registers, Ketchum was able to account in more detail for students who went into various occupations as well as for those who died, moved outside Ontario, or otherwise were eliminated from the workforce. In the later seventies, he finds, half of Whitby's departing students joined the workforce or went on to further non-university education. Of these, 30 per cent entered commercial or clerical jobs; 22 per cent went on to other, non-university (presumably professional) education; 24 per cent entered teaching; and only 10 per cent entered farming.[88] A further 7 per cent of all students went on to university.

What we can conclude from these statistics is not only that students who left school for work entered a variety of jobs, but that primarily they went into occupations in middle-class sectors of the economy. Teaching occupied a large number of school-leavers, but professional careers of other sorts claimed a fair percentage as well. Even the "mercantile" category was probably composed of respectable occupations like merchant or clerk; and by the end of the century, John Seath asserted that almost all those who entered manufacturing establishments from the high schools did so as clerks or office workers.[89] Thus most of the careers we can follow or speculate on had one thing in common. They were all respectable occupations suited to the sons and daughters of the middle class from whom they had largely been drawn in the first place.

CHAPTER FIFTEEN

Conclusion

In his peroration as president of the Ontario Teachers' Association in 1869, Rev. Dr Nelles of Victoria College listed what he believed to be the critical issues facing his generation of educators, and he urged his audience not to rest until they had been resolved. There would be "time enough" for that, he said,

when the leading Educators in Europe and America have come to something like agreement as to what should be taught, how it would be taught, and when it should be taught; what place should be given to Physical Science, and what to Languages; what to ancient Languages and what to Modern; how far the curriculum should be uniform, and how far varied, or special, or optional; what should be done with the girls, whether they should be taught like the boys, or otherwise, whether with the Boys or away from them.[1]

By the late 1880s, on these issues and on others besides, Ontario educators could take their rest. Both the structure of Upper Canadian education, and the assumptions that underpinned it, had been radically transformed. The traditional distinction between a liberal and an ordinary education, institutionalized in the parallel roles of the grammar and common schools, had become a relic of a bygone age. The vertical integration of the education system was now complete and its tripartite divisions clearly delineated, with the secondary and post-secondary sectors extending upwards from the elementary schools. At each boundary line, co-ordinated curricula and examinations ensured a smooth transition from one stage to the next, and at the same time rationed the available school places accordingly to quasi-meritocratic criteria. Latin and Greek had lost their pre-eminence and a number of new subjects had been recognized as co-agents of mental culture and discipline. The high school curriculum was organized around a pattern of core plus options, and the core no longer consisted of the classical languages but English studies. Girls were taught "like the boys" and "with the boys." The schools had gradually ceased to be subordinate to churches and families and were now the creatures of local and provincial governments. The grammar school, with its distinctive purpose and its all-male student body, had become a multi-purpose secondary school serving teenage boys and girls alike, while the common school had been reduced to an elementary school. Together, these various changes, accomplished between the 1840s and the 1880s, established the fundamental shape and character of Ontario's modern system of public education.

Traditionally in our historiography, the creation of the high school has been primarily identified with the school legislation of 1871, and treated almost exclusively as a Ryersonian legacy. We have tried to suggest that some revision of these views is necessary. Taken together, and seen in their proper context, the act and regulations of 1871 are, on the whole, backward-looking measures, Ryerson's last stab at maintaining the distinctions between a liberal and an ordinary education, and the segregation of boys and girls. While some of the key mechanisms survived, the central thrust of his policies was almost entirely abandoned within a few years of his retirement. The act of 1871, moreover, played a relatively limited role in the creation of the modern secondary school. The principle of the entrance examination had been put in place as early as 1855. The principle of local financial support for secondary education was introduced in 1865 and extended in 1877. The curricular principle of core plus options established itself in the wake of the failure of the program of studies contained in the regulations of 1871. There are other examples besides, but our point is that the act of 1871 should be seen as but one of a series of steps in the legislative history of the high school, and not as the definitive one. Nor was the legislation always a product of Ryerson's own work. Others contributed important measures at key points along the way. It was the politicians, for example, who changed Ryerson's "pupils" to boys and girls, and thus established the right of girls to attend the high schools.

The focus on Ryerson, moreover, has obscured the importance of the political struggle of the 1860s over the future of the grammar schools. The expansion of the grammar schools and the lack of central control until the mid-1860s left educational policy in the hands of local people, and they shaped the institutions to fit their resources and their purposes. Ryerson and Young brought all the force they could muster to change the schools, and they won on some points such as the exclusion of beginners through an effective entrance examination. But they failed entirely to uproot other established practices such as the attendance of girls or the teaching of modern subjects divorced from classics. Nor could they raise the entrance standard as high as they would have liked, or preserve advanced instruction in the common schools.

The reasons for their failure deserve reflection. Much recent educational history continues to be animated by the conviction that nineteenth-century school systems were primarily fashioned at the centre by a handful of influential policymakers and that the immediate clientele of the schools had relatively little to say in the matter. The conflicts over the grammar schools in the 1860s, however, hardly lend credibility to such an interpretation, and in our view at least, a more sophisticated formulation is necessary to explain the outcome of this as well as other critical turning-points in the development of the school system. Thus our own approach has been to focus on the interaction between centre and locality, and in particular to stress the role played in policymaking by many actors: Ryerson and his inspectors, provincial politicians inside and outside the cabinet, their municipal counterparts, elected and appointed school trustees, teachers and their organizations, and, above all, the immediate clientele of the schools.

The clientele of the grammar schools was relatively small in numbers but it consisted for the most part of parents who belonged to the respectable classes in a large number of small communities throughout Upper Canada. It included, and commanded the attention of, editors, clergymen, municipal and provincial politicians, and other influential voices. Thus their views did not go unnoticed in the legislature. To put it another way, politicians have constituencies and listen to them, however selectively. Whatever Ryerson and his aides might have preferred, Latin would be offered in every high school, girls would attend to finish their education, boys would be allowed to take the options their parents wanted. Schools, no matter how humble, would be widely dispersed, not concentrated in a few large towns. "Different social groups," writes R.W. Connell, have "radically different capacities to fashion educational arrangements that are favourable to them."[2] If ever there was a classic demonstration of the truth of this maxim it is the outcome of the struggle between the bureaucrats in Toronto and the trustees, parents, and teachers of the grammar schools in small-town Ontario. Ryerson's attempt to reform the grammar schools succeeded only where his policies were congruent, or at least did not conflict with, the interests and wishes of local people, and not otherwise.

This, we want to emphasize, is not to denigrate or belittle Ryerson's impact on Ontario education. While his own vision of the future failed to take hold, he remains, more than any other single individual, responsible for the outcome. If the central thrust of his "reform" policies was always rejected by those with a stake in the grammar schools, and abandoned by policymakers upon his retirement, many of the particular financial and organizational arrangements that underpinned Ontario's secondary schools were Ryerson's achievement, and a permanent legacy of his administration.

Whatever its precise origins, in any case, the school that emerged from the conflicts of the 1860s and 1870s was to become an important and enduring social institution. Unlike the American high school, already beginning to move towards mass secondary education, the Ontario high school would remain the preserve of a minority of adolescents for decades to come. Its importance, in other words, did not lie in the sheer numbers it educated. Rather it lay in its role as gatekeeper for the occupational and social order. In this respect the Ontario high school operated more like a British or European than an American secondary school.[3] Rather like the modern undergraduate arts program, the high school of the late nineteenth and early twentieth centuries controlled the key access points to nearly all the professions and prestigious white collar occupations. Students had to pass the entrance examination and enter a high school just to remain in the pool of potential recruits, and they had to acquire a junior matriculation or other high school certificate to be eligible for entry to professional training. But they did not need an undergraduate degree. The high school gave direct access to the study of law, medicine, dentistry, pharmacy, engineering, and elementary school teaching. It also trained for a wide variety of lower-level white collar jobs. For generations of students, it was a high school and not an undergraduate diploma that mattered in preparing for a vocation.

The high school screened pupils at the key entry and exit points, then, and trained pupils directly for middle-class work. But it did more than that. What Fritz Ringer says of European secondary and higher education is true of Ontario's schools as well. "Higher education," he writes,

can never be truly understood apart from its special relationship to tradition. Of course, secondary schools and universities do prepare and certify students for entry into various professions. But this training function is certainly not their only role; for systems of education also transmit a cultural heritage ... More specifically, institutions of higher education have often concentrated on the perpetuation of especially prized elements in the traditional culture ... More or less consciously they have also transmitted particular lifestyles and norms of conduct derived from the past.[4]

The curriculum debates of the sixties and seventies had thrown up a new configuration of subjects but the aim of the schools remained the development of mental culture and discipline through the study of subjects that had special educational efficacy. Students might now choose between Latin and science but they were still required to draw on a corpus of ideas that constituted the revised version of a liberal education. Shakespeare and Tennyson had to be read, theorems learned, Newton or Virgil dabbled with. For those who stayed long enough, the high school offered a first taste of the intellectual riches of western culture. And for the vast majority of students who would go on directly to professional training or to work, it gave the only general or liberal education they would ever receive. A.R.M. Lower was not one of the latter group, but he makes the point with customary wit in his autobiography. One of his classics teachers at turn-of-the century Barrie Collegiate, he recalls,

was a man named Robertson, who used to pile books on Greece and Rome outside the classroom door and tell us to take them home and look at them. That would have been almost enough in itself, in an Ontario country town, to mark a man as peculiar, but then he used to pass art books around the class, nudes and all. Nudes might have been all right for so "uncivilized" a place as fifth-century Athens, but not for twentieth-century Barrie; so at Christmas time, out went Robertson, never to return.[5]

There were limits to the richness and quality of the curriculum, as we have suggested. Social and educational constraints led to the neglect of the arts and applied skills. The "hegemonic curriculum" prized some subjects and ignored or denigrated others.[6] But this is simply to say what we said at the beginning. The content of the curriculum is never fashioned by educational theorizing alone but also reflects the knowledge esteemed by those groups and institutions that have the power to influence what gets taught in schools. Valued knowledge, however, is not prized simply for its directly utilitarian uses. If culture, however defined, were not an element in determining what teachers and parents make children take in high school, then we would not find 80 per cent of grade 12 students still taking Latin in the 1940s.[7]

The Ontario high school was an important social institution for yet another reason. It gradually obtained a quasi-monopoly on secondary education and the credentialling process that education involved. The high school never, of course, had any sort of legal monopoly, but it acquired advantages that made it difficult for the private sector to compete with it. Obviously the most important advantage was financial. Funded by legislative grants and local taxes, the high school was a local day school, free, or nearly free, and no private school could match that attraction. But the private sector also found it increasingly difficult to distinguish itself in such a way as to make it an appealing alternative to the public high school. At one point in the late 1870s the University of Toronto had begun to administer "local examinations" for women, and more especially for the private girls' schools.[8] Such a development could have laid the basis for a permanent system of certification and matriculation distinct from the state schools, or, at the very least, have allowed the private schools to negotiate with the universities about their own academic programs and thus preserve a degree of curricular independence. But the growth of a system of matriculation examinations and certificates sponsored and organized by the Department of Education, and accepted by all the universities and professional associations, eliminated this possibility. To the extent that upper-class boys and girls needed widely recognized school-leaving and matriculation certificates, the private schools became tied, willy-nilly, to the curricular prescriptions and examination standards set by the department – a bureaucracy whose loyalty was to the high school system and not the private schools. Thus the academic work of the private schools fell hostage to the informal control of the state school system. As early as 1882 private schools were applying, and receiving permission, to hold departmental examinations for their own pupils, and while such integration did not undermine the few existing private schools that existed, it made it harder for new schools to establish themselves.[9] By the early 1880s the public high schools had become the chief source of matriculants in Ontario's universities, and they would maintain that position for the forseeable future. "The shift from essentially private to public, state-supported educational facilities is no surprise," writes David Keane, "but it is assuredly no less important for being predictable."[10]

During the first half of the 1880s a new reform agenda for education was beginning to take shape. Talk of industrial education, kindergartens, new subjects, and new kinds of pedagogy was heard at Ontario Teachers' Association meetings, and the same ideas were being debated in the educational press. Over the next few decades, as reformers gained influential adherents and secure public platforms, much of the rhetoric would focus on the short-comings of the academic high schools, including their formalism and their irrelevance to a changing society. Historians have too often uncritically accepted these charges at face value, assessed the role of the high school according to the canons of educational progressivism, and condemned it for both its irrelevance and its resistance to change. To do so, however, is to miss the point. From the mid-nineteenth century onwards the high school was finely tuned to a particular constituency and to the needs of that constituency in a changing society. It stood at the gateway to some of the most rapidly expanding occupations in the twentieth-century economy, and offered adolescents the arithmetical, written, verbal, and technical skills they needed to enter these occupations. For parents who wanted a profession or other white collar work for their sons and daughters the academic high school was an indispensable and entirely relevant institution. It had always prepared pupils for work. The high school was, in effect, the vocational and pre-vocational school of the middle classes.[11]

It was precisely because of its relevance, then, that the academic high school proved so resistant to substantive change for so long.[12] Technical education made only the slowest of inroads during the first half of the twentieth century, and any student who passed through the system before the 1960s will testify to the fact that progressivism had not yet run rampant in Ontario's secondary schools. Indeed, in many respects the schools of the 1880s would not have seemed alien to the student of the 1950s. Though the entrance examination breathed its last gasp in the 1940s, and the two lowest grades were now crowded with pupils required to stay in school till they were sixteen, the high school remained even as late as the mid-1950s a highly selective institution where the majority of students never proceeded beyond grade 10 and only a small minority reached grade 13. The program of studies continued to consist of core plus options, though in many schools the list of options consisted of only a very limited number of traditional academic subjects. A whopping 77 per cent of students were enrolled in the general (or academic) course, some 14 per cent in the commercial course, and a mere 9 per cent in the technical course, which, in fact, many high schools still didn't even offer.[13] The departmental examinations crowned the work of the high schools, Latin was still taken by a large minority of senior pupils, and the "ladies" and "gentlemen" who taught in the high schools were not only far better educated but even belonged to a union separate from the great mass of their "male" and "female" colleagues in the elementary schools below. Finally, 50 per cent of grade 13 students came from the upper and middle classes, while 71 per cent of all "higher professionals" kept almost three-quarters of their children aged fourteen to twenty-four in school compared to 35 per cent of the unskilled.[14] Though these figures are not strictly comparable to our own analysis of social origins in 1861 or to Anthony Ketchum's for the turn of the century, they are enough to suggest the continuities.

Out of the transformation of the Upper Canadian grammar schools between 1840 and 1880, in sum, came the Ontario high school, a school that was broadly accessible, highly selective, engaged in offering both boys and girls a revised version of a liberal education, preparing students for the universities, professions, and white collar work, and promoting both social mobility and social reproduction. It was an institution that would endure largely unchanged for nearly a hundred years until the early 1960s when Ontarians embraced the notion of an extended secondary education for all young people. That decision changed the face of the high school fundamentally, and probably forever. As an ideal it is resonant with the generous vision pursued by Egerton Ryerson of a common school that not only taught all children the rudiments of learning but offered them richer intellectual fare as well, and in so doing functioned as "the English College of the People." Whether or not we have been any more successful than earlier generations in realizing that ideal, however, remains an open question.

General Tables

Table 1
Selected Occupations, Ontario, 1851–91: Rate of Increase by Decade

	1851	1861		1871		1881		1891	
	N	N	Rate	N	Rate	N	Rate	N	Rate
Accountants/									
Bookkeepers	56	492	779%	1225	149%	2441	99%	5304	117%
Chemists/Druggists/									
Pharmacists	108	355	228%	811	128%	1275	57%	1276	0%
Clergy	963	1716	83%	2211	29%	2876	30%	3283	14%
Clerks	3100	4262	37%	8290	95%	12474	50%	–[a]	
Common school									
teachers									
Male	2541	3031	19%	2641	13%	3362	27%	2621	22%
Female	847	1305	54%	2665	104%	3660	37%	5076	39%
Total	3388	4336	28%	5306	22%	6548	23%	7697	22%
Lawyers	302	632	109%	1152	82%	1394	21%	1886	35%
Physicians	382	886	132%	1565	77%	1778	14%	2266	27%
Ontario population	952004	1396091	46%	1620851	16%	1926922	19%	2114321	10%
Ontario work force	245120	339432	38%	463424	37%	630762	36%	750484	19%

Note   [a]No comparable figures for clerks are given in 1891.
Source   Census of Canada, 1851–91.

Table 2
Grammar Schools and Enrolments, 1838–90; Rate of Increase by Decade, 1850–90

	Schools		Pupils	
	N	Rate	N	Rate
1838	13		300+	
1845	25		700–1000	
1850	57	–	2070	–
1852	60		2643	
1854	64		4287	
1856	61		3386	
1858	75		4459	
1860	88	54%	4546	120%
1862	91		4982	
1864	95		5589	
1866	104		5179	
1868	101		5649	
1870	101	15%	7351	62%
1872	104		7968	
1874	108		7871	
1876	104		8514	
1878	104		10574	
1880	104	3%	12910	76%
1882	104		12473	
1884	106		12737	
1886	109		15344	
1888	115		17742	
1890	120	15%	19395	50%

Note   Figures for 1838 and 1845 are included for comparison; rate of increase is calculated from 1850.

Sources   DHE 4: 254; *JLAC*, 1844–45, appendix c.c.c.; *ARs*, 1850–90.

Table 3
Age Groups and School Enrolment:[a] Rate of Increase, 1851–81

	Ontario Total Population Ages 5–15		Ontario Total Population Ages 10–15		Ontario Grammar School Enrolment		Ontario Common School Enrolment	
	N	Rate	N	Rate	N	Rate	N	Rate
1851[b]	257999	–	119273	–	2643	–	144979	–
1861	348268	35%	169785	42%	4766	80%	310239	114%
1871	440694	27%	207762	22%	7490	57%	437508	41%
1881	478763	9%	233330	12%	13136	75%	476268	9%
1851–71		71%		74%		183%		202%
1851–81		86%		96%		397%		229%

Notes   [a]Enrolments in readers/classes in reading.
[b]1851 statistics used here to compare age groups (from census) and school enrolment; see note b, table 5.
Sources   Census of Canada, 1851–81; ARs, 1851–81.

Table 4
Enrolments in Selected Subjects, Grammar Schools, 1855–88

	1855		1861		1864		1869		1875		1880		1888	
	N	%	N	%	N	%	N	%	N	%	N	%	N	%
Latin	1039	28	2515	53	2825	51	5577	84	3864	46	5559	43	5962	34
Greek	235	6	703	15	726	13	858	13	875	10	1100	9	1126	6
English	3392	91	4618	97	5425	97	6491	98	8130[e]	97	12765[e]	99	17659[g]	99
													17693[h]	99
Arithmetic	3151	85	4555	96	5387	96	6442	98	8146	98	12825	99	17430[i]	98
Algebra	833	22	2194	46	2503	45	3061	46	7038	84	12667	98	17319	98
Bookkeeping	587	16	955	20	1248	22	1539[c]	23	3403[c]	41	4542[c]	35	12344[c]	70
Science	1453[a]	39	2751[b]	58	2911[b]	52	1681[d]	25	2134[d]	26	5736[f]	44	14094[j]	79

Notes   Percentage enrolled in each subject is out of total enrolment in the grammar schools in a given year. The years shown were specifically chosen to avoid temporary enrolment swings due to program changes.

[a] "physical science": includes natural philosophy, chemistry, natural history.

[b] "physical science": includes natural philosophy, chemistry, natural history, physiology, geology.

[c] "bookkeeping and commercial transactions"

[d] "physical science" or "natural philosophy"

[e] "English grammar and literature"

[f] "natural philosophy," "chemistry and agriculture," "natural history," "physiology" – total enrolment

[g] "English grammar"

[h] "composition and prose literature"

[i] "arithmetic and mensuration"

[j] "physics," "chemistry," "botany," "zoology" – total enrolment

Source   ARs, 1855–88.

Table 5
Common School Enrolments, 1852–91: Rate of Increase by Decade

Total Enrolments[a]

	Urban						Rural		Province	
	Cities		Towns		Villages		Counties			
	N	Rate	N	Rate	N	Rate	N	Rate	N	Rate
1852[b]	6162	–	10898[c]	–	2208	–	160319	–	179587	–
1861	19764	221%	21714	99%	11719	431%	276721	72%	329918	84%
1871	28392	44%	37672	73%	21367	82%	358895	30%	446326	35%
1881	46256	63%	50029	33%	–	–	386760[d]	8%	483045	8%
1891	61689	33%	61627	23%	–	–	332257[d]	–14%	455573	–6%

Advanced classes[e]

	Urban		Rural		Province	
	N	Rate	N	Rate	N	Rate
1852						
4th	2935	–	30525	–	33460	–
5th	2351	–	16210	–	18561	–
4th & 5th	5286	–	46735	–	52021	–
1861						
4th	8033	174%	49856	63%	57889	73%
5th	6982	197%	51108	215%	58090	213%
4th & 5th	15015	184%	100964	116%	115979	123%
1871						
4th	13474	68%	61389	23%	74863	29%
5th	9701	39%	51413	1%	61114	5%
4th & 5th	23175	54%	112802	12%	135977	17%
1852–71						
4th		359%		101%		124%
5th		313%		217%		229%
4th & 5th		338%		141%		161%
1881						
4th	14830	10%	58924	−4%	73754	−1%
5th	3463	−64%	9405	−82%	12868	−79%
4th & 5th	18293	−21%	68329	−39%	86622	−36%
1891						
4th	19809	34%	60700	3%	80509	9%
5th	3164	−9%	9764	4%	12928	0%
4th & 5th	22973	26%	70664	3%	93437	8%

Notes   [a]"Total number of pupils of all ages attending school," table A, Statistical Tables, *ARs*.

[b]The more reliable statistics for 1852 are used here as a complement to the 1851 statistics in table 3.

[c]Includes "town municipalities."

[d]Includes "incorporated villages."

[e]Readers/classes: 1871 and 1881 "5th class" include 6th class enrolments.

Source   *ARs*, 1852–91.

Table 6
Advanced Classes in Common Schools, 1852–91

	Enrolments					
	Urban[a]		Rural		Province	
Reader/class	N	% of Total[b]	N	% of Total	N	% of Total
1852[c]						
4th	2935	18	30525	22	33460	21
5th	2351	15	16210	11	18561	12
4th & 5th	5286	33	46735	33	52021	33
1861						
4th	8033	16	49856	19	57889	19
5th	6982	14	51108	20	58090	19
4th & 5th	15015	31	100964	39	115979	37
1871						
4th	13474	16	61389	17	74863	17
5th[d]	9071	11	51413	15	61114	14
4th & 5th[d]	23175	27	112802	32	135977	31
1881						
4th	14820	13	58924	16	73754	15
5th[d]	3463	3	9405	2	12868	3
4th & 5th[d]	18293	16	68329	18	86622	18
1891						
4th	19809	16	60700	18	80509	18
5th	3164	3	9764	3	12928	3
4th & 5th	22973	19	70664	21	93437	21

Notes   [a]"Urban" includes cities, towns, and villages from 1852 to 1871; in 1881 and 1891, "villages" are included with counties in the statistics and are classed as "rural" here.

[b]Percentage of total enrolment in all readers/classes in reading.

[c]See note b, table 5.

[d]Includes sixth class.

Source ARs, 1852–91,

Table 7

Female Students in the Grammar Schools, 1855–90

	5 Towns Total[a]		Inspectors' Estimates		Provincial Totals[b]	
	N	%	N	%	N	%
1855[c]	50	23	–	–	–	–
1861[c]	76	27	–	–	–	–
1866[c]	91	36	798[d]	37	–	–
1868	–	–	1161[d]	42	–	–
1870 (spring)	–	–	1668[d]	40	–	–
1870 (fall)	70[e]	35	1602[d]	43	–	–
1871 (spring)	120[f]	41	1933[d]	41	–	–
1872 (spring)	160[g]	50	2022[d]	45	–	–
1874 (spring, eastern Ontario)	–	–	677[h]	54	–	–
1874 (fall, western Ontario)	–	–	544[h]	50	–	–
1880	–	–	–	–	5880	46
1885	–	–	–	–	6991	49
1890	–	–	–	–	9709	50

Notes [a]Brantford, Stratford, Simcoe, Sarnia, for 1855; includes Strathroy for 1861 and 1866.

[b]From *ARs*.

[c]From school registers in AO, RG2, G1B.

[d]AO, RG2, G1A and G2A; excludes schools for which the inspectors gave no specific numbers for girls enrolled.

[e]AO, RG2, G1A; excludes Brantford.

[f]AO, RG2, G1A: five towns.

[g]AO, RG2, G2A.

[h]These figures are for a small number of schools only and therefore very incomplete, but are included here to indicate the general trend.

Appendices

Sources for the Study of the Private Sector

Though we have relied on a broad range of contemporary comment and opinion for our information about the private schools, we are particularly dependent on two sources. Both have serious flaws, but together they provide us with a range of helpful evidence for our arguments in the paper. One source is the Department of Education statistical series on the private schools, which extends only from 1852 to 1876 The other is a file of "school notices" (advertisements, announcements for the resumption of term, changes of address, etc.) which we have collected from all extant Upper Canadian newspapers between 1830 and 1850, and from selected papers from 1850 to 1870. This file has been supplemented by collecting entries from the city directories when and where these exist. The result has been the accumulation of a file of some 350 voluntary schools between 1830 and 1870. Since many local newspapers are missing or incomplete, and since not all schools advertised, this list is by no means complete. The file is nonetheless invaluable in providing information about fees, curricula, clientele, and a wide variety of other material.

COSTS OF SCHOOLING AT MID-CENTURY

Grant-aided schools such as Upper Canada College and local grammar schools also used newspapers for advertising. Thus it is possible to ascertain that mid-century tuition and boarding fees at aided and non-aided schools were comparable, though growing state subsidies in later years increasingly widened the gap in favour of the public sector.

INSTABILITY OF THE PRIVATE SECTOR

Where long runs of newspapers and directories exist for the mid-nineteenth century, the school notice file can also be used to establish the longevity or survival rates of the private schools by tracking the life-span of each school from first to last notice. Table A.1 indicates the extent of the instability of the private sector in four Upper Canadian communities.

Table A.1
The Longevity of Voluntary Schools, 1830–70

Schools lasting	Toronto		Ottawa		London		Perth		Total	
	N	%	N	%	N	%	N	%	N	%
1 year or less	42	32	14	50	17	57	5	63	78	40
2 years	10	40	4	64	4	70	1	75	19	49
3 years	13	50	2	71	2	77	0	75	17	58
4 years	14	61	2	79	1	80	0	75	17	67
5 years	8	67	0	79	0	80	1	88	9	71
More than 5 years	43	100	6	100	6	100	1	100	56	100
Total	130		28		30		8		196	

Note   For each town, the first column gives the numbers of schools and the second column gives the cumulative percentages.

Sources   Ten newspapers published in Toronto, 1830–70, including for the years after mid-century, the *Globe, Leader,* and *Christian Guardian; Ottawa Citizen,* 1846–70; *London Free Press,* 1849–70; *Bathurst Courier* [Perth], 1846–70. The directories have been used for additional information when newspaper advertisements cease but the directory confirms the continuing existence of a school.

SIZE OF THE PRIVATE SECTOR AT MID-CENTURY

Estimates of the number of private schools are not difficult to obtain. The school notice file alone tells us that for those communities where newspapers and directories have survived, the private sector constituted a "substantial" proportion of the total number of schools. Similarly, both the published and unpublished statistics produced by the Education Office indicate that the number of private schools in urban communities ranged from 40 to 70 per cent of all schools (including grammar, common, and private schools).

However, comparative enrolment figures are more important than the number of schools in estimating the relative size of the private sector. Here we are reduced to one source only – the Education Office statistics. The published statistics for grant-aided schools are reasonably reliable from 1850 onwards, but those relating to the private sector need to be used with extreme caution or not used at all. The provincial and urban aggregates underestimate the size of the private sector because, for a number of communities, no data were ever submitted to the Education Office. In a few important cases the Education Office clerks simply made up the figures themselves. Such is the case with Toronto: the local superintendent never submitted returns on the private sector, but entries were made in the published statistics which are egregious underestimates according to all other contemporary evidence, including comments by Ryerson himself. (For these reasons we have left Toronto out of the local statistics presented here.) Fortunately, the original local superintendents' reports

Table A.2
Proportional Decline of the Voluntary Sector, 1852–66: Cities and Selected Towns

| | Enrolments | | | | | | | |
| | 1852 | | 1855 | | 1861 | | 1866 | |
	N	%	N	%	N	%	N	%
Hamilton	819	37	819	21	250	6	300	6
Kingston	630	37	630	31	500	16	200	6
London	593	26	593	24	30	1	140	4
Ottawa	280	28	280	19	250	7	420	11
Average %		32		23		7		7
Belleville	103	8	110	11	120	7	180[a]	9
Brantford	100	11	80	7	280	12	130	6
Cobourg	228	33	165	28	150	15	150	14
Guelph	106	21	300	35	40	4	155	13
Paris	50	9	60	9	24[b]	4	20	3
St Thomas	50	18	50	12	45	10	0	0
Simcoe	60	17	84	21	50	8	20	4
Average %		15		17		9		8

Notes   [a]1863
    [b]1860
    Percentages of voluntary school enrolment are calculated from the totals for common, grammar, and voluntary schools.
Source   AO, RG2, F3B.

survive for a part of our period (AO, RG2, F3B) and this enables us to separate out and use enrolment figures only for those communities where local superintendents' estimates actually existed. Even then, caution is necessary. Local officials had no incentive to investigate the enrolments in the private sector, and no legal right to do so. Thus, in table A.2 our urban communities were selected not only because data existed in the manuscript returns of the local superintendents but also because newspapers and other sources suggest that their estimates are plausible. At best, the numbers in table A.2 should be treated as "ballpark" figures of informed guesstimates.

The first two columns of table A.2 present the percentage of enrolments in the private sector in 1852 and 1855. Because the local superintendents were new at their jobs in the early 1850s, their reports on the voluntary schools were sporadic. Thus for the cities we give a mean for voluntary enrolments calculated from the F3B reports from 1851 to 1855. The mean is then used to calculate voluntary enrolment as a percentage of the total enrolment in 1852. For comparative purposes we include the same statistics for 1855, when local reporting was probably more reliable.

Our estimates of mid-century private enrolments are about one-third in the cities and 20 per cent in the smaller communities. The difference in the size of the private sector in the cities and towns can be explained as follows. By 1852 all of the towns and cities in our list had grant-aided grammar schools, and these would have provided all of the select and superior educational facilities for boys that the smaller communities needed. The statistics in the *Annual Reports* do not give voluntary school enrolments by sex, but the first grammar school registers, which began in 1855, tell us that most of the pupils were boys. Thus we suspect that the village and town voluntary school enrolments already consisted primarily of girls. The same argument addresses the discrepancy between our calculation in table A.2 of an average private school enrolment of 15 per cent and our claim that 20 per cent is a reasonable estimate for all towns and villages. Our statistics begin only in 1852. But in the late 1840s and early 1850s many communities still did not have a grammar school, nor indeed did some of our selected communities only a few years before 1852. Wherever this was true, boys as well as girls would have been enrolled in private schools and consequently the percentage of enrolments would have been high. In other words, we think our own figures for 1852 in table A.2 underestimate the size of the mid-century private sector.

PROPORTIONAL DECLINE IN PRIVATE
SECTOR ENROLMENTS

Though published aggregate figures exist for the years 1852–76, they must be treated cautiously not only because of underreporting problems but also because category changes render them inconsistent over time. The best statistical information we have is contained in tables A.2 and A.3. Table A.2 presents selected urban areas where we can assure ourselves that the published figures were based on actual reports by local superintendents. Unfortunately, the figures for individual communities do not survive beyond 1866. Table A.3 includes published aggregates for all urban communities (such as Toronto) where data was not reported by the local superintendents and therefore is an underestimate of the voluntary school enrolments.

The quality of the Department of Education data is such that the tables should be read as indicating trends only and not precise arithmetical figures. We are encouraged to think these trends are accurate because our newspaper and directory files for the period 1850–70 tell a parallel story. The number of notices for schools increases over these years but far less rapidly than the number of grant-aided schools. A variety of contemporary comment also suggests similar developments.

After 1876 there are no private school statistics at all. In order to be sure that there is no sudden change in the frequency or number of school notices in the period after the main body of our research ends, we have sampled three newspapers by reading them between 1 August and 30 October, every five years from 1871 to 1896: the *Globe*, the *Ottawa Citizen*, and the *London Free Press*. From roughly the 1870s, school notices that had hitherto been scattered throughout the year began to be

Table A.3
Proportional Decline of the Voluntary Sector, 1852–73: Enrolments in All Urban Places
(Cities, Towns, Villages)

	Enrolments					
	1852		1861		1873	
Total common school	19268	(74%)	53197	(84%)	103611	(88%)
Senior grades of common school	5286		15015		21117	
Grammar school	2643	(10%)	4766	(8%)	8437	(7%)
Voluntary school	4239	(16%)	5429	(8%)	6238	(5%)
Totals	26150	(100%)	63392	(100%)	118286	(100%)

Percentage increase 1852–73

	1852–61	1852–73
Total common school	180	440
Senior grades of common school	180	300
Grammar school	80	220
Voluntary school	30	50

Note   Senior grade enrolments in the common schools in 1852 and 1861 include 4th and 5th readers
and in 1873, 4th, 5th, and 6th classes in reading.
Sources   ARs, 1852, 1861, 1873.

concentrated in the late summer/early fall period and thus we think this procedure is a tolerable method of cross-checking the impressionistic and other evidence we have used. In order to doublecheck our results we have taken counts of private schools from the Toronto directories, 1834–96, and for London from 1856 to 1897. Both exercises produced modest absolute increases but a continuing proportional decline.

Linkage Rates and Problems

There were 286 names recorded on the registers of our five grammar schools in 1861: 210 boys and 76 girls. Of these, we traced 228, or 80 per cent, to their families in the manuscript census. Our success in linking so many students was at least partly because the towns were small enough to make it feasible to trace each grammar school student, using the variables of name and sex, to his or her entry on the census.[1] The record linkage was carried out manually, and in order to make it as complete as possible, it was done twice: first, by collecting the census data on every family in the eligible "target population" (that is, those with children aged ten to twenty living with them) and then matching the grammar school students to the names of the children in these families; second, by searching through each page of the manuscript census for the names of the grammar school students. The second procedure was not as difficult as it sounds, given the small number of students and the use of alphabetical lists, and it was useful to complement the first procedure since it yielded a few additional links – students, for example, who were younger or older than our age limits for the target population. The linkage rules were conservative, with links accepted only when the name of the student on the register matched or was very closely akin to that on the census, when both sources agreed on the sex of the student, and when the student's age fell within reasonable limits. Where there were two equally good links to the census, neither was accepted. The fact that many grammar school students had siblings who were also recorded in the registers made the task of linkage much easier, as in many cases it was possible to confirm one link with a second one.

In this study we have examined only those students resident in the towns in which the grammar schools were located. The percentages of links made from the registers are lower than for the town students listed in the *Annual Report* for 1861, but this fact is at least partly explained by the difficulties of record linkage. No doubt we did not manage to identify every town student in 1861, as some would have moved away and others, despite careful checking, may have been missed. Even the register figures, however, show that nearly two-thirds of the students were town residents.

Table B.1
Linkage Rates for Grammar School Students, 1861: Grammar School Registers to
Manuscript Census

	Stratford	Brantford	Simcoe	Sarnia	Strathroy
Total names on register	47	82	93	40	24
Town students linked	29	58	56	26	14
Percentage linked of total	62%	67%	60%	65%	58%
Township students linked	5	7	13	3	4
Percentage of non-town students	28%	26%	35%	21%	40%
Unlinked	19%	21%	18%	25%	21%

One could legitimately ask why we have neglected to examine the other third of grammar school students: those coming from outside the town. There were at least two reasons for doing so. One major methodological reason is that searching for township pupils is like hunting for the proverbial needle in the haystack – retrieving, from hundreds of names on dozens of pages of the census manuscript for the surrounding townships, the names of a handful of students. In fact, we searched the census lists for contiguous townships and linked a further 10 to 20 per cent of the total cases, ranging from a high of 40 per cent (or four students) of the unlinked cases for Strathroy to about a fifth for Sarnia. The number of students coming from outside the town of Strathroy clearly formed a considerable proportion of the total student body and the effort of tracing these students was well rewarded; nevertheless, a number of unlinked cases remained for all five schools, and we judged a more extensive manual search to be fruitless. There would also have been a major problem created by including the township students in our examination of family backgrounds. We have no comparable group to contrast to their families, as we do in the town. Consequently we cannot distinguish the particular characteristics of the township families juxtaposed against a control group. For these reasons, and since most of the grammar school students were residents of the town, we decided to base our analysis on town students only.

Occupational
Classification

The construction of an occupational classification scheme, especially for the mid-nineteenth century, is an occupational hazard for historians. There is a large literature on the subject and many attempts have been made to fashion a categorization that will adequately capture the reality of a world of work very different from our own.[2] The classification system which we have used is a modification of that devised by Gordon Darroch and Michael Ornstein, which is an attempt to categorize occupations "on the basis of economic sector, skill level, and ownership of capital" and on "individual positions within the division of labour, and not ... income or wealth."[3] Their scheme had several features to recommend it for this study. As an attempt to avoid assumptions about status that are implicit in a ranked continuum of occupations, we felt it to be useful to employ a functional classification rather than one combining the factors of occupation, income, and status. The Darroch/Ornstein classification also includes several categories in which we were especially interested. "Professionals" and "white collar workers" in particular were groups we wished to isolate in our study of school users, as the literature on nineteenth-century superior education generally reports a high rate of participation among these groups.[4]

We have, however, modified the original version of this classification scheme somewhat in order to accommodate the needs of our particular study. An important change was to move "manufacturers" from the Darroch/Ornstein category of "merchants, manufacturers, agents and dealers" to our group of "artisans and manufacturers," justifying the modification on the basis of the time period with which we are dealing. In 1861 our five towns, including Brantford, the largest and most affected by new economic and industrial forces, were still involved mainly in commercial activities, and large-scale manufacturing had yet to be established. In Brantford, for example, the town economy was particularly hard hit by the depression of the late 1850s, and manufacturing on a large scale did not begin until a decade later.[5] For communities in this pre-industrial age, it made more sense to group manufacturers with artisans.

We also created two new categories – "female heads of households" and "gentlemen" – in response to the deficiencies of occupational descriptions on the census.

Table C.1
Darroch/Ornstein Occupational Scale: Household Heads, 1861

	Brantford	Stratford	Strathroy	Simcoe	Sarnia
Merchants, dealers, manufacturers	15%	19%	20%	18%	23%
Professionals, managers	7%	6%	8%	14%	13%
White collar workers	4%	5%	–	4%	5%
Artisans	40%	30%	35%	38%	32%
Semi- & unskilled workers	5%	3%	2%	3%	8%
Labourers	19%	22%	15%	10%	15%
Servants	.4%	–	–	–	–
Farmers	.3%	6%	17%	4%	1%
Outside labour force	10%	9%	3%	10%	2%

Table C.2
Modified Darroch/Ornstein Scale: Household Heads, 1861

	Brantford	Stratford	Strathroy	Simcoe	Sarnia
Merchants, dealers	13%	16%	17%	16%	19%
Professionals, government officials	6%	5%	5%	11%	11%
White collar workers	7%	6%	5%	7%	9%
Artisans, manufacturers	38%	31%	37%	37%	29%
Labourers, semi- & unskilled workers	21%	27%	17%	12%	24%
Female household heads	11%	8%	3%	12%	8%
Farmers	.3%	6%	15%	4%	1%
Gentlemen	3%	3%	2%	1%	–
Outside labour force	.5%	0%	0%	.5%	0%

Women who headed households (most of whom were widows) seldom listed any occupation on the census, and "gentlemen" are unclassifiable in any functional scheme. Thus the Darroch/Ornstein coding scheme places both groups in the category "outside the labour force." However, we needed to include both these categories because both were overrepresented among grammar school users.

The original Darroch/Ornstein classification of occupational distribution and the modified version are illustrated in tables c.1 and c.2 for the household heads of each town. The differences are not great in categories 1 to 4, which are the same in both schemes. From there on the categories are dissimilar and cannot be easily compared, although it is worth noting that in the Darroch/Ornstein classification, category 9, "outside the labour force," is a much larger group – no doubt partly because it includes the "gentlemen" and "female household heads" for whom we created separate categories.

Notes

AO   Archives of Ontario
     CI   AO, RG2, CI
     c6c   AO, RG2, c6c
     GIA   AO, RG2, GIA (manuscript reports on indi-
          vidual schools by the grammar school in-
          spectors)
     G2A   AO, RG2, G2A (manuscript reports on indi-
          vidual schools by the high school inspec-
          tors)

AR   *Annual Report of the Normal, Model, Grammar, and*
    Common Schools in Upper Canada [to 1875]
    Report of the Minister of Education (Ontario) [after
    1875]
     GSIR   General reports of the grammar school in-
          spectors printed in the *ARs*
     HSIR   General reports of the high school inspectors
          printed in the *ARs*

DHE   J.G. Hodgins, *Documentary History of Education in*
     Upper Canada, 28 vols. (Toronto, 1894–1910)
JEdUC   *Journal of Education for Upper Canada*
JLA   *Journals of the Legislative Assembly*
JLAC   *Journals of the Legislative Assembly of Canada*
JLC   *Journals of the Legislative Council*
MTRL   Metropolitan Toronto Reference Library
NA   National Archives of Canada

OTA   Proceedings of the Ontario Teachers' Association
Minutes   Annual Meetings. Various titles referred to:
Report of the Proceedings of the 8th Annual Meeting of the Ontario Teachers' Association, 1868
Constitution, By-Laws, and Rules of Order of the Ontario Teachers' Association; together with the Minutes of the 12th Annual Meeting, 1872
Minutes of the 16th Annual Convention of the Ontario Teachers' Association for the Advancement of Education, 1876
Minutes of the 18th [to 24th] Annual Convention of the Ontario Teachers' Association, 1878 [to 1884]
PRO   Public Record Office
QUA   Queen's University Archives
UCA   United Church Archives
UWORC   University of Western Ontario Regional Collection

CHAPTER ONE

1 *Globe*, 11 Sept. 1856. Similarly see *DHE* 3: 178.
2 AO, RG2, G4, envelope 3, *Rules and Regulations of the Union School, Paris, Canada West* (Paris 1859), 6.
3 See *JLAC*, vol. 5, appendix P (or *DHE* 6: 195–6. J.G. Hodgins italicizes the word but it is not italicized in the original.) Interestingly, Ryerson uses the word "Real School," a Prussian word, later in the text (cf. *DHE* 6: 197) but pairs it with grammar school and never uses the generic "secondary."
4 See *DHE* 7: 50–1. What Ryerson meant by "secondary" were schools such as the German gymnasia, the great English public schools, and the Scottish academies, which were not secondary in our sense but rather were both elementary and secondary.
5 *JEdUC* 6 (Oct. 1853): 146–7.
6 *DHE* 7: 220.
7 *JEdUC* 19 (Jan. 1866): 3.
8 AO, RG2, G4, *Report on the Public Schools of the City of Hamilton, 1861*, 4. For a similar usage see C1, Wm. Elliot (Chairman, Board of Grammar School Trustees), Matilda, 13 July 1855.
9 See for example c6c, A Kirkland (Chairman, Board of School Trustees, Brantford) to Ryerson, 24 Dec. 1851.
10 Compare *JEdUC* 6 (Apr. 1853): 64 (Brantford); c6c, Benjamin Charlton to Ryerson, Brantford, 12 May 1852.
11 *AR* for 1856, 206 [italics added]. For the level of study in the second division in Hamilton, see *DHE* 14: 64.
12 Quoted in Elizabeth Gibbs, ed., *Debates of the Legislative Assembly of*

United Canada, 11 (1852–3), part III, 1748 and 1750.

13 See for example AO, Merritt Papers, Thos. R. Merritt to his grandfather, St Catharines, 28 Oct. 1833; C6C, James Nisbit to Ryerson, 6 Feb. 1860; *DHE* 3: 271 [Report of Commission on Education, 1840].

14 *Ottawa Citizen*, 12 Feb. 1853.

15 See for example *Christian Guardian*, 11 May 1836 (advertisement for Upper Canada Academy).

16 AO, RG2, G4, *Report of the Public Schools in the City of Hamilton, 1861*, 4.

17 AO, RG2, C2, Ryerson to C.R. Brooke, 16 May 1864. But compare *JEdUC* 8 (Feb. 1855): 18, where Ryerson unequivocally describes the grammar school as an "intermediate" school. Similarly see *JEdUC* 18 (Dec. 1865): 179; *DHE* 8: 289–91.

18 See for example Robert Anderson, "Secondary Schools and Scottish Society in the Nineteenth Century," *Past and Present*, 109 (Nov. 1985): 179; Alan Barcan, *A History of Australian Education* (Melbourne: Oxford University Press 1980), 177. The *Oxford English Dictionary* gives credit to Matthew Arnold for providing the earliest usage it cites – in the 1860s. There are in fact earlier examples, but the OED citation does indicate how uncommon the term was in the first half of the nineteenth century.

19 See R.D. Anderson, *Education and Opportunity in Victorian Scotland* (Oxford: Clarendon Press 1983), 163–4; Gillian Sutherland, *Ability, Merit and Measurement* (Oxford: Clarendon Press 1984), 101; R.J.W. Selleck, "State Education and Culture," *Australian Journal of Education* 26, 1 (1982): 12.

20 For Europe see for example Mary Jo Maynes, *Schooling in Western Europe* (Albany: State University of New York Press 1985), 94; Patrick J. Harrigan, *Mobility, Elites and Education in French Society of the Second Empire* (Waterloo: Wilfrid Laurier University Press 1980), 7.

21 David Hogan, "From contest mobility to stratified credentialling: merit and graded schooling in Philadelphia, 1836–1920," *History of Education Review* 16, 2 (1987): 24.

22 Pavla Miller, *Long Division: State Schooling in South Australian Society* (Netley, S.A.: Wakefield Press 1986), 115.

23 John Roach, *A History of Secondary Education in England, 1800–1870* (London: Longman 1986), 9.

24 For two notable exceptions see Ian E. Davey, "Trends in Female School Attendance in Mid-Nineteenth Century Ontario," *Histoire Sociale* 8 (Nov. 1975): 238–54; J. Anthony C. Ketchum, "'The Most Perfect System': Official Policy in the First Century of Ontario's Government Secondary Schools and Its Impact on Students between 1871 and 1910" (Ph.D. diss., University of Toronto 1979). The latter includes an analysis of the surviving registers of Trinity College School.

25 Put another way, it includes the people Peter Russell labels "Respectable," "Marginal Respectable," and the best-off of those he puts in the "Independ-

ent" category. For a fine analysis of Upper Canada's social structure see Peter A. Russell, "Attitudes to Social Structure and Social Mobility in Upper Canada (1815–1840)" (Ph.D. diss., Carleton 1983), esp. 25–30.

26 For the "business class" see Michael B. Katz et al., *The Social Organization of Early Industrial Capitalism* (Cambridge, Mass.: Harvard University Press 1982), chap. 1.

27 For a brief biography see *Dictionary of Canadian Biography* XI. For major studies, see C.B. Sissons, *Egerton Ryerson: His Life and Letters*, 2 vols. (Toronto: Clarke, Irwin 1947), and Clara Thomas, *Ryerson of Upper Canada* (Toronto: Ryerson Press 1969).

CHAPTER TWO

1 See for example Richard S. Tompson, *Classics or Charity? The Dilemma of the Eighteenth-Century Grammar School* (Manchester: Manchester University Press 1971), 20.

2 *DHE* 3: 307–8.

3 Rev. J.H. Harris, *Observations on Upper Canada College* (Toronto, 1836), 16.

4 *Patriot*, 20 July 1845.

5 See for example, *The Church*, 26 July 1848; *British Colonist*, 11 Feb. 1845 and 15 Sept. 1846; *Kingston Herald*, 27 Apr. 1831 and 9 Sept. 1845; *St Catharines Journal*, 17 July 1845.

6 *Christian Guardian*, 11 May 1836.

7 *British Colonist*, 15 Sept. 1846; *Globe*, 30 Nov. 1852.

8 We borrow the phrase and the useful distinction from P.B. Walters, "Occupational and Labor Market Effects on Secondary and Postsecondary Educational Expansion in the United States, 1922 to 1979," *American Sociological Review* 49, 5 (Oct. 1984): esp. 665.

9 *British American Journal*, 27 May 1834. See also NA, RG5, BII, vol. 5, no. 429, Report, Board of Trustees, Ottawa District School, 23 July 1833.

10 CI, Ryerson to George Vardon, 20 May 1847.

11 See for example *Upper Canada Herald*, 27 Apr. 1831.

12 For two full descriptions of the ideal grammar school curriculum, see John Strachan, *A Letter ... On the Management of Grammar Schools* (Toronto 1829), esp. 5–7; and Harris, *Observations on Upper Canada College*, esp. 16–18.

13 Frank M. Turner, *The Greek Heritage in Victorian Britain* (New Haven: Yale University Press 1981), 6. See also Sheldon Rothblatt, *Tradition and Change in English Liberal Education* (London: Faber and Faber 1976), esp. chap. 5.

14 *Globe*, 12 Mar. 1850.

15 *Christian Guardian*, 6 July 1842.

16 *The Presbyterian* (October 1848), 61.

17 *Christian Guardian*, 6 June 1838.

18 *Kingston Chronicle*, 13 Mar. 1830. See also *Kingston Gazette*, 30 Oct.
1810; *JEdUC* 7 (Aug. 1854): 134–5.

19 *Burlington Ladies' Academy* [Prospectus] (Cobourg 1845), 8; similarly see
Circular of the Upper Canada Academy, 1841 (Cobourg 1841), 8–10.

20 For the most important and far-reaching of these reassessments see Marjorie
R. Theobald, "The Accomplished Woman and the Propriety of Intellect: A
New Look at Women's Education in Britain and Australia, 1800–1850,"
History of Education 17, 1 (1988): 21–35. See also Theobald's "'Mere Ac-
complishments'? Melbourne's Early Girls' Schools Reconsidered," *History
of Education Review* 13, 2 (1984): 15–28.

21 For a Canadian introduction see Alison Prentice et al., *Canadian Women: A
History* (Toronto: Harcourt, Brace, Jovanovich 1988), chap. 6.

22 Mrs Holiwell's Address is reprinted in Alison Prentice and Susan Houston,
eds., *Family, School and Society in Nineteenth Century Canada* (Toronto:
Oxford University Press 1975), 244–55. For the passage we have quoted,
see 249–50.

23 Theobald, "The Accomplished Woman," 26.

24 Cf. the argument put forward for the Georgian gentleman by Sheldon
Rothblatt in *Tradition and Change*, chaps. 2–7.

25 For the sequence of correspondence in these paragraphs, see MTRL, R.B.
Baldwin Papers, A86, Maria to Robert Baldwin, Toronto, 18 Apr. 1843;
A86–7, W.W. to Robert Baldwin, Toronto, 21 Apr. 1843; A86, Robert to
W.W. Baldwin, Kingston, 17 Apr. and 16 May 1843.

26 For a rare exception see *North American*, 26 Aug. 1852. It may, however,
be indicative that this cautious endorsement of coeducation appeared in a
radical newspaper.

27 See, for example, *Upper Canada Gazette*, 30 May 1822; *The Packet*
[Bytown], 1 May 1847; *Globe*, 28 Aug. 1865.

28 *AR* for 1852, 136. Similarly see QUA, Kingston Board of School Trustees
Minutes, 30 Mar. 1852; *AR* for 1867, 32.

29 *Christian Guardian*, 10 Apr. 1850.

30 On "class and rank" generally see Asa Briggs, "The Language of 'Class' in
Early Nineteenth-Century England," in *Essays in Social History*, ed. M.W.
Flinn and T.C. Smout (Oxford: Clarendon Press 1974), 154–77. For Upper
Canada see S.F. Wise, "Upper Canada and the Conservative Tradition," in
Profiles of a Province (Toronto: Ontario Historical Society 1967), 20–33;
and the essays by both Wise and W.L. Morton in *The Shield of Achilles*, ed.
W.L. Morton (Toronto: McClelland and Stewart 1968). On economics and
the poor see E.A. Wrigley, "The Process of Modernization and the Industrial
Revolution in England," *Journal of Interdisciplinary History* 3, 2 (Autumn
1972): 240–2.

31 Quoted in Morton, *Shield*, 55. Similarly see *Upper Canada Herald*, 28 June
1836.

32 Among them, some notable family names – the Browns, the Langtons, the

Macdonalds, the Stewarts, the Roebucks. See J.M.S. Careless, *Brown of the Globe* (Toronto: Macmillan 1959), I: 2; W.A. Langton, ed., *Early Days in Upper Canada* (Toronto: Macmillan 1926), xiii–xvi; D.G. Creighton, *J.A. Macdonald: The Young Politician* (Toronto: Macmillan 1952), 5; G.H. Needler, *Otonabee Pioneers* (Toronto: Burns and MacEachern 1953), 67; R.E. Leader, *The Life and Letters of J.A. Roebuck* (London 1897), 3.

33 See G.W. Spragge, *The John Strachan Letter Book, 1812–1834* (Toronto: Ontario Historical Society 1946), 228, n. 1.

34 Mrs Moodie believed that this was the largest group of emigrants of the "higher classes." Susanna Moodie, *Roughing It in the Bush* (London 1852), x–xi.

35 See I. Fidler, *Observations on Professions ... in the United States and Canada* (London 1833), 1; Rev. John Armstrong, *The Life and Letters of the Rev. George Mortimer, M.A.* (London 1847), 173; J. Banks, "The Rev. James Magrath ... ," *Ontario History* 55, 3 (Sept. 1963): 131. The biographies of emigrating doctors can be found in William Canniff, *The Medical Profession in Upper Canada* (Toronto 1894).

36 E.J. Hobsbawm, *Industry and Empire: An Economic History of Britain since 1750* (London: Weidenfeld and Nicolson 1968), 66.

37 In the five towns we have analysed we have isolated those adults with teenage children – i.e. a population in their thirties to fifties and at the height of their wealth and influence in their communities – and of this group 74 per cent were British-born.

38 *The Road to Wigan Pier* (Harmondsworth: Penguin 1962), 108.

39 Moodie, *Roughing It in the Bush*, viii.

40 NA, Hill Collection, vol. 9, Pinhey Papers, Mrs T. Read to Pinhey (two letters), n.d. [1827]. For other examples see NA, Merritt Papers, vol. 11, John Kent to Merritt, 25 July 1836; AO, Strachan Papers, Strachan Letterbook, 1844–49, Strachan to Bethune, 7 Dec. 1846; NA, RG5, CI, vol. 110, no. 5968, Rev. J. Grier to Harrison, Belleville, 6 June 1843.

41 E.G. Firth, *The Town of York, 1815–34* (Toronto: Champlain Society 1966), 144–5. Similarly see *Niagara Gleaner*, 1 May 1824.

42 See for example MTRL, Baldwin Papers, W.B. McVity to W.W. Baldwin, 10 Apr. 1838, 8 and 26 Feb. 1839.

43 See MTRL, Reminiscences of Mrs Elizabeth Grover [typescript]; L.C. Grey, *Maitland: Seaway Village* (Prescott: The Prescott Journal [1967?]), 35–6; PRO, CO 42/379, Barrow to Wilmot Horton, Oct. 1829, and enclosed Memorial.

44 NA, RG5, CI, vol. 107, no. 5087, Petition of the Undersigned Inhabitants of the Town and Township of Niagara, 17 Jan. 1843.

45 C6C, Chairman, School Association, Eastern District, 9 July 1850.

46 Spragge, *Strachan Letterbook*, 75–9.

47 Bruce W. Hodgins, *John Sandfield Macdonald* (Toronto: University of Toronto Press 1971), 5–7.

48 Briggs, "Language of Class," 72.
49 See Peter A. Russell, "Attitudes to Social Structure and Social Mobility in Upper Canada (1815–1840)" (Ph.D. diss., Carleton 1983).
50 For Grantham Academy see AO, W.H. Merritt Papers, Package 28, Grantham Academy, Exhibition, 17 Feb. 1832; NA, RG5, BI I, vol. 4, item 392, Memorial of Trustees of the Grantham Academy. See also C6C, Philip Carman and others to Murray, 5 Jan. 1843; Adam Harkness, *Iroquois High School* ... (Toronto 1896), 16ff; *Christian Guardian*, 26 Jan. 1842 (Markham); *British Colonist*, 3 Apr. 1839 (Streetsville).
51 See R.D. Gidney and W.P.J. Millar, "From Voluntarism to State Schooling: The Creation of the Public School System in Ontario," *Canadian Historical Review* 66, 4 (Dec. 1985): 457.
52 AO, Merritt Papers, Merritt to Dr Jediah Prendergast, 27 Nov. 1831.
53 Firth, *Town of York*, 167.
54 *DHE* 3: 257; Harris, *Observations on Upper Canada College*, 17.
55 MTRL, Anne Macdonell Letters, York, 30 Nov. 1828.
56 AO, Merritt Papers, W.H. Merritt to Catharine Merritt, 28 June 1835.
57 Ibid.
58 MTRL, MacLeod Letterbooks, Donald MacLeod to [unidentified], 1 Jan. 1861. See also MacLeod to Lt. Col. Gallway, 24 Sept. 1851.
59 E.P. Thompson, "The grid of inheritance: a comment," in *Family and Inheritance: Rural Society in Western Europe, 1200–1800*, ed. Jack Goody, Joan Thirsk, and E.P. Thompson (Cambridge: Cambridge University Press 1976), 358. See also David Gagan, *Hopeful Travellers: Families, Land, and Social Change in Mid-Victorian Peel County, Canada West* (Toronto: University of Toronto Press 1981), 50ff.
60 T.W. Acheson, "The Social Origins of the Canadian Industrial Elite, 1880–1885," in *Canadian Business History: Selected Studies, 1497–1971*, ed. David S. Macmillan (Toronto: McClelland and Stewart 1972), 152–4.
61 See, for example, Patrick Harrigan, *Mobility, Elites, and Education in French Society of the Second Empire* (Waterloo: Wilfrid Laurier University Press 1980), 146–7; Sheldon Rothblatt, *The Revolution of the Dons* (London: Faber and Faber 1968), 86–7; David Keane, "Rediscovering Ontario University Students in the Mid-Nineteenth Century" (Ph.D. diss., University of Toronto 1982), 717; Colin B. Burke, *American Collegiate Populations* (New York: New York University Press 1982); R.D. Anderson, *Education and Opportunity in Victorian Scotland* (Oxford: Clarendon Press 1983), 136–9. Our own findings on the Upper Canadian grammar schools are considered in chap. 6.
62 See the grammar school returns in NA, RG5, CI, no. 11,434.
63 See Gidney and Millar, "Voluntarism," 447.
64 Alison Prentice, "Education and the Metaphor of the Family: The Upper Canadian Example," in *Education and Social Change*, ed. Michael B. Katz and Paul H. Mattingly (New York: New York University Press 1975), 110–32.

65 Quoted in Prentice and Houston, *Family, School and Society*, 250. For a helpful discussion of home education in Britain and the colonies, and the traditional preferences for governesses rather than schools, see Elizabeth Windschuttle, "Educating the Daughters of the Ruling Class in Colonial New South Wales, 1788–1850," in *Melbourne Studies in Education, 1980*, ed. Stephen Murray-Smith (Melbourne: Melbourne University Press 1980), 106–16.

66 AO, Blake Papers, 12b, Catherine Hume Blake Papers, "Sketch of Edward by C.H.B."

67 UCA, Ryerson Letters, R.B. Sullivan to Ryerson, Kingston, 20 July 1843.

68 MTRL, MacLeod Letterbooks, MacLeod to John Campbell, 22 Jan. 1851.

69 See for example UCA, Mark Y. Stark Papers, M. Stark to Mother, Dundas, 11 Feb. 1844; Agatha Stark to Mrs Stark, n.d. [Dec. 1846?]; AO, Merritt Papers, Penelope Prendergast to Catharine Merritt, Mayville, 22 Oct. 1827; W.H. Merritt to Catharine, York, 15 Dec. 1832; Catharine to parents, St Catharines, 3 Dec. 1833; AO, A.N. Buell Papers, Buell to Cousin, Toronto, 16 Oct. 1854; AO, John Strachan Papers, Strachan Letterbook, 1844–49, Strachan to Mrs Robt. Cartwright, 8 May 1848.

70 See for example above, 21–2; UCA, Mark Y. Stark Papers, M. Stark to Miss Bannatyre, Dundas, 24 Aug. 1846; Ryerson Letters, John Ryerson to Egerton, St Catharines, 20 Oct. 1842.

71 UCA, Mark Y. Stark Papers, Stark to his aunt, Dundas, 20 June 1844. Similarly see AO, Macaulay Papers, Ann Macaulay to John Macaulay, Kingston, 23 July 1840.

72 See AO, Roe Family Papers, Toronto Boarding School Accounts, 1839–44; AO, David Thorburn Papers, Margaret to David Thorburn, 24 Oct. 1839.

73 MTRL, Reminiscences of Mrs Elizabeth Grover [typescript].

74 Strachan, *On the Management of Grammar Schools*, 23.

75 AO, Blake Papers, 12b, Catharine Hume Blake Papers, "Sketch of Edward by C.H.B."

76 UCA, Ryerson Letters, R.B. Sullivan to Ryerson, Kingston, 20 July 1843.

77 AO, Macaulay Papers, Ann Macaulay to John Macaulay, Kingston, 23 July 1840. For a similar comment see AO, Jarvis-Powell Papers, Samuel P. Jarvis to Mrs Jarvis, Kingston, 23 Mar. 1843.

78 UCA, Mark Y. Stark Papers, Mark Stark to Mother, Dundas, 2 Nov. 1847.

79 *Patriot*, 20 Aug. 1839.

80 [Prospectus] *Burlington Ladies' Academy* (Cobourg 1845), 9.

81 *The Church*, 20 Oct. 1853.

82 *British Colonist*, 14 July 1846.

83 *Bathurst Courier*, 30 Sept. 1853.

84 *The Church*, 26 July 1848.

85 *The Church*, 20 Jan. 1838.

86 For an example, see Gidney and Millar, "Voluntarism," 461.

87 See R.D. Gidney, "Making Nineteenth-Century School Systems," *History of Education* 9 (June 1980): 106ff. The difference between Scottish and English attitudes to government intervention was substantial, and Upper Canadians may have been influenced more by Scotland on this point. See R.D. Anderson, "Education and the State in Nineteenth-Century Scotland," *Economic History Review*, 2nd series, 36, 4 (Nov. 1983): 518–34.

88 *Christian Guardian*, 2 Apr. 1845; *British Colonist*, 20 Feb. 1846.

89 *Globe*, 17 July 1851.

90 The names of the grammar school teachers can be located for each year in the Appendix to the *JLA* which deals with public accounts.

91 Their advertisements are to be found in most newspapers, but typical examples can be found in most issues of *The Church*.

92 Nor is it just a matter of these three familiar names. One of the three members of the committee on education in 1839 was a clergyman, and about half the people consulted by the commission were clergymen. See NA, RG5, BII, vol. 6, no. 754.

93 Until the late 1840s clergymen usually were in the majority as trustees of the grant-aided grammar schools.

94 *Canada Christian Advocate*, 20 June 1855. Similarly see *Christian Guardian*, 2 Apr. 1845.

95 For Victoria see *British Colonist*, 19 May 1846. For Upper Canada College see *DHE* 6: 133.

96 For a more detailed description of the variety of schools in Upper Canada, see R.D. Gidney, "Elementary Education in Upper Canada: A Reassessment," in *Education and Social Change*, ed. Michael B. Katz and Paul H. Mattingly (New York: New York University Press 1975), and Gidney and Millar, "Voluntarism." See also the fine recent review in chap. 2 of Susan E. Houston and Alison Prentice, *Schooling and Scholars in Nineteenth-Century Ontario* (Toronto: University of Toronto Press 1988).

97 See Harris, *Observations on Upper Canada College*, esp. 16–18.

98 See the two school reports in NA, MG24, I3, vol. 3 [McGillivray Papers – Eastern District – Neil McLean]: Report of Trustees, Eastern District School, 29 July 1839 and Report of Hugh Urquhart to Trustees for 1839–40.

99 See above, 27.

100 *Circular of the Upper Canada Academy, 1841* (Cobourg 1841), 8–10, 16, and 20–1. Similarly see *Burlington Ladies' Academy* [Prospectus] (Cobourg 1845). At the latter school in 1845 there were ninety pupils.

101 AO, Macaulay Papers, John to Ann Macaulay, 8 Nov. 1840.

102 For an example see *Kingston Chronicle*, 23 Apr. 1831. See also *York Gazette*, 10 Oct. 1810; *Niagara Gleaner*, 15 Oct. 1825.

103 Indeed one occasionally sees, in the advertisements of the grammar schools and the select private schools, the English branches described as "Common Education." See for example *York Gazette*, 10 Oct. 1812; NA, RG5, BII,

vol. 5, no. 429, Report, Board of Trustees, Ottawa District School, 23 July 1833.

104 *DHE* 8: 290.

105 See the parallel comment by John Roach, *A History of Secondary Education in England, 1800–1870* (London: Longman 1986), 10–11.

106 c6c, Legatt Dounius to R. Murray, 10 July 1844.

107 *Canadian Christian Examiner* (Aug. 1839), 251–2.

108 See for example *Circular of the Upper Canada Academy, 1841*, 11; Harris, *Observations on Upper Canada College*, 16ff.

109 See above, 24.

110 *Circular of the Upper Canada Academy, 1841*, 4–5.

111 Fritz Ringer terms this "horizontal segmentation" in his *Education and Society in Modern Europe* (Bloomington: Indiana University Press 1979), 29.

112 See for example NA, AI, vol. 53, Report of Classes, Midland District School, 28 July 1821; Strachan, *On the Management of Grammar Schools*, esp. 5–7.

CHAPTER THREE

1 For an introduction to the human capital thesis and its difficulties, see Christopher Hurn, *The Limits and Possibilities of Schooling* (Boston: Allyn and Bacon 1978), 35ff.

2 On its relevance for particular sectors of education and the economy, see for example W. Norton Grubb and Marvin Lazerson, "Education and the Labor Market: Recycling the Youth Problem," in *Work, Youth and Schooling: Historical Perspectives on Vocationalism in American Education*, ed. H. Kantor and D. Tyack (Stanford: Stanford University Press 1982), 124–5 and 138–40.

3 For doctors see *Upper Canada Gazette*, 3 May 1832, and *Medical Register for Upper Canada, 1867*, 49. For law, *JEdUC* 17 (Feb. 1864): 24–5; for the Churches of England and Scotland, see for example *Journal of the Third Session of the Synod of the Church of England in the Diocese of Ontario, 1864* (Kingston 1864), 259–60; *The Presbyterian* (Jan. 1864), 9. For the Free [Presbyterian] Church, see *DHE* 19: 267–8.

4 Entry standards can be compared by consulting the calendars of the chartered universities preserved in various university and archival libraries.

5 22 Vict. cap. 77: An Act respecting Land Surveyors and the Survey of Lands, 6th section.

6 See for example *Christian Guardian*, 16 Oct. 1839; *The Church*, 18 July 1840; *Patriot*, 6 Jan. 1846.

7 For some illustrative examples see *Patriot*, 30 July 1844; *London Free Press*, 4 Jan. 1856 and 15 Nov. 1862; *Leader*, 2 Aug. 1861; *Globe*, 3 Sept. 1860 and 26 Mar. 1864; *Ottawa Citizen*, 14 Dec. 1866.

8 Grubb and Lazerson, "Education and the Labor Market," 118. See also David K. Foot, "University Enrolments: Challenging Popular Misconceptions," in *Ontario Universities: Access, Operations, and Funding*, ed. David W. Conklin and Thomas J. Courchene (Toronto: Ontario Economic Council 1985), 171.

9 See for example Michael B. Katz and Ian Davey, "Youth and Early Industrialization in a Canadian City," in *Turning Points: Historical and Sociological Essays on the Family*, ed. John Demos and S.S. Boocock (Chicago: University of Chicago Press 1978), 103; see also the results for grammar school pupils in Upper Canada, chap. 6.

10 For an exposition of this argument see Fritz Ringer, *Education and Society in Modern Europe* (Bloomington: Indiana University Press 1979), 12–22.

11 Katz and Davey, "Youth and Early Industrialization," 114–15.

12 *Upper Canada Gazette*, 2 May 1822; *Patriot*, 6 Jan. 1846 and 19 July 1836.

13 *Upper Canada Law Journal* 1, 3 (Mar. 1865): 79–80.

14 See R.D. Gidney and W.P.J. Millar, "The Origins of Organized Medicine in Ontario," in *Health, Disease and Medicine: Essays in Canadian History*, ed. Charles G. Roland (Toronto: Hannah Institute 1984), 81. On oversupply in medicine see ibid., 78–9.

15 Fred Hirsch, *Social Limits to Growth* (Cambridge: Harvard University Press 1976), 49.

16 There are helpful discussions of these various alternatives by Grubb and Lazerson, "Education and the Labor Market," 122–3, and by Geraldine Clifford, "Educating Women for Work," in *Work, Youth and Schooling*, ed. H. Kantor and D. Tyack (Stanford: Stanford University Press 1982), 248–50.

17 Katz and Davey, "Youth and Early Industrialization," 103.

18 Mary P. Ryan, *Cradle of the Middle Class: The Family in Oneida County, New York, 1790–1865* (Cambridge: Cambridge University Press 1981), 184–5.

19 Joy Parr, "Hired Men: Ontario Agricultural Labour in Historical Perspective," *Labour/Le Travail* 15 (Spring 1985): 99.

20 Bruce Elliott, *Irish Migrants in the Canadas* (Montreal and Kingston: McGill-Queen's University Press 1988), 202ff.

21 c6c, Judith Shore to Ryerson, Nepean, 27 Jan. 1862. Similarly see c6c, Wm. Irvine to Ryerson, 6 June 1855.

22 Calculated from the relevant *ARs*. Some of these pupils may have come from hamlets or villages without grammar school facilities. But a search of the manuscript census for out-of-town residents listed in the grammar school registers, carried out as a subsidiary part of the project described in chap. 6, shows that many pupils came from farms in nearby townships.

23 c6c, Geo. Strauchon to Ryerson, Woodstock, 15 Feb. 1865; GIA, 1863, 54.

24 *Leader*, 23 Dec. 1856.

25 Sheldon Rothblatt, "The Diversification of Higher Education in England," in *The Transformation of Higher Learning, 1860–1930*, ed. Konrad Jarausch (Chicago: University of Chicago Press 1983), 136.

26 *Formation of a Theological Institution by the Baptists of Canada* (New York 1853) [by Archibald Maclay]. Similarly see *DHE* 4: 109–10 [Ryerson to Sydenham, 13 July 1841]; *Christian Guardian*, 7 Sept. 1853; *Canada Christian Advocate*, 1 Aug. 1860.

27 *Ecclesiastical and Missionary Record*, Aug. 1846.

28 *Canada Christian Advocate*, 11 Aug. 1846 and 1 Aug. 1848. Similarly see ibid., 6 Apr. 1853.

29 *Ecclesiastical and Missionary Record*, Dec. 1846, 236. Similarly see QUA, Queen's University Senate Minutes, 7 Mar. 1842; Queen's University Board of Trustees, Minutes, 6 Apr. 1842.

30 *Kingston Chronicle*, 6 Aug. 1842.

31 *JLAC*, 1856, appendix 11. See also David Keane, "Rediscovering Ontario University Students in the Mid-Nineteenth Century" (Ph.D. diss., University of Toronto 1982), 239.

32 For enrolments see QUA, Queen's University Letters, John Campbell to Prof. Williamson, Kingston, 5 Jan. 1852; *Globe*, 15 July 1851; *Christian Guardian*, 28 Feb. 1849 and 3 May 1854.

33 *Canadian United Presbyterian Magazine*, 1 Oct. 1854. Similarly see *Christian Messenger*, 21 June 1855; QUA, Queen's University Board of Trustees, Minutes, Apr. 1848, Instructions to Machar.

34 *British Colonist*, 3 Apr. 1839.

35 *Brantford Expositor*, 20 Sept. 1872. Similarly see *JEdUC* 26 (Oct. 1873): 151.

36 *Christian Guardian*, 16 June 1856.

37 *Christian Guardian*, 23 May 1855 (quoting the *Cobourg Sun*); 30 Jan., 27 Feb., and 27 Oct. 1856; 11 Feb. 1857.

38 See *Kingston Gazette*, 26 Mar. 1811; *JLA*, Appendix: Report of the Select Committee on the Petition of Rev. Robert McDowall and others, 219; CI, vol. 103, #5251, Petition of the President, Secretary and Trustees of the Bath Academy, Feb. 1843.

39 See J.P. Merritt, *Biography of the Hon. W.H. Merritt ...* (St Catharines 1875), 87–8; *Upper Canada Gazette*, 26 Aug. 1830; *Farmers' Journal* [St Catharines], 3 Jan. 1831. For Ancaster see *Patriot*, 6 June 1837; *DHE* 3: 195–8.

40 For details of the growth of the private-venture schools and their numbers, see R.D. Gidney, "Elementary Education in Upper Canada: A Reassessment," in *Education and Social Change*, ed. Michael B. Katz and Paul H. Mattingly (New York: New York University Press 1975); R.D. Gidney and W.P.J. Millar, "From Voluntarism to State Schooling: The Creation of

the Public School System in Ontario," *Canadian Historical Review* 66,
4 (Dec. 1985); and in this volume, appendix A.

41 See *DHE* 3: 138–9; *Upper Canada Herald*, 14 Jan. 1829 and 8 June 1831;
Kingston Chronicle, 16 Sept. 1835. Over the years the school had four different teachers.

42 See *Patriot*, 9 Aug. 1833; *Colonial Advocate*, 3 Oct. 1833; *City of Toronto
and Home District Commercial Directory ... 1837.*

43 For Caradoc see John Morrison, "The Caradoc Academy," *London and
Middlesex Historical Society Transactions 1908–09*, 45–52; *London Herald*,
6 May 1843; *The Church*, 3 June 1845. For Newmarket see *Patriot*, 14 July
1835 and *British Colonist*, 5 June 1839. For Barrie see *Patriot*, 21 June
1839; *Christian Guardian*, 2 Jan. 1839. Despite the title "academy," these
schools were the property of a single teacher and more closely resembled the
private-venture schools than those founded on joint-stock principles.

44 See AO, John Strachan Papers, "Journal of a Tour ... 1828"; NA, RG5, BII,
vol. 4, Gale to Hon. James Gordon, 26 Jan. 1831.

45 See *Brockville Recorder*, 11 Apr. 1833 and 10 Jan. 1834.

46 See *Kingston Chronicle*, 26 July 1834; *Upper Canada Herald*, 27 Apr. and
8 June 1831; Toronto *Patriot*, 8 Sept. 1835; *London Gazette*, 28 Oct. 1837;
London Inquirer, 28 Oct. 1842; *The Church*, 13 July 1839, 20 Oct. 1843,
27 Dec. 1844.

47 J.M.S. Careless, *Brown of the Globe* (Toronto: Macmillan 1959), I: 2–3 and
16.

48 Anne Wilkinson, *Lions in the Way: A Discursive History of the Oslers*
(Toronto: Macmillan 1956), 38.

49 AO, Ridout Papers, Thos. G. Ridout to Mrs Ridout, 21 June 1816.

50 AO, Misc. Coll., Narrative of the Skirving Family by Dr James H. Richardson. For pertinent commentary on Scottish schoolmistresses and their impact
on the colonies, see Marjorie R. Theobald, "Scottish Schoolmistresses in
Colonial Australia," CHEA *Bulletin* 5, 3 (Oct. 1988): 1–17.

51 Edith G. Firth, ed., *The Town of York 1815–1834* (Toronto: University of
Toronto Press 1966), 151; NA, RG5, AI, vol. 55, Bishop Mountain to
Maitland, Quebec, 9 Mar. 1822; *British Colonist*, 11 Aug. 1846. On the
ability of Mrs Cockburn to attract a prestigious clientele, see chap. 2, 28.

52 c6c, Marianne Fuller to Ryerson, 26 Aug. 1861.

53 UCA, Mark Y. Stark Papers, M.Y. Stark to Mrs Stark, 20 Dec. 1834; same
to same, 14 May 1835.

54 For example see the *Patriot*, 1 Dec. 1835 and 29 Aug. 1837; *The Church*,
11 Nov. 1837, 20 Jan. 1838, 26 Jan. 1839, 2 Sept. 1842, 5 Jan. and
7 Nov. 1844; *Kingston Chronicle*, 7 Sept. 1842.

55 *Chronicle*, 24 Jan. 1835; *Christian Guardian*, 27 Apr. 1836; *The Church*,
26 Jan. 1844. For examples of the latter see the *Patriot*, 25 Apr. 1834 and

21 Aug. 1840; *Upper Canada Herald*, 31 Oct. 1826, 22 Jan. 1834, 17 Nov. 1835; *Niagara Gleaner*, 15 Oct. 1825.

56 *DHE* 1: 213.

57 *Christian Guardian*, 10 May 1848. Similarly see UCA, Wesleyan Methodist Church, Foreign Missions: B.N.A. Correspondence, Rev. J. Stimson to Rev. Robert Alder, Kingston, 21 Apr. 1835.

58 For 1838 see *DHE* 3: 254. Unless otherwise noted all the following figures and calculations are based on the relevant *ARs*.

59 See *JLAC*, 1844–45, Appendix C-C-C. The schools of the Midland District are omitted and our enrolment figure is the combined total of the enrolments recorded here plus an estimate for the Midland District based on the average size of the other schools.

60 A word of caution on the growth of Latin is in order here: until 1864 the statistics reflect a high degree of parental choice in the matter; the spectacular growth in Latin between 1865 and 1870 was, however, forced growth, as official policy attempted to turn the grammar schools into purely classical schools. We will return to the story in chaps. 7 and 8.

61 See for example *JLA*, 1831, Appendix: Common School Reports for 1830; *JLA*, 1833–34, Appendix: Common School Reports for 1833; *DHE* 3: 253; NA, RG5, B11, vol. 5, item 466, Quarterly report of a district common school ... London ... 1834.

62 AO, RG2, F2, Report, Common School Commissioners, Ancaster, 1843.

63 Toronto City Council Papers, Local Superintendent (Barber) to Council, 18 Nov. 1844.

64 See for example the comments of Robert Murray and John Strachan to the Commission on Education of 1839, in *DHE* 3: 273 and 278.

65 For a statement of his views, see his report of 1846, printed in *DHE* 6: 140ff. Part 1 deals with the common school curriculum in considerable detail.

66 For the legislation and Ryerson's comments on it, see *DHE* 7: 26–8 and 188–95. This legislation was incorporated directly into the Common School Act of 1850, with two major changes. The boards of school trustees that had been appointed by the municipal councils in 1847 were to be elected directly by the voters from 1850 on, and they were also given direct powers of taxation rather than, as in 1847, having to appeal to the municipal councils for funds.

67 For the first set of these regulations see *DHE* 9: 218–21. They were revised in 1858, and not again until 1871.

68 See *AR* for 1850, 259 (texts) and 311–12 (qualifications). For the fact that Ryerson considered these tantamount to a program of studies, see C1, Ryerson to R.F. White, 5 Apr. 1852. For the Model School program as an example, see *JEdUC* 8, 2 (Feb. 1855): 18.

69 The document is printed as part of the revised regulations in the *AR* for 1858, 153–6. See also *DHE* 14: 63–5.

70 Compare for example the use of Colenso's Algebra in all these institutions: *DHE* 14: 64 (common schools); *JEdUC* 8 (Feb. 1855): 25 (prescribed texts for grammar schools); and *Calendar, University College 1860–1*, 25.

71 *DHE* 7: 189.

72 CI, Hodgins to Sangster, 18 Sept. 1854.

73 See *AR* for 1850, 9, 205; CI, Hodgins to Craigie, 26 Sept. 1854.

74 In table C of the *ARs* for 1847, 1850, and 1852, for example, there are references to Latin being taught, but the number of students is small and declining.

75 CI, Ryerson to J.M. McLaurin, 7 Mar. 1855. See also *JEdUC* 14 (Mar. 1861): 40.

76 For official opinions to this effect see CI, Ryerson to Daniel Morrison, 3 Feb. 1855; *AR* for 1850, 187. For the standards of qualification see *DHE* 9: 220–1, and 14: 62–3.

77 Throughout this chapter there are a large number of simple arithmetical calculations. Unless a separate endnote is provided, all are based on the statistical tables published in the *ARs* between 1852 and 1869.

78 For examples of advertisements by "crammers" see *British Colonist*, 27 June 1848, and *Globe*, 16 Dec. 1854.

79 For a typical argument that lays out the advantages for grading, see *AR* for 1850, 18–21. For a sensible interpretation of the origins of age-grading which eschews the heavy hand of bureaucratization, oppression, and social control, see David L. Angus, Jeffrey W. Mirel, and Maris A. Vinovskis, "Historical Development of Age-stratification in Schooling," *Teachers College Record* 90, 2 (Winter 1988): esp. 215–18.

80 See C6C, A. Kirkland to Ryerson, Brantford, 24 Dec. 1851; GIA (Ormiston), 1855, 24 (Hamilton); *AR* for 1852, 132 (London). All of these schools were later united with the local grammar school. For other examples of classical instruction in common and separate schools, see C6C, Trustees, Village of Embro, to Ryerson, 25 Mar. 1851; James Pringle to Ryerson, Brampton, 14 Dec. 1853; James Noble to Hodgins, Amherstburg, 10 Apr. 1856; *Perth Courier*, 1 July 1864; *JEdUC* 15 (Feb. 1862), 32.

81 See for example, Joel Perlmann, "Curriculum and Tracking in the Transformation of the American High School: Providence, R.I., 1880–1930," *Journal of Social History* 19, 1 (Fall 1985): esp. 34–5; James Albisetti, *Secondary School Reform in Imperial Germany* (Princeton: Princeton University Press 1983), 62ff. and 292ff.; Rupert Goodman, *Secondary Education in Queensland, 1860–1960* (Canberra: Australian National University Press 1968), 200–5; G.E. Saunders, "Public Education in South Australia: the Nineteenth-Century Background," in *Melbourne Studies in Education*, ed. R.J.W. Selleck (1968–9), 133–64.

82 This generalization is not true, however, of instruction in the three Rs. Indeed, in the urban areas at least, the reverse is true. The common schools

were generally overcrowded, and there were not enough school places for the child population.

CHAPTER FOUR

1 See, for example, *Globe*, 2 and 5 Feb. 1852; *Leader*, 23 July 1862, 4 Aug. 1863, 9 Dec. 1864.

2 See, for example, C6C, Chairman, School Association, Eastern District, 9 July 1850; *Leader*, 14 Aug. 1861; C6C, John Paton to Ryerson, 15 Jan. 1862.

3 *AR* for 1855, T.A. Ambridge, Hamilton, 278. See also C6C, W.F. Hubbard to Ryerson, St Catharines, 11 Aug. 1855; C1, James Cummings to Ryerson, Chippawa, 25 June 1856; *Globe*, 31 July 1866.

4 See for example G1A, 1857 (Ormiston), 27; C6C, W.H. Wilbur to Ryerson, Drummondville, 31 Dec. 1861; C6C, James Cameron to Ryerson, Drummondville, 15 July 1865.

5 AO, Hamnett Pinhey Papers, 30 Aug. 1833.

6 AO, Roe Family Papers.

7 UCA, Mark Y. Stark Papers, Mark Stark to mother, [Dec.] 1846 and 12 June 1847; AO, A.N. Buell Papers, account dated 5 July 1850.

8 *JLA*, 1831–32, Appendix: Documents Relating to School Lands. For Kingston, see ibid.

9 AO, Macaulay Papers, Markland to Macaulay, 27 Apr. 1829.

10 MTRL, MacLeod Letterbooks, D. MacLeod to Mrs Gordon, 13 Dec. 1848.

11 AO, John Strachan Papers, John Strachan Letterbook, 1839–43, John Strachan to Mrs Radcliff, 15 Oct. 1842.

12 NA, RG5, C1, 1855, Item 350, Petition, Village of Newboro, Leeds County.

13 UCA, Mark Y. Stark Papers, Stark to mother, Dundas, 20 Dec. 1834.

14 See chap. 6. For other examples see UCA, Ryerson Letters, John Ryerson to Egerton Ryerson, 20 Oct. 1842; AO, Jarvis-Powell Papers, Samuel P. Jarvis to Mrs Jarvis, 33 Mar. 1843; *Christian Guardian*, 30 July 1851 and 13 Oct. 1852; *Globe*, 18 and 23 Sept. 1863; AO, Col. Charles Clarke Papers, A.A. Riddell to Clarke, 15 Mar. 1868.

15 AO, Macaulay Papers, J. Macaulay to Ann Macaulay, Toronto, 23 Sept. 1839.

16 AO, Macaulay Papers, J. Macaulay to Ann Macaulay, Toronto, 8 Nov. 1840.

17 Dianna S. Cameron, "J.G. Hodgins and Ontario Education, 1844–1912" (MA diss., University of Guelph 1976), 17ff.

18 NA, RG5, A1, vol. 225–6, Mrs Blackwood to Arthur, 22 July 1839.

19 *Christian Guardian*, 13 Oct. 1852.

20 For details see appendix A.

21 See above, 48–9.

22 AO, John Strachan Letterbook, 1844–49, Strachan to Miss F. Hodges, 26 Aug. 1848.

23 The school notices reveal a great deal of instability for these reasons; for example, see Mrs Urlin's advertisements in the *London Free Press*, 24 Jan. 1856 and 6 Sept. 1858; Mrs T.C. Campbell, *The Church*, 7 Nov. 1845, and *Leader*, 2 Aug. 1862; Mrs Birnie, *Globe*, 1 Aug. 1866.

24 For example, see MTRL, MacLeod Letterbooks, D. MacLeod to the Rev. E. Coleridge, 6 Nov. 1845, and to Mr Saddell, 18 Dec. 1848; c6c, John Barclay, acting chairman, Grammar School Board of Trustees, to governor-general, Toronto, 6 May 1853; c6c, W.H. Coombs to Ryerson, 4 June 1858; c6c, D.J. Moffatt to Ryerson, 14 Sept. 1861; Miss MacNally's advertisement, *The Church*, 23 Feb. 1854; Ian E. Davey, "Trends in Female School Attendance in Mid-Nineteenth Century Ontario," *Histoire sociale* 8 (Nov. 1975): 244-5.

25 See R.D. Gidney and W.P.J. Millar, "From Voluntarism to State Schooling: The Creation of the Public School System in Ontario," *Canadian Historical Review* 66, 4 (Dec. 1985) and appendix A, table A.1. Compare Susan E. Houston and Alison Prentice, *Schooling and Scholars in Nineteenth-Century Ontario* (Toronto: University of Toronto Press 1988), 67.

26 See *Patriot*, 10 Sept. 1844; *Globe*, 20 Aug. 1860 and 1 Aug. 1866.

27 See *British Colonist*, 11 Sept. 1839; *Globe*, 21 Aug. 1854; *Christian Guardian*, 9 July 1831; *Globe*, 27 Aug. 1866.

28 See *British Colonist*, 24 Oct. 1843; *The Church*, 7 Nov. 1845; UCA, Ryerson Papers, Beaty to Ryerson, Cobourg, Dec. 1862. Table A.1, appendix A, gives the data for 196 schools in four selected communities but it does not include all of the 350 schools we located, and amongst the others there are examples which are helpful in illuminating the experiences of women teachers by showing that, like Mrs Campbell, they moved their schools from one place to another but taught continuously over a long period.

29 When one compares different British colonies in the mid-nineteenth century there are some dramatic contrasts in the way middle-class education developed. The state of Victoria, in Australia, and Ontario share some striking demographic and historical similarities and yet in the former case "secondary" education remained almost exclusively in private hands throughout the whole of the nineteenth century. One key explanatory factor for the different outcomes in Victoria and Ontario may be, quite simply, the different levels of urbanization. In Ontario in 1871, 21 per cent of the population lived in urban places; in Victoria it was 55 per cent. In the same year 3.5 per cent of Ontario's population lived in Toronto; 29 per cent of Victoria's population lived in Melbourne. In Ontario, we suggest, the dispersion of the urban population in a large number of small towns and villages made it far more difficult than in Victoria to sustain schools without some form of subsidy to supplement fees or subscriptions.

30 *Christian Guardian*, 14 Oct. 1863.

31 See for example Theodore Sizer, ed., *The Age of the Academies* (New York: Teachers' College, Columbia University 1964); Brian Heeney, *Mission to the*

Middle Classes: The Woodward Schools, 1848–1891 (London: SPCK 1969);
J.D. Purdy, "The English Public School Tradition in Nineteenth-Century
Ontario," in *Aspects of Nineteenth-Century Ontario*, ed. F.H. Armstrong et
al. (Toronto: University of Toronto Press 1974), 237–52.

32 For example, Burlington Ladies Academy in 1848–49 had nearly 200 pupils:
JEdUC 2, 7 (July 1849): 102; Toronto Academy in 1851 had 170 pupils:
Globe, 17 July 1851; Newburgh Academy in 1846 had 85 pupils: C6C,
H.G. Spafford to Ryerson, 10 Mar. 1846.

33 The sources for this paragraph are as follows: for Grantham Academy the
main source is AO, W.H. Merritt Papers, package 28; for Ancaster, University of Toronto Archives, Office of the Chief Accountant, Financial Records,
vol. 214, General Letterbook no. 1, W. Craigie to J. Wells, 1839; J.G.
Hodgins, *DHE* 3: 220ff.; NA, RG5, B11, vol. 6, item 719, W. Craigie to
S.B. Harrison, 10 Oct. 1839. For Bath, see *JLA*, especially the 1830s, and
NA, RG5, C1, vol. 103, no. 5251, and vol. 109, no. 5861, Feb. and May
1843. For Upper Canada Academy see the *Christian Guardian* in the 1830s;
for the Canadian Literary Institute see *Christian Messenger* [*Canadian
Baptist*] in the 1850s and 1860s; for Belleville Seminary see *Canada Chris-
tian Advocate*, 1850s and 1860s, and UCA, Carman Papers; for Toronto
Academy see *Ecclesiastical and Missionary Record* and *Globe*, 1846–54.

34 See *The Church*, 8 Apr. 1852; *British Colonist*, 2 Apr. 1852; *Globe*,
24 Aug. 1852.

35 See *Ecclesiastical and Missionary Record* and *Globe*, 1846–54.

36 NA, RG5, B11, vol. 5, no. 526, C. Mackenzie to Joseph, 21 Nov. 1836, en-
closing petition of Trustees of Bath School Society (Bath Academy). Two
years earlier the trustees of Grantham Academy had described their plight in
almost identical terms: see *British American Journal*, 5 Aug. 1834.

37 UCA, Carman Papers, Philip Carman to the Rev. S.W. Ladie, 15 Jan. 1857
[punctuation supplied].

38 For example, see NA, RG5, B11, vol. 4, item 244, W.C. Crofton to Mudge,
24 Feb. 1830; NA, RG5, B11, vol. 4, Memorial of Grantham Academy Trust-
ees, 3 Nov. 1832; *JLA*, 14 Dec. 1832; NA, RG5, B11, vol. 6, item 719, W.
Craigie to S.B. Harrison, 10 Oct. 1839; C6C, Rev. Daniel McMullen to
Ryerson, Apr. 1853; C6C, J. Fraser to Ryerson, 30 July 1853; C6C, D.J.
Moffatt to Ryerson, 14 Sept. 1861.

39 For an early example see *JLC*, 1836, appendix K: Report on an Address ...
complaining of the Rejection by the Council of Various Bills.

40 See for example *Globe*, 17 July 1851.

41 Compare, for example, two of Ryerson's statements in 1846 alone, printed
in *DHE* 6: 107–8 and 196–7.

42 See for example *DHE* 6: 261, and *JEdUC* 1, 1 (Jan. 1848).

43 See for example NA, RG5, C1, vol. 202, no. 16774, Extract of a Report of a
Committee of the Executive Council, 7 June 1847 (Burlington Ladies' Acad-

emy); *JLAC*, 5 June 1850 (Petition Re Queen's College School); *JLAC*, 12 Feb. 1849 (Regiopolis); *JLAC*, 8 Sept. 1852 (Petition Re Adelaide Academy).

44 CI, Ryerson to the Rev. Daniel McMullen, 21 Apr. 1853.

45 For this paragraph see AO, W.H. Merritt Papers, package 28, Grantham Academy; *British American Journal*, 6 May 1834; *JLAC*, 9 and 10 Sept. 1841; NA, RG5, CI, vol. 123, no. 1859, W.H. Merritt to Daly, St Catharines, 1 Aug. 1844.

46 For further details see chap. 6.

47 GIA (Ormiston), 1855, 72.

48 *Canada School Journal* 4, 31 (Dec. 1879): 269–70.

49 MTRL, Baldwin Papers, A43–8, W.G. Edmonston to Baldwin, Whitchurch, 23 Feb. 1849. Similarly see ibid., A72–128, Robt.H. Smith to Baldwin, Newmarket, 8 June 1849.

50 See NA, RG5, CI, vol. 258, no. 859, Wellington District Grammar School; MTRL, Baldwin Papers, A45–35, A.J. Fergusson to Baldwin, Montreal, 6 Apr. 1849; ibid., A45–40, Fergusson to Baldwin, Guelph, 11 Aug. 1849.

51 For some examples see NA, RG5, CI, vol. 127, no. 7516, Copy of a Report of a Committee of the Executive Council, 28 Mar. 1844, and Related Materials; vol. 214, no. 18310, Extract from a Report of a Committee of the Executive Council, 11 Nov. 1847; vol. 245, no. 155 [1850], Thurlow Grammar School materials; vol. 282, no. 112 [1850], Palermo Grammar School materials.

52 Quoted in Anne Wilkinson, *Lions in the Way: A Discursive History of the Oslers* (Toronto: Macmillan 1956), 89.

53 David Keane, "Rediscovering Ontario University Students in the Mid-Nineteenth Century" (Ph.D. diss., University of Toronto 1982), 662–3.

54 *AR* for 1858, part III, 96–7.

55 For fees and a list of instructors see the advertisement in the *Globe*, 2 Oct. 1854.

56 For this paragraph generally see chap. 3 above, 54–8 and Alison Prentice, *The School Promoters* (Toronto: McClelland and Stewart 1977), chap. 6. For some Kingston examples see Minutes of the Kingston Board of School Trustees, 11 Dec. 1855 (on teachers' qualifications); 3 Feb. 1859 and 20 June 1861 (on the creation of advanced classes); 10 Mar. 1853 (on separate female departments); and AO, RG2, G4, "Rules for ... common schools in ... Kingston," 1863. The legislation allowing higher common and union schools can be found in *DHE* 7: 189, and 9: 39–40.

57 See, for example, Carl F. Kaestle and Maris A. Vinovskis, *Education and Social Change in Nineteenth-Century Massachusetts* (Cambridge: Cambridge University Press 1980), esp. chap. 4; Patrick Harrigan, *Mobility, Elites, and Education in French Society of the Second Empire* (Waterloo: Wilfrid Laurier University Press 1980), esp. chap. 1.

58 Davey, "Trends in Female School Attendance in Mid-Nineteenth-Century Ontario," 246. See also Ian E. Davey, "School Reform and School Attendance: The Hamilton Central School, 1853–1861," in *Education and Social Change: Themes from Ontario's Past*, ed. Michael B. Katz and Paul H. Mattingly (New York: New York University Press 1975), 294–314; a preliminary analysis of the London Central School in 1870 carried out by Michael Murphy confirms Davey's conclusions: "The Union/Central School and London Education: A Socioeconomic Profile, 1870," unpublished paper, The University of Western Ontario.

59 C6C, W.H. Coombs to Ryerson, Gananoque, 4 June 1859. Similarly see C6C, D.J. Moffatt to Ryerson, Kingston, 14 Sept. 1861.

60 See appendix A.

61 *Leader*, 23 July 1862.

62 Ibid., 14 May 1866.

63 Ibid., 31 July 1862..

64 For a different interpretation see Houston and Prentice, *Schooling and Scholars*, 230–1. Houston and Prentice may well be right that on this score Toronto was different from the places with a central school.

65 *Globe*, 20 July 1852.

66 AO, A.N. Buell Papers, Augusta Miller to Mrs. A.N. Buell, Toronto, 11 Mar. 1877.

67 *Globe*, 28 May 1864. See also letters to the editor, *Leader*, 19 Sept. 1863 and *Globe*, 31 May 1864.

68 See *Globe*, 28 May 1864.

69 C6C, James Morris to J.G. Hodgins, 4 Nov. 1859; *Globe*, 6 May 1859 and 18 Sept. 1865; *Canadian Baptist*, 26 Apr. 1860; C6C, Col. Charles Clarke Papers, A.A. Riddell to Clarke, 15 Mar. 1868.

70 *Globe*, 17 June 1865.

71 *Church Chronicle* (Sept. 1865), 90.

72 *Globe*, 31 May 1864.

73 *Leader*, 19 Sept. 1863; *Christian Guardian*, 14 Nov. 1855. See also *Church Chronicle* (Aug. 1865), 80.

74 The Wesleyan Female College was founded in Dundas in 1858; Bishop Strachan School in Toronto in 1867, among other Anglican schools; the Baptist Canadian Literary Institute at Woodstock, founded in 1857, was defended in the *Christian Messenger*, 23 Oct. 1856, and *JEdUC* 10, 7 (July 1857).

75 For boys, see Purdy, "English Public School Tradition"; for the later nineteenth century generally, see Christopher Podmore, "Private Schooling in English Canada" (Ph.D. diss., McMaster University 1976), 206–9, and Carolyn Gossage, *A Question of Privilege: Canada's Independent Schools* (Toronto: Peter Martin Associates 1977), 59–66.

76 Discounting commercial colleges and convent schools, the figures are: in 1846, 23 schools; 1862, 30; 1877, 14; 1881, 25; 1891, 28; 1896, 29.

CHAPTER FIVE

1 See E.A. Cruikshank, ed., *The Correspondence of Lieutenant-Governor John Graves Simcoe* ... (Toronto: Ontario Historical Society, 1923–6), I: 178–9, and IV: 135, 318–19; E.A. Cruikshank and A.F. Hunter, eds., *The Correspondence of the Hon. Peter Russell* ... (Toronto: Ontario Historical Society, 1932–6), II: 98.

2 For the address and reply, see *Russell Correspondence*, I: 224–5.

3 The report, with appendices, is printed in ibid., III: 2–15.

4 PRO, CO42/325, Portland to Hunter, no. 6, 13 Mar. 1800.

5 Lillian F. Gates, *Land Policies of Upper Canada* (Toronto: University of Toronto Press 1968), 277.

6 The act is printed in *DHE* 1: 60–1.

7 See *DHE* 1: 156.

8 For the only intelligible account of the opposition, see G.H. Patterson, "Studies in Elections and Public Opinion in Upper Canada" (Ph.D. diss., University of Toronto 1969), 309–15.

9 This is our reading of the following petitions: *JLA*, 18 Feb. 1808: Memorial ... London District School; 2 and 11 Feb. 1812: Petitions of the Midland District.

10 *JLA*, 11 Feb. 1812: Petition of the Newcastle District. Similarly see NA, MG24, B7, Charles Jones Papers, "To the Freeholders and Electors of the Province of Upper Canada."

11 *Kingston Gazette*, 12 Feb. 1811.

12 This, we suggest, explains the amended bill proposed by a conservative like Mahlon Burwell in 1814 and passed by the assembly that year.

13 See *JLA*, 18 Feb. 1811 and 26 Feb. 1812.

14 On Strachan and his educational ideas, see G.M. Craig, "John Strachan," *Dictionary of Canadian Biography* IX; J.D. Purdy, "John Strachan and Education in Canada, 1800–1850" (Ph.D. diss., University of Toronto 1962); J.L.H. Henderson, *John Strachan, 1778–1867* (Toronto: University of Toronto Press 1969).

15 59 Geo III, cap. 4. See *DHE* 1: 148–9.

16 Compare *DHE* 1: 156 (his comments in 1819) and AO, RG2, B1, vol. 1, Minutes of the General Board of Education, 56. See also AO, John Strachan Papers, Journal of a Tour through Upper Canada ... 1828; AO, Macaulay Papers, John Strachan to Macaulay, 4 Dec. 1828.

17 John Strachan, *A Letter ... on the Management of Grammar Schools* (Toronto 1829).

18 The standard account of the period remains G.M. Craig, *Upper Canada: The Formative Years* (Toronto: McClelland and Stewart 1963), chaps. 10–13.

19 PRO, CO42/388, Colborne to Hay (Private), 31 Mar. 1829.

20 University of Toronto Archives, King's College Council Minutes, 13 Dec. 1828.

21 See *DHE* 1: 286–7.

22 For a description and photograph see J.G. Hodgins, *The Establishment of Schools and Colleges in Ontario, 1792–1910* (Toronto 1910), II: 188–94.

23 See *DHE* 2: 128–9.

24 For the endowment see PRO, CO43/43, Murray to Colborne, no. 75, 25 June 1830; and *DHE* 2: 129–31. For the annual appropriation see PRO, CO43/43, Goderich to Colborne, no. 1, 20 Dec. 1830 and the annual references in PRO, CO47, Upper Canada Blue Books, 1830–34.

25 See *DHE* 3: 28–31.

26 The sources for this and the preceding sentences in the paragraph are to be found in the records of the "Upper Canada Sundries" (NA, RG5, A1) and NA, RG5, B11. Together these files contain most of the surviving records of the district schools to 1840 – which is not a lot. For typical examples of the problems see RG5, A1, vol. 44, James Mitchell to Hillier, 16 Sept. 1819; vol. 51, Jos. Ryerson to Hillier, 9 Jan. 1821; RG5, B11, vol. 3, Petition of Town of Sandwich, 21 Nov. 1827; vol. 4, item 341, no. 1, McLean to McMahon, 2 Sept. 1831.

27 The number of pupils in the various schools and also details of the curriculum and fees can be found in the successive district school reports printed as appendices to the *JLA* for 1828–36 and 1839. A fourteenth grammar school existed at Peterborough but was financed by imperial revenues and hence did not report to the legislature. See also the *Herald*, 24 Jan. 1837; *Patriot*, 8 Sept. and 30 Oct. 1835, 29 Apr. 1836, 25 Jan. 1839; *The Church*, 20 Oct. 1838. Salaries and fees are listed in PRO, CO47/155, *Upper Canada Blue Book for 1839*. For assistants see *Herald*, 24 Jan. 1837 (Brockville); *Niagara Herald*, 11 Sept. 1828 (Niagara); *Chronicle*, 20 Nov. 1839 (Kingston); *Patriot*, 8 Sept. 1835 (Toronto).

28 As of 1841 the revenue was £861.1.11. See PRO, CO42/471, Mr Macaulay's Report: Statistics of Upper Canada, 1841.

29 2 Vict. cap. 10, An Act to Provide for the Advancement of Education in this Province.

30 The regulations are printed in *JLC*, 1841, appendix no. 12. See also *DHE* 3: 307–8.

31 See NA, RG5, C1, vol. 70, no. 1567, Petition of Sundry Inhabitants of Niagara, Aug. 1841; *The Church*, 4 Sept. 1841; *JLC*, 1 and 16 Sept. 1841; *JLA*, 6 Sept. 1841 [Petitions from various Presbyterian clergy and laymen]. For Morris' part see especially *Christian Guardian*, 8 Sept. 1841, and *JLC*, 3 Sept. 1841.

32 4 and 5 Vict., cap. 19. See *DHE* 4: 55–6.

33 *AR* for 1854, 6–7. The term "senior" was officially introduced in the act of 1853, but for convenience and clarity we will also use it for the grammar schools located in the district or county capitals in the period before that.

34 The actual amounts are reported annually in the various appendices to the *JLA* beginning in 1846 and labelled "Statement of monies arising from the

sale of School lands ... " For the 1848–49 increase see NA, RG5, CI, vol. 261, no. 1010, Inspector General to Jas. Leslie, 26 Apr. 1849.

35 *DHE* 7: 23.

36 See above, chap. 4, 62.

37 See for example NA, RG5, CI, vol. 125, no. 7336, Petition of Householders of Martintown.

38 *Globe*, 15 Nov. 1851.

39 See for example NA, RG5, CI, vol. 104, no. 5301, Warden, Ottawa District to Harrison, 18 Feb. 1843; vol. 113, no. 6274, Report of a Committee of Executive Council, 17 Aug. 1845; vol. 120, no. 6857, H.I. Grassett to Civil Secretary, 16 Dec. 1843; NA, RGI, EI, State Book C, 414, 5 June 1844 (approving a series of recommendations from various district councils).

40 For the acts of 1846 and 1851, see *DHE* 6: 58, and 9: 250. For evidence of local requests for these changes see University of Toronto Archives, Office of the Chief Accountant, Financial Records, vol. 257, Grammar School Records 1838–42, Henry Boys to John Verner, Toronto, 3 June 1841; *JLA*, 13 Apr. 1846, 17 June, and 3 July 1851.

41 GIA, 1867, 776. Similarly see Ormiston's comment in GIA, 1861, 36.

42 The figures and calculations in this paragraph are drawn from the relevant statistical tables for the grammar schools in the *ARs*.

43 See for example NA, RG5, CI, vol. 305 (1850), no. 1718, Grammar School Trustees, Middlesex, to PSO; vol. 314, no. 56, Chairman, Board of Grammar School Trustees, United Cos. of Huron, Perth and Bruce, 28 Feb. 1851.

44 NA, RG5, CI, vol. 273, no. 1829, H.J. Grassett to Provincial Secretary, Toronto, 10 Dec. 1849, and extract of a Report of a Committee of the Executive Council, 14 Dec. 1849.

45 AO, Merritt Papers, package 28, Education, Wm. Hubbard to Merritt, St Catharines, 12 Feb. 1853.

46 See NA, RG5, CI, vol. 183, no. 13973, Memo on Trustees, Johnston District [1846]. See also vol. 271, no. 1631, Wm. Craigie to J. Leslie, Hamilton, 23 July 1849; vol. 272, no. 1736, J. Morris to E.A. Meredith, Brockville, 7 Aug. 1849; vol. 193, no. 15455, Francis Evans to D. Daly, Woodhouse, 26 June 1846 and vol. 199, no. 16321, same to same, 10 Mar. 1847.

47 See for example NA, RG5, CI, vol. 120, no. 6843, H. Patton to Daly, Kemptville, 11 Dec. 1843; vol. 182, no. 13859, S. Givens to Daly, Napanee, 15 May 1846; vol. 242, no. 981, Niagara Grammar School Trustees Materials; vol. 341, no. 1761, Grammar School Trustees, Lennox and Addington Materials; AO, A.N. Buell Papers, Resolutions enclosed in Wm. Grant to Buell, 2 Feb. 1852.

48 On the Provincial Secretary's Office generally see J.E. Hodgetts, *Pioneer Public Service* (Toronto: University of Toronto Press 1955), 87.

49 For examples see AO, RGI, EI, State Books, vol. J, 345, 29 Aug. 1849; NA, RG5, CI, vol. 340, no. 1714, Memorial of Trustees, Kemptville grammar

school, 30 Sept. 1851, and related materials; vol. 365, no. 1615, Extract from a Report of a Committee of the Executive Council, 7 Mar. 1853.

50 AO, RG2, GIC, Provincial Secretary to Ryerson, Quebec, 14 May 1853.

51 See AO, John Strachan Letterbook, 1839–43, John Strachan to Rev. Robert Campbell, Toronto, 22 Oct. 1840; NA, RG5, CI, vol. 45, no. 2551, Rev. Arthur Palmer to Harrison, Guelph, 28 Nov. 1840; vol. 87, no. 3362, Thos. Jones to Harrison, Goderich, 24 Mar. 1842.

52 NA, RG5, CI, vol. 45, no. 2551, Harrison to Rev. A. Palmer, Toronto, 13 Nov. 1840; vol. 87, no. 3362, Harrison to Thos. Jones, 28 Apr. 1842.

53 For an example of the assumption at work see NA, RG5, CI, vol. 37, no. 1822, Memorial of ... Inhabitants of Woodstock, Mar. 1840.

54 See for example NA, RG5, CI, vol. 70, no. 1567, Petition of sundry Inhabitants of Town of Niagara, Aug. 1841; *The Church*, 4 Sept. 1841.

55 NA, RG5, CI, vol. 114, no. 6343, Provincial Secretary to Jas. Fraser, 16 Feb. 1844.

56 See ibid., no. 6343, Francis Evans to Civil Secretary, Woodhouse, 11 Nov. 1843; vol. 116, no. 6530, Memorial of Wm. Craigie, Ancaster, 28 Sept. 1843. For some examples of the reworked boards see NA, RG5, CI, vol. 136, no. 8573, correspondence relating to Ancaster Grammar School; vol. 127, no. 7566, A. Fraser to Hopkirk, 24 July 1843.

57 NA, RG5, CI, vol. 233, no. 494, J.S. Macdonald to R.B. Sullivan, Cornwall, 17 June 1848.

58 MTRL, Baldwin Papers, A49–9, James Hall to Baldwin, Peterborough, 5 June 1848.

59 *DHE* 7: 10.

60 For the numbers in 1855 see GIA (Ormiston), 1855, 72.

61 Because we were directly involved in the appeal to the Supreme Court of Canada in 1987 over the extension of funding to Roman Catholic secondary schools, we thought it would be inappropriate to pursue the issue further in this volume. But it is perhaps worth noting in any case that both sides agreed that the central historical issues focused on the meaning of the common and separate school legislation and the extent of the common and separate school curriculum before 1867. The grammar school legislation unequivocally made no provision for any form of denominational grammar school. Our own views on the larger questions are set out at length in "Affidavit of Robert Douglas Gidney," in the Supreme Court of Canada: In the matter of a reference to the Court of Appeal ... Affidavit submitted as part of the evidence of the appellants against Bill 30, January 1987.

62 The bill is printed in *DHE* 7: 9–12.

63 The bill is printed in *DHE* 9: 21–3. For the opposition, see *Globe*, 18 July 1850. That it was drafted by Ryerson, see CI, Ryerson to Grammar School Trustees, Matilda, 10 Feb. 1852.

64 16 and 17 Vict., cap. 86. Printed in *DHE* 10: 140–5.

65 See NA, RG5, CI, 1854, no. 1322, Inspector-General to Ryerson. Apparently it was only in 1854 that the new schools in county towns began to receive the bounty.

66 According to Ryerson, the government deleted the taxation clauses because they "thought it couldn't be carried in the Legislative Assembly." See CI, Ryerson to Neil Dunbar, 30 Aug. 1852; Ryerson to Rev. Wm. Clarke, 9 Feb. 1854; Ryerson to Thos. Cross, 9 Feb. 1854.

67 CI, Ryerson to Hon. P.J.O. Chauveau, 5 June 1854.

68 See CPI Minutes, *DHE* 11: 168–9 (7 July 1854), and *DHE* 11: 198–9, Circular to Chairmen of Boards of Trustees for each County Grammar School, 10 July 1854.

69 See NA, RG5, CI, 1855, no. 15 [Re Rules and Regulations for Grammar Schools]. The Regulations are printed in *DHE* 11: 188–93. There was a *contretemps* between the executive council and the Council of Public Instruction over the rules for religious observance in the schools but this did not affect the rest of the regulations. See ibid., 194–6.

70 *DHE* 11: 202.

71 See *DHE* 11: 128–9, 202–3; CI, Hodgins to Robertson and Ormiston, 20 Aug. 1855; UCA, Ryerson Papers, Hodgins to Ryerson, 3 Nov. 1855.

72 On Hodgins' reaction to the first trustees' returns, see UCA, Ryerson Papers, Hodgins to Ryerson, 14 July 1855; for the superficial nature of the first inspection, see for example GIA, 1855, 92.

73 See for example GIA, 1856, 2.

74 C6C, Macdonald to Ryerson, 28 May 1855 (telegraph), and AO, Hodgins Collection, J.A. Macdonald to Ryerson, Quebec, 5 June 1855. The details of the clause followed the proposal in CI, Ryerson to Rev. Wm. Clarke, 9 Feb. 1854.

75 See UCA, Ryerson Papers, Hodgins to Ryerson, 2 Sept. 1857.

76 CI, Ryerson to E.C. Campbell, 13 Jan. 1858.

77 NA, RG5, CI, 1857, no. 570, Ryerson to Provincial Secretary's Office, 30 Mar. 1857; see also 1858, no. 324, 11 Feb. 1858, same to same.

78 GIA, 1855 (Ormiston), 24.

79 C6C, D.Y. Leslie to Ryerson, 10 Sept. 1862. For other examples see Thos. Cross to Ryerson, Chatham, 25 Jan. 1855; NA, RG5, CI, 1850, vol. 309, no. 1739 (filed with no. 1972), Report of T. Creen for Trustees, Haldimand and Welland Counties; vol. 340, no. 1753, Arthur Ackland to Leslie, Goderich, 5 Jan. 1852.

80 The financial tables in the *ARs* are useful in indicating which municipalities gave grants, though they do not clearly indicate whether it is the county or particular town that is making the contribution. The best sources are the surviving county records in a variety of archives. The Elgin County Council

Minutes papers are an especially full record relating to educational affairs, though Elgin was atypically active and generous. These records are at UWORC.

81 UCA, Perkins Bull Collection, Education Boxes 4–6, Minutes of Chingua-cousy Township, 13 Mar. 1855.

82 c6c, James Keith to Ryerson, 5 Aug. 1854. Similarly see Benj. Cronyn to Ryerson, London, 21 Aug. 1854; Geo. Salter to Ryerson, Mosa Township, 8 Feb. 1855; *Globe*, 17 Dec. 1856. Councils could, of course, change their minds from year to year, which some did, Brant included, and others did not.

83 See CI, Ryerson to H. Craigie, 31 Jan. 1855, and *Globe*, 11 July 1863.

84 c6c, W.L. Billings to Ryerson, Hamilton, 27 Mar. 1858.

85 *Perth Courier*, 27 Mar. 1863.

86 c6c, no. 7309, Robert Francis to Ryerson, Trenton, 24 Nov. 1866.

87 GIA, 1860 (Ormiston), 21.

88 Ibid., 1855 (Ormiston), 25. Similarly see ibid., 1863 (Checkley), 35.

89 Ibid., 1855 (Robertson), 9–13; 1856 (Ormiston), 28; and 1861 (Ormiston), 23.

90 For examples see ibid., 1858 (Ormiston), 80; 1859 (Cockburn), 29; 1862 (Checkley), 15.

91 See ibid., 1855, 58; 1861, 18; 1864, 480–2.

92 See ibid., 1855, 43.

93 c6c, E.H. Dewar to Ryerson, 11 July 1855.

94 c6c, W.H. Wilbur to Ryerson, Drummondville, 31 Dec. 1861.

95 For inspectors' evaluations see GIA, 1861 (Ambery), 30; 1864 (Young), 487. See also J.C. Sutherland, "At Dr Tassie's," *Canadian Magazine* (Feb. 1924), 261–5; W.G. Wallace, "A Tassie Boy," *Ontario History* 46, 3 (Summer 1954): 169–78.

96 See AO, RG2, G4, envelope 1, Barrie Grammar School 1861 [pamphlet].

97 GIA, 1860 (Ambery), 1–3.

98 J.D. Moodie to Wm. Hutton, 20 Mar. 1848, enclosed in NA, RG5, CI, vol. 245, no. 155 [1850], Thurlow Grammar School Materials.

99 Ibid.

100 See NA, RG5, CI, no. 10748, Demorestville Grammar School Materials, and no. 11879, draft letter to W. Rorke; vol. 282, no. 112 [1850], Gore District, Palermo Grammar School Materials. Demorestville not only survived but was the subject of the same complaint in the late 1850s; see GIA, 1857, 45–7.

101 See for example NA, RG5, CI, vol. 104, no. 5380, Common School Commissioners, Matilda Township to Harrison, 12 Jan. 1843, and c6c, same to Murray, 5 Jan. 1843; NA, RG5, CI, vol. 125, no. 7336, Petition of House-holders of Martintown; no. 11490, Copy of a Report of a Committee of the Executive Council, 3 Oct. 1845; c6c, S. Nelles to Ryerson, Newburgh,

1 Mar. 1847; MTRL, Baldwin Papers, A32–65, J.B. Aylsworth to Baldwin, Newburgh, 17 May 1843.

102 It was also conceded by local people as well. See the comment about nominal Latin enrolments throughout the early 1860s in Hamilton in *DHE* 22: 52.

103 GIA, 1865 (Young), 47.

104 C6C, [illeg.] [Reeve of Port Burwell] to Ryerson, Port Burwell, 8 Jan. 1855.

105 C6C, W.F. Hubbard to Ryerson, 11 Aug. 1855. See also the comment by T.J. Robertson which assumes implicitly that there are "non-grammar school" pupils routinely attending the grammar schools, in *AR* for 1855, 290.

106 Susan E. Houston and Alison Prentice, *Schooling and Scholars in Nineteenth-Century Ontario* (Toronto: University of Toronto Press 1988), 154–5. Similarly, see Bruce Curtis, "Policing Pedagological Space: 'Voluntary' School Reform and Moral Regulation," *Canadian Journal of Sociology* 13, no. 3 (summer 1988): 295.

107 MTRL, R. Baldwin Papers, A64-17, I. Powell to Baldwin, Port Dover, 2 Dec. 1848.

108 Ibid., A32-64, Trustees, Whitby grammar school, to Baldwin, Whitby, 23 June 1850.

109 See above, 101.

110 R.D. Gidney and D.A. Lawr, "Bureaucracy vs. Community? The Origins of Bureaucratic Procedure in the Upper Canadian School System," in *Historical Essays in Upper Canada: New Perspectives*, ed. J.K. Johnson and Bruce W. Wilson (Ottawa: Carleton University Press 1989), 393–4.

111 Michael B. Katz, "The Moral Crisis of the University ... ," in *Universities in Crisis: A Medieval Institution in the Twenty-First Century*, ed. William A.W. Neilson and Chad Gaffield (Montreal: Institute for Research in Public Policy 1986), 16.

112 For the early years see for example MTRL, G.O. Stuart, Account book of York District Grammar School, 1807–10; NA, RG5, A1, vol. 65, Report of Trustees, Gore District School, 31 Jan. 1824; AO, John Strachan Papers, Journal of a Tour Through Upper Canada ... 1828, entry on Sandwich. See also NA, RG5, C1, vol. 133, no. 8132, Trustees, Gore District Grammar School, Report, 2 Aug. 1844; *JEdUC* 3, 1 (Jan. 1850): 9–10.

113 *DHE* 12: 79 and 85.

114 These figures are based on our tally of the number of schools listed as enrolling girls in GIA, vol. 4, 1866, and vol. 5, 1870: Reports filed by inspectors Young and Mackenzie.

115 Young and Mackenzie provided figures for the number of boys and girls on the roll of each school in their reports for 1866 and 1870.

116 For some of the evidence on this point see C6C, Otto Klotz to Ryerson, Preston, 2 Aug. 1852; *AR* for 1855, 285 (Brockville); *Perth Courier*, 2 Oct. 1857; GIA, 1868 (Young), 790–1 (Guelph); 906 (Oshawa); 808 (Kingston).

117 See for example C6C, no. 5892, Rev. James Middlemass to Ryerson, 9 Mar.

1866; *Globe*, 14 Nov. 1853 and 6 May 1859; *AR* for 1852, Galt Board of School Trustees, 136.

118 AO, Col. Charles Clarke Papers, A.A. Riddell to Clarke, Toronto, 15 Mar. 1868.

119 *Canadian Baptist*, 26 Apr. 1860. Similarly see *Globe*, 6 May 1859, 18 Sept. 1863, and 28 and 31 May 1864; *Leader*, 7 and 8 June 1864; C6C, Geo. Stewart to Ryerson, 16 Apr. 1863; *DHE* 20: 252–3.

120 Quoted in *JEdUC* 23 (Oct. 1870): 156–7.

121 See for example the fate of the proposals to fund a girls' high school in Toronto, in Toronto Board of School Trustees Minutes, 4 May, 8 and 29 June 1864; *Globe*, 30 June 1864, 11 July 1865.

122 See R.D. Anderson, *Education and Opportunity in Victorian Scotland* (Oxford: Clarendon Press 1983), 135; Lindy Moore, "Invisible Scholars: Girls Learning Latin and Mathematics in the Elementary Public Schools of Scotland before 1872," *History of Education* 13, 2 (1984): 121–37.

123 CI, Ryerson to Rev. H.B. Scopp? [illeg.], Chairman, Board of Grammar School Trustees, Vienna, 3 Mar. 1855.

124 For a pertinent comment see *Globe*, 23 Sept. 1863, letter from "Justicia," Port Hope.

125 The incorporated urban areas can be identified by comparing the undifferentiated list of grammar schools in the *ARs* with the list of geographical places for the common schools, which is broken down into villages, towns, and cities. The unincorporated places are those that appear neither on the common school list nor in the census of 1861.

126 See for example *AR* for 1857, 211; GIA, 1857 (Robertson), 69; *Perth Courier*, 20 Nov. 1857; *Annual Report of the Local Superintendent of Public Schools, Toronto, for 1863*, 38.

127 See *Brantford Expositor*, 4 Jan. 1867; *DHE* 22: 52; *Perth Courier*, 11 Dec. 1863, 15 Jan. and 26 Feb. 1864.

128 *DHE* 13: 75.

129 Our calculation from the *AR* for 1861 is that the average income from all sources for non-union schools in towns and villages was $1237.95 and for union schools, $846.34.

130 See *Globe*, 2 Oct. 1854, 21 Dec. 1863, and 8 Feb. 1864.

131 See C6C, James Coyne to Ryerson, St Thomas, 6 Feb. 1850; GIA, 1865, 47.

132 See for example GIA, 1859 (Ormiston), 8; *DHE* 19: 127; *AR* for 1859, GSIR (Cockburn), 160–1.

133 *AR* for 1850, 197.

134 AO, RG2, F3E, Belleville Board of School Trustees Minutes, 28 Feb. 1854.

135 *AR* for 1865, part III, 59.

136 *Stratford Beacon*, 16 Sept. 1859.

137 GIA, 1863 (Checkley), 24.

138 Ibid., 1857 (Ormiston), 24. For other examples see ibid., 1855 (Robertson), 38; 1859 (Cockburn), 29 and 41.

139 UWORC, Elgin County Council, Correspondence and documents filed by the Elgin County Clerk, Report of the Chairman of the Board of Trustees, St Thomas County Grammar School, 23 Jan. 1866, par. 7.

140 C6C, James Nisbet to Ryerson (Oakville), 6 Feb. 1860. For other examples see *Bathurst Courier*, 26 Jan. 1849; *AR* for 1864, 67.

141 C6C, Geo. Cox to Ryerson, London, 13 Jan. 1859.

CHAPTER SIX

1 GIA, 1857 (Ormiston), 4 (Toronto).

2 Ibid., 1864, 574–5 (Welland).

3 *JEdUC* 10 (Feb. 1857): 19–20.

4 GIA, 1855 (Ormiston), 63.

5 Ibid., 36–7.

6 Ibid., 1856 (Robertson), 44.

7 Ibid., 1859 (Ormiston), 30; 1861 (Ambery), 49–50. Ormiston in 1860 reported that fifteen of the twenty union schools in the western half of the province were housed in "large, recently erected, airy and well arranged buildings"; *AR* for 1860, GSIR, 198.

8 GSIR, 1861 (Ormiston), in *DHE* 17: 13–14.

9 See for example GIA, 1860 (Ormiston), 5; 1861, 44.

10 See comments in GSIR, 1861 (Ormiston), in *DHE* 17: 13–14, and in Young's report for 1864 in ibid., 18: 203.

11 UWORC, Correspondence and Files of the Elgin County Clerk, Report of the Grammar School Trustees, Elgin County, 26 Jan. 1864.

12 GIA, 1855 (Robertson), 63 (Bath).

13 Ibid., 1855 (Ormiston), 5–6 (Toronto).

14 GIA, 1861 (Ormiston), 13 (Brockville).

15 Ibid., 1855 (Robertson), 54 (Perth).

16 *AR* for 1865, statistical tables.

17 GSIR, 1862 (Ormiston), *DHE* 17: 230.

18 GSIR, 1858 (Ormiston), *DHE* 14: 94.

19 GSIR, 1860 (Ormiston), in *DHE* 16: 145.

20 UCA, G.H. Kenney Papers, Reminiscences [manuscript], 19–20.

21 GSIR, 1860 (Cockburn), *DHE* 16: 146–7. See also GSIR, 1861 (Ormiston), *DHE* 17: 15.

22 See for example GIA, 1859 (Ormiston), 43 (Vienna).

23 AO, Benson Family Papers, Subject Files, Schools: C.R. Luscombe to Benson, 15 June 1855.

24 GIA, 1856 (Robertson), 29, and 1863 (Checkley), 183. See also ibid., 1862 (Ormiston), 7 (Weston); 14 (Collingwood).

25 Ibid., 1859 (Cockburn), 23 (Ashton).
26 Ibid., 1859 (Ormiston), 10 (Barrie). This pattern of turning public schools into private ventures continued well into the next decade; see for example the comments on Milton school in 1873: it "seems to be simply a small private boarding and day school at which high fees are charged"; G2A, vol. 1, 1873, 420.
27 GIA, 1862 (Checkley), 36–7.
28 Calculated from the relevant tables in *AR* for 1861. Little was different by 1865: 71 per cent of schools had only one teacher, the pupil/teacher ratio was identical, and the size of the average enrolment was virtually the same: see relevant tables in *AR* for 1865.
29 The program of studies is printed in *DHE* 11: 201.
30 AO, RG2, G4, envelope 2, *Report of the Public Schools in the City of Hamilton, 1861*, 14.
31 For an example of such organization see ibid., 4; see also the comments on Rev. Mulholland, headmaster in Simcoe grammar school: GIA, 1864 (Young), 466–9; *Norfolk Reformer*, 8 June 1865.
32 *Perth Courier*, 15 July 1851. See also *Report of the Public Schools in the City of Hamilton, 1861*, 4; *Synopsis, Timetable, and Course of Instruction in Brantford Public Schools* (Brantford 1857).
33 *Regulations, Programme and Course of Instruction in the Oakville Grammar School* (Oakville 1857).
34 GIA, 1861 (Ambery), 99–100.
35 C6C, [illeg.] (Reeve of Port Burwell and Chairman, Board of Education) to Ryerson, Port Burwell, 8 Jan. 1855; GIA, 1866 (Young), 472 and 483; ibid., 1865 (Young), 47 (Paris).
36 C6C, Geo. Blair to Ryerson, Bowmanville, 12 Jan. 1864. See also C6C, John King to Ryerson, Peterborough, 12 Dec. 1864; GIA, vol. 5 (McKenzie), Port Hope, Oct. 1868, 28.
37 Ibid., 1865 (Young), 36.
38 *AR* for 1861, 210.
39 QUA, Queen's University Letters, School Business Report, 31 Dec. 1854.
40 C6C, Timetable [Cornwall Grammar School], enclosed in W.H. Davies to Ryerson, Cornwall, 31 Jan. 1861.
41 GIA, 1865 (Young), 90–2.
42 Ibid., 1855 (Robertson), 95–6 (Cobourg); GSIR, 1858 (Ormiston), *DHE* 14: 93.
43 GIA, 1855 (Robertson), 51–2 (Perth); 108 (Bowmanville); 95–6 (Cobourg); 11 (Kingston).
44 *Perth Courier*, 8 May 1863.
45 UWORC, Elgin County Correspondence and Documents filed by the Elgin County Clerk, Report of the Chairman of the Board of Grammar School Trustees, St Thomas, 24 Jan. 1865.

46 *AR* for 1859, 162–3.

47 GIA, 1865 (Young), 39–42.

48 These registers are located at AO, RG2, GIB. See appendix B for an explanation of sources and methodology.

49 Aggregate education statistics for 1861 are from the relevant tables in the *AR* for 1861.

50 The figures are from the published census for 1861.

51 Calculated from *AR* for 1861, table G. This fact helps to justify our selection of urban grammar schools rather than those in unincorporated places; a fortunate circumstance, given the difficulty of record linkage where no manageable boundaries to the school's geographical catchment area exist. See also appendix B.

52 This population excludes families whose only "children" were teenagers with different surnames as well as an occupational designation, on the assumption (admittedly arbitrary) that these children were employed non-relatives and therefore unlikely candidates for grammar school. We chose the age limits after a preliminary examination of the registers and linkage with the census, and they have proven reasonably accurate – in 1861, only 1 per cent of 196 students linked from these registers were younger than ten and 1.5 per cent were over twenty. Out of the total 578 students linked to 1861 from all the registers, 8.7 per cent entered grammar school under ten and 2.9 per cent after twenty years of age. The youthful entries occurred mainly in the 1850s; by the 1860s, the ages of grammar school students tended to fall within our age limits.

53 The "non-school" household heads were considerably younger than other heads and form a distinct subgroup. Many of them had young families with presumably unrelated teenage boarders or servants who were not identified as employed (that is, with an occupation) on the census.

54 Calculated from the 1861 manuscript census.

55 Analysing the patterns of over- and underrepresentation by religion or birth-place separately gives less revealing results than combining the two factors, as we have done here.

56 Only Irish Roman Catholics were, in the longitudinal analysis, still underrepresented (by some 10 per cent).

57 We would like to acknowledge the assistance of Fred Ellett on the question of preference-rankings: that is, the probability that those at a given level of wealth would choose the grammar school over other alternatives. Examining the preferences which school-users exhibited for a particular kind of school allows us to compare the choices made at each level of wealth rather than only for the resultant distributions within each group of school users. We return to the question of probability in endnote 63 below.

58 See appendix C for a detailed explanation of the categories employed.

59 C6C, Marianne Fuller to Ryerson, 26 Aug. 1861.

60 Few women are listed on the assessment rolls, but several gave figures for "capital invested" in the census; most female household heads in Simcoe were well below the median rank of economic standing.

61 Over the entire period of thirteen years, by comparison, the proportion of very wealthy families decreased in almost every occupational category, and the percentage of those in the middling or poorer ranks increased; but the same relative standings of occupations in terms of school use were maintained. In particular, merchants remained much more wealthy than other users, and professionals fell more into the middling economic sector.

62 See above, chap. 2, 25–6.

63 The following paragraphs analyse the resultant distribution of families within the two school-using groups – that is, the interplay of occupation, wealth, and family size after the choice of school had been made. To ascertain that this distribution was not affected by the probability that any particular occupational or economic group would choose the grammar school, we examined the relationship between their schooling preferences and the average number of children and found the following probabilities of choosing the grammar school:

Wealthy/large families	.43 (19 out of 44 household heads)
Poor/large families	.17 (24 out of 129)
Wealthy/small families	.17 (8 out of 48)
Poor/small families	.08 (17 out of 196)

These numbers broken down into occupational categories are small, but they tend to suggest the same pattern: the effect of family size in determining the choice of the grammar school was largely independent of occupation or wealth.

64 Calculated from the manuscript census, 1861. The difference in family size does not appear to be a function of the maturity of the family. Controlling for the age of the household head, we find the relationship to hold for almost every age cohort: that is, whatever the parent's age, his or her decision to use the local grammar school as opposed to other schools appears to have depended in part at least on the number of children in the family.

65 The following paragraphs are based on an analysis of the entire cohort of grammar school users – that is, those who attended grammar school at any time between 1855 and 1867, linked to the 1861 census information on their families. These families were divided into three groups: "sibling families," or those sending more than one child to grammar school; "one-student families," or those sending one child only out of several; and "only-children families." It should be noted that our figures on the number of siblings will be on the low side because some siblings had left home by 1861 and could not be traced from registers in the 1850s to their families on the census, and because others attended before 1855 or after 1867 and therefore their names do not appear on the extant registers.

66 The percentages for students are out of *all* students, including only children (who constituted 5 per cent of the total 574 students).

67 Parents who used other schools may well have followed the same strategy: if they were going to invest in schooling at all, they did so for more than one child. However, without other school registers we have only the census information on these school attenders, and while this will show many siblings attending in 1861, equally it will miss many more who attended in other years. Ian Davey found that in the Central School in Hamilton in 1861, some 86 per cent of students were the sole students sent by their families; see Ian Davey, "School Reform and School Attendance: The Hamilton Central School, 1853–1861" (MA diss., University of Toronto 1972), 86. We suspect, however, that the numbers of siblings would rise dramatically if they were traced over the entire run of registers.

68 None are reported in the *ARs* of 1861–6.

69 Those families with only one child were eliminated from the following analysis in order to limit the comparison to students from families who had the choice of sending one or several of their children.

70 The wealth of sibling families does not appear to have affected this pattern: at every level of wealth, the percentage of children educated at the grammar school depended rather on the number of children in the family.

71 See general table 7.

72 There was substantial variation amongst our towns on this matter. In Strathroy, Sarnia, and Simcoe, the girls were considerably older than the boys. In Strathroy, indeed, the gap was enormous, the girls averaging 16 years and the boys 13. In Brantford, boys and girls had the same median age of 14 but the mean age of the girls was 14.5, while that of the boys was 13.8. However, in Stratford the girls were younger than the boys. We have no easy explanation for these differences. There are no clear patterns of girls being sent because older brothers already attended; indeed, in Stratford, more girls than boys were the eldest students in their families. By the years around 1861, some of the rural grammar schools were already being used by boys and girls to prepare for first- and second-class county teaching certificates and that might explain the 16-year-old girls at Strathroy. Whatever the explanation, in any case, boys generally tended to be younger, not older, than the girls.

73 Robert Anderson, "Education and Society in Modern Scotland: A Comparative Perspective," *History of Education Quarterly* 25, 4 (Winter 1985): 463.

74 Ian Davey, "Patterns of Inequality: School Attendance and Social Structure in the Nineteenth Century, Canada and Australia," in *Childhood, Youth and Education in the Late Nineteenth Century*, ed. John Hurt (Leicester: History of Education Society 1981), 9–10.

75 The median persistence might be greater if township students were included in this group (since most township students that we have traced, at least,

were from farmers' families and attended grammar school for long, if frequently broken, intervals of several years' duration). The median is also artificially low because it includes those at either end of the run of registers, some of whom would have attended before 1855 or after 1867 but whose complete records are missing.

76 Curiously, both boys and girls from labourers' families rated highest in taking no breaks from school. However, since both sexes also rated very low in persistence, this may be simply an artifact of the statistics, in that if labourers' children went to grammar school at all, they went for a short, concentrated period of time.

77 *AR* for 1861 (Ormiston), 209; *AR* for 1859, 160; GIA, 1862, 35 (Gananoque); 1864, 606–7 (Kincardine); 1865, 23 (Iroquois), 76 (Drummondville), 95 (Scotland).

78 See Ian E. Davey, "The Rhythm of Work and the Rhythm of School," in *Egerton Ryerson and His Times*, ed. Neil McDonald and Alf Chaiton (Toronto: Macmillan 1978), 225. For other examples of historians using a standard of 100 days per year, see Chad Gaffield, *Language, Schooling, and Cultural Conflict* (Kingston and Montreal: McGill-Queen's University Press 1987), 110; Haley P. Bamman, "Patterns of School Attendance in Toronto, 1844–1878: Some Spatial Considerations," in *Education and Social Change: Themes from Ontario's Past*, ed. Michael B. Katz and Paul H. Mattingly (New York: New York University Press 1975), 237.

79 Our reiterated caution about the effect of small numbers applies, of course, here as well.

80 Miss J. Turnbull attended Brantford grammar school from 1858 to 1860, taught at Brantford Central School, and then received an appointment to Toronto Model School; see *Brantford Expositor*, 21 July 1865. Miss Sylvia Pottinger, who attended Sarnia grammar school intermittently from 1859 to 1865, was appointed to Sarnia Collegiate Institute in 1878 and remained on its staff for at least fifteen years; see *AR* for 1893, appendix O, III.

CHAPTER SEVEN

1 *JEdUC* 5, 9 (Sept. 1852): 134. Similarly see ibid., 2, 12 (Dec. 1849): 181.
2 Ibid., 3, 5 (May 1850): 72.
3 *Christian Guardian*, 28 Apr. 1841. Similarly see *JEdUC* 3, 5 (May 1850): 72–3.
4 *DHE* 6: 142.
5 Ibid., 197.
6 Ibid., 8: 290.
7 *AR* for 1850, 21–2.
8 *DHE* 8: 289.
9 Ibid., 290.

10 *DHE* 7: 50.
11 *AR* for 1850, 22.
12 *DHE* 7: 189.
13 CI, Ryerson to Rev. Wm. Clarke, 9 Feb. 1854.
14 *AR* for 1853, 11 [italics added].
15 See *DHE* 11: 189–90 and 201.
16 CI, Ryerson to D.S. Roberts, 10 Mar. 1854.
17 *AR* for 1855, 4; CI, Ryerson to J.R. Griffin, 20 Sept. 1856.
18 See for example CI, Hodgins to John Smith, 17 Mar. 1856; Ryerson to Chairman, Board of Common School Trustees, Belleville, 18 Dec. 1857; Ryerson to J.D. Murray, 9 Feb. 1857.
19 See *JEdUC* 11 (Aug. 1858): 21; *AR* for 1857, 335–42.
20 See *AR* for 1858, 153–6.
21 AO, RG2, C2, Ryerson to J.F. Pringle, 19 Nov. 1862.
22 AO, RG2, C2, Ryerson to Wm. Davies [?], Grammar School Teacher, Newcastle, 11 Mar. 1864.
23 AO, RG2, C2, Ryerson to Chas. R. Brooke, 16 Mar. 1864; see also *Globe*, 29 July 1865.
24 Ryerson himself was born in 1803. Birth dates and biographies, including the relevant educational information, are drawn from the *Dictionary of Canadian Biography* and from W. Stewart Wallace, ed., *The Macmillan Dictionary of Canadian Biography*, 3rd ed. (London and Toronto: Macmillan 1963). For the classical emphasis at the Edinburgh High School see R.D. Anderson, *Education and Opportunity in Victorian Scotland* (Oxford: Clarendon Press 1983), 22. For additional detail on G.R.R. Cockburn, see AO, RG2, EI, box 2, folder 6, Cockburn to Ryerson, 30 Dec. 1857.
25 For this paragraph see Sheldon Rothblatt, *Tradition and Change in English Liberal Education* (London: Faber and Faber 1976), esp. chap. 17; George Elder Davie, *The Democratic Intellect: Scotland and Her Universities in the Nineteenth Century* (Edinburgh: Edinburgh University Press 1961); Frank M. Turner, *The Greek Heritage in Victorian Britain* (New Haven: Yale University Press 1981), esp. chap. 1.
26 The generalizations in this and the succeeding three paragraphs are based on our reading of the inspectors' private school-by-school reports in AO, RG2, GIA, 1855–64, and on their general reports, published annually in the *ARs* for the same years.
27 GIA, 1864, 607.
28 Quoted in *DHE* 16: 147.
29 GIA, 1857 (Robertson), 20. Similarly see ibid., 1855 (Robertson), 1; ibid., 1865 (Young), 149; ibid., 1866 (Young), 347–8.
30 Though schools did in fact close down during the period, their demise seems to have been entirely due to local circumstances and not central initiative. Moreover, while some weak schools closed, other weak schools opened de-

spite vigorous objections by Ryerson and the inspectors. See for example GIA, 1857–58 (Robertson), where closures and openings are noted and re-marked upon.

31 AO, Hodgins Collection, Ryerson to J.A. Macdonald, Quebec, 21 Mar. 1860.

32 The bill and an explanatory memo are printed in *DHE* 17: 294–305.

33 *JEdUC* 16 (Mar. 1863): 40.

34 Ibid. [Italics added.]

35 AO, RG2, C2, Ryerson to Rev. D.K. Smith, 2 Jan. 1864.

36 Ryerson and his colleagues were well aware of the rising numbers of girls in the schools – the inspectors often noted it in their private reports. But all of them were extremely circumspect in their public comments, the issue rarely being addressed directly anywhere before the middle 1860s. In his official correspondence Ryerson occasionally expressed doubt about the wisdom of sending girls to a grammar school, but he always emphasized that the appor-tionment rules made no reference to sex but only to enrolment of *pupils* in Latin. See CI, Ryerson to H.B. [illeg.] (Chairman, Board of Grammar School Trustees, Vienna), 3 Mar. 1855, and cf. Ryerson to W.A. Caldwell, 8 Feb. 1864, and Ryerson to John King, 14 Dec. 1864.

37 C.B. Sissons, *The Life and Letters of Egerton Ryerson* (Toronto: Clarke, Irwin 1947), II: 480. Generally on the progress of the bill see ibid., 476ff.

38 UCA, Ryerson Papers, Ryerson to Hodgins, 29 Apr. 1863.

39 See for example *Leader*, 21 Mar. 1863; *Belleville Intelligencer*, 3 Apr. 1863; *Globe*, 21 Apr. 1863; NA, Buchanan Papers, "Mr Tassie's Remarks on the Proposed Grammar School Act 1863."

40 NA, RG5, CI, 1863, no. 1072, Ryerson to Provincial Secretary, 18 July 1863; Hodgins in *DHE* 17: 302.

41 *Leader*, 27 Mar. 1863. See also *Globe*, 23 Mar. 1863; Canadian Library As-sociation, *Parliamentary Debates*, Legislative Assembly, 17 Mar. 1863.

42 There is a brief biography of Young in *Dictionary of Canadian Biography* XI. He was formally appointed grammar school inspector on 7 Apr. 1864: *DHE* 18: 180. For his unofficial but continuing influence on Ryerson's poli-cies, see UCA, Ryerson Papers, Ryerson to Edward Blake, 10 Feb. 1872. For the role of the Central Committee of Examiners during Adam Crooks' tenure as minister of education, see *JEdUC* 29 (Dec. 1876): 178.

43 *AR* for 1867, 35.

44 The report is to be found in *DHE* 18: 199–205.

45 NA, John A. Macdonald Papers, Ryerson to John A. Macdonald, 27 Jan. 1865.

46 Sissons, *Life and Letters of Egerton Ryerson*, II: 503.

47 Ibid., II: 504.

48 The drafts of the new regulations can be found in AO, RG2, C2, Memoran-dum, Minutes of the Council of Public Instruction, 14 Mar. 1865. See also

c6c, Wm. McDougall to Ryerson, 13 Apr. 1865, no. 3289. The official circular and regulations were printed in *JEdUC* 18 (Apr. 1865) and are reprinted in *DHE* 18: 252–61.

49 *DHE* 19: 28.

50 AO, RG2, C2, Ryerson to Rev. S. Ramsay, 11 July 1865.

51 *JEdUC* 18, 8 (Aug. 1865): 113–17.

52 *JEdUC* 18, 10 (Oct. 1865): 149–50.

53 See for example *Perth Courier*, 26 May 1865; *Sarnia Observer*, 2 June 1865; *Norfolk Messenger*, 28 Sept. 1865.

54 c6c, S.F. Ramsay to Ryerson, 4 July 1865. Similarly see ibid., Principal, Union School, Simcoe, to Ryerson, 14 June 1865; John Scoon to Ryerson, Strathroy, 30 June 1865; Peter Lindsay to Ryerson, Arnprior, 5 July 1865.

55 c6c, James Wilson to Ryerson, 10 Aug. 1865.

56 c6c, Alexander Burdon to L. Wallbridge, 13 Sept. 1865. Similarly see in the same file a clipping from *Welland Telegraph* of 7 Sept. 1865, file no. 5601.

57 *JEdUC* 18, 10 (Oct. 1865): 150 and 152.

58 AO, RG2, E1, box 1, folder 6, Hodgins to Ryerson, Quebec, 25 Aug. 1865.

59 AO, RG2, C2, Ryerson to Rev. S. Ramsay, 11 July 1865.

60 See *DHE* 19: 35, and c6c, telegraphs, Hodgins to Ryerson and Ryerson to Hodgins, 15 Sept. 1865, no. 5620.

61 AO, RG2, E1, box 1, folder 6, Hodgins to Ryerson, 25 Aug. 1865, and ibid., Hodgins to Ryerson, 29 Aug. 1865.

62 AO, RG2, C2, Ryerson to Wm. McDougall, Provincial Secretary, 31 Oct. 1865, no. 3410.

63 UCA, Ryerson Papers, Hodgins to Ryerson, Quebec, 13 Sept. 1865.

64 *JEdUC* 18, 9 (Sept. 1865): 129. See also the *Globe*'s assessment, 19 Sept. 1865.

65 The act and Ryerson's explanatory memorandum highlighting its most significant points are printed in *DHE* 19: 25–9.

66 Ryerson had actually tried to introduce an average attendance regulation in the later 1850s but it expressly contradicted the provisions of the act of 1853, which required apportionment according to a ratio of population amongst the counties.

67 Hodgins to Ryerson, 5 Sept. 1865, quoted in *DHE* 19: 33–4.

68 See *DHE* 19: 33–4; AO, RG2, E1, box 1, folder 6, Ryerson to Hodgins, 8 Sept. 1865; *AR* for 1867, GSIR, 1866, 46; and *DHE* 26: 267.

69 The key sections of the November regulations are printed in *DHE* 19: 46–9. A full set are in *AR* for 1865, part III, 79–89.

70 AO, RG2, C2, Ryerson to C.F. Farnsworth, 1 Sept. 1865.

71 *JEdUC* 18, 9 (Sept. 1865): 129.

72 This point is not specified in the regulations but was the Education Office's "interpretation" for correspondents. See AO, RG2, C2, Hodgins [?] to Rev. K. Maclennan, 4 Apr. 1866. Girls, however, could enter the classical pro-

gram at the lower standard *if they took Latin*, because only the English program explicitly excluded girls – a Trojan horse, as it turned out, of gargantuan proportions.

73 AO, RG2, C2, Ryerson to Wm. McDougall, 31 Oct. 1865.

74 AO, RG2, C2, Hodgins [?] to W.N. Hossie, 30 Oct. 1866.

75 See for example *AR* for 1865, part III, 79.

76 AO, RG2, C2, Ryerson to Rev. J. Fraser, 26 Aug. 1867.

CHAPTER EIGHT

1 *AR* for 1865, part III, GSIR, 1865, 75.

2 Young's inspectoral tours and the details of the failure rates, year by year and school by school, are recorded in AO, RG2, GIA. For a very brief published description by Young himself, see *AR* for 1865, part III, 75–6.

3 His instructions are printed in *AR* for 1865, part III, 88–9. For his school-by-school assessments, again see the files in GIA. For an example of his impact see the explanatory note on the semi-annual return in C6C, Robt. Rodgers to Ryerson, Collingwood, 31 Dec. 1865, no. 159.

4 AO, RG2, C2, Ryerson to Chairman, United Board of School Trustees, Renfrew, 1 Feb. 1866, no. 695; same to Ryerson, 8 Feb. 1866, no. 1479. Similarly see ibid., Ryerson to Chairman, Grammar School Board of Trustees, in Ottawa, 1 Feb. 1866, no. 696; Fonthill, no. 697; Cobourg, no. 742; Port Hope, no. 760.

5 AO, RG2, C2, Hodgins to Thos. Hart, 18 Aug. 1866, no. 2678; the issue is set out in C6C, Hart to Ryerson, 14 Aug. 1866, no. 5896. Similarly see AO, RG2, C2, Ryerson to H.W. Peterson, 18 Jan. 1866, no. 439.

6 AO, RG2, C2, Hodgins or Ryerson to W.H. Peterson, 9 Oct. 1866, no. 3007.

7 See *AR* for 1865, part I, 25, and *AR* for 1867, part I, 40.

8 See *AR* for 1867, part I, 40; *DHE* 22: 31.

9 *AR* for 1865, part III, 73.

10 GIA, 1866 (Young), 385. Similarly see ibid., 325.

11 C6C, W.R. Biggs, Principal, Brockville Central School, to Ryerson, 2 Sept. 1867, no. 6113.

12 GIA, 1866 (Young), 339.

13 Ibid., 378.

14 See for example AO, RG2, C2, Ryerson to Rev. Duncan Morrison, 23 Jan. 1866, no. 503.

15 AO, RG2, C2, Hodgins to J.W. Connor, 14 Jan. 1867. See also ibid., Ryerson to H.H. Hulton, 30 Jan. 1866, no. 619, and Hodgins [?] to E.C.W. McCallum, 6 Sept. 1866, no. 2782.

16 *JEdUC* 20 (May 1867): 81–2.

17 See *AR* for 1867, part I, 32–3.

18 *AR* for 1867, part i, 33.
19 *JEdUC* 21 (June 1868): 85.
20 The two reports are printed together in the *AR* for 1867, 39–66. His 1867 report, however, is dated July 1868, and reflects the events of spring and summer that year. In the following paragraphs we have paraphrased or quoted from both reports without distinguishing between them. The quotations are all from the *ARs* but more accessible versions are to be found in *DHE* 20: 98–128.
21 *AR* for 1867, part i, 30–9.
22 c6c, James Cameron to Young, 15 July 1865, no. 4809 [italics in original].
23 *Brantford Expositor*, 7 Aug. 1868.
24 *London Free Press*, 7 July 1865. For other examples see Duncan Morrison to Hodgins, Beckwith, 15 Apr. 1866; *Stratford Beacon*, 16 Nov. 1866; c6c, Charles Farnsworth to Ryerson, Kingston, 29 Aug. 1865, no. 5475; H.W. Peterson to Ryerson, Guelph, 3 Oct. 1866, no. 6460.
25 See for example *Norfolk Messenger*, 28 Sept. 1865; GIA, 1867, 701 and 712.
26 c6c, Petition to Council of Public Instruction from Trustees, Streetsville Grammar School, 21 Oct. 1858.
27 c6c, C. Underhill to Ryerson, 23 Apr. 1860.
28 *Globe*, 12 Aug. 1865. Similarly see c6c, Albert Andrews to Ryerson, Kincardine, 12 Aug. 1865; *Brantford Expositor*, 7 Aug. 1868.
29 c6c, Rev. Geo. Blair to Ryerson, Bowmanville, 12 Jan. 1864.
30 *Norfolk Messenger* (Simcoe), 28 Sept. 1865. Similarly see GIA, 1867 (Young), 701 and 712.
31 For two sharply contrasting opinions see *Globe*, 6 July 1867, and *Brantford Expositor*, 7 Aug. 1868.
32 OTA *Minutes* (Toronto 1868), 24 and 33. For other examples see *JEdUC* 21 (Aug. 1868): 123 and 126; *Brantford Expositor*, 28 Aug. 1868.
33 See *JEdUC* 21 (Aug. 1868): 126–7.
34 *DHE* 20: 240.
35 Ibid., 238.
36 Ibid., 239.
37 *JEdUC* 21 (Aug. 1868): 123. The relevant OTA motions and debates are in *JEdUC* 18 (Oct. 1865): 152; *JEdUC* 20 (Oct. 1867): 165; OTA *Minutes* (Toronto, 1868), 11.
38 See *DHE* 20: 245.
39 *Globe*, 5 Aug. 1852.
40 *JEdUC* 13 (Aug. 1860): 121. For some examples of similar views see UWORC, Records of the Huron County Council, John Hadden to County Council, Goderich, 30 June 1851; *AR* for 1852, 75 and 229; *AR* for 1858, part iii, 25; *AR* for 1861, 182; *AR* for 1864, part iii, 57–60.

41 *Leader*, 28 July 1860; *Globe*, 10 Oct. 1856.
42 For a parallel argument see R.D. Anderson, *Education and Opportunity in Victorian Scotland* (Oxford: Clarendon Press 1983), 124 and 338, and Robert Anderson, "In Search of the 'Lad of Parts': The Mythical History of Scottish Education," *History Workshop* 19 (Spring, 1985): 82–104.
43 *DHE* 21: 10.
44 *Brantford Expositor*, 28 Aug. 1868. Similarly see ibid., 7 Aug. and 27 Nov. 1868; *London Advertiser*, 9 Nov. 1868; *Globe*, 17 July, 7 Aug., and 11 Nov. 1868; *Leader*, 20 Nov. 1868.
45 For the number of petitions see *DHE* 20: 304ff. (Proceedings of the Assembly with regard to Education); for typical examples of the content of these petitions see AO, RG8, I-I-D, nos. 922 and 1001, Provincial Secretary's Correspondence 1868, Petition of Trustees, Colborne Union Grammar School and Petition of Municipal Council and Grammar School Trustees of Oshawa.
46 AO, RG8, I-I-D, no. 993, Provincial Secretary's Correspondence 1868, Petition, Board of Grammar School Trustees, Farmersville Grammar School, 12 Nov. 1868.
47 OTA *Minutes* (Toronto 1868), 16–36.
48 The resolutions are printed in ibid., 11.
49 See *DHE* 20: 303; 22: 28.
50 *Leader*, 19 Jan. 1869; *DHE* 21: 270. Generally on these matters see C.B. Sissons, *The Life and Letters of Egerton Ryerson* (Toronto: Clarke, Irwin 1947), II: 562–3; and "Egerton Ryerson," *Dictionary of Canadian Biography* XI: 792.
51 For an example see the pencilled query on the back of C6C, no. 2832, Headmaster, St Catharines Grammar School to Ryerson, 22 Mar. 1869, and compare it to Ryerson's comments in the *Globe*, 27 Nov. 1869.
52 See for example C6C, Headmaster, Manilla to Hodgins, 25 Mar. 1869; Secretary, Grammar School Board to Ryerson, Cayuga, 12 Apr. 1869; A. Mitchell to Ryerson, St Catharines, 26 Apr. 1869; James Fleming to Ryerson, Brampton, 7 Aug. 1869.
53 For two examples see AO, RG2, F3E, Belleville Board of Common School Trustees Minutes, 6 Apr. 1868 and Belleville Board of Grammar School Trustees Minutes, 8 July 1868 and 3 Aug. 1869; *Globe*, 7 Aug. 1868.
54 *DHE* 22: 54–5.
55 *DHE* 20: 253.
56 *DHE* 21: 28.

CHAPTER NINE

1 Quoted in Suzanne Zeller, *Inventing Canada* (Toronto: University of Toronto Press 1987), 147.

2 The bill of 1868 is printed in *DHE* 20: 293–5. That the 1869 bill was essentially the same, see *Globe*, 12 Nov. 1869. For the 1870 bill see *DHE* 22: 191–3.

3 All had formed part of Ryerson's abortive 1863 grammar school bill, for example.

4 *DHE* 23: 146.

5 For Ryerson's own idea of a three-tiered hierarchy, see *DHE* 22: 296.

6 *DHE* 22: 296.

7 *DHE* 21: 20–1.

8 See *DHE* 21: 52ff. and *JEdUC* 18, 8 (Aug. 1865): 113–17.

9 See *DHE* 22: 297; and AO, RG2, C2, Ryerson to H. Peterson, 4 Jan. 1872.

10 See *Oxford English Dictionary*, "College," esp. 4A to F.

11 See for example *DHE* 20: 305; 16: 6–7; *JLA*, 12 Oct. 1843; *JLAC*, 5 Apr. 1861; *Minutes of the Annual Conferences* [Methodist], 1837, 180.

12 See the discussion in UCA, Ryerson Papers, Hodgins to Ryerson, 5 Sept. 1865.

13 See the comment by Young in the *Globe*, 22 Dec. 1869.

14 AO, RG2, C2, Ryerson to E.B. Wood, Provincial Treasurer, 6 Dec. 1870.

15 *JEdUC* 22 (Sept. 1869): 141.

16 *AR* for 1868, 31.

17 See for example, *Globe*, 15 Nov. and 10 Dec. 1869; and the phraseology of the two private members' bills in *DHE* 20: 304, and 22: 6.

18 *DHE* 22: 26–8, and 129–30; AO, RG8, I-I-D, no. 922, 1868, Provincial Secretary's Correspondence, Petition of Trustees, Colborne County Grammar School, Oct. 1868; *Globe*, 15 Nov. 1869; *Leader*, 29 Dec. 1869.

19 *DHE* 22: 31.

20 *DHE* 20: 304.

21 *DHE* 22: 27–8.

22 *JEdUC* 22 (Sept. 1869): 140.

23 See for example, C6C, no. 2398, Wm. Tassie to Hodgins, 8 Mar. 1869; *Leader*, 27 Nov. 1869; *Ottawa Citizen*, 7 Dec. 1869; *Globe*, 22 Nov. 1869; *JEdUC* 22 (Sept. 1869): 140.

24 *Globe*, 22 Nov. and 1 Dec. 1869.

25 *DHE* 22: 131. Similarly see *Globe*, 22 Nov. and 1 Dec. 1869; *JEdUC* 22 (Sept. 1869): 140.

26 *DHE* 22: 131.

27 *Globe*, 1 Dec. 1869.

28 For the references see note 2 above.

29 The final version of the act is printed in *DHE* 22: 213–22.

30 *DHE* 22: 294.

31 *DHE* 23: 83.

32 *DHE* 22: 285.

33 *DHE* 24: 274.
34 The new public school program of studies is printed in *DHE* 23: 83–94.
35 *DHE* 22: 283.
36 *DHE* 24: 246.
37 *DHE* 25: 242–3.
38 *DHE* 23: 109.
39 See *DHE* 23: 108.
40 See for example ibid., and compare that to Ryerson's views only a few years earlier in, for example, AO, RG2, C2, Ryerson to H.J. MacDonell, 13 Apr. 1867.
41 See *DHE* 23: 179–80.
42 For this point see Ryerson's comments, *DHE* 24: 300, and *DHE* 25: 175.
43 *DHE* 23: 108.
44 The new high school program of studies is printed in *DHE* 23: 109–16.
45 *DHE* 15: 123–4.
46 *DHE* 24: 178–9.
47 *DHE* 25: 175. See also *DHE* 24: 300–1, and AO, RG2, C2, Hodgins to J. Battrany, 25 Jan. 1872.
48 *DHE* 24: 300–1.
49 *DHE* 23: 115.
50 For the first extended discussion of the proposal, see *DHE* 23: 172–9. For the need for additional inspectors see *DHE* 23: 265.
51 *DHE* 23: 170.
52 *JEdUC* 25 (June 1872): 85–6.
53 For a detailed account see C.B. Sissons, *The Life and Letters of Egerton Ryerson* (Toronto: Clarke, Irwin 1947), II: chaps. 15 and 16.
54 Much of the conflict during 1872 is recorded, issue by issue, in *DHE* 24.
55 All of the core documents relating to the conflict over the high school entrance examination are filed together in AO, RG8, I-I-D, Provincial Secretary's Correspondence, no. 1216, 1872. The quotation is from ibid., H.W. Peterson to Provincial Secretary, 12 Sept. 1872. Some, but not all, of this material is reprinted in *DHE* 24: chap. 16.
56 *DHE* 24: 159.
57 See Inspector McLellan's report for 1872 in *DHE* 24: 237–42.
58 The regulations for 1873 are printed in *DHE* 25: 168–71.
59 For the relevant clauses of the legislation of 1874 see *DHE* 26: 20–1.
60 See *DHE* 26: 20.
61 For a list of exceptions in 1873 and a justification for using discretion on the matter, see G2A, vol. I, 1873, 459, Memo: "Assistant Teachers."
62 *DHE* 27: 199–200.

CHAPTER TEN

1 For examples of the support it had even during the 1870s, see *AR* for 1873, appendix B, 22; *AR* for 1877, appendix B, 21; *AR* for 1876, appendix B, 123; AO, RG2, D3C, G. German (Strathroy) to Department, 27 Jan. 1877.

2 For the amount of the grants and the various estimates of per pupil spending, see *DHE* 25: 147 and 156; *JEdUC* 28 (May 1875): 7.

3 *AR* for 1873, appendix B, 38. Similarly see ibid., 22.

4 G2A, vol. 1, 1872, 193.

5 See *AR* for 1872, 138–41. See also the argument put forward on this point by the editor of the *Brantford Expositor*, 25 July 1873, and *DHE* 26: 249.

6 G2A, vol. 1, 1874, 268; similarly see *AR* for 1874, appendix B, 85; *AR* for 1873, appendix B, 22; *Globe*, 20 Apr. 1875.

7 *Brantford Expositor*, 25 July 1873.

8 For some examples see AO, RG8, I-I-D, 1874, #279, Petition, Board of High School Trustees, Berlin; G2A, vol. 1 (2), 1874, 343, 362, 366; C6C, #2336, Clerk, Co. Lambton to Education Department, 1 Feb. 1876; AO, RG2, G2C, box 2, J.M. Buchan to A. Crooks, 14 Oct. 1876.

9 AO, RG2, D2, W.W. Elliott, Head, Kemptville High School, 4 Jan. 1877, #478.

10 C6C, box 300, Petitions of Arnprior, Vankleekhill, Williamstown, etc. to Lt. Governor in Council, Province of Ontario, 27 Jan. 1876.

11 See AO, D2, box 1, Department to H. Watt, Public School Board, Meaford, 11 Oct. 1876, and RG2, D3C, box 116, #13414, Reeve and Councillors, Township of Euphrasia to Dept., 26 Aug. 1876. Similarly see G2A, vol. 1, 1873, 460, Memo, "The High School District Question."

12 For the relevant changes in certification see below, 223–4. For new family strategies see above, chap. 3, 41–2.

13 Quoted in *JEdUC* 30, 3 (Mar. 1877): 40.

14 The legislation is summarized in *AR* for 1877, part I, 15.

15 See the comment by the high school inspectors in *AR* for 1877, part III, 3–4.

16 See *AR* for 1880–81, 207–11.

17 See ibid., 198. Our count is higher than that in the printed table because we have included as free those schools that only charged tuition fees to *non-residents*. Then, as now, it was a conventional practice to charge tuition fees for any non-resident, and therefore non-taxpayer, who used a local school.

18 *Globe*, 7 Mar. 1862. The literature on payment by results in Britain is now substantial. For helpful introductions, however, see James Winter, *Robert Lowe* (Toronto: University of Toronto Press 1976), chap. 11, and Thomas Wilson, "A Reinterpretation of 'Payment by Results' in Scotland, 1861–72," in *Scottish Culture and Scottish Education 1800–1980*, ed. W.M. Humes and H.M. Paterson (Edinburgh: John Donald 1983), 93–114.

19 See chap. 7, 171–2.

20 Quoted in *DHE* 23: 144.

21 For the various stages in the development of the scheme see *DHE* 23: 172–9; 24: 245–6; 25: 154–5; 26: 256–62.

22 *DHE* 27: 202.

23 *AR* for 1876, 84.

24 See AO, RG2, D2, box 2, Memo to all High School Boards and Headmasters, 27 Nov. 1876.

25 See for example UWORC, East Elgin District High School Board Minutes, 22 Dec. 1877, 11.

26 *JEdUC* 29 (Aug. 1876): 117.

27 George Bruce, "An On-looker's View of 'Payment by Results,'" *Educational Monthly* 1 (May-June 1879): 280. Similarly see "Editorial Notes," *Educational Monthly* 1 (Oct. 1879): 539–40.

28 See for example "Departmental Reports and the Intermediate Examination," by a Headmaster, *Educational Monthly* 1 (Apr. 1879): 217–22; "The Intermediate," ibid., 3 (Nov. 1881): 461–62; "High School Department," ibid., 452–7.

29 *AR* for 1879, 98 and 103–4.

30 Bruce, "An On-looker's View," 281.

31 For examples see AO, RG2, D2, #13623–5 and 13628–31, Reports to the Presiding Examiners from Kingston, Grimsby, Iroquois, Berlin, St Thomas, Collingwood.

32 *Globe*, 7 Aug. 1876.

33 A set of instructions that gives some sense of the complexity of administering the examination is printed in *AR* for 1877, 94–6.

34 G2A, vol. 10, 1880, Resolutions of the Clinton Board, attached to Report on Clinton.

35 Ibid. Similarly see *AR* for 1880–81, HSIR, 25, and AO, RG2, D2, Minister to J. Mills, Head, Brantford Collegiate Institute, 19 Oct. 1877, #18031.

36 See *AR* for 1882, 18.

37 *AR* for 1871, appendix B, 131.

38 *DHE* 28: 62.

39 There is a useful historical sketch covering the developments outlined in this and the following paragraph in the *AR* for 1880–81, 223–5. For the 1871 and 1877 certification requirements see *AR* for 1872, 172–5; *AR* for 1877, 107–12.

40 See *JEdUC* 30 (Mar. 1877): 39; *Canada School Journal* 1, 1 (June 1877): 4–5; ibid., 1, 2 (July 1877): 18; *AR* for 1880–81, 225; *AR* for 1882, 19–22 and 34–9.

41 See for example the comments of the high school inspectors in G2A, vol. 1, 1873, 371, 477; vol. 1 (2), 1874, 167–8, 191, 329, 350.

42 Total enrolment calculated from tables in the relevant *ARs*.

43 Adam Crooks, the minister of education, estimated 50 per cent in 1877; see AO, RG2, D2, Memorandum of the Minister, 14 Apr. 1877, #6645. For the lower estimate see *Canada School Journal* 2, 9 (Feb. 1878): 25. In the late eighties it stood at about 40 per cent; see for example *AR* for 1887, appendix A, 45 (table H).

44 *AR* for 1876, 87.

45 *Educational Monthly* I (Jan. 1879): 20. For similar sentiments see *AR* for 1877, appendix B, 33; *AR* for 1878, appendix D, 117; *AR* for 1882, 116–17.

46 *London Advertiser*, 4 Feb. 1874; similarly see *AR* for 1872, appendix B, 118.

47 OTA *Minutes*, 1875, 48.

48 AO, RG2, D3C, box 17, #13885, Public School Board to Department, Port Hope, 29 Sept. 1876; RG2, D3C, #10891, W. Coburn, Oshawa Board Trustees, 28 May 1879.

49 AO, RG2, D2, box 1, #15285, Minister to Chairman, Port Hope Public School Board, 3 Oct. 1876; RG2, D2, #15334, Hodgins to W. Coburn, Oshawa, 4 June 1879.

50 Calculated from *AR* for 1880–81, 184.

51 G2A, vol. 1 (2), 1874, 55.

52 *AR* for 1875, appendix B, 9. Similarly see *AR* for 1874, appendix B, 76.

53 AO, RG2, G4, envelope 7, Representatives of Public Schools, County of Waterloo, 1875. Similarly see *JEdUC* 26 (Oct. 1873): 145–6; *AR* for 1874, appendix B, 69.

54 See R.D. Gidney and W.P.J. Millar, "Rural Schools and the Decline of Community Control in Nineteenth-Century Ontario," in *Fourth Annual Agricultural History of Ontario Seminar Proceedings* (Guelph: University of Guelph 1979), esp. 74ff.

55 AO, RG2, G4, envelope 6, Second Annual Report of the Inspectors, Victoria County, 1873; see also ibid., Report of Public School Inspector, Lanark County, 1873; UWORC, Miscellaneous records, Oxford County, B673, Report of W. Carlyle, 9 Dec. 1871.

56 UWORC, Norfolk County Council Papers, B838, Report of J.J. Wadsworth for 1871. See also *AR* for 1871, appendix B, 22, A.W. Ross, Glengarry County.

57 For pertinent commentary on these points see *AR* for 1875, appendix B, 31 and 38; *AR* for 1876, appendix B, 101 and 128; *AR* for 1877, appendix B, 37; *AR* for 1878, appendix D, 121 and 124–5; *AR* for 1882, 118; UWORC, Report of W. Carlyle, Public School Inspector, Oxford County, to Oxford County Council, 17 June 1884.

58 See for example *AR* for 1883, 134; UWORC, Report of J.S. Carson, 1883, Middlesex County Minutes, June 1884, 37.

59 For the relevant regulations see *AR* for 1877, appendix F, 114–20; *AR* for 1882, 13–16.

60 *AR* for 1873, appendix B, 58.
61 *AR* for 1878, part I, 16.
62 *AR* for 1885, 14.
63 Ibid., 166.
64 *AR* for 1887, xxxvi.
65 See for example *AR* for 1876, 123; *Canada School Journal* 1, 4 (Sept. 1877): 57; *AR* for 1885, 90.
66 Calculated from *AR* for 1880–81, 197–8.
67 *AR* for 1879, 72.
68 *Educational Monthly* 6 (Sept. 1884): 332–3.
69 Calculated from the relevant tables in the *ARs*.

CHAPTER ELEVEN

1 See chap. 9, 198–9 and 208–9; despite the changes over the decade, the three-tiered scheme remained in the regulations as late as 1878. See Ontario Education Department, *Regulations of the Public, Separate and High Schools* (Toronto 1878), 54.
2 *AR* for 1871, appendix A, 2.
3 Calculated from the relevant tables in the *ARs*.
4 *AR* for 1871, appendix A, 2.
5 See *DHE* 23: 116.
6 *DHE* 25: 237–8. For a similar private comment see G2A, vol. 1, 1873, 461.
7 *DHE* 26: 260.
8 For an example of this see AO, RG2, G2C, Buchan and Marling to Ryerson, 18 Sept. 1874.
9 The key memorandum from the inspectors is printed in *DHE* 26: 256–64. On the link between the revised program and payment by results, see 260. For their own program recommendations see 262–4.
10 The final version is printed in *DHE* 27: 216–18.
11 See *DHE* 27: 219.
12 The standard introduction is Walter B. Kolesnik, *Mental Discipline in Modern Education* (Madison: University of Wisconsin Press 1958). For an illuminating short commentary see Sheldon Rothblatt, *Tradition and Change in English Liberal Education* (London: Faber and Faber 1976), 126–32.
13 *DHE* 23: 165.
14 Until recently, the definition of culture maintained this usage exclusively: the *Concise Oxford Dictionary* (cf. 6th ed., 1976) defines "culture" as "tillage of the soil; rearing, production, (of bees [etc] ... Improvement by (mental or physical) training; intellectual development; ... *v.t.* Cultivate." For a brief note on changing usage see Raymond Williams, *Culture and Society 1780–1950* (Harmondsworth: Penguin 1961), 16.
15 *Christian Guardian*, 20 July 1842.

16 *DHE* 16: 57–8.

17 *AR* for 1886, appendix A, 21.

18 *Canada Educational Monthly* 6 (Sept. 1884): 330–1.

19 *DHE* 16: 58.

20 *Christian Guardian*, 6 July 1842. For other typical expositions or set pieces on the meaning of mental discipline and the centrality of the classics, see *JEdUC* 10 (Sept. 1857): 129–31, "Mr Gladstone on Classical Education"; 11 (Sept. 1858): 139, "The Benefits of Classical Education," by Dr Lewis of Brockville.

21 *DHE* 20: 110. Similarly see William Tassie's comments, *JEdUC* 22 (Sept. 1869): 138.

22 *Ottawa Citizen*, 27 Nov. 1852.

23 *JEdUC* 10 (Dec. 1857): 181. For other examples see *DHE* 15: 170, 183 and 235 (evidence of Daniel Wilson and John Langton before the University Committee).

24 Rothblatt, *Tradition and Change*, 131.

25 For two classic texts by Huxley see his addresses titled "On the Educational Value of the Natural History Sciences" [1854] and "A Liberal Education; and Where to Find It" [1868]. These are printed in a variety of places, including *Science and Education; Essays by Thomas H. Huxley*, International Science Library (Akron, Ohio: Werner Co. [1893?]). Passages from Huxley were often reported in the Upper Canadian press. See for example *JEdUC* 22, 11 (Nov. 1869): 161–3. For Dawson's arguments, see his "Inaugural Discourse" as principal of McGill, printed in *JEdUC* 8, 11 (Nov. 1855): 165–70.

26 *AR* for 1870, appendix A, 5.

27 *DHE* 25: 244.

28 *DHE* 15: 235.

29 *DHE* 23: 165.

30 *Canadian Monthly and National Review* 5, 1 (Jan. 1874): 90.

31 Ibid., 3, 3 (Mar. 1873): 234.

32 *AR* for 1872, part III, 5.

33 *JEdUC* 10 (Dec. 1857): 181.

34 *DHE* 15: 29.

35 The testimony is printed in *DHE* 15. It is a gold mine for contemporary attitudes about a wide variety of curricular issues, and one that has yet to be adequately exploited.

36 *DHE* 15: 215. For a comparison of the "Ryersonian" curriculum at Victoria in 1860 and the contemporary curriculum at University College, see Robin S. Harris, *A History of Higher Education in Canada* (Toronto: University of Toronto Press 1976), 42–4.

37 *Globe*, 25 Nov. 1865.

38 *DHE* 21: 28.

39 This, it must be emphasized, was no mere *canard* launched by enemies of the University. See AO, George Brown Papers, Daniel Wilson to Brown, 30 Apr. 1860 and 11 May 1860. See also *Globe*, 10 June 1857. The necessity of such an adjustment had been vigorously argued earlier by G.P. Young in the *Globe*, 23 Jan. and 6 Feb. 1854.

40 *JEdUC* 23 (Jan. 1870): 14.

41 *JEdUC* 20 (Apr. 1867): 6.

42 For an example see *DHE* 27: 64–9.

43 The estimate for 1874 is based on our tally of pupils listed in G2A, vol. 1 (2), 1874. The list is, however, not entirely complete, so our figure is a "ballpark" estimate. Published statistics on the number of boys and girls enrolled in the high schools are printed in the *ARs* from 1880; see general table 7.

44 The sources for our figures here are the same ones cited in note 43 above.

45 See the address by J.M. Buchan in OTA *Minutes*, 1874, 38–47, and the OTA debate about it in *JEdUC* 27 (Sept. 1874): 136–7. See also the comment of the three inspectors in *AR* for 1876, 87.

46 *Educational Monthly* 1 (Oct. 1879): 483. See also ibid., 1 (May-June 1879): 288–94; *Canada School Journal* 2, 43 (Dec. 1880): 269.

47 See for example *Canada School Journal* 4 (Nov. 1879): 251–3.

48 Quoted in J.G. Hodgins, *The Establishment of Schools and Colleges in Ontario, 1792–1910* (Toronto 1910), II: 233.

49 *Educational Monthly* 6 (Mar. 1884): 142 and 421.

50 *Canada School Journal* 4, 30 (Nov. 1879): 252. The author was principal of Ottawa Ladies' College.

51 See for example G2A (Marling), vol. 1 (2), 1874, 346. Our own reading of these reports suggests such references were very infrequent.

52 Again, see G2A, 1871–4, where the inspectors list the subjects taught and the numbers of girls and boys in each.

53 *Canadian Monthly* 3, 1 (Jan. 1873): 42.

54 *DHE* 25: 243. Similarly see ibid., 26: 250.

55 *Brantford Expositor*, 7 Aug. 1868.

56 *JEdUC* 18 (Oct. 1865): 152.

57 *London Advertiser*, 8 Feb. 1877; D.C. McHenry, "The Higher Education of Women," OTA *Minutes*, 1879, 75–80. Similarly see President's Address, OTA *Minutes*, 1868, 26.

58 For examples see ibid., 26; Remarks by J.H. Thom, *JEdUC* 21 (Aug. 1868): 123; McHenry, "Higher Education," 79; Richard Lewis, "The Higher Education of Women," OTA *Minutes*, 1872, 34–6.

59 See "Higher Education for Women," *Canadian Journal of Science, Literature and History* (Nov. 1869), 308–20.

60 G.M. Grant, "Education and Co-Education," *Canada Educational Monthly* 1 (Oct. 1879): 477–87. The passages quoted will be found on 481–2, 484, and 479.

61 The phrase is from Rosalind Rosenberg, *Beyond Separate Spheres: Intellectual Roots of Modern Feminism* (New Haven: Yale University Press 1982), chap. 4.

62 *Canada School Journal* 2, 9 (Feb. 1878): 25.

63 *DHE* 23: 164.

64 See for example *London Advertiser*, 8 Feb. 1877; Grant, "Education and Co-Education," 484; McHenry, "Higher Education," 78.

65 Veronica Strong-Boag, *"A Woman with a Purpose": The Diaries of Elizabeth Smith, 1872–1884* (Toronto: University of Toronto Press 1980), xi.

66 For the 1871 regulations see *DHE* 25: 136ff. For those of 1877 see Education Department (Ontario), *Regulations Respecting the Public, Separate, and High Schools* (Toronto, 1878), 94–5.

67 See for example G2A, vol. 1, 1872, 199–360, which indicates enrolment patterns for girls and boys.

68 In the statistical tables of the *ARs* the subjects for the non-professional certificate commonly have enrolments of 90 per cent or more of the students.

69 *Canada Educational Monthly* 2 (Jan. 1880): 41.

70 See *AR* for 1879, 103; *Canada Educational Monthly* 2 (Feb. 1880): 99.

71 *AR* for 1879, 99.

72 Calculated from the financial tables in the *ARs*.

73 *Canada Educational Monthly* 1 (Dec. 1879): 636.

74 See for example *Canada Educational Monthly* 2 (Feb. 1880): 102–3 and 2 (Oct. 1880): 464; 3 (Feb. 1881): 84; *Canada School Journal* 4, 31 (Dec. 1879): 269–70; 5, 41 (Oct. 1880): 222–3.

75 For examples of these criticisms see *Canada School Journal* 5 (Feb. 1880): 35–6; 5 (Oct. 1880): 231; *Canada Educational Monthly* 1 (Dec. 1879): 635–6; 2 (Feb. 1880): 98–100; OTA *Minutes*, 1879, 22.

76 *Globe*, 22 Feb. 1881.

77 See *AR* for 1880–81, 93–4, 127, 243–4; *Canada Educational Monthly* 3 (Feb. 1881): 80.

78 See *AR* for 1882, 19.

CHAPTER TWELVE

1 For the Churches of England and Scotland see, for example, *Journal of the 3rd Session of the Synod of the Church of England in the Diocese of Ontario, 1864* (Kingston 1864), 259–60; *The Presbyterian*, Jan. 1864, 9. The Free Church required classics but not an arts degree. See *DHE* 19: 267–8.

2 On pre-Confederation medical education generally see R.D. Gidney and W.P.J. Millar, "The Origins of Organized Medicine in Ontario," in *Health, Disease and Medicine: Essays in Canadian History*, ed. Charles G. Roland (Toronto: Hannah Institute 1984), 65–95.

3 See *JEdUC* 17 (Feb. 1864): 24–5.

4 *AR* for 1853, 119 and 125; *DHE* 19: 28.

5   See "An Act respecting Land Surveyors and the Survey of Lands," 22 Vict. (1859), cap. 77, sections 6 and 8.
6   For the various standards referred to in this paragraph, see Queen's University, *Course of Study, 1855–56* (Kingston 1855), 8; *JEdUC* 10, 10 (Oct. 1857): 158 [Victoria]; *Rules of the Law Society of Upper Canada, 1859* (Toronto, 1859), 11; "An Act respecting Land Surveyors"; *JEdUC* 10, 6 (June 1857): 81 [University of Toronto]. See also the lengthy comparisons in a series of letters on the universities in the *Globe*, 1, 11, 24 Sept. and 19 Nov. 1856.
7   The degree of overlap in the mid-1850s can be gauged by comparing the grammar school program printed in *JEdUC* 8, 2 (Feb. 1855), and the various references in note 6 above.
8   See for example the comments by Paxton Young, *Globe*, 23 Jan. 1854.
9   R.D. Anderson, *Education and Opportunity in Victorian Scotland* (Oxford: Clarendon Press 1983), 3–4. For the United States, see Jurgen Herbst, "Diversification in American Higher Education," in *The Transformation of Higher Learning, 1860–1930*, ed. Konrad H. Jarausch (Chicago: University of Chicago Press 1983), 198.
10 King's College, Toronto, *Regulations Relative to the University ... Established by the College Council, October 1846*. See also the comment by Daniel Wilson, *DHE* 15: 213–14.
11 *Globe*, 23 Jan. 1854.
12 *Globe*, 6 Feb. 1854. For Wilson's version of the struggle see AO, George Brown Papers, Daniel Wilson to Brown, Toronto, 30 Apr. and 11 May 1860.
13 *Globe*, 2 July 1855.
14 *Globe*, 10 June 1857. To compare the two standards see *JEdUC* 8, 2 (Feb. 1855): 18–19, and 10, 6 (June 1857): 81.
15 *DHE* 15: 213–14. Similarly see Langton's arguments in ibid., 28–9 and 250–1.
16 See *JEdUC* 13 (Jan. 1860): 3, and *DHE* 15: 206–7.
17 *DHE* 15: 118.
18 Compare *Calendar, University College 1860–61*, 25; *JEdUC* 8 (Feb. 1855): 25 (prescribed grammar school texts); *AR* for 1861, table E, 43 (texts used in common schools).
19 David Keane, "Rediscovering Ontario University Students in the Mid-Nineteenth Century" (Ph.D. diss., University of Toronto 1982), 260.
20 See *DHE* 15: 111 and 119.
21 C.B. Sissons, *My Dearest Sophie: Letters from Egerton Ryerson to His Daughter* (Toronto: Ryerson Press 1955), 88. Generally on the phenomenon of cramming see Donald Leinster-Mackay, "Competitive Examinations in Victorian England: The Development and Decline of 'Cramming,'" *Journal of the Australian and New Zealand History of Education Society* 10, 1 (Autumn 1981): 24–34.

22 See for example the rules in *University College Calendar 1860–61*, 13, or *JEdUC* 10, 6 (June 1857): 81.
23 Keane, "Rediscovering Ontario University Students," 29.
24 Ibid. The figure of 70 per cent includes medical students.
25 Ibid., 239.
26 *JEdUC* 16, 11 (Nov. 1863): 175.
27 *JLAC*, 1856, appendix 11.
28 See for example the comments of Paxton Young, *Globe*, 6 Feb. 1854.
29 See for example *Ecclesiastical and Missionary Record*, July 1854, August 1855, August 1856: Reports to Synod by College Committee.
30 *DHE*, 15: 283–4.
31 See *Annual Report ... of the University of Queen's College* (Kingston 1860), 30–1.
32 For the period 1854 to 1863 see *JEdUC* 16, 11 (Nov. 1863): 175. For 1880 see Keane, "Rediscovering Ontario University Students," 819, and *AR* for 1880–81, 368.
33 To compare the new matriculation standards and the new grammar school program, see J.G. Hodgins, ed., *Grammar School Manual* (Toronto 1866), 35–6 and 59–60. For the introduction of these changes see *JEdUC* 17, 12 (Dec. 1864): 187–8.
34 See *JEdUC* 17, 2 (Feb. 1864): 22–5; *The Medical Register for Upper Canada, 1867*, Schedule z and 48.
35 See *Medical Register*, 48.
36 The relevant tables in the *ARs* give the numbers of university matriculants from early on but include the professional matriculants only from 1871.
37 G2A, vol. 1, 1872, 313.
38 Ibid. Similarly see ibid., 1, 1873, 485, and 1, 1874, 14.
39 *DHE* 27: 202. For a similar complaint see OTA *Minutes*, 1872, 19–20.
40 OTA *Minutes*, 1874, 13. For other examples see *JEdUC* 21 (Jan. 1868): 14–15; OTA *Minutes*, 1875, 15.
41 *DHE* 15: 197. Similarly see *Canada School Journal* 1, 2 (July 1877): 15–16; *AR* for 1884, 189.
42 *Canada Lancet* 13, 6 (Feb. 1881): letter to the editor from W. Tytler.
43 AO, RG2, D2, Memorandum for consideration by Central Committee ... by Adam Crook, no. 6645, 14 Apr. 1877.
44 See *JEdUC* 21, 1 (Jan. 1868): 14–15; ibid., 21 (Aug. 1868): 123.
45 The Law Society actually widened the gap between its matriculation and the high school course when it revised its regulations in 1872. For the reaction from headmasters and inspectors, see *DHE* 25: 243, and OTA *Minutes*, 1872, 19–20.
46 For the different options available in articulating secondary and higher education see Harold S. Wechsler, *The Qualified Student: A History of Selective College Admissions in America* (New York: John Wiley 1977).
47 OTA *Minutes*, 1876, 23–4.

48 See *DHE* 27: 202; *Canada School Journal* 1, 1 (Jan. 1877): 4–5, and 2, 10 (Mar. 1878): 48–9.

49 *Canada Law Journal* 12 (Oct. 1876): 296; *DHE* 28: 94–6 and 111–12.

50 See *Canada School Journal* 2, 10 (Mar. 1878): 48–9, and 3, 15 (Aug. 1878): 66; *Canada Lancet* 13, 2 (Oct. 1880): 57–8. For the key change at Victoria see UCA, Victoria University Senate Minutes, 21 May 1879.

51 See Keane, "Rediscovering Ontario University Students," 854; *Educational Monthly* 6 (July-Aug. 1884): 316–17.

52 *Canada School Journal* 3, 14 (July 1878): 32. Similarly see *Educational Monthly* 2 (Sept. 1880): 414–15.

53 *Canadian Journal of Medical Science* 5, 8 (Aug. 1880): 236.

54 See ibid., 2, 8 (Aug. 1877): 283–4.

55 *Canada Lancet* 21, 11 (July 1880): 347.

56 For the arguments in favour of the combined examination see QUA, Grant Papers, box 1, 2491, Memorial by George Ross to the Senate of the University of Toronto, Oct. 1889. See also *AR* for 1887, xxix–xxx; *AR* for 1893, xxx–xxxi.

57 *Canada School Journal* 1, 1 (June 1877): 7.

58 UCA, Victoria University Senate Minutes, 23 Dec. 1880.

59 During the last decades of the nineteenth century the length of time needed to prepare for junior matriculation varied. In the 1870s and 1890s it seems to have required four years of study, and in the 1880s, three.

60 *Journal of the Methodist General Conference* (Toronto 1878), 240.

61 *Announcement, School of Dentistry, Toronto*, 1881–82.

62 *AR* for 1885, 165.

63 See for example *Canada School Journal* 3, 15 (Aug. 1878): 56, and 5, 33 (Feb. 1880): 28; *Educational Monthly* 2 (May-June 1880): 288–90, and 4 (Feb. 1882): 72; *Globe*, 21 Feb. 1881.

64 See *Educational Monthly* 3 (Oct. 1881): 406–7, and 6 (May-June 1884): 247. For the number of junior and senior matriculants, see *AR* for 1880 and 1881, 166–7; *Educational Monthly* 6 (July-Aug. 1884): 258.

65 Keane, "Rediscovering Ontario University Students," 848–9.

CHAPTER THIRTEEN

1 See general tables 2 and 3.

2 See for example GIA, 1859 (Cockburn), 77; 1866 (Young), 328 and 466; 1867 (Young), 560–1; 1868 (McKenzie), 67 and 361–2.

3 GIA, 1865 (Young), 142.

4 *DHE* 23: 179–80.

5 See for example AO, RG2, F3D, box 4, Letters to Department from School Inspectors, etc., G.H. Porter, Bradford, 9 Aug. 1871; G2A, vol. 1, 1873, 480.

6 See for example G2A, vol. 1, 1873, 480, Vankleekhill High School; 416, Oakville.
7 *DHE* 25: 170, regulation no. 19. See also the restatement of the principle, ibid., 173.
8 See *Globe*, 18 Feb. 1874, and the comment of the high school inspectors in *DHE* 27: 199.
9 *JEdUC* 27, 3 (Mar. 1874): 33–4.
10 AO, RG2, G2C, box 2, High School Inspectors to Ryerson, 11 Feb. 1874.
11 OTA *Minutes*, 1875, 51.
12 The figures are reported in various columns of the high school tables in the *ARs* between the late seventies and mid-eighties.
13 See AO, RG2, P2, 59, no. 182, Memorial of Parents to Minister of Education, 14 Apr. 1891, and *Globe*, 10 Apr. 1891.
14 See *AR* for 1884, 31. The figures for 1880 are only marginally different; see *AR* for 1880–81, 81.
15 *Educational Monthly* 6 (Sept. 1884): 326.
16 Quoted in *DHE* 28: 13.
17 *JEdUC* 30, 3 (Mar. 1877): 39.
18 J. Anthony C. Ketchum, "'The Most Perfect System': Official Policy in the First Century of Ontario's Government Secondary Schools and Its Impact on Students between 1871 and 1910" (Ph.D. diss., University of Toronto 1979).
19 For the following two paragraphs see chap. 6, 132–3, and Ketchum, "System," 168–75, and appendices E1–E7. There is some difficulty in comparing our parental occupations to Ketchum's, particularly since he studied all students including those from farmers' families in his analysis, whereas we deliberately excluded non-town students and thus a great many farmers' children. The occupational categorization is also somewhat different. In order to compare the two studies, we have excluded all cases of female-headed households in our population. The results are then as follows. If we include all our township students and assume that most of their fathers were farmers, we arrive at the percentages in column A. If we exclude all farmers, the proportions are those in column B.

Parents using grammar school in 1861	A Including farmers (%)	B Excluding farmers (%)
Merchants & dealers	15	28
Professionals, government service	10	19
White collar workers	8	16
Artisans, manufacturers	15	28

Labourers	1	3
Farmers	47	–
Gentlemen	4	7
	N = 219	N = 116

20 There is a problem in comparing these tables to our analysis so far: we have been examining the *parents* in both our schools and Ketchum's, while the figures in the *ARs* are for *students*. Thus if siblings attended the high schools in great numbers, as they did at mid-century, the proportions reported in occupational categories in the *ARs* will be somewhat skewed according to whether parents in one or another occupational category sent several children or had larger or smaller families. Nevertheless, we use these reports as supplementary evidence on a question where little data exists. The figures can be found in the *ARs*, but Ketchum also conveniently summarizes them in his appendix E3.

21 See Ketchum, "System," appendix E3.

22 Calculated from Ketchum, "System," appendix E4.

23 See *AR* for 1896.

24 See above, chaps. 2 and 3.

25 R.W. Connell et al., *Making the Difference: Schools, Families and Social Division* (Sydney: George Allen and Unwin 1982), 140–3.

26 *Canada School Journal* 1, 5 (Aug. 1877): 27. Similarly see ibid., 4, 31 (Dec. 1879): 269–70.

27 Quoted in *DHE* 28: 2. For a helpful commentary on the limits and ambiguities of nineteenth-century notions of equality of opportunity, see Fred Hirsch, *The Social Limits to Growth* (Cambridge, Mass.: Harvard University Press 1976), 161–3.

28 The published data can be found in the various *ARs*, but they have also been conveniently summarized by Ketchum in his appendix C3.

29 See Ketchum, "System," 199–201.

30 G2A, vol. 7, 1878, Brantford, July; Owen Sound, Dec.; Ottawa, Dec.; ibid., vols. 25–6, 1895, Belleville, Brantford, Perth, Sarnia, Simcoe, Stratford, Strathroy, Richmond Hill, Ottawa. The three schools in which girls were always in a majority were Belleville, Brantford, and Ottawa – perhaps significantly, these were in the three largest towns, where more jobs for teenage boys may have been available. For other references in 1878, see also ibid., vol. 7, 1878, Carleton Place and Kingston.

31 *AR* for 1875, appendix A, HSIR, 4–5.

32 Ketchum, "System," 140. Ketchum notes that as late as 1911, the equivalent percentage was over 75 per cent: see ibid.

33 See above, chap. 6, 127, and appendix B.

34 G2A, vol. 10, 1880; *AR* for 1890, table 1 (statistics for 1889). See also G2A, vols. 25 and 26, 1895, reports on Ottawa, Richmond Hill, Strathroy, Stratford, Simcoe, Sarnia, Perth, and Brantford; 35 per cent of the students were non-residents.

35 *AR* for 1887, appendix E, Ontario Teachers' Association Proceedings, 96.

36 *AR* for 1893, appendix: Special Reports, 120.

37 *AR* for 1889, 125; similarly see *AR* for 1891, 136.

38 See the relevant public school tables in the *ARs*.

39 *AR* for 1880–81, 96 [italics in original].

40 The phrase in quotation marks is from *AR* for 1878, part 1, 16.

41 *DHE* 25: 242.

42 *Canadian Monthly* 3, 1 (Jan. 1873): 42.

43 Though the figures in this paragraph can be worked out from each of the *ARs*, the department often summarized them. See for example the *AR* for 1893, XVI (Pupil Classification), and XXX (Entrance Examinations).

44 We will return to the gender variation of this question below, 292–4.

45 Calculations are based on the *AR* for 1889 (statistics for 1888).

46 Joel Perlmann, "Curriculum and Tracking in the Transformation of the American High School: Providence, R.I., 1880–1930," *Journal of Social History* 19, 1 (Fall 1985): 48.

47 Fritz K. Ringer, *Education and Society in Modern Europe* (Bloomington: Indiana University Press 1979), 29.

48 David F. Labaree, *The Making of an American High School: The Credentials Market and the Central High School of Philadelphia, 1838–1939* (New Haven, Conn.: Yale University Press 1988), 37.

49 See for example A.J. Halsey, Anthony Heath, and J.M. Ridge, *Origins and Destinations: Family, Class and Education in Modern Britain* (New York: Oxford University Press 1980). For a review of some of the pertinent literature, see Patrick J. Harrigan, "Social Mobility and Schooling in History: Recent Methods and Conclusions," *Historical Reflections* 10, 1 (Spring 1983): 127–42.

50 For a summary see *AR* for 1890, xxvi.

51 *AR* for 1893, xxxii.

52 *Canada Lancet* 13, 3 (Nov. 1880): 89.

53 See for example the new program of studies in Ontario, *Statutes and Regulations Respecting Public and High Schools* (Toronto 1885), no. 93.

54 Professor Nicholson of the University of Toronto, quoted in *DHE* 25: 207.

55 For some examples see *Ottawa Citizen*, 27 Nov. 1852; *Globe*, 25 Nov. 1865; *JEdUC* 22 (Apr. 1869): 51–3; ibid., 24, 3 (Mar. 1871): 33.

56 See for example *JEdUC* 14 (Sept. 1861): 140; *Globe*, 3 Dec. 1863, 29 Jan. 1864; *Leader*, 9 Oct. 1866; *JEdUC* 19 (Feb. 1866): 22; 20 (Sept. 1867): 156; 21 (Dec. 1868): 180; 22 (Mar. 1869): 38; 24 (Mar. 1871), entire issue.

57 *DHE* 22: 181.

58 *DHE* 21: 113–14.

59 See for example *Canada School Journal* 4, 31 (Dec. 1879): 271.

60 *DHE* 27: 84. Generally, see C.R. Young, *Early Engineering Education at Toronto, 1851–1919* (Toronto: University of Toronto Press 1958), chap. 3.

61 *Globe*, 14 Jan. 1874. See also *Globe*, 20 Jan. 1874. For a fine introduction to Loudon see A.B. McKillop, *Contours of Canadian Thought* (Toronto: University of Toronto Press 1987).

62 *DHE* 27: 89.

63 *AR* for 1891, 289.

64 See for example *Educational Monthly* 3 (Mar. 1881): 140–1; 3 (Oct. 1881): 387–9; 4 (July-Aug. 1884): 285–6.

65 *AR* for 1880–81, 252.

66 *AR* for 1884, 205.

67 *AR* for 1887, 246.

68 *AR* for 1886, appendix A, 21.

69 *Canada School Journal* 2 (Feb. 1878): 25.

70 See *Globe*, 29 Jan. 1864; *Belleville Intelligencer*, 25 May 1866; *DHE* 23: 220–1; John E. Bryant, "A Commercial Department in High Schools," *Educational Monthly* 6 (Sept. 1884): 339–46; Ontario, *Statutes and Regulations Respecting the Public and High Schools* (Toronto 1885), no. 100. For a stimulating recent study of the rise of commercial education see Nancy S. Jackson and Jane S. Gaskell, "White Collar Vocationalism: The Rise of Commercial Education in Ontario and B.C., 1870–1920," *Curriculum Inquiry* 17, 2 (1987): 179–200.

71 Summary statistics for enrolment by subjects are printed in *AR* for 1889, xvii. Figures for music exist only for 1883. For the number of schools offering music, see *AR* for 1889, table H.

72 *DHE* 25: 210–12.

73 G2A, vol. 1, 1874, 86.

74 See for example *Ottawa Citizen*, 2 and 21 Feb. 1882; Adam Harkness, *Iroquois High School …* (Toronto 1896), 146; AO, Col. Charles Clarke Papers in Possession of the Wellington County Archives, Calendar and Transcription, Charles Clarke to "My dear girls," Elora [1875].

75 See for example the comments on this point in *Canada School Journal* 1, 2 (July 1877): 15–16; 2, 9 (Feb. 1878): 25–6; *AR* for 1883, 89; *AR* for 1889, 182.

76 *AR* for 1889, HSIR, 187–8, 191.

77 Calculated from *AR* for 1887, table H; Ontario, *Statutes and Regulations respecting Public and High Schools, 1885*, 118–20 (form I requirements), and 133 (requirements for third-class non-professional teachers' certificates).

78 For the revised course of studies see *DHE* 27: 216–17. A rough estimate of

the enrolment in the lower school is available in the *AR* for 1879, 80–1, where the average attendance figures are given.

79 *Canada School Journal* 6, 52 (Sept. 1881): 200. See also ibid., 6, 46 (Mar. 1881): 54.

80 *AR* for 1880–81, 247.

81 See *AR* for 1882, 17 and 20.

82 See *AR* for 1885, 28–9, and successive revisions of the course of study printed in the *ARs*. The major revision was in 1890.

83 Ann Margaret Gray, "Continuity in Change: The Effects of Coeducational Secondary Schooling in Ontario, 1860–1910" (MA diss., University of Toronto 1979), esp. 102 and 163.

84 Marjorie G. Cohen, *Women's Work, Markets, and Economic Development in Nineteenth-Century Ontario* (Toronto: University of Toronto Press 1988), 152.

85 Carol Dyhouse, *Girls Growing Up in Late Victorian and Edwardian England* (London: Routledge and Kegan Paul 1981), 60.

86 See *AR* for 1883, 141.

87 See J.G. Hodgins, *The Establishment of Schools and Colleges in Ontario, 1792–1910* (Toronto 1910), II: 232.

88 Quoted in Ramsay Cook and Wendy Mitchinson, eds., *The Proper Sphere: Woman's Place in Canadian Society* (Toronto: Oxford University Press 1976), 143.

89 Hodgins, *Schools and Colleges*, II: 233.

90 See for example Ontario, *Regulations respecting ... High Schools* (Toronto 1878), 67; *Statutes and Regulations Respecting ... High Schools* (Toronto 1885), no. 97.

91 Gwyneth Dow, "Family History and Educational History: Towards an Integration," *Historical Studies* 21, 84 (Apr. 1985): 431.

CHAPTER FOURTEEN

1 The high school inspectors' reports on individual schools have all survived and are filed in AO, RG2, G2A. But after the early 1870s they become routine statistical reports containing little detailed commentary.

2 For descriptions and pictures of the new physical plant, see for example Suzanne I. Tanguay, *The History and Development of Welland High and Vocational School, 1854–1979* ([Welland, Ont.] 1975), 11; Greta M. Shutt, *The High Schools of Guelph* (Toronto: University of Toronto Press 1961), 35; Ottawa Collegiate Institute Ex-Pupils' Association, *A History of the Ottawa Collegiate Institute, 1843–1903* (Ottawa 1904), 12–14; David Judd, ed., *Simcoe: County Town of Norfolk* (Simcoe, Ont.: Norfolk Historical Society 1985), 90; J.G. Hodgins, *The Establishment of Schools and Colleges in Ontario 1792–1910* (Toronto, 1910), esp. vol. I.

3 Robert Anderson, "Secondary Schools and Scottish Society in the Nineteenth Century," *Past and Present* 109 (Nov. 1985): 180.
4 Shutt, *High Schools of Guelph*, 35; O.C.I. Ex-Pupils' Association, *Ottawa Collegiate Institute*, 13; John M. Lees, *Thorold Secondary School, 1857–1975: An Illustrated History* (Pelham, Ont. [1975]), 19.
5 See for example the various high school inspectors' reports in the *ARs* of 1876, 1878, 1879, 1887, 1889; *Brantford Expositor*, 27 June and 8 Aug. 1873 (Brantford); G2A, vol. 1, 1873, 507 (Galt); *Canada School Journal* 2, 9 (Feb. 1878): 35 (Stratford); Tanguay, *Welland High*, 10; *Globe*, 14 Mar. 1872 (Toronto); *London Advertiser*, 8 Jan. and 1 Feb. 1879 (London).
6 Quoted from H.H. Page Atlas of Lincoln and Welland, 1876, in Lees, *Thorold Secondary School*, 5.
7 G2A, vol. 7, 1878, July, Brantford C.I. Floor Plan.
8 G2A, vol. 10, 1880, Harriston. For other examples, see ibid., vol. 14, 1885, Fergus; *Educational Monthly* 6 (Apr. 1884): 187 (Dundas).
9 *Ottawa Citizen*, 27 Jan. 1872 and 24 Dec. 1874.
10 Quoted in R.J. Bolton, *History of Central Public School, Peterborough, 1860–1960* ([Peterborough 1960]), 4, 11. See also the case of Sarnia, in GIA, 1861, 3; G2A, vol. 14, 1885, Sarnia.
11 G2A, vol. 1 (2), 1874, 202, and vol. 14, 1885, Belleville; AO, RG2, H3, Belleville Board of Education Minutes, vol. 56 (1887): 31 and 46–8.
12 *AR* for 1885, 149.
13 Ibid., 153.
14 For more optimistic comments citing improvements in equipment, see *AR* for 1889, appendix I, HSIR.
15 *AR* for 1893, xxvii.
16 All calculations in this paragraph are from the relevant tables and appendices in the *ARs*. See also J. Anthony C. Ketchum, "'The Most Perfect System': Official Policy in the First Century of Ontario's Government Secondary Schools and Its Impact on Students between 1871 and 1910" (Ph.D. diss., University of Toronto 1979), appendix G6, for the growth of the student body at four high schools from 1871 to 1910. In our own high schools, student numbers grew from an average size of 57 in 1861 to 249 by 1886; see relevant tables in *ARs* for 1861 and 1887 (statistics of 1886).
17 Calculated from the retrospective table in *AR* for 1887, xxiii.
18 Calculated from relevant tables in *AR* for 1872, and from *AR* for 1887, xxiii.
19 Calculated from relevant tables in the *ARs*.
20 See for example Tanguay, *Welland High*, 10; *Brantford Expositor*, 7 Mar., 27 June, 8 Aug. 1873; *London Advertiser*, 1 Feb. 1879.
21 *AR* for 1887, xxv. See also G2A, vol. 14, 1885, Collingwood C.I.
22 *AR* for 1891, table G. The numbers of free and fee-charging high schools are recorded each year in the financial tables for the high schools in the *ARs*.

23 See Ketchum, "System," appendices H1 and H2. His tables show that the proportion of total income raised by tuition fees grew from 7 or 8 per cent in the mid-seventies to 13 per cent a decade later. The collegiate institutes were much more likely to charge fees than the high schools; almost three-quarters of the collegiate institutes levied fees in 1888, compared to just half the high schools.

24 *AR* for 1880–81, part I, 100–1.

25 AO, RG2, G2A, vol. 14, 1885: Brantford, Stratford, Simcoe, Sarnia, and Strathroy.

26 *AR* for 1890, appendix M, 373–86.

27 For example, the staff of Brantford C.I. was 14 per cent female; Strathroy, 20 per cent; London, 13 per cent; Guelph, Ottawa, and St Catharines, no female teachers.

28 See for example G2A, vol. 1, 1872, Goderich; vol. 7, 1878, Hamilton; vol. 10, 1880, Peterborough (timetable); vol. 14, 1885, Brantford and Sarnia.

29 Ontario, *Statutes and Regulations Respecting Public and High Schools* (Toronto 1885), 134. The percentages in these paragraphs are calculated from *AR* for 1890, appendix M.

30 G2A, vol. 14, 1885, Newcastle.

31 See for example the remark that several teachers at various schools were leaving to "join the ever-increasing army of ex-teachers" in such jobs as insurance agent and merchant, in *Educational Monthly* 6 (Jan. 1884): 46–7; and Adam Harkness, *Iroquois High School* ... (Toronto 1896), 67.

32 G2A, vol. 14, 1885, Brantford and Sarnia.

33 G2A, vol. 1, 1872, 74–5, Brampton; see also ibid., Weston.

34 Calculated from the listings in G2A, vol. 1 (2), 1874, western Ontario; and ibid., vol. 14, 1885.

35 Calculated from *AR* for 1890, appendix M, "List of Headmasters and Assistants of Collegiate Institutes and High Schools, December 1890."

36 G2A, vol. 1, 1873, 428. See also ibid., vol. 1 (2), 1874, 205 (Sydenham).

37 See for example comments in *Educational Monthly* 6 (Jan. 1884): 46–7; Harkness, *Iroquois High School*, 67; G1A, vol. 5, 1870, 541 (Caledonia); G2A, vol. 1 (2), 1874, 351 (Whitby), and 360 (Brampton).

38 *Canada School Journal* 6, 54 (Nov. 1881): 264.

39 See for example the St Thomas case in 1883, in which the classics master, offered $1100 by another board, settled for a raise from his own trustees. UWORC, St Thomas Board of Education Minutes, Managing Committee 1882–1906, 7 Mar. 1883.

40 Compare the average salaries listed in the *AR*s of the 1880s with Ian M. Drummond, *Progress without Planning: The Economic History of Ontario from Confederation to the Second World War* (Toronto: University of Toronto Press 1987), 227 and table 13.2.

41 *DHE* 17: 231. See also c6c, T.J. Lundy, Chairman, Board of Trustees, Beamsville County Grammar School, to Ryerson, 25 Jan. 1855; c1, Ryerson to George Brown, Secretary, Owen Sound Board of Grammar School Trustees, 13 Jan. 1857; *AR* for 1859, GSIR, 161.

42 *AR* for 1875, appendix A, 5.

43 G2A, vol. 14, 1885.

44 *AR* for 1880–81, table D, 188–9.

45 Compare the statement of salaries for both public and high school teachers in Campbellford in 1890, where only the public school headmaster made as much as the lowest-paid high school assistant ($600), and all the (female) public school assistants received less than $350 a year. AO, RG2, P2, 62, no. 483, Detailed Statement of High and Public School Accounts, 1890, Campbellford.

46 *AR* for 1893, xix, table M, and appendix M.

47 For reminiscences of a good teacher, see for example the account of headmaster J.M. Dunn at Welland (Tanguay, *Welland High*, 13); but compare this to his regime at Guelph (Shutt, *The High Schools of Guelph*, 25). For examples of bad ones, see GIA, 1867, Farmersville, 592; ibid., vol. 5, 541, Caledonia, Nov. 1870; G2A, vol. 1, 1873, 419, Streetsville; ibid., vol. 1 (2), 1874, 360, Brampton.

48 AO, Col. Charles Clarke Papers in Possession of the Wellington County Archives, Calendar and Transcription, Charles Clarke to "My dear girls," Elora [1875]. The principal of Elora public school was David Boyle, the future archaeologist and curator of the provincial museum, who according to his biographer stimulated an "intellectual awakening" in Elora; see Gerald Killan, *David Boyle: From Artisan to Archaeologist* (Toronto: University of Toronto Press 1983), chap. 3. In the same passage quoted here, Clarke comments that "even David Boyle is in rapture."

49 GIA, vol. 5, 1868, Bowmanville, 46; ibid., Port Hope, 28. See also ibid., 1865, Ingersoll, 36; ibid., vol. 5, 1870, Peterborough, 503–4.

50 GIA, vol. 5, 1871, Belleville, 745–9. A similar expedient was tried at Barrie, where boys and girls were separated by a partition extending from the back of the room to the headmaster's area in front of the pupils: see ibid., 1867, Barrie, 671.

51 G2A, vol. 1, 1874, 179.

52 For examples of separate facilities, see the references in notes 7 and 8 above. For examples of common facilities, see GIA, vol. 5, 1871, Stratford, 882–3; Strathroy, 887–8; G2A, vol. 1, 1874, 176, Morrisburg; vol. 14, 1885, Berlin, Cayuga, Fergus.

53 G2A, vol. 14, 1885, Toronto. See also ibid., vol. 1, 1874, Toronto, 112–13; vol. 7, 1878, Toronto. For examples of separate washrooms, cloakrooms, and the like, but common classrooms, see ibid., vol. 7, 1878, Brantford Floor Plan; vol. 1, 1874, Goderich, Clinton, Listowel, Barrie, Cobourg.

54 See G2A, vol. 10, 1880, Almonte, July. Seating all the girls in the front and all the boys in the back, or in rows at one side of the room or the other, may well have been common; the authors remember Ontario public school classrooms of the 1950s in which seating arrangements attempted to separate the sexes. See note 50 above for examples of possible forerunners.

55 AO, RG2, P2, 1892, box 62, no. 480, Listowel.

56 *AR* for 1883, HSIR (J.A. McLellan), 140.

57 *AR* for 1885, HSIR, 165.

58 See for example Paxton Young's revealing description of his inspection visit to Alexandria grammar school in 1867 in which he writes of examining boys "in Virgil," "in the 2nd Ode of the first book of Horace," and classes "in Spencer's Arnold and Caesar": GIA, 1867, 564. See also above, chap. 6, 125–6.

59 G2A, vol. 1 (2), 1874, Omemee, 353.

60 G2A, vol. 1, 1873, St Catharines, 423.

61 G2A, vol. 1, 1873, 454. Similar arrangements existed in other schools for years to come: see for example ibid., vol. 14, 1885, Colborne.

62 G2A, vol. 7, 1878, Hamilton; ibid., vol. 1, 1872, Goderich, 1.

63 OTA *Minutes*, 1876, advertisement on inside back cover.

64 *AR* for 1879, 101.

65 G2A, vol. 10, 1880, Timetable and Course of Study, Peterborough Collegiate Institute, 1879, encl. in Peterborough report, July.

66 Ketchum, "System," appendix A2.

67 G2A, vol. 1, 1873; 2, 1873–4; 1, 1874; and 1 (2), 1874: various schools.

68 Ketchum, "System," 161. For persistence records in Ketchum's schools, see also ibid., 162 and appendices B1, B2.

69 See for example G2A, vol. 7, 1878, Perth, Sarnia, Strathroy; vol. 10, 1880, various schools.

70 Ketchum, "System," 161.

71 Relevant tables in the *ARs*, summarized by Ketchum, "System," 164 and table 4.3.

72 In chap. 6 we used *median* persistence, which was 1.5 years. Here we use the *mean* in order to compare our results to Ketchum's.

73 Ketchum, "System," appendices B1 and B2.

74 The percentages are for 1888 and are calculated from the *AR* for 1889, 49–53. For 1889 see *AR* for 1890, 49–53.

75 For the relevant regulations see Ontario, *Statutes and Regulations Respecting Public and High Schools* (Toronto 1885), nos. 160–8 (teachers' non-professional certificates), no. 100 (commercial diploma), nos. 98–9 (course of study and matriculation requirements).

76 W.G. Fleming, *Education: Ontario's Preoccupation* (Toronto: University of Toronto Press 1972), 40.

77 In 1892 there was, on the face of it, a startling rise in the numbers enrolled

in the third and fourth forms. But this, we suspect, was entirely due to the reorganization of the program which made form III the standard for pass junior matriculation and form IV the standard for senior matriculation. Once that is taken into account, the percentages in the pre-matriculation forms in 1892 are just about the same as in 1888.

78 See *Regulations*, 1885, no. 95.

79 *AR* for 1956, s-89.

80 *AR* for 1877, appendix A, HSIR, 9; similarly see *AR* for 1879, part II, HSIR, 101–2; *AR* for 1884, part II, HSIR (Hodgson), 188–9.

81 *AR* for 1879, part II, HSIR (S. Arthur Marling), 101–2; G2A, vol. 14, 1885, Berlin.

82 *AR* for 1889, appendix I, HSIR (J.E. Hodgson, Eastern Division), 180. Some schools may in fact have provided for their girls; see *AR* for 1877, appendix A, HSIR, 9.

83 See 304 above.

84 AO, RG2, G4, envelope 2, Report of the Board of the City of Hamilton, 1875 (Report of George Dickson, Headmaster, Collegiate Institute, 1 May 1876), 5. See also comments of Inspector Hodgson on the large number of literary societies and on their activities, in *AR* for 1884, part II, HSIR, 189.

85 The information from the *ARs* is conveniently summarized by Ketchum in "System," appendix D9. For the data on his schools, see the other tables in appendix D.

86 Calculated from *AR* for 1880–81, table L. In the same year, 1307 students obtained third-class teaching certificates, and nearly 500 more received first and second-class certificates, making a total nearly equal to those leaving from all schools for "other occupations"; see ibid., 224. We cannot assume that all those who received certificates went into teaching; presumably many went on to further education; others might have gone into different occupations than teaching; others may have moved out of the province, etc. Nevertheless, it seems likely that many, if not most, students intending to enter "other occupations" were in fact going into teaching.

87 See Ketchum, "System," appendix D9.

88 Recalculated from Ketchum, "System," appendix D6.

89 *AR* for 1900, 243.

CHAPTER FIFTEEN

1 Quoted in *DHE* 21: 291.

2 R.W. Connell et al., *Making the Difference: Schools, Families and Social Division* (Sydney: George Allen and Unwin 1982), 190. For a parallel account of the politics of reforming secondary education see R.D. Anderson, *Education and Opportunity in Victorian Scotland* (Oxford: Clarendon Press 1983), chaps. 5 and 6.

3 For relevant commentary on the effects of these differences, see Burton Clark, "Academic Differentiation in National Systems of Higher Education," *Comparative Education Review* 22 (1978): 247–8.

4 Fritz Ringer, *Education and Society in Modern Europe* (Bloomington: Indiana University Press 1979), 6. Similarly see R.J.W. Selleck, "State Education and Culture," *Australian Journal of Education* 26, 1 (1982); James C. Albisetti, *Secondary School Reform in Imperial Germany* (Princeton: Princeton University Press 1983), 9.

5 Arthur R.M. Lower, *My First Seventy-Five Years* (Toronto: Macmillan 1967), 30.

6 The phrase is from Connell, *Making the Difference*, 120.

7 *AR* for 1943–44, 178.

8 *Canada School Journal* 1, 6 (Nov. 1877): 87; ibid., 4, 26 (July 1879): 148.

9 For examples see *AR* for 1882, 25; *Educational Monthly* 4 (May-June 1882): 250–1. See also Jean Barman, *Growing Up British in British Columbia: Boys in Private Schools* (Vancouver: University of British Columbia Press 1984), 65–9.

10 David Keane, "Rediscovering Ontario University Students in the Mid-Nineteenth Century" (Ph.D. diss., University of Toronto 1982), 854.

11 For a parallel comment see Daniel T. Rodgers and David B. Tyack, "Work, Youth and Schooling: Mapping Critical Research Areas," in *Work, Youth and Schooling*, ed. Harvey Kantor and David B. Tyack (Stanford: Stanford University Press 1982), 274.

12 For an example see B. Anne Wood's enlightening references to the Ottawa collegiate institute, scattered throughout her *Idealism Transformed: The Making of a Progressive Educator* (Kingston and Montreal: McGill-Queen's University Press 1985).

13 Calculated from *AR* for 1956, S-73.

14 John Porter, *The Vertical Mosaic* (Toronto: University of Toronto Press 1965), 180–2.

APPENDICES

1 The linkage rate would undoubtedly be much lower if we had been searching a large population base; Ian Davey, for example, could link only one-third of the pupils at Hamilton Central School in 1853 to their families, and a similar low number in 1861. See Ian Davey, "School Reform and School Attendance: The Hamilton Central School, 1853–1861" (MA diss., University of Toronto 1972), 45 and 87.

2 For example, see Michael B. Katz, in *The People of Hamilton, Canada West: Family and Class in a Mid-Nineteenth-Century City* (Cambridge, Mass.: Harvard University Press 1975), appendix 2; Michael B. Katz, Michael J. Doucet, and Mark J. Stern, *The Social Organization of Early In-*

dustrial Capitalism (Cambridge, Mass.: Harvard University Press 1982), esp. chap. 1; Theodore Hershberg and Robert Dockhorn, "Occupational Classification," *Historical Methods Newsletter* 9, 2 and 3 (March/June 1976): 59–98.

3 A. Gordon Darroch and Michael D. Ornstein, "Ethnicity and Occupational Structure in Canada in 1871: The Vertical Mosaic in Historical Perspective," *Canadian Historical Review* 61, 3 (1980): 305–33.

4 See for example Patrick J. Harrigan, *Mobility, Elites, and Education in French Society of the Second Empire* (Waterloo: Wilfrid Laurier University Press 1980), chap. 1.

5 See David G. Burley, "The Businessmen of Brantford, Ontario: Self-Employment in a Mid-Nineteenth Century Town" (Ph.D. diss., McMaster University 1983), chap. 1.

Index

408   Index